COST AND MANAGEMENT ACCOUNTING
Made Simple

The Made Simple series
has been created
primarily for self-education
but can equally well
be used as
an aid to group study.
However complex the subject,
the reader is taken
step by step,
clearly and methodically,
through the course. Each volume
has been prepared by experts,
using throughout the
Made Simple technique of teaching.
Consequently the gaining
of knowledge now becomes
an experience to be enjoyed.

Accounting
Acting and Stagecraft
Additional Mathematics
Advertising
Anthropology
Applied Economics
Applied Mathematics
Applied Mechanics
Art Appreciation
Art of Speaking
Art of Writing
Biology
Book-keeping
British Constitution
Calculus
Chemistry
Childcare
Commerce
Commercial Law
Company Administration
Computer Programming
Cookery
Cost and Management
  Accounting
Data Processing
Dressmaking
Economic History
Economic and Social
  Geography
Economics
Electricity
Electronic Computers

Electronics
English
French
Geology
German
Human Anatomy
Italian
Journalism
Latin
Law
Management
Marketing
Mathematics
Modern European History
New Mathematics
Office Practice
Organic Chemistry
Philosophy
Photography
Physical Geography
Physics
Pottery
Psychology
Rapid Reading
Russian
Salesmanship
Soft Furnishing
Spanish
Statistics
Transport and
  Distribution
Typing

COST AND MANAGEMENT ACCOUNTING
Made Simple

Joseph Baggott, BSc (Econ), ACMA, FSCA

Made Simple Books

W. H. ALLEN   London

A Howard & Wyndham Company

Printed and bound in Great Britain
by Richard Clay (The Chaucer Press) Ltd
Bungay, Suffolk
for the publishers W. H. Allen & Co. Ltd.
44 Hill Street, London W1X 8LB

First Edition, September 1973
Reprinted (with revisions), June 1976

ISBN 0 491 01420 1 Paperbound

Acknowledgements

The publishers and the author gratefully thank the Ronald Press Company (New York) for allowing the inclusion of Fig. 29, adapted from *The Accountants Cost Handbook* edited by R. I. Dickey; the Controller of Her Majesty's Stationery Office for extracts from the *Report of the Committee on the Working of the Monetary System, Cmnd. 827 (the Radcliffe Report)* and the Institute of Cost and Management Accountants for the Present Value Table in Appendix One (from I.C.M.A. publication *Mathematical Tables for Students*).

Our thanks are also due for permission to include in the exercises at the end of each chapter questions taken from the examinations of the Association of Certified Accountants (A.C.A.), the Association of Cost and Industrial Accountants (C.A.A.), and the Institute of Cost and Management Accountants (C.M.A.).

To FRANCES
whose encouragement and understanding over many years
has made this book possible

Preface

There has been a growing awareness of the importance of cost and management accounting during the present century and a recognition of its contribution to business efficiency within an increasingly complex economic environment. During this period, cost and management accounting has adopted progressively more sophisticated techniques to meet the needs of management for a reliable information service as a basis for decision-making. The demands made on a management accountant call for that flexibility of mind which springs from an understanding of the influences governing business activity. Today's management accountant must know **how**, but more especially **why**, there are clear causal relationships between the various factors which determine management performance.

This book has been written to fill the need for a book on cost and management accounting that goes beyond a statement of the elementary principles. It is written, therefore, from a conceptual approach rather than the more usual recitation of accounting rules. At the same time, it is intended for the non-mathematician, so that the more advanced mathematical techniques used by accountants have been omitted. It is in this latter sense that the book purports to show cost and management accounting made simple, rather than being restricted to the elementary principles of the subject.

Cost and Management Accounting Made Simple is derived from the author's experience of teaching professional students, degree students and those on many other types of courses. Therefore, it is intended for students of the professional examinations of the major bodies of accountants in the United Kingdom: the Institute of Chartered Accountants, the Institute of Cost and Management Accountants, the Institute of Municipal Treasurers and Accountants and the Association of Certified Accountants, as well as the examinations of other accountancy bodies. It is also appropriate for undergraduates studying management accounting in a wide spectrum of degrees in accounting, business studies, and economics. Students on courses for the HND/HNC in business studies will find it satisfies their needs, as will those on other advanced or professional courses including the subject of cost and management accounting.

The businessman, the manager, the executive, the engineer, and the salesman will also find it helpful in gaining an appreciation of the role of accountancy in business and the ways in which accounting data can assist them to be more effective in their particular work. The general reader, too, will discover that the explanation of management accountancy is now within his grasp, and this should dispel some of the mystical awe frequently accorded to accountancy by the layman.

My special gratitude is due to Mr. John F. Keen and Mr. W. Hingley, who have read through the complete manuscript and made many helpful suggestions and comments. The book is all the better for their advice, but full responsibility for it rests with me.

My thanks are also due to my colleagues at the City of Birmingham Polytechnic and the Institute of Cost and Management Accountants, who have contributed in many ways to my ideas and so to this book, although the responsibility for the text is again mine. I am grateful to the publishers (especially Margaret Anderson) for their considerable help in preparing the manuscript; to my sister-in-law, Margaret, who prepared the typescript from my frequently amended notes; and to my wife for preparing the index and assisting me with the book generally.

JOSEPH BAGGOTT

Table of Contents

CHAPTER ONE

COST CLASSIFICATION AND ANALYSIS

The Role of Management

The fundamental role of management is to make decisions, the continuous function of choosing between several courses of action. This is also the concern of economics—choosing between various alternatives to maximize satisfaction. Thus business management is concerned with economic activity within the context of the firm (**micro-economics**) and accountancy is economics since it evaluates these micro-economic decisions *ex post facto*, as well as providing *ex ante facto* financial data as a basis for future decisions.

For many years after the *Companies Act, 1844*, the role of business accounting was primarily concerned with the statutory requirements for **stewardship accounting**. The increasing complexity of business organization, the growth in size of manufacturing units, and the increasing mechanization of production methods, steadily created the need for more and more financial data to be provided for the day-to-day management of a business. Financial, or stewardship, accounting failed to provide this information because it was not designed to do so and gradually a new concept of accountancy, **costing**, evolved which has developed rapidly over the last fifty years. Cost accounting arose from the needs of business management for decision-making criteria and eventually became known as **management accounting**. All other things being equal, management will tend to maximize profits within the limits and constraints of given resources or a given capacity, a given economic environment and a given business policy. Profit is the fundamental criterion of business efficiency within a self-adjusting, competitive economy and, indeed, it is essential for business survival since profit is the source of capital growth, whilst losses erode capital.

Decision Data

A system of cost accounting is designed to provide the financial data, which will form the basis of managerial decisions—from those at the top through all levels of management right down to the shop floor. Every decision taken within a business will influence the overall profit performance in a variety of ways. Consequently, cost is a factor in every business decision—sometimes the least important, but usually the most significant. For example, in decisions within the sphere of employee welfare the cost may be relatively unimportant, in comparison with improved morale or good relations. Nevertheless, it cannot be ignored because it determines whether or not a business can afford an otherwise desirable scheme.

The problem underlying this type of decision arises, of course, from the inability to measure its impact upon profit performance, so that it becomes a *social*, rather than an *economic*, decision. In contrast, most management decisions are economic ones and can be made only with the knowledge of the economic consequences. Generally, this means that management decisions depend on an awareness of the probable effect upon the company's profits—in other words the influence exerted on the gap between revenue and costs.

Rational decisions (as opposed to pure guesswork) can only be made when the person making a decision is aware of the probable consequences of all the available alternatives. A man who arrives at a fork in the road has to choose which road to take in order to reach his destination. Should a signpost indicate his destination the decision is simple, but if there are two roads shown, leading to places other than his destination, he requires further information. He may know the two places and be aware that one is nearer to his final destination than the other and, again, he can readily decide. However, if he does not know either place, or there is no signpost at all, he cannot decide, but only guess or take a chance with a 0·5 probability of being correct. Obviously a wrong choice will be costly in additional time taken for travelling and probably be more expensive too. Whereas, he could have bought a map of the area and so had available an appropriate information system to provide the necessary guidance for the relevant decision-making on his journey.

The Contribution of Accountancy to Management

Accounting is the business manager's map. It is an information service providing data to 'show the right way' towards the desired profit result for a business. Unfortunately, accountancy is too often viewed as an end in itself, rather than its true role of assisting management by providing relevant data for decisions. The blame for this rests squarely and fairly on the accountants' shoulders. As with other professionally qualified people and specialists, accountants are confident in their ability to 'know what is *best* for others' and frequently insist on furnishing data they believe should be wanted, instead of that which will be used. There is, for example, no advantage in a motorist taking a map, however beautifully prepared, if it does not include his destination. Nor will he derive much benefit from a general map showing only main trunk roads when his destination lies within a maze of minor roads. It is also true, conversely, that a finely detailed map may cause confusion on a journey between principal cities. During one year the motorist will make many different journeys: for some he will need the general map of principal routes; for others he will require detailed maps; or perhaps a suitable admixture of several, including a street guide in his destination town. The **accounting information service** must be similarly flexible in contributing to effective managerial decision-taking. The starting-point and destination should be considered, together with the most suitable route, for all the 'journeys' to be taken by the firm.

Performance Evaluation

The accounting function, however, does more than this. It not only provides financial data as an aid to business decisions, but it also evaluates the decisions already implemented. An accounting system is designed to measure the effect on the company's profit performance of each decision taken by management. In this way, the accountant is able to evaluate managerial performance throughout the organization and also to determine the individual manager's responsibility for the ultimate result. (Hence the use of the term **responsibility**

accounting in this context.) This forms the basis of the various **accountancy control systems** which are designed to receive, from all the myriad **decision points** or 'nerve ends' of the business, the **feedback** which acts as a stimulus signal designed to correct any deviations from the pre-determined norms. This indicates to individual managers their personal effectiveness within the business structure and provides them with the guidelines for future action. Furthermore, it acquaints superiors with the managerial efficiency of their subordinates and the contribution of the subordinates to the corporate effort.

The accounting function performs a fundamental and vital role in the harmonious and efficient operation of a business enterprise. In a way it can be compared with the part the heart plays in the body's circulation system —pumping the **lifeblood of information** throughout the body's trunk to its members and, especially to the brain (scientists, technologists, designers, engineers, and administrators) of the firm.

Functional Accounting

In order to fulfil its purpose adequately, accountancy must concern itself with very considerable detail in furnishing the relevant data to management. This is so because many managerial decisions are concerned with detail, sometimes with trivia, especially at the lower levels of the administrative structure. Furthermore, consequent upon the requirements by management for decision data, accountancy must compile this by **functions or activities** rather than by the **financial classification by types of expense.**

Herein lies the basic distinction between the two arms of the accountancy dichotomy—**financial accounting** analyses revenue and expenditure according to types of transaction, whereas **cost accountancy** pursues a functional, or activity analysis of data. In many ways financial accounts resemble the small-scale map giving the main routes between principal towns, while costing is akin to the large-scale map indicating the minor roads or by-ways and, in some cases, the detailed town roads' atlas, too. Nevertheless, each will guide the 'traveller' from a starting-point to a desired destination and will reveal the overall profit result of a business. Modern thinking has moved a long way towards the abandonment of this binary system and this will be discussed in Chapter Two.

Unique Conditions

The demands on a costing system for fine detail in the data it provides require considerable attention to be given to the development of an appropriate framework. Ultimately, each business requires a unique costing system —one which is *tailor-made* to its needs, for just as no two people are quite identical, so one business will differ from all other businesses. This applies even within the same industry or trade as each business will be located in a different place, and this alone can create enormous physical variations, for example in the size of the plot and its shape. Then the buildings will have been erected at different times, by varying methods of construction or from different materials. The plant, machinery, and equipment installed in one factory will differ from another, as will the various products manufactured with their distinctive characteristics in design, function, and quality.

The most important distinction between one business and another is found in the employees since no two people are actually alike, no combinations of people will be alike either—even though the law of statistical regularity tends to operate with large groups of people and so lead to greater *uniformity* in the groups—each group of people has its own ethos. After all, a business is a group of individuals united in a corporate endeavour to produce goods or services to satisfy human wants and the individual personalities of these people are welded together to give the business its distinctive and unique character.

Dynamic Environment of Management Accounting

This is a matter of some significance to the cost accountant who is designing a costing system: not only must he take into account the physical features, but also the business personnel. The cost accountant in developing an information service for people, must consider the individual managers who will use this service and model the system to yield the data they require in a manner appropriate to their positions, personalities, and intellects.

Beyond this, however, he must look to the data-processors who will be involved in his system, not only those engaged in the cost department but also the staff employed in 'feeder' departments providing the basic accounting information. It is not always easy or even possible to recruit ideal staff, nor to dispose of less able personnel within one's own department and it is far more difficult to do so in other departments, especially if such people are suitably qualified for their work. The cost accountant who creates a costing system must 'cut his coat according to his cloth'.

The establishment of a costing system is not, however, simply a 'once-and-for-all' operation but a continuous exercise. Personnel will change from time to time, bringing new ideas to modify an established pattern and new products; improved materials; technological innovation; better education; raised living standards; modified social customs and changes in fashion or taste, will all influence the changes within a business. The costing system should also be subject to change because it serves a dynamic organism evolving within the changing economic and social pattern of the nation and of the world. If the accounting system is to be the information service it should be, it must be able to show the same dynamism that is apparent within the company and society as a whole. Any costing system, which for several years has shown no signs of change, is likely to be of little or no value to the firm that shelters it, and the sooner it is replaced, the sooner the company's profit will improve.

A 'tailor-made' costing system does not, of course, have to be unique in every respect. A man who visits a bespoke tailor, for example, will come away with his own individual suit. The tailor, however, will cut other suits out of the same roll of cloth and the same style of suit from different materials. All the suits cut will conform to the basic conventions of a jacket and trousers, buttons and pockets. Similarly, a costing system may vary from others in matters of detail within the universally accepted concepts; the degree of application and in the adoption of alternative techniques or practices but, at the same time, will have many features in common. Thus it is possible to establish fundamental accounting theories to provide the conceptual framework in which to create a unique costing system for a particular business. This book attempts to explain current accounting theories and the application of these theories in the business situation so as to provide a **data information**

service for management, which will aid decision-making through the use of financial criteria.

Precision in Accountancy

Contrary to popular opinion, the degree of accuracy in much accounting data is more apparent than real. Accountancy is by no means the exact science it is supposed to be but, frequently, much more a matter of opinion than of fact. It is not uncommon for business men—and even accountants—to refer to 'true costs' from time to time. This is absurd in the sense of absolute verifiable accuracy since accounting data is too dependent on estimation, approximation, and arbitrariness to yield such figures. In multi-product businesses, certain costs are *common* to two or more products and are arbitrarily apportioned between the relevant products. Materials issued to production are often priced on arbitrary bases: period costs are averaged over the period's output; fixed assets are assumed to have an 'estimated life period' and asset depreciation is calculated by an arbitrarily chosen method.

The degree of imprecision in any accounting data is, however, less important than knowing the limits of error and properly appreciating its significance. Indeed, it is the ever-present need for accountants **to make arbitrary decisions and to use imprecise data** that creates the necessity for them to be capable of analytical thought, of assessing the relative significance of accounting data, and of appreciating the economic implications of business decisions. Were the intellectual demands on accountants to be no more than those of book-keeping, there could be neither professional nor economic justification for the current educational policies of the professional bodies.

The Elements of Cost

Cost is essentially a compound term—even at its simplest it is the product of quantity and price. In the highly complex environment of modern manufacturing businesses it embraces many diverse components and activities. Initially, it is possible to identify **three separate elements of cost**, namely, **materials, labour,** and **services,** for which the manufacturer must pay. Since 'products' of all kinds are tangible objects, it is apparent that they are made from materials of one kind or another. Furthermore, the term **manufacturing** implies 'changing the form' of materials in some way or another—this clearly requires the application of labour (even where machinery is used). In the service industries, too, there will customarily be found all three elements of cost. The use of labour and the consumption of other services are readily apparent, but materials are also usually required in one form or another. Some 'service' businesses really *manufacture* a product as in the case of restaurants and similar catering organizations; but others simply perform a service in the sense of a **change of place** and/or a **change of ownership** in the case of material products or, alternatively, provide personal services such as hairdressing.

Consumable Materials

Consideration of the service industries illustrates clearly that some materials are not necessarily passed on to the customer in one form or another but are **used up** in providing an efficient service: the detergents and other cleaning agents used by office cleaners are never seen or mentioned to the bank's clients; the tyres on buses are essential to an efficient public transport, yet they have no direct relationship with the passengers; and the computer tabulations in insurance companies are used for internal administration and not handed to the insured. Hairdressers use a prodigious quantity of cosmetics in satisfying their clients and the entertainment industry, too, consumes a wide variety of materials. The various manufacturing industries also embrace similar examples of materials which are consumed in the business, but do not form part of the company's products.

Direct and Indirect Costs

Those costs that can be readily identified with the particular products or services which the business produces and sells to its customers are designated **direct costs**. The raw material, from which a product is made, would be direct, as would the labour engaged in converting that raw material into a saleable form. **Indirect costs**, on the other hand, are not so easily identified with the firm's products or services, such as *inter alia* lubricating oil for machinery or vehicles; fuels to provide space heating; stationery and printing for administration forms; building repairs and so on. Thus, the cost accountant classifies the three basic elements of cost into two groups—direct and indirect. The three direct elements are referred to collectively as **prime cost** while **overhead** is the collective term for indirect costs as illustrated below.

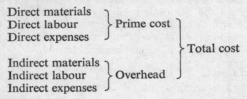

$$
\left.\begin{array}{l}\text{Direct materials}\\ \text{Direct labour}\\ \text{Direct expenses}\end{array}\right\}\text{Prime cost}\;\left.\begin{array}{l}\\ \\ \\ \\ \\ \\ \\ \end{array}\right\}\text{Total cost}
$$
$$
\left.\begin{array}{l}\text{Indirect materials}\\ \text{Indirect labour}\\ \text{Indirect expenses}\end{array}\right\}\text{Overhead}
$$

Functional Analysis of Costs

Overhead Classification

Overhead represents the revenue expenditure incurred in the provision of the business facilities which are required for production to take place. Every manufacturing business needs at least two fundamental activities for which these 'facilities' must be provided, namely, manufacturing and marketing. In most organizations there are likely to be additional **activity groups** forming overhead sub-divisions. In particular, marketing is frequently separated into selling and distribution; while administration is recognized as an independent activity serving all sections of the business. Many firms spend large sums on research and development and in these cases the relevant overhead will be analysed into this further classification.

Clearly, the three indirect elements of cost call for a functional analysis so that not only is the cost of providing all the business facilities known, but it is ascertained in a meaningful manner. Consequently, overhead will be categorized into the **principal activity groups of manufacturing, administration, selling, distribution, and research**. This is not simply an analysis for its own sake, which would be pointless, but is made because the **incidence of cost** is likely to vary from one activity to another. Put simply, the factory overhead is likely to vary with the volume of factory output, whereas the incidence of selling overhead will be dependent on the sales promotion activity, and distribution costs are determined by the quantities of goods dispatched. Research as an independent function will differ from all these other activities, while administration 'activity' is partly independent and partly influenced by the activities of all the functions.

Prime Cost Classification

A consideration of the functional analysis for overhead will naturally beg the question of its relevance for prime cost, too. A study of current literature on cost accountancy indicates a general acceptance of the view that prime cost is solely a works characteristic with the corollary that all the costs of other functions are essentially overhead. Nevertheless, this traditional view of prime cost can be challenged as unrealistic, and is frequently contradicted (by implication) when the separate functions are discussed in detail. Administration, by its very nature, is not related to individual products but to products and functions as a whole, so it will normally be a wholly indirect cost. Selling and distribution costs, on the other hand, can frequently be related to the products or to orders and therefore qualify to be classed as **direct costs**. Obvious examples will be found in a jobbing business (where goods are made only against customers' specific orders) when both the manufacturing order and the sales order will refer to the same item or items. Such examples include:

(1) **The commission paid to salesmen or agents for securing an order.** This payment arises solely from the particular order and is capable of direct analysis to it, so that sales commission can be recognized as a direct cost equally with the raw materials from which the item is made.

(2) **The charges paid for delivery or transportation of the customer's order.** Again, without the order this cost would not be incurred. Therefore, since it arises directly from the particular job it can be identified with it and so becomes a direct expense.

Research and development costs will normally be treated as wholly indirect—if only as a matter of expediency. Most *product-related* research costs will have been incurred in advance of production and even prior to receiving the order from a customer, but patently they are derived from the particular product concerned; in some ways this is not dissimilar to the familiar 'chicken and egg' problem. Difficulty in dealing with the costs of research stems largely from the inability to foresee the outcome of particular investigations, which may frequently be abortive in their contribution to the immediate objective (this topic is dealt with more fully in Chapter Twelve). Nevertheless, at least in theory, we can separate the costs of research too into direct and indirect categories.

The simple classification of the elements of cost (above) can now be supplemented by the functional classification on page 8.

Analysis Through Expediency

Later chapters will explain the need for a more detailed analysis of costs within this functional classification, but a further point to be made here is that there is some danger in trying to pursue a *rigid* classification of costs for circumstances alter cases. Numerous instances occur of nominally direct costs being treated as overhead—particularly with materials. Many products contain materials in relatively small quantities or of insignificant values such as glue, string, tape, nails, screws, rivets, nuts and bolts, and so on. A strict

	Direct Costs £	Indirect Costs £	Total Costs £
Factory prime cost	xxx		xxx
Factory overhead		xxx	xxx
	—	—	—
FACTORY COST	xxx	xxx	xxx
Selling prime cost	xxx		xxx
Selling overhead		xxx	xxx
	—	—	—
SELLING COST	xxx	xxx	xxx
Distribution prime cost	xxx		xxx
Distribution overhead		xxx	xxx
	—	—	—
MARKETING COST	xxx	xxx	xxx
Research prime cost	xxx		xxx
Research overhead		xxx	xxx
Administration overhead		xxx	xxx
	—	—	—
TOTAL COST	xxx	xxx	xxx

application of theory demands the inclusion of such items as direct costs, but expediency suggests treating them as overhead since this is administratively far easier and less costly. Since the value of such items in both absolute and relative terms tends to be small, any inaccuracy in cost analysis must also be small as a result of this practice.

There are other instances where costs are allocated to products on a 'recovery' basis which is similar to the manner of charging overhead. However, such items are **not treated as overhead, but similarly to overhead.** For example, a man may be employed in a jobbing foundry to trim castings. It is plain that he works directly upon the products (castings) and so his remuneration is classified as direct labour. Were he obliged to record the time spent on each casting for the purpose of determining the proportion of his wages to be allocated to each such casting, this could occupy up to one-third of his working time. The absurdity of such a situation is apparent! The cost accountant overcomes the problem by initially charging the man's wages to a castings trim recovery account and then transferring to products the 'recovered' amounts of trim direct labour calculated on an arbitrary basis, such as the weight of castings or the cost of moulding or some other suitable basis. Under this procedure the direct wages remain direct even though apportioned to products in this arbitrary way: had they been treated *as* overhead they would have been aggregated with the various indirect costs for the particular activity concerned.

There is one further instance of 'circumstances altering cases' in the classification of costs, namely in the categorization of **types of expenses.** A good illustration of this is to be found in the wages paid to factory supervision. The foreman of a production department may be responsible for a group of direct workers although he himself does not work directly on the products—but only indirectly, through the supervision of his subordinates. In such a case, his wages or salary would be analysed as factory overhead. Most elementary texts on costing assume that all such supervision will always be an overhead, but this is not necessarily so. In determining whether to classify a particular item as a direct or indirect cost, the guiding principle to follow is that costs should be included as direct whenever possible. In the process industries it is quite common for a single department to be concerned with a single process or perhaps a chain of several linked processes. In this situation the cost accounts will be designed to provide the cost of operating the process rather than finding the costs of individual jobs. Since the foreman in charge of the department is engaged in this one process, his salary can be identified with it and is clearly direct wages of that process. Consequently, prime cost tends to be a relatively greater proportion of total cost in the process industries than would be the case for jobbing businesses.

At the outset the student should beware of developing rigid attitudes of mind to cost concepts and cost terminology. As previously mentioned accounting is frequently more a matter of opinion than a matter of fact, which means that everything should be considered objectively, particularly within the context of a given situation. The ability to form opinions on business situations depends on keeping a flexible and open mind coupled with analytical reasoning and breadth of vision. The study of accounting develops these qualities and prepares the accountant for his advisory role to management.

Exercises

1. The main function of accounting is to record, summarize and report various business facts. To do this requires a measurement of these facts and an accounting measurement, like most others, is an approximation not a precisely accurate statement. Why are accounting figures approximations? Give examples of three items which appear in the published accounts of a limited company and which are approximations. What basic requirements of a management accounting system add to the degree of approximation in accounting figures?   [A.C.A.]

2. One of the prime functions of the management accountant is to prepare financial data on which management will base decisions. Outline the reasons why in the preparation of such data the management accountant should relate this information to a system of 'responsibility' accounting.   [A.C.A.]

3. 'Costing is an instrument of management control.'
   'Costing is nothing more than a detailed analysis of expenditure.'
Reconcile these two statements, quoting examples to illustrate the truth of each.
                    [A.C.A.]

4. Explain fully the advantages that a manufacturer should derive from an efficient costing system which will assist him in running his business.   [C.A.A.]

5. (*a*) Explain the difference between direct and indirect labour.
   (*b*) Classify the following into direct or indirect, giving your reasons:
     (i) Factory wages.
     (ii) Stoker's wages for firing a boiler to heat the offices and factory.
     (iii) A setter's wages where he services four cost centres.
     (iv) A foreman's salary where he controls a single cost centre.
     (v) A factory floor sweeper's wages.
     (vi) Holiday pay.   [C.A.A.]

6. Define the following and state how you would deal with them in cost accounts:
     (i) Notional Rent.
     (ii) Waiting time.
     (iii) Deferred maintenance.
     (iv) Depreciation.
     (v) The amortization of a lease.
                    [C.A.A.]

CHAPTER TWO

THE COST DEPARTMENT

Information to Management

If managers are to derive any help from cost accounting in decision-making, then data must be communicated to them in an intelligible form. Management should not be expected to deduce from ledgers and other accounting records the facts which they could use advantageously in the operation of a business. The accounts department is essentially a **service department** for all levels of management from the managing director to the foreman; it contributes nothing to the profits itself but its information services enable other departments to increase earnings by performing more effectively. The ultimate effectiveness of accounting data for decision-making depends on its being used which, in turn, depends on the form and timing of its presentation. Information, as the life-blood of a management system, needs to be both relevant and punctual and the accounting system must be seen as a means to an end, not an end in itself: as designed for the 'customer' departments and not for the accountant.

Design of a Costing System

The first essential is to determine management information requirements so as to devise a system to satisfy them. Certain routine reports will need to be submitted at regular intervals and the system should be constructed to produce them. From time to time, *ad hoc* reports will be called for but it is clearly impossible to create a system which will provide all, or even most, requirements for special reports. The structure of an accounting system will be influenced by both the data input and the data output of the department. Data output—reports, analyses, summaries, and so on—depends upon the needs of the recipients. Top management requires comprehensive reports in broad outline, while lower management needs progressively narrower, but more detailed, information relating to specialized functions or activities.

When designing accounting information systems it is essential to consult the 'customers' regarding their needs. This not only ensures the relevance of accounting data, but frequently induces valuable suggestions and encourages co-operation on all aspects of accounting. Input data for the cost department is critical in determining the reliability of the output data, since no amount of mathematical wizardry will impart a greater degree of accuracy to numerical data than that contained in the original inputs. The cost and management accountant, therefore, must carefully study the information fed in from other departments.

Both input and output data demand a thorough understanding of company organization and activities on the part of the management accountant—production technology, product design, manufacturing processes, marketing strategy, and so on. In general, the simplest system is likely to be the most efficient. Where possible, any new system should use the existing forms amended, if necessary, in preference to devising and introducing a completely new set. Personnel will be familiar with forms in current use and will adapt to the new system more readily if the old forms are retained. It is also essential to avoid a 'text-book' mentality and not to be hidebound to costing principles at the expense of a satisfactory system. Practical considerations may require the adoption of what are theoretically 'second-best' methods, if the costing system is to be 'tailor-made' to the needs of the business.

Installation of a Costing System

It is obviously easier if the complete change-over to a new system can be made at one time, say, the beginning of the company's financial year. Normally, however, a major system change will be piecemeal and be spread over several months. This makes it vital to draft a carefully phased programme for the introduction of the different aspects of the cost system. The various items in the programme should be arranged in the expected order of attainment and completion dates given to the individual parts of the system. The use of **network analysis** is invaluable in this context and indicates the final completion date for the whole project. It is desirable to keep the programme fairly flexible as regards specific times, since there will be inevitably some unexpected delays as well as certain gains on the time-table.

The cost accountant should seek the active co-operation of all the people who will be affected by the new system, particularly subordinate managers and foremen. It is helpful to arrange special briefing meetings at which the system can be explained, problems considered and doubts removed. In some cases it will be necessary to discuss the changes with the employees or trade union representatives, and this will be **essential** if wages are affected in any way at all. The staff of the accounts department, too, should be kept fully informed, so as to avoid ill-founded rumours about their employment prospects under the new system. When planning the new system, it is essential to anticipate staff requirements at the successive stages of the phased programme. A re-allocation of duties may be sufficient but it may be necessary to retrain staff, particularly when new pieces of office machinery are to be installed, and to engage additional staff. The existing system will also have to continue while the new one is being introduced which could make it difficult to re-allocate duties in some cases.

Post Installation Appraisal

A much neglected exercise is the carrying-out of a post-installation appraisal of any new system. Even in the most carefully designed systems unexpected difficulties may arise and actual conditions differ from expectations. Consequently, there are many systems of cost and management accounting which are less effective than they should be, because no honest re-appraisal is made after they become fully operational. A regular review at reasonable intervals afterwards is also desirable so that the system can be adapted to changing conditions. Cost and management accounting operates in the dynamic environment of business, and rigidity in the accounting system is prone to emasculate its usefulness, especially where the submission of routine reports is concerned. It is desirable to review periodically all reports emanating from the cost department and check them against their usefulness to the recipients. Redundant reports are a waste of time and effort and should be eliminated.

Cost Office Manual

A manual containing all the various tasks performed in the cost department will prove to be very useful in several ways—reviewing the costing systems and routines, recruiting additional or replacement staff, and as a guide for newcomers. The manual should be arranged in sections for ease of reference. One section comprises the *job specifications* for each individual person employed in the department, defining each separate task performed, its frequency, and the forms or records involved. Another section describes each task performed in the department, classified by the frequency of performance, for example, daily, weekly, monthly, annually, and so on (including typical *ad hoc* exercises). A third section is a schedule of all the forms which originate in the department specifying the purpose of each, the person preparing it, and its distribution. There should be a further section describing the account code in use and detailing the code numbers which have been allocated. The manual is best prepared in loose-leaf form to facilitate amendments as well as enabling *personal* sets to be made-up for individuals rather than issuing the master set to each person.

Design of Forms

Forms provide a cornerstone of any clerical system in standardizing procedures and simplifying the collation and analysis of data. Therefore, the care and attention given to form design can make a significant contribution to the general efficiency of the clerical routines of which they are a part. Good form design needs to be approached from two aspects—use and printing—and must be based on a thorough understanding of the relevant office routines as well as an appreciation of printing and layout.

Use of the Form

A list should be compiled detailing each item of information to be recorded on the new form, which should include general details such as a serial number, a date, a signature, and so on. Against each item should be noted the person who enters or records it; the source of the information; the expected manner of recording (by hand or by machine); and the place (cost office, stores department, work-point, and so on) where the item will be entered. Finally, a note should be made against each item indicating those who will read and use the information. This exercise should ensure the inclusion of the necessary matter and an appreciation of the importance of each item relative to all the other items.

Form Layout

An apt title should indicate the form's purpose, which should be brief, a single word wherever possible. There is little point in the company's name appearing on internal forms, which would add to the printing cost.

Arrangement. The information on the form should follow a logical sequence to assist both the recorder and the reader. Where entries are made by several people on the same form, each recorder's information should be grouped. Items transferred from one form to another should be arranged in the same sequence on each form. An outlined *box* is recommended for emphasizing a small but significant part of the information. If several boxes are used they should be aligned to prevent giving a patchwork appearance.

Pre-printing. Pre-printing standard data is a useful time-saver where it is practicable. It also diminishes errors and improves legibility, particularly where the information is recorded by manual workers.

Spacing. This should be adequate for each item, but no more. Ruled lines are useful for handwritten entries of several words; four lines to the inch being recommended for clerks, but three lines per inch for manual workers.

Columns. These should be given a clear horizontal title. The width of columns is determined by the information to be entered and not by the length of column heading. Upcasting of figures should be made in preference to cross-casting, but in either case there should be a straight cast without the need to skip lines or columns. The use of bold lines is often useful in emphasizing particular columns.

Printing the Form

Simple forms can be produced most cheaply on the office duplicator and will normally prove satisfactory in use. However, if printing is decided upon, the printer should be given specific instructions together with the draft layout; as his advice can be invaluable, he should be consulted before an order is placed. The print on the form should not be so conspicuous as to distract the reader's attention from the recorded information. In this context, pale printing ink is helpful, as is a small typeface for internal forms where the entries are made by people who are familiar with them. Bold type provides emphasis but should be used sparingly as should a variety of types.

There are various extras which increase the printing cost and should not be asked for unless they are really needed. These include: serial numbering, required only where it is desirable to maintain a strict control of the forms; the use of more than one colour, as this requires a separate run for each colour; perforation to provide detachable sections which often calls for a separate production process; and binding in pad form which is expensive and seldom necessary.

Where possible, standard sizes of paper or card should be used, to minimize costs. Furthermore, non-standard binders or filing cabinets are always relatively much more expensive than standard ones. The size of a form should be adequate for the *average* quantity of data (the use of continuation sheets is cheaper than catering for maximum volume) but very small pieces of paper are easily lost and very large sizes are awkward to handle. The quality and texture of the paper used for forms are influenced by the extent to which the form is handled; whether or not both sides are used; the need for retention and the method of filing; and the manner in which information is entered on the form.

Ad hoc Reports

From time to time the management accountant will be asked to prepare special reports on particular aspects of the company's activities which, to be of any real value, need to be prepared with considerable care and skill. First, the report must be addressed to a particular person by name or office and indicate all the people receiving copies of it. The report should be dated and signed by the person responsible for it. The form and content of the body of a report will depend on the particular circumstances, but it should be given a suitably descriptive title including any time period to which it relates. A good report is a well-planned one with carefully chosen words to convey the necessary message simply, briefly, and precisely.

Most *ad hoc* reports should be arranged in three distinct parts—fact, comment, and recommendation. The first part of the report includes a statement of the terms of reference, followed by an unembellished statement describing the situation covered by the report. It is important that this should be a factual report, void of all personal opinions, so that the reader can form his own judgments.

The second part of the report contains the writer's own assessment and interpretation of the situation described in the first part. This gives the reader an opportunity to compare the writer's views with his own.

Finally, the report should indicate the author's recommendations on the possible courses of action to be taken arising from his assessment of the present situation. This, too, should be straightforward and unequivocal, otherwise the essential message will be lost in a cloud of words and the purpose of the report may be frustrated.

In writing reports it is necessary to be objective and unemotional; to eschew dogmatic assertions and sweeping generalizations; and to suppress personal antagonisms. The main body of the report must not be cluttered up with statistics, tables, and other detailed data, which should be contained in an appendix. (Students preparing for examinations would do well to ponder carefully on these points for report writing and learn to apply them to examination answers, as the situations are very similar.)

Cost Book-keeping

The Cost Ledger

Ledger is the collective noun used for accounts and hence the cost ledger embraces all the various individual cost accounts of a business. Most businesses will have a considerable number of separate cost accounts, which could result in a large cost ledger. The accounts are arranged, therefore, into smaller homogeneous groupings to form subsidiary ledgers within the cost ledger. The stores (or materials) ledger contains all the materials stock accounts; the overhead ledger embraces the sectional overhead accounts; the work-in-progress ledger holds the job or process accounts; etc. The particular grouping of cost accounts into subsidiary ledgers varies from one business to another, but normally there will be at least the stores ledger, the overhead ledger, the work-in-progress ledger and the finished goods ledger. The cost ledger could contain a sales account and so arrive at a profit.

Double Entry Principle

As in all methods of book-keeping, cost accounts are firmly based on the principle of double entry; that is, a recognition of the dual nature of **giving** and **receiving** in every transaction. Thus, each costing transaction will create a debit entry in the **receiving account** and a credit entry in the **giving account**. Nevertheless, the traditional format for accounts of debits on the left and credits on the right will seldom, if ever, be apparent in cost accounts, as the format is designed to suit **particular conditions**. In some cases, the debits are recorded in the upper part of a page and the credits in the lower part. As the entries in many cost accounts are debits (credits frequently being totals of several debits) it is not customary to separate debits from credits but to post the debit entries in black and credit entries in red.

There are other instances where an account only appears to have debits, such as a **job cost account**, which is removed from the work-in-progress ledger on completion and transferred to the finished stock ledger but, as will be explained in Chapter Eight, this is more apparent than real. Yet again, the overhead accounts may be kept in the form of an analysed apportionment schedule as illustrated in Chapter Seven. Nevertheless, the double-entry principle is always observed.

Ledger Control Accounts

In accountancy two types of ledger control are usually found in practice, the first one being used to make a ledger self-balancing. Provided that the double entry is correctly completed for each transaction, then the total debit balances within the ledger will be equal to the total credit balances. For this reason, agreement between debits and credits is taken to be *prima facie* evidence that the double entry has been completed satisfactorily, apart from a risk of compensating errors.

If both debit and credit entries are made correctly in the same ledger there is no question of the debits not equalling the credits, but for many transactions the debits appears in one subsidiary ledger and the credits in another. There-fore, although in neither subsidiary ledger will the debits equal the credits, they will be equal in the cost ledger as a whole. The subsidiary ledgers are rendered self-balancing by the introduction of a **ledger control account** and a separate trial balance can then be extracted from each ledger, which localizes any differences revealed. The control account enables the double entry to be completed within each ledger, so that a transaction involving two ledgers will call for **four entries** to be made. To illustrate this point, consider an issue from the stores of the cast-iron frames to job number M319. The journal entry for this transaction in its simplest form would be:

Dr. Job M319 (in the work-in-progress ledger).

Cr. Cast-iron frames (in the stores ledger).

However, in neither ledger would the double entry be completed unless a control account is introduced, when the journal entry for the transaction would appear as:

(1) Dr. Job M319.
   Cr. Work-in-progress control account.
(2) Dr. Stores control account.
   Cr. Cast-iron frames.

The use of the control accounts thus requires four entries for inter-ledger transactions. The balance on a cost control account will normally be a credit and equal to the aggregate debit balances on individual cost accounts. Thus the value of work in progress (an asset or *debit balance*) is equal to the *credit balance* on the work-in-progress ledger control account—a possible source of confusion.

To overcome this risk ·of confusion it is more usual to find in practice the second form of ledger control account. This is the **summary control account**—as distinct from the self-balancing control account—which provides a summary of all the transactions recorded in the individual or subordinate accounts of the ledger. Consequently, every debit in one of the subordinate accounts gives rise to a debit in the ledger control account and *vice versa*. Thus the journal entry using the previous example would be:

(1) Dr.   Job M319.
     Dr.   Work-in-progress control account.
(2) Cr.   Stores control account.
     Cr.   Cast-iron frames.

In this way, the control account provides a summary of the transactions posted to the ledger and its balance is the total of the balances appearing in the subordinate accounts. It also possesses the qualities of a self-balancing control account in that the total of a list of subordinate balances should be the same as the control account balance: thus providing *prima facie* evidence of the accuracy of posting. The debit balance in the work-in-progress control account, therefore, represents the value of work-in-progress and will be the figure shown as a current asset in the balance sheet at that date as will stores and finished goods.

Relationship between Cost and Financial Accounts

Both cost accounting and financial accounting use the same basic data but in different ways—rather as a builder can construct many different types of house from the same bricks, doors, and windows. Financial accounting analyses revenue and expenditure according to types of transaction such as purchases, sales, wages, travelling expenses, and so on. This century has witnessed an increasing awareness of the irrelevance for management decision-making of this kind of classification. Variations in the total expenditure or revenue of individual types of transaction are much less significant than the causes of such variations. This requires a recognition of the **source** of each transaction which is only possible under the **functional analysis** pursued by cost accountancy.

Every item of revenue or expenditure springs from a management decision of one kind or another, consequently the source of each transaction is a particular management decision. Since all management structures tend to be functionally orientated, the sources of revenue and expenditure transactions will also be related to management functions, so that cost and management accounting follows a functional analysis of data. Costs are expenditures incurred by particular sections of an organization and it is the aggregate costs for individual sections which are important rather than the total expenditure by all sections collectively on particular types of expense. The functional analysis of transactions has also stimulated an awareness of cost behaviour by demonstrating the effect on cost incidence of changes in the level of activity. It thus becomes possible under the functional analysis of cost accounting to assess the significance of cost movements and especially to provide realistic forecasts of future revenues and expenditures as a basis for management policies. (Chapter Three is devoted to a study of cost behaviour.)

These two different concepts of accounting have led to the separate evolution of financial and cost accounting. The increasing recognition of the importance of cost and management accounting has led to a growing awareness of the irrelevance of the financial accounting approach. Nevertheless, both are concerned with the analysis of the same data with the same ultimate objective in view, and modern practice recognizes the mutual interdependence at least of these two arms of accountancy, while a significant body of opinion rejects the accountancy dichotomy altogether and proclaims the **indivisibility of accounting**. The actual relationship between cost accounts and financial accounts tends to vary quite widely in different companies but it is possible to classify them all into four groups ranging from complete independence to full integration. In the first two methods it is necessary to introduce into the cost ledger a master control account to permit completion of the double entry for items which originate outside the cost ledger or are ultimately transferred out.

Independent Systems

Although using much the same basic data, the financial accounts are completely separated from the cost accounts and there is usually little or no general exchange of information. The most likely exceptions are the valuations of stocks and work in progress, which may be taken from the cost accounts to prepare the final accounts and the balance sheet, but this is by no means certain. This is really an unfortunate situation as each set of accounts will produce a profit figure which differs from the other and can only foster doubts as to the reliability of both. With reason too, for where the two *profits* are not reconciled, both are just as likely to be wrong as is either one and this reckless independence does a disservice to both management and accountancy.

Reconciled Accounts

Although the cost accounts are independent of the financial accounts, it is recognized—since there will be a different result from each set of figures—that it ought to be possible to account for and justify the difference between the two profits figures. To effect a reconciliation between the financial accounts and the cost accounts it is necessary to recognize the areas of difference, and the reasons for the difference.

Points of Agreement. Between the two sets of accounts these will normally be found in:

(1) *Wages.* The postings in both sets of accounts are derived from the pay-roll, and so exactly the same figure should be used.
(2) *Materials.* Postings are prepared from the suppliers' invoices in both cases.
(3) *Expenses.* Each system will be posted from the same original documents —invoices.
(4) *Sales.* Copy invoices form the basis of postings in each case.

Points of Difference. The differences between cost accounts and financial accounts fall into four categories and represent the points calling for reconciliation. Although all four points will not be present in every example of reconciled accounts, they do indicate the most probable differences:

(1) *Valuation of Stores, Work-in-Progress, and Stocks.* In the cost accounts these items will normally be valued at cost, whereas the financial accounts valuation may accord with the accountancy precept of prudence and follow

the **cost or market rule** by taking the lower value of cost or current market price (*see* Chapter Four for a fuller treatment of this topic).

(2) *Items Included in Cost Accounts Only.* These include **notional costs** such as rent where the premises are owned; interest on the capital employed in the business; or, where assets are fully written-off but retained in use, the cost accounts may continue to include depreciation in order not to vitiate the comparison of costs between different periods.

(3) *Items Included in Financial Books Only.* They usually comprise those items which are not normal trading or manufacturing items such as donations to charities; income from investments; rents receivable; profits and losses on the sale of investments and assets; and so on. In most cases the items also include the costs of capital such as interest on overdrafts, loans, and debentures.

(4) *Depreciation.* This is often treated differently in the two sets of accounts, apart from the point mentioned in (2) above. The financial accounts may use the 'annual allowance' rate, related to the expected asset life. The financial accounts will usually adopt a time basis such as diminishing value or straight-line, whereas the cost accounts may take the machine-hour basis or some similar usage basis.

Where such points of difference occur a reconciliation between the results reported by the two systems can be effected by means of a **Reconciliation Statement**. This commences with the costing profit, followed by the various points of difference, and so ends with the financial profit. The reconciliation is necessary not only to avoid a loss of confidence by management in both sets of accounts (as the average non-accountant will find difficulty in accepting that both are correct), but also to use each set of figures as a reliability check on the other.

Interlocking Accounts

This arrangement recognizes the interdependence of the two accounting systems and attempts to reduce the points of difference by adopting common procedures as far as possible. In general, this means that the valuation of stores, work in progress, and stocks are taken from the cost accounts and both sets use the same bases for depreciation. Normally, all items of expenditure and revenue will originate in the financial books but 'cost data' will be transferred into the cost accounts. This is done through opening special control accounts in each set of accounts. In the cost ledger a **financial ledger control account** is introduced (in place of the cost ledger master control account) which acts as the channel between the two systems. There will be also a cost ledger control account opened in the financial books to complete the interlocking of the two systems. The two sets of accounts with their inter-locking control accounts function similarly to the system already described for the subsidiary ledgers in the cost accounts. The payment of wages provides a good illustration of this and the simplified journal entries follow:

Financial Books

    (1) Dr.   Wages account.
           Cr.   Bank account.
    (2) Dr.   Cost ledger control account.
           Cr.   Wages account.

Costing Books

(3) Dr. Wages control account.
    Cr. Financial ledger control account.
(4) Dr. Work-in-progress control account.
    Dr. Overhead control account.
    Cr. Wages control account.

At the close of the accounting year, the costing profit is transferred through the interlocking control accounts into the financial books. The balance then remaining on the cost ledger control account (in the financial books) will equal the aggregate balances remaining in the cost ledger, so that a costing trial balance provides an analysis of this figure for the preparation of the final accounts and balance sheet. This system of interlocking accounts is fairly widely practised, but usually wrongly described as integrated accounts. It is often accompanied by the so-called 'third-entry method' which is a less than practical way of using the interlocking control accounts and is best avoided.

Integrated Accounts

This is a single unified system of accounts which rejects the concept of an accounting dichotomy. It is based on the premise that accounting is undivided, so that financial accounts and cost accounts are parts of a whole rather than being two parallel but related systems. At its simplest, integrated accounts means starting with the financial records but substituting the cost ledger for the nominal ledger so there is one set of accounts embracing all the transactions of the business. The earlier example of the journal entry for wages under an integrated system would be:

(1) Dr. Wages control account.
    Cr. Bank account.
(2) Dr. Work-in-progress control account.
    Dr. Overhead control account.
    Cr. Wages control account.

A further example of the integration of cost and financial accounts is found in the annual provision for depreciation:

    Dr. Overhead control account.
    Cr. Provision for depreciation account.

There are clearly sound objections to the unnecessary duplication of accounting records, especially when one of the systems provides an analysis by types of expense which is irrelevant to the present day needs of management. Accounting exists to provide data for management decision-making and, in this sense, all accounting is management accounting—or it is nothing. The preparation of published accounts or accounts for the Inland Revenue is important, but these are, nevertheless, only by-products of management accounting. Therefore, the accounting system should be structured to provide the necessary data for management and this is best done within a properly integrated accounting system.

Illustration of Integrated Book-keeping

The following illustration shows how the book-keeping entries would appear under integrated accounting systems. The Apollo Moonstone

Company Limited maintains its ledger in integral form and the following data has been taken from the company's books for the month of May.

	£
Opening Balances	
Ordinary Share Capital Account	500,000
Profit and Loss Appropriation Account	8,277
General Reserve Account	39,600
Bought Ledger Control Account	40,293
Buildings—freehold (cost £180,000)	155,200
Plant and Machinery (cost £200,000)	166,283
Investments (at cost)	12,500
Stocks—Raw materials	58,564
—Work in progress	63,114
—Finished goods	44,334
Sales Ledger Control Account	82,948
Cash at bank	5,227
Transactions for the month	
Sales invoiced to customers	95,832
Works cost of goods sold	75,840
Purchases of raw materials	56,822
Payments made to creditors	68,607
Cash received from debtors	107,690
Cash drawn from bank for wages and salaries	42,229
P.A.Y.E. deducted from wages and salaries	7,550
National Insurance and Graduated Pension	2,856
Completed production transferred to Finished Stock	93,412
Sundry expenses (all received on credit)	7,200

	Wages and Salaries £	Raw Materials £	Sundry Expenses £
Direct costs	28,960	25,024	2,400
Production Machine Shop	6,450	3,246	2,600
Production Assembly Department	4,280	2,464	1,450
Service Department 'A'	4,593	3,388	242
Service Department 'B'	3,512	1,936	387
Selling and Administration	4,840	—	121

Additional Information

	Value of Buildings £	Value of Machinery £	Apportion Dept. 'B' £
Production Machine Shop	54,000	159,000	50%
Production Assembly Department	48,000	12,000	30%
Service Department 'A'	18,000	18,000	—
Service Department 'B'	24,000	15,000	—
Selling and Administration Office	36,000	6,000	20%

Service Department 'A' is apportioned to all other departments in the ratio of their respective plant and machinery values.

Depreciation: Buildings at five per cent per annum on cost.

Plant and machinery at ten per cent per annum on cost.

Overhead Absorption: Machine Shop—£25,200

Assembly Department—£10,600

Selling and Administration—£6,900

JOURNAL ENTRIES

	£	£
Sales Ledger Control A/c	95,832	
Sales Account		95,832
Being sales during May		
Trading Account	75,840	
Finished Goods Stock A/c		75,840
Being cost of sales for May		
Raw Materials Stock A/c	56,822	
Bought Ledger Control A/c		56,822
Being purchases for May		
Bought Ledger Control A/c	68,607	
Bank Account		68,607
Being payments to suppliers		
Bank Account	107,690	
Sales Ledger Control A/c		107,690
Being payments by customers		
Wages and Salaries Account	52,635	
Bank Account		42,229
P.A.Y.E. Account		7,550
Nat. Ins. and Grad.		
Pensions A/c		2,856
Being gross wages paid for May		
Finished Goods Stock A/c	93,412	
W.I.P. Control Account		93,412
Being output completed in May		
Sundry Expenses Account	7,200	
Bought Ledger Control A/c		7,200
Being general expenses in May		
W.I.P. Control Account	28,960	
Machine Shop Overhead A/c	6,450	
Assembly Overhead A/c	4,280	
Service Department 'A' A/c	4,593	
Service Department 'B' A/c	3,512	
Selling and Administration		
Overhead A/c	4,840	
Wages and Salaries Account		52,635
Being wages analysis for May		
W.I.P. Control Account	25,024	
Machine Shop Overhead A/c	3,246	
Assembly Overhead A/c	2,464	
Service Department 'A' A/c	3,388	
Service Department 'B' A/c	1,936	
Raw Materials Stock A/c		36,058
Being stores issues in May		

	£	£
W.I.P. Control Account	2,400	
Machine Shop Overhead A/c	2,600	
Assembly Overhead A/c	1,450	
Service Department 'A' A/c	242	
Service Department 'B' A/c	387	
Selling and Administration		
Overhead A/c	121	
Sundry Expenses Account		7,200
Being analysis of expenses		
incurred during May		
Machine Shop Overhead A/c	225	
Assembly Overhead A/c	200	
Service Department 'A' A/c	75	
Service Department 'B' A/c	100	
Selling and Administration		
Overhead A/c	150	
Freehold Buildings Account		750
Being depreciation provided		
on buildings for May		
Machine Shop Overhead A/c	1,325	
Assembly Overhead A/c	100	
Service Department 'A' A/c	150	
Service Department 'B' A/c	125	
Selling and Administration		
Overhead A/c	50	
Plant and Machinery A/c		1,750
Being provision for deprecia-		
tion on plant and machinery		
in May		
Machine Shop Overhead A/c	6,996	
Assembly Overhead A/c	528	
Service Department 'B' A/c	660	
Selling and Administration		
Overhead A/c	264	
Service Department 'A' A/c		8,448
Being apportionment of cost		
Machine Shop Overhead A/c	3,360	
Assembly Overhead A/c	2,016	
Selling and Administration		
Overhead A/c	1,344	
Service Department 'B' A/c		6,720
Being apportionment of cost		
W.I.P. Control Account	35,800	
Machine Shop Overhead A/c		25,200
Assembly Overhead A/c		10,600
Being overhead absorbed		
Profit and Loss Account	6,900	
Selling and Administration		
Overhead		6,900
Being overhead absorbed		
Sales Account	95,832	
Trading Account		95,832
Being balance transferred		
Trading Account	19,992	
Profit and Loss Account		19,992
Being gross profit for May		

THE LEDGER

Ordinary Share Capital Account

May 1 Balance b/for	500,000

Profit and Loss Appropriation Account

May 1 Balance b/for	8,277

General Reserve Account

May 1 Balance b/for	39,600

Bought Ledger Control Account

May 31 Bank Account	68,607	May 1 Balance b/for	40,293
31 Balance c/d	35,708	31 Raw Material Stock	56,822
		31 Sundry Expenses	7,200
	£104,315		£104,315
		June 1 Balance b/d	35,708

Freehold Buildings Account

May 1 Balance b/for	155,200	May 31 Sundries (depn.)	750
		31 Balance c/d	154,450
	£155,200		£155,200
June 1 Balance b/d	154,450		

Plant and Machinery Account

May 1 Balance b/for	166,283	May 31 Sundries (depn.)	1,750
		31 Balance c/d	164,533
	£166,283		£166,283
June 1 Balance b/d	164,533		

Investments Account

May 1 Balance b/for	12,500

Raw Materials Stock Account

May 1 Balance b/for	58,564	May 31 W.I.P. Control A/c	25,024
31 Bought Ledger	56,822	31 Machine Shop Overhead	3,246
		31 Assembly Overhead	2,464
		31 Service Dept. 'A'	3,388
		31 Service Dept. 'B'	1,936
		31 Balance c/d	79,328
	£115,386		£115,386
June 1 Balance b/d	79,328		

Work-in-progress Control Account

May 1	Balance b/for ..	63,114	May 31	Finished Goods	93,412
31	Wages and Salaries	28,960	31	Balance c/d	61,886
31	Raw Materials Stock	25,024			
31	Sundry Expenses ..	2,400			
31	Machine Shop Overhead ..	25,200			
31	Assembly Overhead	10,600			
		£155,298			£155,298
June 1	Balance b/d	61,886			

Finished Goods Stock Account

May 1	Balance b/for	44,334	May 31	Trading Account	75,840
31	W.I.P. Control A/c	93,412	31	Balance c/d	61,906
		£137,746			£137,746
June 1	Balance b/d	61,906			

Sales Ledger Control Account

May 1	Balance b/for	82,948	May 31	Bank Account	107,690
31	Sales Account	95,832	31	Balance c/d	71,090
		£178,780			£178,780
June 1	Balance b/d	71,090			

Bank Account

May 1	Balance b/for	5,227	May 31	Bought Ledger	68,607
31	Sales Ledger	107,690	31	Wages and Salaries	42,229
			31	Balance c/d	2,081
		£112,917			£112,917
June 1	Balance b/d	2,081			

P.A.Y.E. Account

		May 31 Wages and Salaries	7,550

National Insurance and Graduated Pension Account

		May 31 Wages and Salaries	2,856

Wages and Salaries Account

May 31	Bank Account	42,229	May 31	W.I.P. Control A/c	28,960
31	P.A.Y.E. Account	7,550	31	Machine Shop Overhead	6,450
31	Nat. Ins. and Grad. Pension	2,856	31	Assembly Overhead	4,280
			31	Service Dept. 'A'	4,593
			31	Service Dept. 'B'	3,512
			31	Selling and Administration	4,840
		£52,635			£52,635

Sundry Expenses Account

May 31 Bought Ledger	7,200	May 31 W.I.P. Control A/c			2,400
		31 Machine Shop			
		Overhead			2,600
		31 Assembly Overhead			1,450
		31 Service Dept. 'A'			242
		31 Service Dept. 'B'			387
		31 Selling and Admini-			
		stration			121
	£7,200				£7,200

Machine Shop Overhead Account

May 31 Wages and Salaries	6,450	May 31 W.I.P. Control A/c	25,200
31 Raw Materials Stock	3,246		
31 Sundry Expenses	2,600		
31 Building depreciation	225		
31 Machinery depreciation	1,325		
31 Service Dept. 'A'	6,996		
31 Service Dept. 'B'	3,360		
31 Balance c/d	998		
	£25,200		£25,200
		June 1 Balance b/d	998

Assembly Department Overhead Account

May 31 Wages and Salaries	4,280	May 31 W.I.P. Control A/c	10,600
31 Raw Materials Stock	2,464	31 Balance c/d	438
31 Sundry Expenses	1,450		
31 Building depreciation	200		
31 Machinery depreciation	100		
31 Service Dept. 'A'	528		
31 Service Dept. 'B'	2,016		
	£11,038		£11,038
June 1 Balance b/d	438		

Service Department 'A' Account

May 31 Wages and Salaries	4,593	May 31 Machine Shop	
31 Raw Materials Stock	3,388	Overhead	6,996
31 Sundry Expenses	242	31 Assembly Overhead	528
31 Building depreciation	75	31 Service Dept. 'B'	660
31 Machinery depreciation	150	31 Selling and Admini-	
		stration	264
	£8,448		£8,448

Service Department 'B' Account

May 31	Wages and Salaries	3,512	May 31	Machine Shop	
	31 Raw Materials Stock	1,936		Overhead	3,360
	31 Sundry Expenses	387		31 Assembly Overhead	2,016
	31 Building depreciation	100		31 Selling and Admini-	
	31 Machinery depreciation	125		stration	1,344
	31 Service Dept. 'A'	660			
		£6,720			£6,720

Selling and Administration Overhead Account

May 31	Wages and Salaries	4,840	May 31	Profit and Loss A/c	6,900
	31 Sundry Expenses	121			
	31 Building depreciation	150			
	31 Machinery depreciation	50			
	31 Service Dept. 'A'	264			
	31 Service Dept. 'B'	1,344			
	31 Balance c/d	131			
		£6,900			£6,900
			June 1	Balance b/d	131

Sales Account

May 31	Trading Account	95,832	May 31	Sales Ledger	95,832

Trading Account

May 31	Finished Goods Stock	75,840	May 31	Sales Account	95,832
	31 Profit and Loss (Gross Profit)	19,992			
		£95,832			£95,832

Profit and Loss Account

May 31	Selling and Administration	6,900	May 31	Trading Account	19,992
	31 Net Profit c/d	13,092			
		£19,992			£19,992
			June 1	Balance b/d	13,092

TRIAL BALANCE AT MAY 31, 1973

	£	£
Ordinary Share Capital Account		500,000
Profit and Loss Appropriation Account ..		8,277
Profit and Loss Account		13,092
General Reserve Account		39,600
Bought Ledger Control Account		35,708
Freehold Buildings Account	154,450	
Plant and Machinery Account	164,533	
Investments Account	12,500	
Raw Materials Stock Account	79,328	
W.I.P. Control Account	61,886	
Finished Goods Stock Account	61,906	
Sales Ledger Control Account	71,090	
Bank Account	2,081	
P.A.Y.E. Account		7,550
National Insurance and Graduated Pensions		2,856
Machine Shop Overhead Account		998
Assembly Department Overhead Account	438	
Selling and Administration Overhead Account		131
	£608,212	£608,212

Exercises

1. As the cost accountant of The Fiume River Limited you have been submitting monthly costing profit and loss accounts which show that the company is making an average profit of £20,000 per month. The managing director is now apt to doubt your figures because the financial accounts show an average profit of only £16,000 per month.

Required:

Submit a report to the managing director explaining the possible cause of this difference between the two sets of results and outline any possible action you would propose to take in future periods with regard to this situation. [C.A.A.]

2. Describe in detail how you would set about the installation of a costing system in a medium-sized manufacturing concern, in which at present only annual financial accounts are produced. [C.A.A.]

3. Your company has an efficient system of costing which is independent of the company's financial accounts. Discuss the likely causes of possible differences in the profit performance as shown by the two sets of accounts and explain the steps you would take to reconcile the figures. [C.A.A.]

4. Compare the advantages and disadvantages of a system of integrated accounting with that of reconciled accounting. [C.A.A.]

5. State the major factors of effective form design and describe how these might be achieved in a large organization. [C.A.A.]

6. The following accounts appear in the ledger of a manufacturing company. You are required to:

    (i) explain briefly the meaning of each of the entries labelled (*a*) to (*s*), and

    (ii) write a short note to explain the function of each of the accounts and the significance of the word 'control' in their titles.

Stores Ledger Control Account

	£		£
(a) Balance b/for	8,192	(c) Suppliers	59
(b) Suppliers	13,654	(d) Work in progress	12,184
		(e) Production overhead	1,379
		(f) Stores discrepancies	17
		(g) Balance c/d	8,207
	£21,846		£21,846

Work-in-progress Control Account

	£		£
(h) Balance b/for	7,123	(l) Finished goods	32,093
(i) Stores ledger	12,184	(m) Balance c/d	4,179
(j) Wages	9,292		
(k) Production overhead	7,673		
	£36,272		£36,272

Production Overhead Control Account

	£		£
(n) Suppliers	4,121	(r) Work in progress	7,673
(o) Stores ledger	1,379	(s) Overhead adjustment	23
(p) Wages	2,179		
(q) Stores discrepancies	17		
	£7,696		£7,696

[A.C.A.]

7. C Limited operates an integrated accounting system.
The trial balance at May 1, 1973 was as follows:

	£'000	£'000
Raw material stock	138	—
Work in progress	34	—
Finished goods stock	62	—
Debtors	200	—
Creditors	—	140
Expense creditors	—	58
Wages accrued	—	11
P.A.Y.E. tax	—	45
Bank	40	—
Freehold buildings	360	—
Plant and machinery, at cost	240	—
Provision for depreciation, plant and machinery	—	60
Issued share capital	—	600
General reserve	—	120
Profit and loss account	—	40
	£1,074	£1,074

The following information is given of the transactions that took place in May 1973:

	£'000
Sales	320
Purchases of raw materials	92
Raw materials returned to supplier	4
Production overhead incurred	88
Selling and distribution costs incurred	42
Administration costs incurred	37
Direct wages incurred	42
Raw materials issued:	
to production	80
to production maintenance department	10
Raw materials returned to store from production ..	2
Abnormal loss in process	5
Cost of finished goods sold	210
Payments received in respect of sales	330
Payments made for raw materials purchased.. ..	101
Discounts allowed	11
Discounts received	3
Payments made to expense creditors	140
Direct wages paid	34
P.A.Y.E. tax deducted from wages	16

You are informed that:
(i) depreciation of plant and machinery is provided for at ten per cent per annum of cost;
(ii) production overhead is absorbed on the basis of 250 per cent of direct wages incurred;
(iii) selling and distribution costs and administration costs incurred in May 1973, are charged against the profit of May 1973;
(iv) work in progress was valued on May 31, 1973 at £39,000.

You are required to:
(a) open and write up the accounts for May 1973;
(b) prepare a profit and loss account for May 1973.

[C.M.A.]

CHAPTER THREE

COST BEHAVIOUR PATTERNS

A study of cost behaviour reveals that an increase in activity, for example a higher level of output, will always result in an increase in total cost. The converse is equally evident—lower costs will be incurred at lower levels of activity. In other words, there tends to be a more or less direct relationship between output and the cost of manufacturing that output. Closer investigation reveals that this is a common characteristic not only of individual products and functions but also of business activity as a whole, be it in the manufacture of tangible articles or the provision of services. However, although costs do move in sympathy with output changes, the cost movement tends to be less sensitive than the activity change. Therefore, for double the volume of output, costs will tend to increase by less than one hundred per cent, while there will be a proportionately smaller decline in total cost in relation to a given reduction in the activity. Common sense indicates that costs should behave in this manner, but (for such to be of value to the accountant) it must be possible to anticipate or predict the cost changes which will follow from any given rise or fall in the volume of production. This creates the need to establish a clear relationship between costs and output, where possible.

Influence of Activity Level

A detailed study of each item of cost under varying conditions of activity shows that there are two broad groups of cost behaviour patterns. Cost items in one group tend to vary more or less *directly* with activity, while costs in the other group remain largely unaffected by volume changes. These two types of cost behaviour are known as **variable costs** and **fixed costs**.

Variable costs are defined as those cost items which vary more or less directly with changes in the level of activity.

Fixed costs are defined as those cost items which will be relatively unaffected by changes in the level of activity.

In each case these definitions relate to the **total expenditure** on that particular item of cost for a given volume of output. It follows, therefore (if these distinctions are *valid*), that the distinction is one of fundamental importance in the determination of cost, since the incidence of cost depends on the level of activity, or output achieved or expected. Consequently, it is essential to test the validity of these concepts of cost behaviour first and only then is it possible to develop further the theory from that point, in accordance with the results obtained.

Variable Cost

Direct costs (prime costs) can be expected to display variable characteristics, since each additional unit produced will consume extra materials and require the application of further labour in its production. Whilst there tends to be a direct relationship between output and prime cost, there will be some minor deviations from an **absolute direct variability.**

A consideration of direct materials reveals that higher output will increase the rate of consumption and so the purchase of larger quantities may enable the company to take advantage of quantity discounts or other favourable terms. In this case, the expenditure on materials will increase by a slightly smaller proportion than the rise in output which generated it. However, increased demand for materials may necessitate finding additional sources of supply at less favourable prices, or a search for substitutes at higher prices. Similar considerations apply to direct labour costs. Extra labour may be 'obtained' by overtime working, but the workers will expect to be *compensated* through the payment of an overtime allowance in addition to their normal earnings. Two- or three-shift working could be introduced to increase the capacity of existing resources but, here again, shift allowances will be payable over and above the normal earnings to compensate the workers for the personal inconvenience engendered by the shift-work. Labour costs may rise at a lower rate than output where the labour force is currently under-employed, so that some economy is effected in *taking-up the slack.*

Variable Overhead

Certain overhead also will display variable characteristics while the remainder will be more or less fixed in nature. Variable overhead includes indirect materials and indirect manual labour in production departments. Fuel and power consumption will also tend to vary with output: higher output, all other things being equal, will be derived from more hours of operation, which creates higher power usage. Also, the payment of royalties is customarily determined by the volume of output (or sales in some instances), so that this cost, too, will have variable characteristics. Variable expenses may be distinguished as being of three types, as illustrated in Fig. 1. In practice,

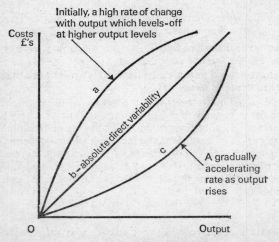

Fig. 1. Types of cost variability

the deviation from *b*—the curve of absolute direct variability—towards curves *a* or *c* is not usually significant for most practical situations and can be safely ignored. Where, however, a cost item is known to behave similarly to either *a* or *c* in a significant manner, or it is significant in amount, it should be treated accordingly. Even so, it will only be really significant over the whole range of output and, under normal business conditions, fluctuations in output are likely to be contained within a much narrower range; within which the characteristics of *a* and *c* curves become rather less significant. It should also be kept in mind that the aggregate variable costs will tend to approximate much more closely towards curve *b* as the *a* items are offset through the inclusion of *c* items. Thus, for all practical purposes, variable costs can be presumed to behave similarly to the *b* curve of Fig. 1.

Validity of the Variable Concept

Nevertheless, some accountants reject any general concept of variable cost and suggest that in the short term, at least, most costs are fixed and this is especially true of labour. It is, of course, evident nowadays that it is no longer possible to lay off men or put them on short time at 'the drop of a hat'—nor should it be! Experience shows that the day-to-day fluctuations in output do not markedly affect the total wages bill which tends, therefore, to remain constant. However, there are two distinct aspects to this particular problem. First, direct wages will, all other things being equal, tend to display variable characteristics, so that payments for **direct labour** will always tend to vary more or less directly with activity. Secondly, close scrutiny shows that for a given level of activity (say, normal capacity) any cut-back in production will give rise to 'make-up' payments designed to maintain the workers' expected earnings level, so that the total wages bill remains unchanged. Conversely, any increase in output beyond the 'normal' will usually be matched by a corresponding rise in direct wages. The point here is that direct wages do remain variable throughout—the 'make-up' element of wages being analysed as an indirect cost.

This practice in turn *begs the question* of the wisdom of continuing to follow this traditional analysis of costs. It is apparent that we are inevitably moving steadily towards a **salaried manual workforce**, which can but result in **fixed labour costs** in the short term, say, weekly or monthly. There are, therefore, good grounds for recognizing these *de facto* weekly payments under make-up agreements with a consequent amendment to the rules of cost analysis. If we do so, however, the whole of an operator's wages would be treated as direct costs and we would lose track of the various forms of idle time with their supposed labour costs. It is true that the payment of wages for lost time certainly reflects a failure on the part of management, but it is now questionable that this serves any really useful purpose nowadays. It is only significant under historical costing systems because, paradoxically, all standard costs are variable and changed conditions are reflected in the variances. Whatever reservations may be retained regarding the existence of **truly** variable costs, the concept of variable costs has sufficient validity to merit the description of a **law of cost behaviour**.

Variable Cost per Unit

Since, by definition, the total expenditure on an item of variable cost will fluctuate more or less directly with output, it follows that the variable cost

per unit of output will remain constant at all levels of activity. If it is assumed that a certain variable cost is £800 for 4,000 units of product, then the cost rises by £1 for each additional 5 units manufactured, and the total expenditures for successive increases in output will be:

Output (units)	4,000	5,000	6,000	7,000
Total costs	£800	£1,000	£1,200	£1,400

A simple arithmetical calculation shows that at each level of output the unit cost is the same at £0·20 as shown in Fig. 2. This characteristic of a variable

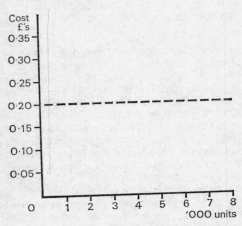

Fig. 2. Variable unit costs

cost, that unit costs will remain constant at all levels of activity, is clearly a matter of considerable significance to management in its decision-making role. All other things being equal, variable costs will vary directly with output. As far as variable costs are concerned there are no **economies of scale** as output rises. In fact, the **law of diminishing returns** is much more likely to operate in such a situation. (Note that in the present context a substitution in the factors of production, such as machinery for labour, is being ignored.) It is also apparent that the margin between selling price and variable cost per unit will tend to remain constant at all levels of output. (This is developed further in Chapters Nineteen and Twenty on marginal costing.)

Fixed Cost

Certain overhead expenses tend to be fixed in nature, that is, they will be the same at all levels of activity. Thus, in Fig. 3 the fixed cost is represented by a linear curve parallel to the abscissa (or *X* axis) used for the independent variable—the output. If it is assumed that a certain item of cost is fixed at £2,000, then the unit costs at successive levels of activity will be:

Output (units)	4,000	5,000	6,000	7,000
Fixed unit cost	£0·50	£0·40	£0·33	£0·29

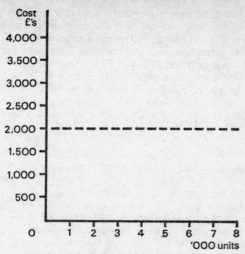

Fig. 3. Total fixed expenditure curve

It follows from the definition that unit costs for fixed expenses will tend to vary inversely with the volume of output, as shown in Fig. 4. The characteristics of a fixed cost will also be of significance for management decisions

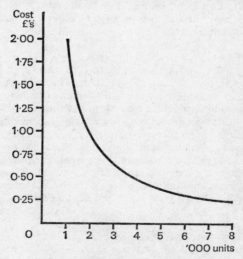

Fig. 4. Fixed expenditure per unit

since total (that is, fixed plus variable) costs per unit will fall as output rises and *vice versa*. This suggests economies of scale from operating at higher levels of activity. Examples of fixed costs include management salaries, rent and rates of premises, insurance on buildings and plant, patents, and licences.

The discussion of fixed costs so far has been made on the assumption that such costs do, in fact, exist—a view that does not go unchallenged in many quarters and a continuing source of controversy amongst both accountants and economists. It is necessary to weigh up the arguments for and against a concept of fixed costs in order to establish whether there is any validity for it, either in general or under specific conditions. The usual premise for dismissing the concept of fixed costs may be summed up in the expression that 'in the long run all costs are variable'. A careful study of the 'long-run' argument indicates two possible and separate interpretations of the usage of the term 'long run'.

Long-term Considerations

The first argument is that, 'No cost is static in a dynamic economy for—at the very least—incipient inflation will ensure a "cost creep" so that all costs will tend to *rise in the long run*. It is true that this may be more or less offset by technological innovation, new sources of supply, a more capital-intensive production and other factors leading to reductions in costs, nevertheless, it is apparent over a period of several years that *all* costs must vary.'

It is indeed true that all costs will vary from time to time for experience shows this to be so and it would be foolish to even attempt a rebuttal of the point. However, this argument does not invalidate in the slightest degree the fixed cost concept. This argument uses 'long run' in the sense of 'long term' (or period), whereas the definition of a fixed cost refers to the influence on the incidence of cost exerted by changed activity. Reference to any other factors influencing cost behaviour is irrelevant and this argument can be rejected unhesitatingly, leaving the fixed-cost concept as acceptable within the terms of its definition.

Long-range Influences

Alternatively, critics use the term 'long run' to refer to all possible levels of output between zero and infinity. This is a much more serious challenge for significant increases in output are unlikely to be met without the provision of additional manufacturing facilities. It will obviously follow that fixed expenses, too, will rise concurrently with the capital expenditure for expansion. Extra buildings attract increased demands for local rates, and insurance premiums will rise to cover the additional plant, buildings, work in progress, personnel, etc. An augmented labour force makes heavier demands on personnel services such as pay-roll preparation, medical and welfare services, canteen facilities, personnel and training organization. Depreciation, if treated as a fixed cost, will also be higher with more production facilities in use.

Stepped Growth

The **variable** characteristics of so-called 'fixed costs' over long-range changes in output can be illustrated by reference to shop-floor supervision which is remunerated on a salary basis. In a particular production department, the labour force required to produce up to X units of output can be supervised by a single foreman at a salary of £Y. To manufacture between X and $2X$ units means, say, doubling the labour force and appointing another foreman so that supervision salaries now total £$2Y$. Further expansion of output to $3X$ units will mean recruiting an additional foreman, so that supervision salaries rise to £3Y for the output range 2X to 3X. Supervision salaries of £4Y are payable when the output capacity reaches 4X units, and so on. This situation is illustrated graphically in Fig. 5. It is plain from this graph that supervision is 'keeping pace' with output and, far from being a fixed cost, is variable over the output range from zero to 4X units and beyond. (For ease of illustration it is assumed that no 'output related' bonus is paid as a supplement to a supervisor's salary, even though its introduction would not invali-

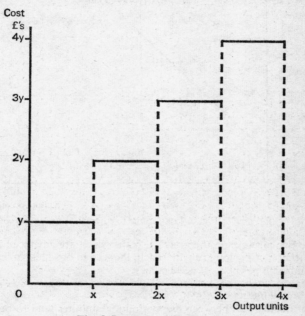

Fig. 5. Incremental fixed costs

date the basic argument in any way.) Figure 6 illustrates that the average cost of salaries for supervision is almost entirely variable, any fixed element being equal to $\frac{1}{2}Y$ (that is, the point on the Y axis where the *average* curve intersects it). In other words, although this expense is fixed for small ranges of output, in the long run it is clearly variable. Thus, it appears to be true that **in the long run all costs are variable**, and consequently the theory of a fixed-cost concept can not be sustained, except within the limitations of a relatively narrow range of volume fluctuations, that is, in the short run.

The 'Fixed-cost School', however, responds to this argument with the charge that it is largely theoretical and unrelated to the practical day-to-day situation which is the environment of cost accountancy. This attitude will be recognized as a normal response to criticism. 'Customary practice' does not always provide sufficient theory in itself, nor is any contradiction of 'customary practice' necessarily academic theorizing without relevance to *real life*. Such an attitude is by no means rare in accountancy which has had little in the way of a conceptual framework until quite recent times. Nevertheless,

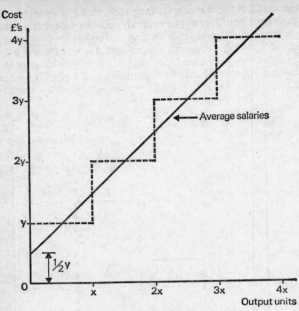

Fig. 6. Long-range fixed costs

there are two answers on the practical plane which are advanced in support of the rejection of the long-run approach, the second of which, at least, merits recognition as a **postulate of accountancy**.

Wide-range Output Fluctuations

Output fluctuations between one period and another tend to be relatively small. Under normal manufacturing conditions, activity on the average will lie within the range of 'normal capacity ± ten per cent'. Catering for peak demands is always expensive as capacity must be available to meet the peak loading yet much of it remains idle during the off-peak periods. Consequently, it is unrealistic to suggest that output fluctuations will range from zero to maximum capacity under normal conditions, especially with the competition experienced by the majority of manufacturers, where price (and therefore cost) is critical in winning orders. The management of a business will naturally wish to see the plant being used at, or near, normal capacity throughout the year, and deviations from this normal level being kept to a minimum. Within the normal fluctuation in activity experienced by industry fixed costs will be found within the normal range of output, say, $3X$ to $4X$ as shown in Fig. 5. It may be concluded, therefore, that the fixed-cost concept is valid within the normal range of activity and so acceptable for most practical situations.

The limitations of this argument are, however, readily apparent to those who have had any real practical experience of cost behaviour. In the *short term* there may well be *long-range* fluctuations in output which go far beyond the 'normal' limits suggested above and arising from a whole spectrum of causes. These will include *inter alia*: unforeseen shortages of materials; power failure; transport delays; rifts in labour relations; fire or other natural hazards; plant breakdown; trade recessions; government restraints and cyclical fluctuations. Any of these events could generate a 'cut-back' in production activity far in excess of ten per cent and even reduce output to zero for a time. Furthermore, it matters little whether this relates to the factory as a whole or to some section of it, for in either case there is lost output from the affected area. Nevertheless, these are clearly 'temporary' reductions in output and there is unlikely to be any consideration by management of the disposal of the **surplus** capacity created by this fall-back in activity; it will be retained in readiness for the next 'upswing' or return to 'normal activity'. It may be postulated that, all other things being equal, significant changes in **capacity** between zero and infinity will generate corresponding changes in the level of fixed expenditure, so that fixed cost will settle at some higher or lower amount than previously. It may be also postulated that each business, as a matter of management policy, will establish a given capacity to produce which will attract certain fixed expenses of operation and that these fixed expenses will remain unaffected by changes in capacity utilization (that is, output) for this given capacity. This being so, the latter postulate can be illustrated graphically in the following manner (Fig. 7)

Capacity to produce	Fixed expense
x units	£y
2x units	£2y
3x units	£3y
4x units	£4y

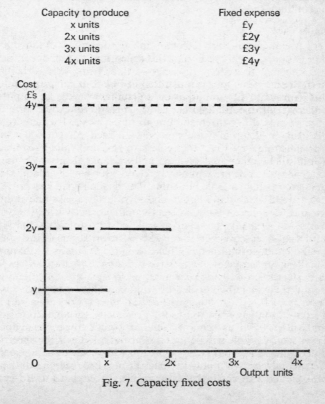

Fig. 7. Capacity fixed costs

using the data from the previous example of supervision salaries. This chart shows that the fixed cost will remain at £4Y for any output level where the *capacity to produce* is 4X units—and similarly for different capacity levels.

Since, therefore, neither the *long-term* argument nor the *long-range* argument can be sustained, the fixed-cost concept can be accepted as valid. Nevertheless, the definition of a fixed cost will be more precise—and perhaps more universally acceptable—were it to be re-phrased as:

A fixed cost is one which will be relatively unaffected in total by changes in the level of activity for a given plant capacity.

The incidence of a fixed cost is thus dependent on the size of the plant capacity, which is determined by **management policy**, so that fixed costs are often known as 'policy costs'. Some accountants shrink from using the term 'fixed cost' because they consider it to be at best misleading and find the term 'policy cost' more acceptable. There are still others who, feeling dissatisfied with both policy costs and fixed costs, formulate alternative terms—sometimes in the belief that they have also formulated a new concept. Some people appear to be more concerned with terminology than—what really matters— with the underlying concepts! It is still true that *a rose by any other name would smell as sweet* and exercises in semantics are particularly unrewarding in the context of accounting, apart from the brake they apply to the development of accounting theory.

Semi-variable Cost

There are certain cost items which tend to vary directly with the volume of output, but proportionately less than the generating movement in activity; and such cost items are customarily referred to as being **semi-variable costs**. This pattern of cost behaviour is illustrated in Fig. 8. It can be seen that the cost of this item is £3Y for an output of '2X' units, whereas an output of 4X units (an increase of one hundred per cent) generates an expenditure of £4Y (an increase of only thirty-three and one-third per cent). It is apparent that this cost is really made up of two components, a fixed element and a variable element, as illustrated by Fig. 9. Needless to say, individual semi-variable costs will not all be composed of fixed and variable elements in the same proportions. Some will be predominantly fixed with a small variable element, while others are mainly variable but containing a small fixed element. (These two extremes are illustrated in Figs. 10 and 11.) This has led some authorities to make a nice distinction between semi-variable costs where the variable element forms at least fifty per cent of total cost at normal activity (as in Fig. 10) and **semi-fixed costs** where the fixed element forms at least fifty per cent of total cost at normal activity (as in Fig. 11). This is a classification which has all the appearances of excessive pedantry. It is hard to give credibility to any suggestion that the cost incurred in such a detailed analysis of expense could in any way be justified by what can only be negligible, if any, gains in accuracy. It will be appreciated that *all* costs must lie within the spectrum from absolutely fixed to absolutely directly variable. In this sense, most costs will be seen as semi-variable, although those costs normally recognized as semi-variable will be found near the middle of the spectrum.

Undoubtedly, three groups of cost behaviour would call for a more complex system of cost analysis than if only two such groups are recognized, therefore to minimize the 'cost of costing' it is more usual to avoid a third group if

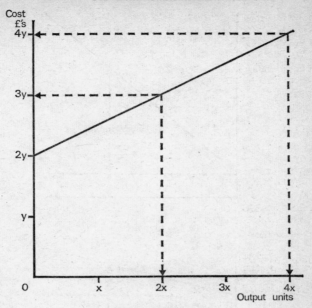

Fig. 8. Semi-variable costs

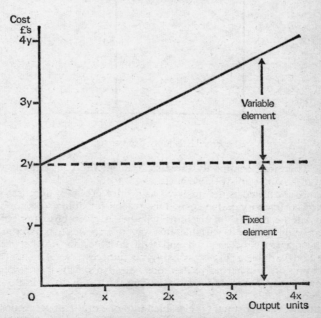

Fig. 9. Elements of semi-variable costs

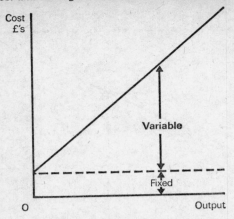

Fig. 10. Mainly variable costs

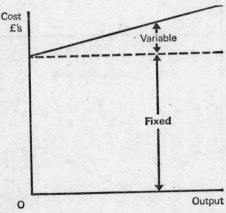

Fig. 11. Mainly fixed costs

possible. There are commonly three separate methods of dealing with the problem of having semi-variable costs.

(1) Semi-variable costs are analysed as a third group of expenses separate from fixed costs and variable costs. One reason for doing so is to avoid the problem 'at the margin' of deciding whether a given cost item should be treated as being fixed or as variable. In a way, this creates two lesser problems: (*a*) at the margin between fixed and semi-variable, and (*b*) between semi-variable and variable. This is probably an unnecessary refinement in most cases, as one of the alternative methods will give satisfactory results under most conditions. There can be no universal rule in this, it depends on circumstances.

(2) Initially, each cost item is classified into one of the three groups—fixed, variable, and semi-variable. Each item of semi-variable cost is then analysed

into its fixed element and its variable element: the fixed elements of all semi-variable costs being aggregated with the fixed costs, while the aggregate variable elements are added to the variable costs, leaving only two classifications of fixed and variable costs. In this manner, the problem of semi-variable costs is overcome by eliminating them through a procedure which is certainly less sophisticated than the former method, but rather more precise than the following one.

(3) No separate classification is made of semi-variable cost items, each cost item is simply analysed into either fixed or variable costs, according to its dominant characteristics under conditions of changing activity. The limits of error from incorrectly classifying the smaller part of the cost incurred are likely, generally speaking, to be minimal, and there will naturally be compensating influences found in each category. A consideration of individual semi-variable cost items leads one to reject this method for its imprecision, although within the context of aggregate costs it has much to commend it, and it is in this context that the cost accountant must ultimately decide. Clearly it raises problems in the control of costs—a matter which is discussed in Chapters Eight to Seventeen.

Conclusion

Cost will always be a factor in business decision-making, though not the only consideration. Sound business decision-making is dependent on an appreciation of cost behaviour as cost is frequently the most critical factor in choosing the **least-cost alternative**. However, cost behaviour is rather more subtle than the simple (almost naive) dichotomy which categorizes every expense as being *per se* either fixed or variable. Each expense will display both fixed and variable characteristics from time to time, depending on the relevant time scale and the influence of changing conditions of operation. It is the cost accountant's responsibility to recognize this fact and, in the individual situation, to identify the prevailing characteristics in each relevant cost item.

Exercises

1. (*a*) Say what you understand by the terms fixed, variable and semi-variable costs.
   (*b*) Give your classification of the following expenses under those headings:

1. Indirect wages.	5. Rent.	9. Machine repairs.
2. Factory insurance.	6. Light and heat.	10. Foreman's wages.
3. Legal expenses.	7. Direct materials.	11. Small tool replacement.
4. National insurance.	8. Lift operator's wages.	12. Plating solutions.

[C.A.A.]

2. 'In the short run, all costs are fixed—in the long run, all costs are variable.' Discuss.

3. Most cost accounting systems are designed to produce data which will enable management to control costs; however, much of this same information is also used for planning purposes. Discuss some of the problems which this presents to the management accountant and what steps are required to overcome them. In particular, you should refer to the distinction between fixed and variable expenses, and the assumption of short-run considerations where nothing will change which underlies the preparation of cost control data.

[A.C.A.]

4. What do you understand by the terms fixed and variable expenses? What is the purpose of such a classification of expenditure in costing?

[C.A.A.]

5. The concept of 'capacity' appears frequently in readings on management accounting. Explain what you understand by (*a*) theoretical capacity; (*b*) normal capacity and (*c*) practical capacity, and how they might be useful in management accounting.

[A.C.A.]

CHAPTER FOUR

MATERIALS COSTING

Importance of Materials

The relative importance of materials costs varies widely between different industries. In sugar refining, materials may represent over ninety per cent of the total production cost; whereas in the extractive industries there is really no direct materials cost at all. Clearly, all industries lie somewhere within this spectrum but, in most industries, materials represent a significant proportion of total costs of production. There is also a wide range in the relative values of individual materials, for example from precious metals to iron ore. Perhaps one of the most frequently overlooked qualities of materials is that it represents **money's worth**. It is an odd trait of human nature that £1 in cash will often be accorded far more respect and attention than will £5 in goods. Materials call for very careful consideration from the cost accountant because they do represent money's worth.

Control of Materials

The ascertainment of materials cost is derived from two primary documents —the supplier's invoice setting out the value of goods purchased and the stores requisition detailing the materials issued to production. Behind these two documents lies a whole complex organization of control. The data recorded on these forms must be reliable, and any cost accounting system which fails to ensure the reliability of basic information will be as 'a house built on sand'.

Furthermore, the **cost of materials** calls for much wider considerations than just the amounts paid to suppliers. Production delays can be expensive in the wages paid to idle workers, in the cost of providing unused facilities, and in the reduced profits through lost output. Consequently, it is necessary to ensure where possible that such delays do not arise from either a general lack of materials or a shortage of particular materials.

The cost accountant, therefore, is concerned with creating the environment which will achieve this, even though the material control department is frequently independent of the accounting function. Management accountancy is directly concerned with the introduction of an effective and efficient system of stores control. Indeed the accountant frequently takes the initiative in setting up the system and will always have a useful contribution to make in its formation.

Influence of the Nature of Materials

The importance of materials as a cost requires the cost accountant's attention in the **control aspects** of all materials. Nevertheless, different materials call for varying degrees of attention according to their relative values and for the risks of deterioration during storage. Precious or valuable metals represent a far higher risk of loss than base metals, since their intrinsic value for a given quantity is far greater, and they are also inherently more attractive to dishonest persons. Consequently, it is necessary to keep a tighter control over the more valuable items. Deterioration risks during storage will also vary widely, and greater care and closer control is required for the perishable materials, than is necessary for the non-perishable ones.

The Purchasing Function

The purchase of materials should be a specialized function in all businesses, and one person in each organization should be given the overall responsibility for placing orders with suppliers. In large companies there will usually be a well-staffed department under the chief buyer; in very small companies the buying may be no more than the *part-time occupation* of one man who also holds other responsibilities. It is, however, essential that the overall responsibility for buying is invested in a single person to avoid waste and inefficiency.

In recent years there has been a continuing debate on the position of the purchasing department within a company's organization structure. Traditionally, buying has been considered to be a **commercial function**, largely because of the opportunities for gains through favourable prices obtained by commercial sagacity. This is particularly true with natural materials where prices will tend to vary throughout the year and also with imported **strategic materials** whose prices are influenced by world political activities. An intelligent anticipation of future prices can yield considerable cost benefits to a business in buying at the right time.

Relationship to Production Control

In the twentieth century there has been a gradual evolvement of the principles of production planning and control, with their application to all kinds of business. This has led to the emergence of a whole range of specialists in production techniques and the implementation of sophisticated schemes in the integration of production activities.

Specialists engaged in production control have also become increasingly aware of the relative significance of its **related aspects**, and nowhere is this more true than in materials. It is argued that **buying** calls for an understanding of the uses to which materials are put and an appreciation of the significance in specified dimensions or qualities, and that this is likely to be lacking in the commercial buyer. The requirements of production, therefore, will only be satisfied where production materials purchasing is accepted as a function of the production control department. However, all buying includes commercial considerations so that the practice of placing the buying department within the production control function has never become widely adopted. Instead, it is customary for the production control to draw up precise specifications of materials required and to communicate these to the buying office in a materials purchase requisition. The buyer then uses his commercial expertise in buying within these specifications.

Centralization of Group Purchasing

Another twentieth-century phenomenon has been the growth of mergers, with a consequential increase in the size of businesses. Companies have linked in both vertical and horizontal structures, and in recent years the **conglo-**

merate has emerged embracing quite different industries to provide diversification. One of the earliest policy problems on amalgamating two businesses lies in a consideration of the advantages from centralizing the various common activities—purchasing being one of the first. It is true that economies can be gained from the centralization of the buying function, but they are normally dependent on the prior rationalization and integration of manufacturing facilities. Experience shows that where the production units remain independent, it is usually better to forgo group centralized purchasing as well.

The Purchasing Model

The first control applied to materials is in the procedures established for the procurement of materials from the company's suppliers. This is achieved in building the **purchasing model**. The authority to place orders is restricted to prevent errors of commission, omission, or duplication and the buying officer is given the sole authority to issue purchase orders. This is by no means a licence to buy anything, at any time, from anywhere, and is circumscribed by withholding authority to initiate specific purchases. This general authority to purchase remains 'dormant' until activated by the receipt in the buying office of a *purchase requisition* originated by a properly authorized and specified official. These officials are authorized to issue purchase requisitions which instruct the buying office to make the purchase, but do not themselves place orders with the supplier. Furthermore, the requisitioning authority is limited to particular categories of goods. 'Stock' materials may be requisitioned by the stores controller, or the storekeeper or the progress department, but 'special' materials may depend on purchase requisitions originating in the design office or the planning department. The plant engineer might be the sole authority for maintenance materials and stationery purchases could be initiated by the office manager. Purchasing control is thereby exercised through the limitation of authority vested in officials, but care is needed to avoid the creation of a bureaucracy which leads to excessive administrative costs, and 'usual channels' which impede prompt action. The buying office will be responsible for placing orders and the selection of the particular supplier after receiving quotations from several potential suppliers of the required materials.

The Purchase Order

Placing an order with a supplier should always be done in writing, preferably in a standard form, since it is the basis of a legal contract. For this reason, too, it is necessary to include all the essential details to avoid any possibility of dispute later on. The company's name and address should be clearly printed on the order form and the supplier's name and address should be legibly written or typed. The purchase order should contain a full description of the materials to be supplied, including any relevant code, catalogue, or other reference numbers. It is important to specify a definite quantity or number of items and not to order vague or approximate quantities. The contractual nature of a purchase order also requires that it quotes the purchase price at which the goods are ordered, together with the terms of payment including any discounts or allowances. The expected delivery period or delivery date forms part of the contract and should be entered on the purchase order, as should be the *place* of delivery. Finally, the purchase order should

Purchase Order				
Neoplant Limited			No.	
Scrambler Street,			Date	
Wellertown, Essex, WE5N 8XQ			Reqn. No.	
⌐ ￢			A/C ref.	
			Delivery Required	
Quantity	Description	Price	Per	Amount

Please state the Order Number in all communications

Please supply the above in accordance
with the conditions stated overleaf

For Neoplant Limited

Buyer

Please complete this slip and return it within seven days

To Neoplant Limited: Your Purchase Order_____dated_____
is hereby accepted in accordance with the conditions therein.

Signed_____ For_____

Fig. 12. Purchase order

be validated by the signature of a properly authorized official of the company, usually the buyer or his deputy. It is helpful to provide a *tear-off slip* at the foot of the order which would be signed by the supplier and returned as an acceptance of the order with its conditions.

Copies of the purchase order will be circulated to interested departments including:

(1) The department which originally requisitioned the purchase as a notification that the goods have been ordered.
(2) The goods inwards department as an advice to prepare for the delivery of the materials on the due date.
(3) The accountant for verifying the supplier's invoice and for authorizing the payment in settlement of the debt.

The purchase department will normally hold several copies filed in different series such as order number sequence, alphabetically by suppliers, and materials description. In this way it becomes possible to locate particular purchase orders where full information is not available. The buying office should arrange a system for **progressing purchase orders** to ensure prompt delivery on the due date and to receive early warnings of a possible late delivery, so that the production departments can be given advance notification of possible delays.

Goods Received

When the ordered materials are delivered to the goods inward department they should be checked against the purchase order and the packing note as well as being examined for damage or shortage. It is desirable at this stage for a **goods received note** to be prepared as a record of the delivery and as a notification to interested parties.

(1) The buying office as an advice that the order has been delivered.
(2) The requisitioning authority to inform them of the arrival of their material.
(3) The accountant for 'marrying' with the purchase order copy prior to payment.
(4) The storekeeper (with the goods themselves) for information purposes and for up-dating the stores records.

Within the system as outlined there is contained yet another and important control, namely, payment to suppliers. The accountant, quite independent of the control system so far, will arrange payment of the supplier's invoice. Neither the requisitioning authority nor the buying office has any right to authorize payment, this is reserved to the accountant. Needless to say, the accountant will only make payment when he is satisfied that the goods have been delivered (goods received note) and that they are as ordered (purchase order) against an authorized requisition. Thus, the purchasing model provides a comprehensive control system designed to prevent inefficiency and to avoid dishonesty or corruption amongst employees.

Storage Control

After clearance from the goods inward department the materials are transferred to the custody of the storekeeper. It is his responsibility to store the materials in an appropriate manner to avoid deterioration and to prevent unauthorized withdrawals. Storage control is founded in the storekeeper's twin responsibilities of preservation and security.

Stores Environmental Control

Environmental control is fundamental to the avoidance of storage deterioration which can clearly be a source of considerable loss and represent a significant increase in effective material costs. The building of air-conditioned rooms to provide the correct temperature and humidity is expensive, but cheaper than the losses that may arise without it. Relatively few manufacturers require such elaborate methods to preserve their stocks of materials, but all need some form of environmental control, even if it is only four walls and a sound roof. Within the stores building, environmental control will embrace the methods of storage: such as racks, shelves, bins, tanks, vats, etc. Unless the physical facilities for storage are appropriate to the nature of the items retained in the stores, there will be a risk of loss through damage, fracture, evaporation, or rusting. Therefore, dry chemicals will *not* be placed in damp rooms; delicate instruments will be stored away from strong vibrations; fragile objects will not be crushed under heavy ones and volatile liquids will be kept away from excessive heat.

Environment control also extends to the stores layout and ensures an efficient arrangement of locations within the stores, so that wanted materials are found easily and quickly to avoid the delays and time wasted from having to 'search' for particular items.

Finally, the stores must be kept clean and tidy to prevent accidents to both staff and materials. Containers should be removed immediately they have been emptied; aisles and passageways must be kept free of all obstructions; receptacles should be provided for the disposal of wrappings and litter and dust and dirt need to be cleaned up frequently and regularly. Good environment control will minimize the storage costs and so increase profitability.

Stores Security Control

To prevent the unauthorized removal from the stores of materials placed in the storekeeper's charge, it is necessary to introduce stores security control. Access to the stores is confined to the stores personnel and certain other authorized persons such as stores auditors and senior officials. Unauthorized persons should not be permitted 'beyond the counter' under any circumstances whatsoever, and the stores should be locked securely when there are no stores personnel on duty. The issue of materials from stores is made only against a properly authorized stores requisition (*see* Fig. 13) which is an important document in both storage control and in cost ascertainment. Initially it authorizes the storekeeper to issue specified materials to the originator or to

Stores Requisition					No. 30718
Account Code: _Job No. M472_					Date 8/7/73
Description	Stores Code	Quantity	Price	Value	For Office Use Only
D Shackles size 5 Galvanised	7785G	20	25p	5.00	Priced by: *EB*
					Extended by: Comptometer **16**
					Stores Ledger *M Allen*
					Cost Ledger *RJM*
Issue authorised by: Signature *J Williams* Status *Assy Shop Foreman*					

Fig. 13. Stores requisition

some other person. When exchanged at the counter for the materials concerned, it becomes the storekeeper's receipt and thereby also his discharge from accountability for those materials. Subsequently it is the basis for up-dating the inventory and ultimately for posting the cost accounts with the value of materials used.

The 'Closed' Stores

It is generally true that a 'closed' stores is necessary to prevent undue waste of materials and/or pilferage, but there will be some instances where potential losses will be less than the cost of preventing them. I have come across a factory where there were two 'closed' stores properly managed and one 'open' stores. When workers required further materials from the 'open' stores they simply walked in and took what they needed, without let or hindrance and with a complete absence of 'paperwork'. The management justified the practice by claiming that the materials, steel tubes in six-foot lengths of varying diameters, were not likely to be attractive to pilferers, and in any case they could not be carried through the works gate without detection. In reply to the argument that excessive usage may be going undetected, it was pointed out that a reconciliation between purchases, stocks, and consumption (estimated from the finished output) indicated that this wastage was not serious. Making a 'closed' stores for tubes would attract additional costs of at least £2,000 per annum, which was twice the estimated maximum loss for excess usage. The store remained 'open' (**'circumstances alter cases'**).

Accounting for Materials

Receipts of Materials

The basic accounting record for materials is the **stores ledger**, which contains an account for each separate item held in stock. The stores account is debited with materials received and credited with issues from stock. The debits are raised from the goods inwards note, which has been priced from a copy of the purchase order and, in this way, the ledger postings can be up-dated daily. There will be exceptions, especially for non-standard materials where the price is subject to negotiation, but the great majority of materials can be dealt with promptly. It will be noted that the accounts copy of the goods inwards note becomes effectively a journal voucher and, as postings are made direct from goods inwards note to ledger account, the file of goods inwards notes also forms a part of the journal. Under systems of integrated accounts, the goods inwards note can also be used to credit suppliers' accounts, completing the double entry. In non-integrated systems the credit would be made in the master control account of the cost department while the financial books would be posted from the purchase journal.

Issues from Store

The materials issued against stores requisitions will be priced from the stores ledger account and credited thereto. Thus, the stores requisition is also a journal voucher and the file of posted requisition forms another section of the journal. The corresponding debits for stores issues will be posted to the work-in-progress ledger, for direct materials, and to the appropriate standing order or overhead account for indirect materials. (This aspect will be dealt with in more detail at later stages of this book. In Chapter Fourteen it is further suggested that the stores ledger might form the stores record for control purposes and that this requires some modification to the conventional form of ledger accounts.)

Pricing Stores Issues

In the preceding paragraph it was glibly suggested that the stores requisitions are priced from the stores ledger accounts and that the quantity extended at this price provides the value of the issue and, by implication, the crediting of this value to the ledger account adjusts the balance on the account. Unhappily the practice is likely to be much less straightforward. Prices are not static but influenced by many varied factors, sometimes pulling in different directions such as competition and inflation, or supply and demand. Thus, the stock of one particular item may be made up of quantities from several separate consignments delivered at different prices. This creates a problem in deciding which price, or prices, should be used for a particular requisition. There is no easy solution to this problem since, when components are lying together in one bin, there is normally no means of separately identifying each piece with its delivery consignment, and this is generally undesirable anyway in the accounting context.

It is necessary to consider the pricing method in the context of product costs, since the values so determined are debited to work in progress, and thus the effect on product costs becomes an important influence. Also, the value accorded to stores issues is credited to the stock accounts and influences the valuation of the stock balances.

Another important factor is the **stock concept**. Materials purchased for stock may be thought of as being bought in anticipation of future use. When the use opportunity occurs, then replenishment stocks are ordered against some other anticipated future use. In other words, materials are bought in advance of expected usage. The alternative stock concept sees the stock as a fund of materials which can be 'borrowed' from time to time to satisfy production needs. Since the 'loan' must be repaid, an equivalent quantity must be purchased to restore the stock to its original level. Thus, the **real cost** of the issue is seen as being the cost of replenishment rather than the cost of first purchase. It is, therefore, customary for the pricing method adopted for stores issues to be influenced by considerations of product costs, inventory valuation, and the stock concept. It should be remembered that the various methods are not mutually exclusive so that separate groups of materials may require different methods of pricing.

Specific Prices

In the issue of special purchase materials there is little or no difficulty in determining the price since the items will have been bought especially for a particular job and can be readily identified with the relevant invoice. Requisitions for these materials will be valued at the **specific price** charged by the supplier.

First in–First out (F.I.F.O.)

This method is based upon the presumption that the first items to be received will be issued first. In a sense this is an **accounting fiction** for it is not necessarily related to the physical movements in the stores—apart from coincidence—since common sense suggests that it might be better to issue materials in this way and minimize deterioration risks. (It is important to recognize this distinction between the physical movements and the accounting fiction in other pricing methods too.) The operation of F.I.F.O. is illustrated by the following example:

CHROMIUM-PLATED TOGGLETHONGS

		Receipts				Issues	
Date		Quantity	Price		Date		Quantity
Jan.	1	40	£1·00		Jan.	2	20
	11	50	£1·20			9	15
	21	30	£1·15			16	40
	3	40	£1·25			23	25
						30	20

STOCK ACCOUNT
CHROMIUM-PLATED TOGGLETHONGS

		Receipts		Issues		Balance	
Date		Quantity	Price	Quantity	Price	Quantity	Price
Jan.	1	40	£1·00			40	£1·00
	2			20	£1·00	20	£1·00
	9			15	£1·00	5	£1·00
	11	50	£1·20			{ 5	£1·00
						50	£1·20
	16			{ 5	£1·00	15	£1·20
				35	£1·20		
	21	30	£1·15			{ 15	£1·20
						30	£1·15
	23			{ 15	£1·20	20	£1·15
				10	£1·15		
	30			20	£1·15	—	—
	31	40	£1·25			40	£1·25

When surplus materials are returned to stores they should be credited at the issue price and then 'charged out' on the next requisition.

Characteristics of F.I.F.O.

(1) It is based on a clear-cut assumption regarding the identification of issues with particular receipts.
(2) It is based on actual cost incurred and avoids the problem of unrealized profits or losses.
(3) The resulting valuation of the stock balance reflects current market values.
(4) Product costs tend to lag behind current conditions. In periods of inflation this leads to **under-costing** and an overstatement of profits— and *vice versa* during periods when prices are falling.
(5) With a high stock turnover and frequent price changes, the pricing of stock balances becomes unwieldy.

Average Price

It ought to be taken for granted that average price is always a **weighted average**, but there has been a tendency in recent years for some texts to include a **simple average** as an apparent alternative. A simple average price cannot possibly have any justification at all for it must lead to absurd results. The average price needs to be re-calculated after each new receipt of materials, even where the supplier's price is unchanged for successive deliveries as this price will probably be different from the average price of items in stock owing to the influence of earlier deliveries. It is better to express all average prices in pounds rather than some in pounds and others in pence, while the number of significant figures in the average will be influenced by the size of individual issues. Generally speaking, prices should be calculated to three decimal places for issue quantities up to fifty units; four decimal places for issue quantities up to 500 units; and five decimal places up to 5,000 units. The previous example is re-worked using average price as follows:

STOCK ACCOUNT

CHROMIUM-PLATED TOGGLETHONGS

	Receipts		Issues		Balance	
Date	Quantity	Price	Quantity	Price	Quantity	Price
Jan. 1	40	£1·000			40	£1·000
2			20	£1·000	20	£1·000
9			15	£1·000	5	£1·000
11	50	£1·200			55	£1·182
16			40	£1·182	15	£1·182
21	30	£1·150			45	£1·161
23			25	£1·161	20	£1·161
30			20	£1·161	—	—
31	40	£1·250			40	£1·250

Surplus materials returned to store should be credited at the issue price and a new average price should be calculated if necessary. It is frequently the practice in process industries to price issues on a weekly or a monthly basis and the average price is usually re-calculated at the same time.

Characteristics of Average Price

(1) It is based on actual costs incurred and (like F.I.F.O.) it does not give rise to unrealized profits and losses.
(2) It is particularly useful with fluctuating prices since it tends to even out the price changes.
(3) Stock balances will be valued at a single price but lag further behind current values than when using F.I.F.O.
(4) The lag behind current prices of product costs will be less than under F.I.F.O.
(5) The calculation of the average price is an opportunity for error which will be reflected in all issues until the next receipt of materials when the average is re-calculated.

Standard Price

Under a system of standard costing (fully described later, *see* page 229 *et seq*.) it is necessary to use a standard price for the issue of materials from store.

However, it may also be convenient to use a *fixed* price in costing systems not using standard costs. The fixed (or standard) price for materials is really a **predicted average price** for a future period as it is based on anticipated conditions and price movements to provide a stable price. During the specified period, all issues and returns to store are valued at the same price.

Characteristics of Standard Price

(1) It imparts stability to product costs through the elimination of fluctuations in prices.

(2) The differences between actual and standard prices are written off to a price adjustment (variance) account and the year-ended balance transferred to the profit and loss account.

(3) The stock account can be simplified as there will be no need to provide columns for prices, all being the same.

(4) It is an estimated price and, not being based on actual costs incurred, may present problems in inventory valuation.

Last in–First out (L.I.F.O.)

This basis of pricing stores requistions is designed to reflect current prices in product costs by valuing issues at the price of the most recent receipt. This, it is argued, will also result in greater earnings stability from year to year and so provide a better guide for management decision-making. Generally, these claims will only be valid when issues are priced from recent receipts as the objective is frustrated when prices are taken from 'old' stock. The working of L.I.F.O. is illustrated by using the previous example.

STOCK ACCOUNT

CHROMIUM-PLATED TOGGLETHONGS

Date	Receipts		Issues		Balance	
	Quantity	Price	Quantity	Price	Quantity	Price
Jan. 1	40	£1·00			40	£1·00
2			20	£1·00	20	£1·00
9			15	£1·00	5	£1·00
11	50	£1·20			{ 5	£1·00
					{ 50	£1·20
16			40	£1·20	{ 5	£1·00
					{ 10	£1·20
21	30	£1·15			⌈ 5	£1·00
					{ 10	£1·20
					⌊ 30	£1·15
23			25	£1·15	⌈ 5	£1·00
					{ 10	£1·20
					⌊ 5	£1·15
30			5	£1·00		
			10	£1·20		
			5	£1·15	—	—
31	40	£1·25			40	£1·25

Surplus materials returned to stores are credited at the issue price and then 'charged-out' against the next requisition.

Characteristics of L.I.F.O.

(1) It is based on a clear-cut assumption regarding the identification of issues with particular receipts, but it conflicts with the probable physical movement in stores.
(2) It is based on actual costs incurred and does not generate unrealized profits and losses.
(3) Closing stock valuation is determined by the oldest prices remaining in the account.
(4) When issues are heavier than usual, current prices may have been 'used up' and the older prices will distort product costs.
(5) The recording of prices for stock balances is cumbersome and balances often consist of 'residual' amounts from several consignments—especially if price changes are frequent.

Next in–First out (N.I.F.O.)

This method recognizes the **fund of materials stock concept** while attempting to reflect current prices in product costs. It presupposes an ability to predict the price of the next delivery from the supplier—an assumption likely to be found wanting. Nevertheless, margins of error in prediction are claimed to be small in most cases and more than offset by the enhanced significance of product costs and the resultant profit performance. The use of N.I.F.O. is particularly suitable in preparing cost estimates for pricing decisions.

Characterists of N.I.F.O.

(1) It creates considerable administration problems in using 'future' prices —both in prediction and recording.
(2) Unless replenishments are received at an early date, product costs reflect future rather than current conditions.
(3) Considerable adjustments to stock accounts are needed in reconciling actual expenditure with issue valuations and with resultant profit performance distortions.
(4) The valuation of stock balances has to be made independently of the prices used for stores issues if absurd valuations are to be avoided.
(5) In periods of rising prices, product costs tend to be inflated and *vice versa* with falling prices.

Replacement (or Market) Cost

This is another method which recognizes the fund of materials stock concept. Whilst variations will be found in practice, the general principle is that materials issued from stores are valued at the buying price ruling on the day of issue. Clearly, this does result in materials being charged to production at current prices, and so it is claimed that product costs will indicate realistic profit performances. The fundamental difficulty in this method lies in ascertaining ruling prices and the volume of work involved in up-dating price lists can be tremendous, even if done monthly instead of daily. Furthermore, it is often impossible to find market prices for non-standard materials without obtaining quotations from suppliers.

Characteristics of replacement cost are the same as for N.I.F.O. plus:

(6) Most issue prices will not represent *actual* buying prices since daily replenishment is patently uneconomic.

(7) Product costs and profits may not be as *realistic* as is claimed since they represent what costs might have been had the operating conditions been different.

(8) On the other hand, where the opportunity is taken to analyse the differences between current market price and actual purchase price, the variance becomes a **purchase performance indicator**. (Even so, the volume of work involved will usually preclude this exercise being done.)

Highest in–First out (H.I.F.O.)

The adoption of this method is justified on the basis of a long-standing accounting convention that **losses should always be anticipated, but profits are never anticipated**. Therefore, the highest prices are absorbed into production at the earliest opportunity. The operation of H.I.F.O. is illustrated by using the earlier example of chromium-plated togglethongs.

STOCK ACCOUNT

CHROMIUM-PLATED TOGGLETHONGS

	Receipts		Issues		Balance	
Date	Quantity	Price	Quantity	Price	Quantity	Price
Jan. 1	40	£1·00			40	£1·00
2			20	£1·00	20	£1·00
9			15	£1·00	5	£1·00
11	50	£1·20			{ 5	£1·00
					{ 50	£1·20
16			40	£1·20	{ 5	£1·00
					{ 10	£1·20
21	30	£1·15			{ 5	£1·00
					{ 10	£1·20
					{ 30	£1·15
23			{ 10	£1·20	{ 5	£1·00
			{ 15	£1·15	{ 15	£1·15
30			{ 5	£1·00	—	—
			{ 15	£1·15	—	—
31	40	£1·25			40	£1·25

Characteristics of H.I.F.O.

(1) Materials costs tend to decline as the higher prices are 'used up' until a new consignment is received at a higher price.

(2) Materials cost movements and trends do not reflect market price movements and trends.

(3) Closing stocks will be valued at lowest prices and thus tend to be under-valued.

(4) In periods of rising prices, there will be **stock residuals** from several consignments in the actual balance, which complicates the recording.

Inventory Valuation

At the close of accounting periods it is necessary to value the closing stock. The balances recorded on individual accounts form the inventory and their aggregate valuation provides the value of closing stock (*see also* references to perpetual inventory and stocktaking in Chapter Fourteen). In the first instance, inventory valuation will depend upon the basis (or bases) adopted for pricing stores issues. This valuation, however, will frequently be modified to conform to the accounting principle of anticipating losses but not profits.

Cost or Market Rule

It is a traditional practice for accountants to value year-end inventories at the **lower of cost or market value**—a practice which is defended on the grounds of conservatism since it departs from incurred cost. It should be recognized, however, that accounts are prepared for different uses and each purpose requires a relevant format. Year-end accounts are normally prepared for three different groups: management, the shareholders, the Inland Revenue, and each set of year-end accounts will not only vary in content but may report separate profit figures. It is in the accounts for the last two groups that it is usual to apply the cost or market rule to inventory valuation. The application of this rule will result in lower valuations for stock than would the use of incurred costs.

There are three customary methods of applying the cost or market rule to inventory valuation.

Individual Method. Each item of stock is considered separately in the application of the cost or market rule. The quantity in stock is extended at whichever is the lower of cost price and current market price. The summation of the individual valuations provides the inventory valuation.

Global Method. Each item in stock is valued at cost and the aggregate cost valuation is obtained. Then the exercise is repeated by using the current market prices. The adopted inventory valuation is the lower of the two aggregates.

Group Method. This is a modified global method in that separate groups of materials are valued at both cost and market value to provide group aggregates of each—the lower of the two valuations being adopted. The inventory valuation is then obtained from summing the adopted valuations for each group.

In comparing these three methods it will be noticed that the individual method yields the lowest final valuation and the highest valuation is obtained by the global method. The individual method is less demanding in clerical effort as only one extension is required, whereas the other methods require the quantity to be extended twice—at cost price and at market price.

Exercises

1. (*a*) Describe briefly the steps to be taken by the purchasing department of an engineering company in connection with the purchase of a new component. It may be assumed that the component will be purchased for about £50 each and that delivery will be taken in quantities of 1,000 frequently.

   (*b*) In connection with the procedure described above, design the following forms: (i) schedule of quotations; (ii) purchase contract record.   [C.M.A.]

2. What are the advantages of a centralized purchasing procedure in an organization where there is a vast number of different types of materials and components? Describe how you would institute such a system and the difficulties you would expect to encounter, on its introduction into a large manufacturing business where previously the individual divisions had their own separate buying departments. [C.A.A.]

3. Describe in detail a procedure and the documentation for the ordering of foods, recording and checking the receipt of these goods, and the subsequent action for approving for payment and paying for the goods. In your answer indicate what departments will be involved in the documentation. [A.C.A.]

4. 'In some circumstances the best interest of a manufacturing unit are served by one central stores, whilst in others smaller stores scattered around the works is the best solution.' Describe the situations where these contrasting conditions are likely to occur and list the major factors which govern the layout of stores in general. [C.A.A.]

5. Describe carefully the principles to be followed in planning the layout and organization of a production materials stores in a large factory. Assume that there is a varied and wide range of items including:

(*a*) Raw materials—such as sheet, rods, tubes, circles, etc.

(*b*) Semi-finished items—such as castings, fittings, components, etc.

(*c*) Sub-assemblies and bought-out motors, etc.

(*d*) Process materials—such as acids, oils, greases, etc. [C.A.A.]

6. The stores ledger account for a certain material for the month of October, includes the data given below.

You are to assume the following alternative methods are being considered and are required to calculate the values of:

(*a*) the stores loss at October 31, 19.. using the F.I.F.O. system:

(*b*) issues of five of the following:

    (i) October 27 using the L.I.F.O. system;

   (ii) October 22 using the H.I.F.O. system;

  (iii) October 14 using the N.I.F.O. system;

  (iv) October 9 using weighted average system;

   (v) October 19 using the F.I.F.O. system;

 (vi) October 5 using periodic weighted average system.

Date	Ordered			Received			Issued			Balance in stock		
	Q.	P. £	A. £	Q.	P. £	A. £	Q.	P. £	A. £	Q.	P. £	A. £
October												
1										420	1·20	
2	500	1·25										
5							200					
7				300	1·25							
9							400					
10				200	1·25							
12	500	1·20										
14							200					
15	500	1·30										
16				400	1·20							
19							300					
20				100	1·20							
21				200	1·30							
22							300					
23	500	1·35										
24				300	1·30							
26				200	1·35							
27							400					
28				300	1·35							
29	500	1·25										
30							200					
31		Actual stock in hand								380		

Key Q=Quantity P=Price A=Amount   [C.M.A.]

7. The Kwikgro Fertiliser Company uses as one of the ingredients in its products, a compound known as XYZ which it buys from several suppliers both in the U.K. and abroad. Issues to production are in units of 1 cwt and are charged out on the weighted average basis.

On November 1 the stock of XYZ was 60 cwt. valued at £2·45 per cwt.

Receipts for November were as follows:

4th   500 cwt at £3 per cwt less ten per cent trade discount, carriage paid. The consignment was delivered in ten containers included on the invoice at £10 each, £6 per container being credited on return.

20th   1,000 cwt from Sweden for £2,000 bulk price, plus freight £150 and insurance £40.

Issues for November were as follows:

2nd	40 cwt	22nd	500 cwt
10th	100 cwt	29th	300 cwt
18th	300 cwt		

Prepare an account for November for compound XYZ indicating clearly the value of each intake, the unit issue prices and the value of the closing stock. Your calculations should be taken to three decimal places.   [A.C.A.]

8. The following information relates to some of the stores transactions for the month of May, at the Togglethong Engineering Company Limited:

Receipts					Issues	
Date	Reference	Quantity	Price	Date	Job	Quantity
Account—TIMING GEAR K67						
May 1	Balce.	8 sets	£7·50	May 4	P612	6 sets
2	GR218	12 sets	£7·80	9	P982	12 sets
10	GR223	12 sets	£8·10	11	P342	4 sets
16	GR237	12 sets	£8·40	18	P1092	14 sets
23	GR250	12 sets	£8·70	24	P552	15 sets
25	GR262	12 sets	£9·00	28	P612	15 sets
Account—SALIC CRYSTALS B60						
May 1	Balce.	30 bags	£0·60	May 2	P982	20 bags
4	GR220	40 bags	£0·55	7	P612	15 bags
10	GR228	20 bags	£0·71	8	P403	25 bags
18	GR241	12 bags	£0·61	11	P322	10 bags
21	GR269	10 bags	£0·69	15	P672	12 bags
28	GR281	56 bags	£0·60	25	P803	16 bags
Account—BRACKETS PB18						
May 1	Balce.	5 units	£2·00	May 3	P342	4 units
4	GR221	6 units	£2·00	7	P552	6 units
10	GR227	10 units	£2·40	14	P612	6 units
17	GR239	8 units	£2·40	21	P672	4 units
25	GR259	6 units	£2·66	24	P503	4 units
30	GR274	6 units	£2·66	28	P552	8 units

Required:

Prepare suitable stock accounts for the above and enter these transactions therein showing the quantity and value of the balances at May 31.

In pricing issues:

(*a*) Use the average method in any **one** account.

(*b*) Use L.I.F.O. in **one** of the other two accounts.

(*c*) F.I.F.O. for the remaining account.

In selecting the method of pricing issues you should consider carefully which is likely to be most suitable for conditions pertaining to that account. Add a footnote account stating the reasons for the chosen pricing method.   [C.A.A.]

CHAPTER FIVE

LABOUR REMUNERATION

Significance of Labour Cost

Labour forms the second element of cost and, in a sense, is the true **primary** cost of production, since it will always be required. In some service industries there is no direct materials cost at all, while primitive industries may have little or no expenses—but labour is always needed in one form or another. Therefore, labour is a significant element of cost, although its relative importance varies from one business and, indeed, from one task to another. This will be relatively more significant within the contexts of **conversion cost** and **added value**—topics which will be developed in Chapters Eight to Twelve. Generally speaking, wage rates may be more readily controlled than materials prices since they are more amenable to internal influences. Although there are many external factors influencing wage rates—such as cost-push inflation, local labour demand and supply, national wage agreements, and so on—the effect on labour costs tends to be rather less significant than is the case with materials costs. Another difference between labour and materials is seen in the relative stability of wage rates which do not fluctuate as do many materials prices. The most significant contrast between labour and materials is that labour costs are **time related**, whereas no such relationship is found in materials costs.

The Basis of Remuneration

In general, there are two distinct bases of employee remuneration in that it tends to be either **time related** or else **output related**. The cost of labour is clearly derived from the remuneration of workers and this in turn is dependent on the number of hours worked relative to the reward for particular skills. It is quite common, however, to find earnings being wholly or partly determined by output quantities. At first sight this would appear to deny the postulate that remuneration is time related. A closer look at output-related earnings schemes, however, discloses the **remuneration syllogism** that:

> **Wages depend on output.**
> **Output depends on time worked.**
> **Therefore, wages depend on time.**

It is apparent then that all labour costs are time related since output, too, is time related as longer working hours lead to higher output levels (and *vice versa*).

Cost Behaviour Patterns

Until fairly recently, it has been generally accepted that wages costs tend to be variable, and by re-framing the remuneration syllogism it can be said that:

Wages vary with time.
Output varies with time.
Therefore, wages vary with output.

This clearly identifies both direct wages and indirect wages as being variable costs. Nevertheless, it is recognized that there is in fact some semi-variable element present in wages but this has not been significant for the derivation of unit costs. The activities of the trades unions in improving conditions have also tended to yield stabilized earnings at given rates of pay, reflected in such benefits as the guaranteed week, holiday pay, and 'make-up' allowances. Consequently, a definite movement towards the **salaried labour force** is emerging—which tends to accelerate as businesses become more **capital intensive**. Under these conditions the remuneration of workers will be fixed relative to output, although direct wages remain variable because it is customary accounting practice to analyse the various 'supplementary payments' made to direct workers as overhead. It is being argued nowadays, when workers are virtually salaried, that any distinction between the fixed and variable components of wages is both unnecessary and unrealistic. An acceptance of the fixed nature of wages cost it is claimed would lead to: (*a*) a more sensible approach to wages policy; and (*b*) a more positive attitude to labour costs. There is certainly much to be said in favour of this view but, apart from some of the larger employers—notably the nationalized industries, the motor industry, the petroleum industry, and some large-scale retailers—it is likely to be some time before such progressive thinking finds general acceptance.

Variable Overhead

By definition, variable cost tends to vary with output or activity and, consequently, variable cost per unit tends to remain constant. This is certainly true in **machine-determined** output situations as the physical output will tend to vary directly with the number of actual operating hours. Variable overhead, too, will vary with the operating hours, so that variable overhead varies directly with the quantity of physical units produced.

In **operator-determined** output situations, the quantity produced will vary with the effort made by the operator and consequently there may well be some divergence from a strict application of the postulate that output is directly related to hours worked. For example, in a given period of time one operator may achieve a higher level of output than another would under identical operating conditions. Should the variable overhead be **time related**, for example, power usage, then the incidence per unit of this variable cost will not be constant. The example of power is used in the following illustration.

In a department there are ten machines of the same type, each having a power consumption cost of £1·00 per hour. In a certain week, three operators achieved varying performances as shown.

Operator	Hourly output	Power per piece
'A'	8 pieces	£0·125
'B'	9 pieces	£0·111
'C'	10 pieces	£0·100

In this example where the incidence of the variable cost is time related, fluctuations in labour productivity lead to fluctuations in variable costs per unit. In many cases any divergence from strict variability will not usually be significant, but this topic will be further explored in dealing with standard costs.

Fixed Overhead

By definition, the fixed overhead for a given capacity to produce will remain unchanged irrespective of movements in output levels. The importance of this characteristic lies in the fact that fixed cost per unit of output will vary inversely with the output volume. It is for this reason that managements should attempt to obtain, everything else being equal, high levels of productivity to maximize profit performance. This principle underlies all forms of wage incentives as they all seek to encourage workers to maintain their best efforts and, therefore, to obtain the highest possible level of output. This is especially important in all capital-intensive situations where high output levels are essential to earn even moderate profits. All businesses, however, need to maximize output in order to minimize fixed overhead cost per unit produced.

Time-related Earnings

Normal Hourly Rates

This method of remuneration simply rewards the worker in proportion to the number of hours worked. The cynics suggest that it is really payment for *time attended* since he is paid according to his 'clock' hours without any consideration being given to the amount of 'effort' he has made during his time in the factory. Although there is indeed no incentive to contribute more than minimum effort on a consistent basis, other than that imposed from good supervision, this assertion is only a half truth. It is true that wages are computed on attendance time, but the implication that hourly paid workers stand about in idleness for the whole, or even a significant part, of the working week is rather absurd for such a state of affairs is unlikely to be tolerated even by indifferent supervisors.

The use of day wages (that is, hourly rates of pay) is often appropriate for unskilled workers where it is not possible to find objective measures of effort or performance, which could provide a basis for an incentive scheme of remuneration. This is frequently the situation with indirect labour and most forms of unskilled labour. Time wages are also applicable to highly skilled work where quality is more important than quantity such as in toolmaking, pattern-making, sign-writing, plant-repairing, etc. The cost of imperfect work of a skilled nature is likely to be very much higher than any potential savings yielded by increased productivity through a wage incentive.

High Time Rates

It is sometimes suggested that the introduction of a **high time rate** will yield better results than can be obtained from any conventional output-related incentive scheme, because high wages will attract the better workers with a high productivity potential and that this higher output per worker yields lower costs per unit of product. In a way this is a form of **negative incentive** to high productivity as there is always the risk of dismissal for any failure to achieve set tasks or performance standards, and so adverse effects on staff relationships. Workers, who are recruited through the attraction of higher wages, will strive to maintain required productivity to avoid the necessity to leave and thereby receive lower wages. High time rates are not really quite as negative as this argument suggests, for advertised vacancies will stimulate a high response from those seeking rewards commensurate with their skills. The management is then able to select the better applicants for the vacancy with the ensuing benefit in higher productivity. This approach can be most successful for highly skilled workers, but with the following two provisos:

(1) It must be supported by a progressive and efficient management, a determination to maintain sound human relations and a framework of good working conditions. The scheme will be undermined where there is over-strict supervision arising from a 'hire and fire' attitude with near slave-like conditions. The better workers will seldom think the extra wages worth the over-exacting demands of management and some will certainly leave. The company will then be left with less than the best workers—those who are prepared to tolerate the conditions for the sake of high earnings. There can be little doubt that in such situations lie the seeds of future serious industrial unrest.

(2) The success of high wage rates in attracting the better skilled workers will be achieved only where the rates offered are above the prevailing rates in local industry generally. (In much the same way that companies offering relatively poor rates of pay will only recruit those who cannot obtain employment elsewhere.) If all the employers in a particular local area decide to match one company's high rates in order to obtain a reasonable share of the available labour, the exercise becomes self-defeating and inflates labour costs without any corresponding benefit in productivity. Clearly, the high-wage-rate policy can only be successful where it is an exception to current local wage rates.

Output-related Earnings

As an encouragement to achieve high output levels, workers are frequently offered inducements in the form of output-related remuneration. Clearly this has the twofold advantage of rewarding the worker in proportion to his personal endeavour and of encouraging him to work harder in order to improve this income. At the same time the employer also benefits from being able to spread his fixed costs over a larger output and, even with higher labour costs per unit, reducing the total unit cost of his products.

It is generally true of all wage incentive schemes that their success depends on the accuracy with which task standards are set and on the precision of measuring attainment. Incentive schemes also require mutual confidence and trust between workers and management, or else they will become a continuing source of friction which vitiates good labour relations. Industrial history is a catalogue of bad faith between the two sides, especially in the context of wages. There have been innumerable examples of poorly set standards which have led to very high earnings on the part of the workers being followed by undisguised efforts by management to restrict the individual's earnings. Alternatively, there have been instances where workers have made ridiculous demands or even used dishonest means to inflate earnings. It is, however, the responsibility of management to create the right environment for good industrial relations and equally so for the establishment of a sound wages structure.

Principles of Incentive Schemes

In creating a system of payment by results there are certain basic principles which need to be observed. It must be possible for the average worker to earn more than his time wages, and it is widely recognized that earnings under an incentive scheme should be about one-third higher than time wages. Targets set under incentive plans should be reasonably attainable by the average worker or else the incentive will be lost. Research into the motivation of standards suggests that where a target is set beyond the possibility of attainment the actual performance tends to be **lower** than it would have been where, in effect, the operator sets his own standard. There should be no limit imposed on a worker's earnings, and the safeguard to management lies in the careful setting of standards at the outset and also once a rate is set and agreed by both sides it should not be altered unilaterally. (Blatant abuses such as minor modifications to tasks in order to substantially reduce earnings quickly erodes mutual confidence.) Finally, to be economically viable, the plan should not increase the wages cost per unit beyond the *effective* savings in overhead costs per unit.

Piecework Incentive Plans

The following example is used throughout to illustrate the structure of various plans as it provides a basis of comparison for contrasting the characteristics of the different schemes:

The average time taken to perform a particular machining operation is estimated to be thirty minutes per casting. The basic time rate for this task is £0·72 per hour. Fixed cost is £80 per week.

The effect on earnings and costs of differing operator efficiencies is demonstrated by taking weekly outputs in the range 50–120 castings.

Straight Piecework

The basic principle of straight piecework is that a **fixed price per piece** is paid as wages for each piece produced. Earnings vary directly with the number of pieces produced, and the incentive is the opportunity to increase earnings by working harder. There is also a clear recognition of the principle of **equity** between workers of differing abilities or application. In the early part of the twentieth century, pieceworkers' wages were calculated strictly on their attained outputs, even if this meant paying below time rates to the less able. Happily, trade union activity has removed this injustice and minimum time wages are now normally guaranteed.

Accepting the assumption that an average worker's wages under an incentive plan should be one-third higher than time wages, then the **allowed time** per casting must be set at forty minutes. This means that an average performance will complete one casting in thirty minutes but merit forty minutes pay. Thus, the piecework rate would be $40/60 \times 72p = 48p$ per casting. The effect on unit costs induced by varying performances is shown in Fig. 14. Here it can be seen that wages is a truly variable cost under piecework. By contrast, time wages are fixed, and so the wages cost per unit varies inversely with the output per week. The heavy incidence (£80 weekly) of the department fixed costs provides an opportunity to achieve significant cost savings from higher output yields. This is demonstrated by the 'aggregate' curve combining wages and fixed overhead. The effect on hourly earnings and, of course, on weekly wages is shown in Fig. 15. Earnings rise steeply as efficiency improves, offering a real inducement to attain the highest possible outputs each week.

Straight piecework is not by any means an unrelieved blessing and does possess certain inherent disadvantages. As in all incentive schemes, the increased output is often gained at the expense of quality. It is usually necessary to draft the agreement so that only 'good' work is paid for, but

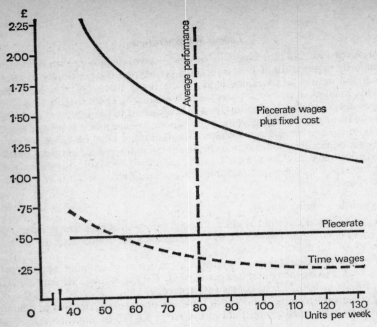

Fig. 14. Unit costs for straight piecework

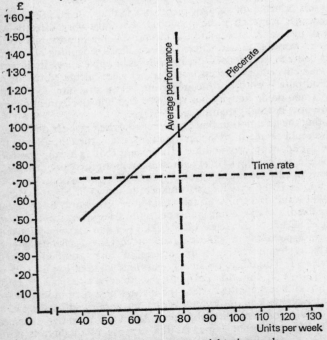

Fig. 15. Hourly earnings at straight piecework

this throws an additional burden on to the quality control or inspection staff. Steps must also be taken to verify quantities produced as 'over-booking' is by no means an uncommon occurrence. It is clear from Figs. 14 and 15 that some of the poorer operators can earn more than time wages even though their performance fails to achieve the standard or average. Although Fig. 15 shows that the earnings rise steeply as efficiency improves, the incentive tends to diminish as the output per week increases. There are two reasons for this: first, the **proportionate** increase in earnings falls with each additional **increment** of output and, secondly, the incidence of personal income tax bears more heavily as weekly earnings rise. Poor timekeeping and absenteeism can become a serious problem when workers are able to 'earn enough in less than a normal week', especially as they consider (wrongly) themselves to be the only sufferers from this malpractice. Differential piecerates have been developed to overcome the problem of diminishing incentives when workers set their own earnings levels.

Differential Piecework

The earliest differential plans were rather crude and adopted two piecerates: the lower for sub-standard performance and the higher being applied to super-standard performance. Using the data in the standard example on page 63, differential piecerates might be set as follows. Standard task is set at eighty pieces per week, therefore, where efficiency is at or above standard performance the piecerate is 48p per piece produced. When efficiency fails to reach standard, the piecerate is, say, 32p per piece produced. Figure 16 shows the unit costs for differential piecerates and the **penalty** of less than time wages

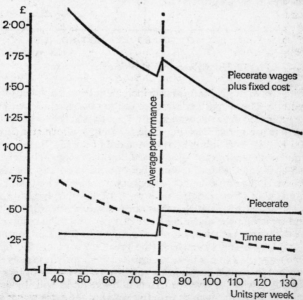

Fig. 16. Unit costs for differential piecerates

for failure to achieve standard performance. It will also be noticed that earnings for seventy-nine pieces per week will be 79 × 32p = £25·28, but eighty pieces earn £38·40—the one extra piece earning £13·12 (an increase in wages of fifty-two per cent). This plan provides a strong incentive to achieve standard efficiency but, thereafter, the incentive once again starts to fall away as shown by the earnings curve in Fig. 17. It is difficult by any criteria (other

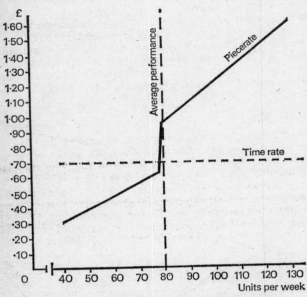

Fig. 17. Hourly earnings at differential piecerates

than a punitive one) to justify this large increment between seventy-nine units and eighty units. There is little difference in the relative efficiencies and only a negligible reduction in fixed cost per unit. Present practice tends to guarantee time wages and use an accelerating scale for output above standard performance (*see* Fig. 18). Here it has been assumed that the piecerate is calculated by the formula—actual output ÷ standard output × 40p. (This gives a price in pence which is equal to half the number of units produced per week.) The piecerate curve rises at an even rate as output increases. The total cost curve (on the assumption of guaranteed time wages) falls sharply until the break-even point is reached, after which it falls fairly slowly as the wage cost per unit is rising and offsetting the declining fixed cost per unit. The resulting hourly earnings at the various efficiency levels are shown in Fig. 19. Up to a weekly output of seventy-six units per week (the break-even point) the operator is paid his time wages of 72p per hour. Thereafter the hourly rate rises at a faster rate than output increases, providing a strong incentive for workers to attain their maximum efficiency. Over-generous allowed times will, however, give rise to exceptionally high earnings with the risk that the extra wages will more than absorb any savings of fixed unit costs. It was this very problem of setting

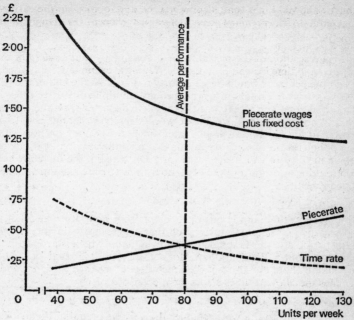

Fig. 18. Unit costs for accelerating piecerates

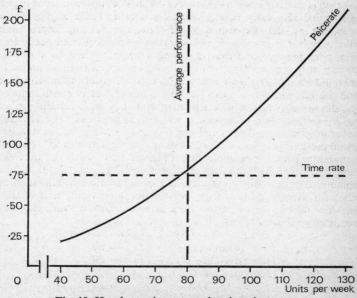

Fig. 19. Hourly earnings at accelerating piecerates

reliable or allowed times that encouraged the development in the early years of this century of the **premium bonus plans** as wage incentives to higher output.

Standard Time Plan

This is a variation of the piecerate method whereby the *standard* or allowance is given in time instead of in money. With the example already used, the allowed time per piece would be set at forty minutes. At the end of the period (daily or weekly) the total units produced are multiplied by forty to give the total allowed time. The actual time taken is then deducted from the total time allowed to obtain the **time saved**. The worker receives a bonus equal to the time saved at the appropriate bonus rate. Where the bonus coincides with the worker's time rate (72p per hour in this example) the earnings will be exactly as shown in Figs. 14 and 15 for piecework. Once again, the difficulty experienced in setting accurate allowed or standard times led to the introduction of modified schemes.

Premium Bonus Plans

While various premium bonus plans differ from each other in detail, they all possess two common features. Full-time wages are paid for the whole working period and this is supplemented by a bonus which is proportional to the **time saved** out of the **time allowed** for a given task. It is usual for the bonus to be equal to about one-third of the time wages at average efficiency and this determines the allowed times set under the various plans.

Time sharing

The bonus paid to the worker under the various premium bonus plans is usually calculated on only a **proportion** of the time saved. In other words, the time saved is shared between the worker and his employer in some previously agreed ratio. The early management consultants (such as Halsey, Weir, Rowan, Taylor, Bedaux) would argue plausibly that any improvement in productivity was partly due to the worker's own efforts and partly to good management practice and that this should be recognized by time-sharing. Naturally, this is a viewpoint which would commend itself to management who would be flattered by a recognition of their contribution to efficiency. At the risk of cynicism, one can feel sure that these early consultants appreciated the **selling value** of this argument and they were certainly making a living by selling their professional services to business. The real reason, however, undoubtedly lay in their inability to formulate precise standards as time and motion study was still primitive by comparison with today's practice.

A premium plan, for example, might include a 50/50 ratio of time-sharing which is illustrated with the data used previously. The average time taken to machine a casting is thirty minutes. The **premium time** should then be ten minutes for average performance, but this represents only half of the **time saved** which needs to be twenty minutes. To ensure this, the **time allowed** must be set at fifty minutes. Thus,

$$
\begin{array}{ll}
\text{Time Allowed (TA)} & = 50 \text{ min} \\
\text{Time Taken (TT)} & = 30 \\
\text{Time Saved (TS) (TA$-$TT)} & = 20 \\
\text{Premium Time (PT)} & \\
\quad (\tfrac{1}{3}\text{ TT and } \tfrac{1}{2}\text{TS)} & = 10 \\
\text{Earned Time (ET) (TT$+$PT)} & = 40
\end{array}
$$

Earnings at the different efficiency levels shown in Table 1 are derived from the above data.

Table. 1. Comparison of Standard Time and Time-sharing

Output Units	Standard time		50/50 Time-sharing				
	TA (*min*)	Wages £	TA (*min*)	TS* (*min*)	PT (*min*)	ET* (*min*)	Wages £
50	2,000	24·00	2,500	100	50	2,450	29·40
60	2,400	28·80	3,000	600	300	2,700	32·40
70	2,800	33·60	3,500	1,100	550	2,950	35·40
80	3,200	38·40	4,000	1,600	800	3,200	38·40
90	3,600	43·20	4,500	2,100	1,050	3,450	41·40
100	4,000	48·00	5,000	2,600	1,300	3,700	44·40
110	4,400	52·80	5,500	3,100	1,550	3,950	47·40
120	4,800	57·60	6,000	3,600	1,800	4,200	50·40
130	5,200	62·40	6,500	4,100	2,050	4,450	53·40

*TT=40 hours per week (i.e. 2,400 min).

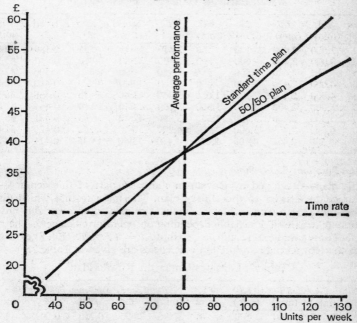

Fig. 20. The 50/50 plan and the time-sharing plan compared

Earnings under the two plans are shown in Fig. 20. In each case, the earnings are the same at standard efficiency—an output of eighty units per week. If, however, the estimate of standard performance was set too high, say, average performance is sixty or seventy units per week, then this will be far less serious under the 50/50 plan since a bonus becomes payable at fifty units per week. Higher earnings will be received under the 50/50 plan for sub-standard performance. However, had the standard been set so low that average workers could produce, say, one hundred units weekly, then lower wages will be paid under the 50/50 plan. Thus, time-sharing plans embrace a 'built-in' safety factor against the risk of inaccurate standard setting. On the whole, this is probably desirable although it does tend to diminish the incentive.

Halsey Time-sharing Plan

There are a number of schemes based on Halsey's plan which differ in the ratio of time-sharing—the most common being the 50/50 (other versions had ratios of 3:1 and 2:1). The basic features of the Halsey plan are that time wages are guaranteed and a bonus is paid on the basis of time saved. Table 2 shows the earnings under the Halsey 50/50 plan at the different levels of operating efficiency. It is apparent from this table that the hourly earnings will rise as operating efficiency improves, but that wages cost per unit falls simultaneously. The employer benefits from lower unit costs in both labour *and* fixed overhead with higher productivity.

Table 2. Earnings Under Halsey 50/50 Plan

Output (units)	TA (min)	TT (min)	TS (min)	PT (min)	ET (min)	Wages £	Per hour £	Per unit £	Per unit (min)
50	2,500	2,400	100	50	2,450	29·40	0·735	0·588	49·0
60	3,000	2,400	600	300	2,700	32·40	0·810	0·540	45·0
70	3,500	2,400	1,100	550	2,950	35·40	0·885	0·506	42·1
80	4,000	2,400	1,600	800	3,200	38·40	0·960	0·480	40·0
90	4,500	2,400	2,100	1,050	3,450	41·40	1·035	0·460	38·3
100	5,000	2,400	2,600	1,300	3,700	44·40	1·110	0·444	37·0
110	5,500	2,400	3,100	1,550	3,950	47·40	1·185	0·431	35·9
120	6,000	2,400	3,600	1,800	4,200	50·40	1·260	0·420	35·0
130	6,500	2,400	4,100	2,050	4,450	53·40	1·335	0·411	34·2

Rowan Premium Bonus Plan

This plan—developed by Rowan in the early part of this century—has similar characteristics to the Halsey plan. The main feature which distinguishes the Rowan plan is that the bonus is calculated on a **variable ratio** of the time taken (itself a variable depending on operator efficiency). The ratio is that of time saved to time allowed, so that $PT = TT \times TS/TA$. The earnings under the Rowan plan at different efficiencies are given in Table 3.

Table 3. Earnings Under the Rowan Plan

Output (units)	TA (min)	TT (min)	TS (min)	PT (min)	ET (min)	Wages £	Per hour £	Per unit £	Per unit (min)
50	2,500	2,400	100	96	2,496	29·95	0·750	0·599	49·9
60	3,000	2,400	600	480	2,880	34·56	0·864	0·576	48·0
70	3,500	2,400	1,100	754	3,154	37·85	0·946	0·541	45·1
80	4,000	2,400	1,600	960	3,360	40·32	1·008	0·504	42·0
90	4,500	2,400	2,100	1,120	3,520	42·14	1·054	0·468	39·1
100	5,000	2,400	2,600	1,248	3,648	43·78	1·094	0·438	36·5
110	5,500	2,400	3,100	1,353	3,753	45·04	1·126	0·409	34·1
120	6,000	2,400	3,600	1,440	3,840	46·08	1·152	0·384	32·0
130	6,500	2,400	4,100	1,514	3,914	46·97	1·174	0·354	30·1

One interesting feature of the Rowan plan is that the worker can never earn double his time wages as the bonus will always be less than TT since TS/TA must be less than unity. It will also be noticed that both Halsey and Rowan yield the same result when $TS = \frac{1}{2}TA$ (or $TS = TT$).

Bedaux Premium Point System

This is an interesting variation, being a hybrid Halsey/Standard Time scheme. The Bedaux system is highly flexible in that the basic time unit is the **minute** and one minute of allowed time is known as a 'Bedaux point' or **B**. Initially, the Bedaux system resembles the Standard Time plan since there is no time-sharing between employer and employee and, consequently, the company experiences constant unit costs for labour above standard performance. However, although the company pays out the full bonus, the direct worker only receives seventy-five per cent of it, the other twenty-five per cent goes into a 'kitty' and is shared amongst the foremen, supervisors, inspectors, and other indirect workers, so that it is similar in effect to a Halsey 75/25 plan.

Table 4. Earnings Under Bedaux 75/25 Plan

Output (units)	TA (min)	TT (min)	TS (min)	PT (min)	ET (min)	Wages £	Per hour £	Per unit £	Per unit (min)
50	2,000	2,400	0	0	2,400	28·80	0·720	0·576	48·0
60	2,400	2,400	0	0	2,400	28·80	0·720	0·480	40·0
70	2,800	2,400	400	300	2,700	32·40	0·810	0·463	38·6
80	3,200	2,400	800	600	3,000	36·00	0·900	0·450	37·5
90	3,600	2,400	1,200	900	3,300	39·60	0·990	0·440	36·6
100	4,000	2,400	1,600	1,200	3,600	43·20	1·080	0·432	36·0
110	4,400	2,400	2,000	1,500	3,900	46·80	1·170	0·425	35·5
120	4,800	2,400	2,400	1,800	4,200	50·40	1·260	0·420	35·0
130	5,200	2,400	2,800	2,100	4,500	54·00	1·350	0·415	34·6

The Bedaux system originated in the U.S.A. but was widely introduced to the United Kingdom during the 1920s and 1930s. In fact, any U.K. premium bonus system is probably a modified Bedaux system. Nowadays it is customary to give direct workers one hundred per cent of time saved and to use the average efficiency of direct workers for paying a bonus to indirect workers. For example, an average worker is expected to achieve eighty B's per hour (thus $TS = \frac{1}{3}TT$), and this is described as an eighty-unit hour efficiency. The indirect workers of a given department would be paid a bonus calculated at their personal hourly rates on the **overall average unit hour** achieved by all the direct operators. An important feature of the Bedaux system is that the incentive scheme is only one part of a comprehensive management control system designed to reduce costs and improve plant-wide efficiency and managerial effectiveness. The various premium bonus plans are contrasted in Fig. 21.

Measured Daywork

This is a relatively recent development in remuneration which endeavours to combine the best features of time wages and incentive schemes. Measured Daywork also has the merit of being readily applicable to either individual or group situations and is particularly useful for machine-dominated output.

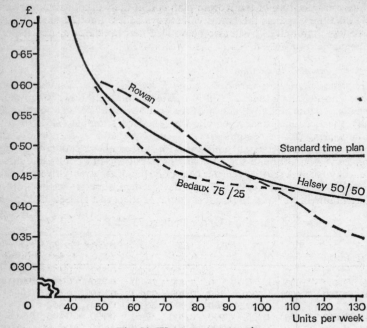

Fig. 21. Wages cost per casting

This last factor has led to its introduction into capital-intensive plants, notably in the automobile industry. In effect, the approach is to pay high time rates on an individual worker basis and to expect a good day's work at bonus efficiency—the actual rate is determined by past performance and reviewed at regular intervals. Inevitably, there will be found several variations on this particular theme, but the general principle is demonstrated by the following typical method.

Initially, work measurement is used to determine a reasonable week's work (or hour's work, perhaps) and the incentive element is agreed. For example, as discussed earlier, the piecework basis of 48p per casting may be taken to calculate the incentive earnings per hour at various efficiencies. This hourly rate then becomes the worker's time rate according to his expected efficiency. Table 5 shows the hourly rates payable in the *future* based on *past* performance. Suppose that a certain operator had regularly machined an average of eighty castings a week, then he would be given an hourly rate of 96p and would receive this time rate henceforth, irrespective of actual outputs attained. At some future day, say, in three months' time, his performance would be reviewed. If his performance over that period fell within the range 76–85 his hourly rate would remain unchanged, but if it had been within the range 86–95, his hourly rate would be raised to 108p, and so on. When average performance consistently falls below expected efficiency, the foreman, or supervisor, and the worker together attempt to discover the cause.

Measured Daywork has the merit of high time rates in that workers'

Table 5. Measured Daywork Ratings

Piecework Basis			Measured daywork			Conversion costs			
Output (units)	Earnings £	Per hour £	Efficiency rate (units)	£	Per unit £	Wages £	O'head £	Total £	Per unit £
50	24·00	0·60	46–55	0·72	0·576	28·80	80·00	108·80	2·18
60	28·80	0·72	56–65	0·72	0·480	28·80	80·00	108·80	1·81
70	33·60	0·84	66–75	0·84	0·480	33·60	80·00	113·60	1·62
80	38·40	0·96	76–85	0·96	0·480	38·40	80·00	118·40	1·48
90	43·20	1·08	86–95	1·08	0·480	43·20	80·00	123·20	1·37
100	48·00	1·20	96–105	1·20	0·480	48·00	80·00	128·00	1·28
110	52·80	1·32	106–115	1·32	0·480	52·80	80·00	132·80	1·21
120	57·60	1·44	116–125	1·44	0·480	57·60	80·00	137·60	1·11
130	62·40	1·56	126–135	1·56	0·480	62·40	80·00	142·40	1·09

earnings will not fluctuate with output, and consequently there are no disputes regarding the number of pieces nor is there any need to bother with 'make-up' payments for lost time. It enables workers to be paid on their merits and the periodic reviews give the system flexibility. It is also found in practice that workers will more readily accept new tasks since their rates are unaffected and there is a general improvement in industrial relations. There is much less paperwork and clerical work than under traditional incentive schemes and usually an improvement in the quality of supervision.

Share of Production Plans

The basic concept behind this type of plan is that wages tend to form a constant proportion of **added value** (defined as the sales value of output less the cost of external inputs that is, broadly speaking, conversion cost plus profit). The ratio of wages to added value, whilst slightly varying between different companies, tends to remain almost constant at about forty per cent. Any event which upsets this balance tends to be followed by correcting pressures until the ratio is restored. For example, the introduction of a new transfer machine may well improve productivity considerably, so that initially the ratio of wages to added value is reduced. However, the tendency is for this to be followed by claims to higher wages—now harder to resist and certainly easier to meet from increased earnings—thus restoring the ratio.

The promoters of these plans (notably Rucker in the U.S.A. and Bentley in the U.K.) claim that a recognition and acceptance of this ratio leads to an automatic payment to the workers of their **share of production** as a right. Most industrial unrest is generated by unsatisfactory wage systems where each side attempts to gain a larger 'share of the cake' to the detriment of the other side. The share of production ratio—in recognizing each side's share—leads to improved industrial relations and increased co-operation between management and workers. It is claimed that the introduction of the plan encourages workers to eliminate all forms of waste since the workers are less careless in spoilage, stop wasting materials, economize in power usage, and so on. Certainly, its introduction into some factories has given rise to spectacular savings for less waste means there are lower external inputs, higher added value, and therefore increased wages.

There are two major difficulties in this plan: the absolute necessity for strong mutual trust between management and workers; and since it is in effect a group wages plan for the whole factory one of the incentive schemes may need to be introduced as a means of determining the relative rewards of individuals. Another difficulty may be found in the payment of the bonus at monthly intervals. The operation of the plan is illustrated in the following example (on the assumption of a ratio of thirty-six per cent to labour) for a given month:

	£
Sales value of production	356,600
Less Materials and Supplies	204,400
ADDED VALUE IN OUTPUT	152,200
36% of production value	54,792
Factory wages paid	45,218
Balance due as BONUS	£9,574

The bonus of £9,574 is then payable to the workers and is usually distributed amongst individuals in proportion to their wages already paid for the month. (It is customary to pay out about seventy-five to eighty per cent of this sum, the balance being retained for supplements in low-output months, at Christmas and for the annual holiday.)

Group Incentive Plans

The incentive plans already discussed have been taken within the context of measuring the effort and efficiency of individuals. There are many instances of team activity for groups of workers for whom it is desirable to provide an incentive scheme. Generally, all the plans are readily applicable to groups of workers, the only problem being that of recognizing the varying contributions in skill, experience, and responsibility. This is not really a problem in fact, since these differences are reflected in scales of pay. Premium bonus plans are particularly well suited to teamwork as each worker has his personal rate, but all bonuses are calculated on the same unit hour or efficiency rating—thus giving differing *amounts* of bonus. Measured daywork is also readily applicable to group situations, which is why it is so often introduced for assembly-line departments.

Exercises

1. The chairman of E. Limited, a company which operates a conventional piece-rate system, has recently discussed, with fellow members at his club, the subject of 'Piecework Abandoned'. A number of the club members are directors of local companies which have abandoned piecework systems of remunerating labour in favour of a variety of systems. The high-day-rate system is one now particularly favoured by them.

The chairman intends at the next board meeting to propose that piecework should be abandoned at E. Limited. He has asked you, as cost accountant, to prepare a report to enumerate the advantages and disadvantages of both the piecework system and the high-day-rate system.

You should in your report to the chairman set out clearly four advantages and four disadvantages inherent in each system, piecework and high-day-rate, and in the conclusion of your report state which of the two you favour, giving your reasons. [C.M.A.]

2. (*a*) Distinguish between: (i) straight piecework; (ii) differential piecework.

(*b*) Calculate the earnings arising under each method for each of the following jobs issued to make a common product. Under one system a rate of 3p per unit is paid. Under the other, the first 480 units for each job are paid at 1p per unit increasing by the same amount for each subsequent 240 units produced.

Job	Units
'D'	720
'E'	1,200
'F'	480
'G'	1,680

(*c*) For each method give: (i) the total cost of the total output; (ii) the average cost per unit. [C.M.A.]

3. A company is considering installing a workers' profit-sharing scheme in lieu of an individual bonus scheme.

You are required to specify the disadvantages of the former and to give an example of each point you list. [C.M.A.]

4. (*a*) The XYZ Company operates the Rowan premium bonus scheme for its production workers. During week ended November 8, employee 'A', whose basic hourly rate of pay is 40p was assigned the following jobs which he completed:

Job no.	Time allowed hours	Time taken hours
123	24	18
345	40	25

You are required to calculate:
    (i) 'A's remuneration for the week in question; and (ii) his effective hourly rate of pay for that week.

(*b*) What would 'A's remuneration for the week have been if the Halsey 50/50 premium bonus scheme had been in operation? [A.C.A.]

5. 'A', 'B', and 'C' work together as a team making simple metal components which they pack into boxes ready for despatch to the main assembly department. The expected output is 6,000 components per week, each operative working forty hours and being paid a basic rate of 62p per hour.

A productivity index is calculated each week by expressing actual production per hour as a percentage of the expected production per hour. The percentage so calculated is then applied to the basic hourly rate of pay to compute the actual rate used in the calculation of wages.

From the following data which relate to three consecutive weeks, you are required to calculate:
    (*a*) the productivity indices; and
    (*b*) the actual hourly rates of pay.

Hours worked

	Week 1	Week 2	Week 3
Operative 'A'	40	39	40
Operative 'B'	38	40	40
Operative 'C'	39	37	39
Production	6,201	5,916	6,426

[A.C.A.]

6. Cyclo-Reflex Limited is a medium-sized engineering company producing a wide range of components for the motor industry. All workers are remunerated by one

system or another of payment by results—the method of payment depending upon the nature of the task performed. In the heavy machine shop, workers' earnings are computed under the company's own premium bonus system which has the following features:

(*a*) Workers receive time wages at the appropriate rate for all hours worked.
(*b*) Each task is allotted a 'standard value' of allowed minutes.
(*c*) 'Bonus' time is the difference between the 'standard values' and the actual time taken to complete the task.
(*d*) Bonus earnings are calculated by multiplying the bonus time at the relevant bonus rate of pay.

The following data is taken from the factory records for a week in June:

Worker	Time rate per hour	Bonus rate per hour	Standard values earned	Hours worked
'A'	£0·60	£0·20	3510	40
'B'	£0·70	£0·25	3000	38
'C'	£0·80	£0·30	3440	42

The works manager has recently written to the managing director suggesting that the whole matter of workers' remuneration now requires a thorough re-appraisal It is ten years since the last major review and during this time several anomalies have grown up. In particular there is an urgent need to improve incentives as bonus rates are (on average) only one-third of time rates. As an interim measure, he proposes that all 'standard values' should be doubled immediately—rather than use 'time rates' for bonuses (as suggested by a foreman) which would treble the bonus rates.

Required:
Write a report to the managing director giving your opinion on the works managers' proposals.
[C.A.A.]

7. Using the information given below you are required to:
   (*a*) Calculate the amounts earned by each employee under each of the following remuneration methods:
      (i) piecework (with guaranteed hourly rates);
      (ii) hourly rates;
      (iii) bonus system (under which the employee receives 66⅔% of time savings).
   (*b*) Calculate the gross wages paid to each employee under each of the above methods:

	Employee 'A'	Employee 'B'	Employee 'C'
Time allowed: hours per 100 units	23	32	38
Price per unit	6p	5p	8p
Guaranteed hourly rate	30p	38p	25p
Actual time taken: hours	40	42	39
Actual units produced	200	125	150

[C.M.A.]

CHAPTER SIX

LABOUR COSTS

Time-recording

The whole basis of accounting for labour costs depends on the establishment of satisfactory methods of recording labour time. In this context, a clear distinction is made between **attendance time** (or **gate time**) and **activity time** (or **job time**). Put simply, attendance time is the actual number of hours that the worker spends in the factory, whereas activity time is the record of how he has spent that time on various tasks. All time-related remuneration plans require attendance time records, while output related remuneration plans need activity time records. (Of course, premium bonus schemes need both.) The existence of both kinds of record provides a useful control check through a reconciliation of the attendance time with the activity time. Certainly, any significant difference between them requires an investigation.

Mechanical Time-recorders

As with all business data, the value of time records is proportional to their reliability and accuracy. This is best ensured by introducing mechanical time-recorders. It is now common practice for attendance time to be mechanically recorded, but rather less so in the case of activity time. The introduction of mechanical time-recorders for activity time usually depends upon the frequency of **activity change** for each individual worker. Several changes per day call for a high level of precision in delineating the starting and finishing times of each task. Fifteen minutes in an average job time of two hours represents a possible error of twelve and a half per cent; but thirty minutes in an average job time of twenty hours is only two and a half per cent error.

Period-related Activity Time Records

There are two kinds of activity time records, those which are period related and those which are task related. Records of the first type are usually known as **time sheets** and are prepared for defined periods of time—daily or weekly. The time sheet is a chronological record of the successive activities undertaken during the relevant period. The reconciliation between attendance time and activity time is relatively simple with time sheets since both records are coterminous. Most time sheets are handwritten by the employee with a consequent risk of error in recording starting and finishing times of individual tasks.

Time Sheet Inaccuracies

The risk of inaccuracy stems mainly from the practice of 'filling-in' time sheets at the end of the period or, more probably, at the commencement of the following period. The use of daily time sheets minimizes this risk, whereas the times shown on weekly time sheets are very much approximations. Weekly time sheets are commonly used for *indirect workers* engaged in a single activity throughout the week where there is, consequently, no real need to use mechanical time-recorders. For example, the weekly time sheet (Fig. 22)

Weekly Time Sheet				Dept:		
Clock No			Name		Wk. Edg	
To be completed by worker				For Office Use		
Day	Start	Finish	Details	Code	Hrs.	Amount
Foreman's Signature:				Gross Wages		

Fig. 22. Weekly time sheet

is frequently used for maintenance personnel who, although performing various tasks, will not find it convenient to use time-recorders because of the peripatetic demands of their work. The daily time sheet is more generally adopted for direct workers and does lend itself in many cases to the use of mechanical job time-recorders for recording the times of job changes. The principal drawback to the use of time sheets for direct workers is that job times are seldom coterminous with working periods. This is especially true of daily time sheets and prompts the introduction of task-related time records to avoid the use of several records for a single operation.

Task-related Activity Time Records

The use of task related time records means that there is a separate record for each job, or task, or operation and such records are variously known as **job sheets, operation cards,** and **piecework tickets.** They are often adopted in conjunction with output-related remuneration schemes (especially for direct workers) and are particularly appropriate for job costing systems. The accuracy and reliability of task-related activity records are generally higher than for time sheets, especially as they are more readily used with mechanical time-recorders (*see* Fig. 23).

```
┌─────────────────────────────────────────────────────────────────────┐
│ Operation Card                                                       │
│   Start Date April 5. Operator JOHNSON E.G.    Clock No 2074         │
│   Finish Date April 6. Dept MACHINE SHOP NO. 3. Job No M816          │
│   Quantity 50 Operation GRIND FACES            M/c No 39/46          │
├─────────────────────────────────────────────────────────────────────┤
│            Inspection Report              │  Foreman's Signature     │
│   Remarks OK           Signed EW          │    RMEvans               │
└─────────────────────────────────────────────────────────────────────┘
```

					Hrs.	Rate	£	p
TU 12.00 / TU 8.00	4.0	Finish / Start	Time Allowed	16.00				
TU 3.30 / TU 2.30	1.0	Finish / Start	Time Taken	12.30	Time Wages	12.30	60p	7.50
W 9.10 / W 7.00	2.10	Finish / Start	Time Saved	3.30	Bonus	1.45	50p	88
					Total Wages	12.30		8.38
W 5.00 / W 10.40	5.20	Finish / Start	Bonus Time	1.45	Overhead	12.30	1.50	18.75

Fig. 23. Operation card

Relationship to Attendance Time

One of the problems in using operation cards linked to a remuneration plan is that the job times will not be coterminous with the pay period. This means that most workers are engaged on partly completed tasks at the end of the pay week which will be continued in the following pay week. It is occasionally possible to arrange with trade union representatives for the workers to be paid at time rates for part-completed work and the bonus to be paid in a lump sum on completion. On the whole, however, workers expect full payment in a given pay week for work done during that week. There are two practical ways of overcoming this problem.

Weekly Reconciliation

In the first method, job sheets are sent to the wages department at the end of the pay week so that earnings can be calculated. After completing the calculations, the job sheets are returned to the operators for the next pay week; and so on until the job is finished. This is unsatisfactory in most cases because of the great pressure imposed on the wages staff in dealing with the partly completed job cards, and the inconvenience on the shop floor if there is any delay in returning the job sheets. In most cases it will be found more practicable to adopt the alternative method, whereby the work completed by the end of the pay week is entered on the operation card and a fresh operation card is issued for the unfinished balance at the start of the next week.

Lost Time Analysis

The reconciliation of gate time with job time can be difficult with task-related activity records, but it is particularly important as a means of ensuring a complete record of time spent within the factory. One of the principal reasons for this reconciliation is to discover the incidence of **lost time** and through an analysis of causes to seek means of minimizing such wastage of labour.

Payroll Preparation

There are three basic operations in the payroll routine: preparation of the payroll; making up the cash into pay packets; and paying out the wages to individual workers. Large sums of money are involved in the payment of wages, which necessitates the introduction of security checks throughout all three stages to minimize the risk of fraud. The risk of fraud tends to vary inversely with the number of different people involved at the various stages of the payroll routine. Collusion between individuals is much less likely when large numbers of people are involved. In small organizations particular care is needed to introduce checks as only one or two persons may be engaged on payroll work. In large organizations, horizontal specialization—responsibility for one particular operation—is preferable to a vertical specialization where one clerk is responsible for all operations in respect of a given group of workers.

The major risk in payroll routines is 'ghosting' or the introduction of fictitious employees, which becomes possible where a single clerk has responsibility for all stages of the payroll routine. Another avoidable risk is over paying a worker who has a confederate in the wages department. Checks should also be made from time to time of each employee's national insurance card and income tax deduction card to prevent the addition of fictitious persons to the payroll. Additional payments such as overtime pay, special bonuses, tool allowances, loans, etc., should only be made after authorization by a responsible official. 'See through' wage packets enable the worker to check the contents without opening the envelope as it is always difficult to deal with complaints of short payment when the packet has been opened outside the wages department.

Gross Wages

The remuneration of each worker is calculated initially from his clock card (attendance record) since time wages are normally guaranteed. Time wages will be increased by any bonus earned under an incentive plan, or piecework earnings will be paid in lieu of time wages. The earnings so calculated will be supplemented by any additional payments such as **overtime premium**—a payment over and above time rate for hours worked outside the normal week; **shift allowance**—another hourly payment over and above time rate as compensation for shift working outside the normal day; **service bonus**—a payment for punctuality and regular attendance sustained over a period of, say, three months; **tool allowance**—a weekly sum to compensate a skilled worker who buys his own small tools to use in the factory. The total sum due to the worker is known as **gross wages,** and it is essential that the calculation of this sum is subject to check, partly to ensure accuracy and partly to prevent fraud.

Net Wages

The development in modern society of a whole spectrum of social benefits has imposed a burden on employers to act as government agents in the collection of taxes related to the payroll. Personal income tax is deducted by the employer under the scheme of P.A.Y.E. (pay-as-you-earn) and remitted to the Inland Revenue. Social security benefits are financed by weekly *per capita* payments made by both employer and employee. The employer is responsible for making the combined contribution to the Ministry of Social Security and therefore deducts the employee's contribution from the gross wages. Also, the worker may authorize his employer to make other deductions from gross wages. In many cases, these deductions are a condition of service for sports and social clubs, hospital services, holiday savings, trade union subscriptions, protective clothing, etc. Many of these deductions are not only constant from week to week, but also identical for groups of workers and it is possible to simplify the payroll procedure by grouping together all such deductions into a single figure referred to as the **standard deduction**. The gross wages less *all* deductions leaves the **net wages** which is the sum payable in cash to the employee. In some cases a memorandum column will be used to create a provision for annual holiday pay.

Cash Analysis

After completion of the payroll, the **cash analysis** is prepared from the net wages, and forms the basis for drawing cash from the bank to pay the workers. The payroll cash analysis is a summary of the quantity of each coin or note required to make up the pay packets. Many companies now have arrangements with the trade unions whereby net wages are paid rounded up to a given monetary denomination such as the nearest £1, 50p, 10p, or 5p. In the case of the first two it is usually possible to recover in subsequent weeks any over-payment from 'rounding up', and this is sometimes possible in 'rounding up' to 10p too. This recovery of over-payment is usually forgone with rounding up to the nearest 5p as the extra payment (an average of 2½p per worker) is considered to be justified by the gains of convenience by not having to use the small-denomination bronze coins, and in not needing to carry forward the over-payment for subsequent recovery.

Making-up Pay Packets

Conditions vary quite widely from one business to another, but it is essential in all cases to introduce a well-ordered routine for making up pay packets. The cash is drawn from the bank against the cheque for the total net wages in denominations according to the payroll cash analysis. The exact amount of cash should be counted out for each paysheet so that the total cash drawn is exactly disbursed to the various paysheets. This provides a further check on the amount drawn and also helps to localize any errors which may subsequently arise in filling the pay packets.

Employees' Pay Advices

Several copies of the payroll sheets are normally prepared and the first copy is usually perforated between each worker's entry to provide **payslips** for insertion in the pay packets. It is also customary practice to advise each worker of his gross wages and net wages before the payout so that queries can be settled in advance. This advice may take the form of a payslip or, more frequently, the details are entered on the relevant clock card which is returned to the worker through his foreman.

Making-up Routine

Clerks in pairs are detailed to make up the various payroll sheets. They are given the paysheet with the necessary cash, the pay packets and the payslips. The first clerk using the paysheet calls out the clock number and amount for each worker. The second clerk checks these details against the payslip, counts out the cash, and then hands both to the first clerk for checking and insertion in the pay packet which is left unsealed. This procedure is repeated for each entry on the paysheet, so that when the last name is reached the remaining cash is exactly equal to that man's net wages. Should any discrepancy occur at this point, the contents of the pay packets are immediately re-checked. When all is satisfactory the pay packets can be sealed. Some companies prefer to be double sure by having the unsealed pay packets checked by another pair of clerks, but this is usually unnecessary.

The clerks engaged in preparing a particular paysheet should not be involved in making up the pay packets for that sheet, nor in checking the pay packets. In practice this means that each wages clerk is engaged in preparing some paysheets, making-up others, and paying out still others. The use of automatic cash machines will greatly improve the speed and efficiency of this operation of making-up the pay packets. After the pay packets are sealed, they are placed in trays or boxes and then locked away until just prior to the time of paying out. Each tray or box should relate to one particular **pay station**.

Paying Out Wages

At a suitable interval before the paying out commences, the various pay clerks report to the chief wages clerk. Each pay clerk counts the number of pay packets in his box and signs for them in the **paying-out register**. He then takes his box to the appointed pay station where the foreman or his deputy is present to identify each worker in turn. The workers then come forward individually in clock number sequence, which may be reversed in alternate weeks. As the worker comes forward he hands to the foreman his clock card which he has signed as a receipt for the payment. The foreman reads out the worker's number and name, which the pay clerk checks against the next pay packet before handing it to the worker. After payout is completed, the pay clerk returns to the wages department with the collected clock cards and any unclaimed packets. These details are recorded in the paying-out register against the original entry and initialled by the pay clerk and by the issuing clerk.

Unclaimed Pay Packets

There are unclaimed pay packets most weeks when workers are absent through sickness or other cause. In some cases severe hardship can be caused to individuals and their families if the payment of wages is withheld. It becomes necessary in such circumstances to make alternative arrangements to enable the absent worker to receive his pay. There are normally three ways of dealing with this problem. The money can be sent through the post as a **money order**; taken by the company's **welfare officer** when visiting the sick person; or sent through one of the worker's **colleagues**. In the latter case, it is essential to insist that written authorization for this procedure is first received from the absent employee so as to avoid subsequent difficulties or claims for non-payment.

Payroll Accounting Entries

The payroll is not an account but really a rather large **journal voucher** which is used to post the relevant accounts on completion of the payroll routine. The payroll is prepared in sections, usually on a departmental basis, and sub-totals are extracted for each item in the payroll such as time wages, bonus, gross wages, deductions, net wages. The total wages bill for the employer is represented by the gross wages of workers plus the employer's contributions to social security benefits. It is the totals of these various items which provide the data for posting to the relevant ledger accounts. The entries are summarized in the following composite journal entry which is the overall payroll summary for the week:

Dr. Wages account.
(At gross wages plus employer's social security contributions and any provision for annual holiday pay.)
Cr. Bank account (at net wages).
Income tax account (deductions).
Social security account.
Provision for holiday pay account.
Sports and welfare club account, etc., etc.

Ultimately, the whole debit to the wages account is represented by credits to the bank account. The income tax deducted from workers' gross wages is remitted to the Inland Revenue, usually each month. The social security contributions (both employer's and employees') are payable to the Ministry of Social Security through the purchase of adhesive stamps or by cheque. The provision for annual holiday pay is finally paid out prior to the firm's annual holiday. Sports and welfare subscriptions are paid into the account of the social club, and so on.

Labour Cost Accounts

The amounts debited to the wages account represent the total wages cost incurred week by week. Under the traditional pattern of financial accounts, the weekly amounts will be accumulated and at the close of the financial year transferred to the **manufacturing account**. Where an integrated accounting system is adopted, however, the wages account balance is 'cleared' to the various cost accounts. Where interlocking accounts are in use, the wages account balance is transferred to the cost ledger through the two primary control accounts. Under systems of independent cost and financial accounts, the payroll journal is used also for raising the transaction in the cost accounts. The corresponding debits to the credit in the wages control accounts are made in the various cost accounts and are derived from the costing wages analysis.

Functional Analysis of Wages

The total payroll bill is analysed functionally to enable the cost accounts to be posted. This analysis of wages is based on the **activity time** obtained from the time sheets, operation cards, piecework tickets, and so on. In the first instance it will be made on a departmental basis and then (within each department) there will be a further analysis into the various categories of direct labour (jobs or operations) and indirect labour (activities or lost time). The usefulness of the wages analysis depends largely on the reliability of the basic documents recording activity time—hence the need to introduce automatic time-recorders, where practicable, as well as arranging for most of the data to be *pre-printed* by the production control department.

Weekly Time Sheets

Wages analysis is easiest with weekly time sheets since the whole week's activities are recorded on a single form. A suitable time sheet for maintenance workers is shown in Fig. 22 (*see* p. 78) and illustrates the features of weekly time sheets. The worker enters details of his various tasks down the left-hand side and these are confirmed by the foreman who signs the sheet. In the accounts department the analysis is made in the columns on the right from the details given by the worker. It is not uncommon to apportion the maintenance worker's **gross wages** over all tasks in proportion to the time spent on each, on the premise that all maintenance costs are indirect and that in this context there is little merit in making nice distinctions between different types of indirect wages. In many cases this is true for the smaller and medium-sized businesses, but in larger companies the maintenance department needs to have a more sophisticated costing system (*see* Chapter Eleven) where it is necessary to distinguish between the direct costs and indirect costs of maintenance. The procedure for analysing wages, when weekly time sheets are used, is to complete the analysis by hours first, and then take the gross wages from the payroll and enter it on the time sheet. The gross wages, when analysed between the respective tasks, is posted to the various accounts represented by the account code numbers. A summary of the wages analysis will be prepared for the whole department from all the workers' time sheets to provide the departmental supervisor with a comprehensive picture.

Daily Time Sheets

There are primarily two problems in wages analysis stemming from the use of daily time sheets: there will often be an 'overnight' job carried forward to the next time sheet and it is rather more troublesome to make the analysis from five, six, or seven separate sheets. The best way of simplifying the situation is to operate on a daily basis and calculate the gross daily wages from the time taken, plus any earnings under an incentive scheme. The sum of the individual daily sheets will not, of course, exactly equal the week's gross wages as shown on the payroll. Unless there has been an error, this difference will be very small and can safely be transferred to an adjustment account (or to a departmental general overhead account). In a given department there will be some self-cancelling so the departmental net difference will also usually be negligible. This practice has a benefit which far outweighs the small discrepancies in gross wages, in that time sheets can be extended independently of the payroll. The advantage of this lies in the opportunity to post to the various cost accounts the gross wages of one day, by the following day, to ensure that all costs accounts are kept right up to date. The gross wages for Monday can be posted to the cost accounts on Tuesday, always assuming that the appropriate routine is adopted, whereas waiting for the payroll first will necessitate a delay of about ten or eleven days in making the postings.

Operation Cards

The use of operation cards (*see* Fig. 23, p. 79) reduces the number of postings to the cost ledger but creates a problem of reconciling the gross wages debited to the cost accounts with the payroll—mainly because the operation cards are not co-terminous with the payweek (as explained earlier in this chapter). As with daily time sheets, it is possible to calculate the earnings for each operation card on completion of the task, in advance of the payroll preparation. This is especially true under the various kinds of incentive scheme where the earnings are task-related and the bonus or piecework earnings are calculated from the operation card for inclusion in the payroll. The separate calculation of earnings for the payroll and the operation cards will lead to small differences which should be transferred to an adjustment account, or a departmental general overhead account, as explained for daily time sheets.

Indirect Wages Analysis

It is useful to analyse indirect wages according to activity, such as supervision, instruction, inspection, idle time, internal transport, overtime premium, clerical duties, and so on. Weekly results compared with past averages will often indicate suitable areas for investigation. This is particularly true of idle time as its inclusion in indirect wages gives some indication of the cost of inefficiency in production control; while an analysis by causes of idle time will stimulate attempts to reduce its incidence through eliminating the causes.

Overtime Premium and Shift Premium

It is customary practice to pay a premium over and above time rate to employees who work outside the normal hours of a working week. This additional payment is made to compensate the worker for **overtime or shift working**. In the cost accounts, these premiums are frequently analysed as a separate category of indirect wages, but there are exceptions found in practice. The maintenance department is often an exception to the rule as mentioned earlier in this chapter (page 84) with regard to the use of gross wages. There are also examples in process industries where the premium for regular overtime and shift working is treated as a direct process cost. Since process costs are essentially average costs over a defined period time, the overtime and shift premium is averaged over all the units produced and so bears equally on each. Industries using job costing, however, must always treat overtime and shift premium as overhead or it will only be charged against work done during overtime periods. This is clearly inequitable as it is purely fortuitous that a particular order is done during either normal or extra time.

Direct/Indirect Wages Ratio

Factories usually prepare a summary wages analysis for each department every week. This summary details the total payroll figure by distinguishing between direct wages and indirect wages, the latter being analysed according to expense categories. The first purpose of this analysis is to show the relative amounts of direct and indirect labour. The summary will usually include either a direct/indirect ratio or, alternatively, express indirect wages as a percentage of the direct wages, the one being a reciprocal of the other. A common variation on this theme is to express both the direct wages and the indirect wages as a percentage of the total wages. It is useful to have an indication of the relative amounts spent in these two categories as a simple control tool. Clearly, any significant variation in the ratio or percentage from expected or standard calls for further investigation which is followed by any necessary corrective action.

Cost Control Ratio

This is a very crude cost control device, as will be appreciated from a study of Chapters Thirteen to Eighteen—yet it contains the essence of all control systems. All data in isolation is quite meaningless and needs to be compared with other known data to have significance. For example, if the ratio of direct wages to indirect wages for a given department was 2·89 in a particular week, this ratio only has significance when compared with some other relevant ratio. The ratio may be 4·16 for another department which immediately invites a comparison of the two ratios and a deduction regarding the relative labour structures of the two departments. Nevertheless, there is a very limited usefulness in this particular comparison as operating conditions vary widely in the two departments, so that like is not really being compared with like. The first ratio of 2·89 may be more usefully compared with the first department's average ratio for the past three months, say, 3·60. It is now apparent that there is a significant increase in this week's proportion of indirect wages—a matter demanding some immediate attention.

Significance of Ratio Changes

Care is needed by the managment accountant in assessing the significance of such movements. Suppose that the ratios are derived from the following data:

	This week £	Weekly average £
Direct wages	520	540
Indirect wages	180	150
Total	£700	£690
Ratio	2·89	3·60

It appears that some four per cent of direct wages (about £20) has become indirect wages and perhaps the lost time of a direct worker has caused this but, because the direct wages have fallen and the indirect wages have risen, the effect on the ratio is exaggerated.

Classification Problems

A difficulty sometimes experienced by management accountants is the attitude that all overhead is a 'burden' to be kept as light as possible. The story is told of the young cost accountant who found on taking up his post that it was company policy to treat the whole of a direct worker's wages as a direct cost despite the regular incidence of lost time. In his youthful zeal he seized the chance to show his mettle and arranged for the analysis, by causes, of idle time as overhead. The managing director, however, was greatly disturbed by this marked increase in overhead and refused to accept the idle-time analysis as being relevant. The cost accountant saved his face and integrity by henceforth preparing an analysis of wages paid to direct workers and wages paid to indirect workers.

A similar case arose in another factory where a foreman enhanced his reputation in improving the ratio of direct wages to indirect wages. This was achieved without changing either the total payroll or the output, but by the simple device of re-classifying one or two indirect workers as direct operators.

Exercises

1. In a production shop a man generally works on several jobs each day, and it is necessary to keep a record of what a man has earned as well as the labour cost of each job. Outline a method whereby the wages department and the cost department can maintain accurate records. [A.C.A.]

2. Describe the various methods which can be used to record the attendance time of the workers in a factory employing about 500 people and give the disadvantages of each method. [C.A.A.]

3. The management of a company is worried by the apparent lack of control over wages (labour costs) in its manufacturing departments.
   (*a*) You are asked to assist in the control of wages by designing for weekly issue by the cost office:
       (i) a departmental wages (labour costs) control statement which will give information;
       (ii) a summary of departmental statements for the general works manager.
   (*b*) Tabulate and briefly describe each of ten internal checks to be installed against fraud in the calculation and payment of wages. [C.M.A.]

4. Give a detailed explanation of the routine to be followed in a large factory for each of the three stages of wages procedure. [C.A.A.]

5. The Langham Engineering Company Limited has a number of factories, one of which is situated in a busy industrial region. The managing director is concerned to learn of the apparently high rate of labour turnover in this factory and has asked you, as cost accountant, to prepare a report to help him to understand and improve the situation.

You are required to prepare a formal report to the managing director and in it to:
   (*a*) show how labour turnover is calculated;
   (*b*) explain the influences it can have on costs; and
   (*c*) suggest steps that could be taken in an attempt to reduce the rate of labour turnover. [C.M.A.]

6. (*a*) Distinguish between (i) production and (ii) productivity.
   (*b*) Name and define a cost accounting ratio used in measurement of each of (i) and (ii).
   (*c*) Illustrate your answer by calculating the appropriate ratio from the following data.
   (*d*) State the significance and the shortcomings of each.

Machine Department:

	Model 'A'	Model 'B'
Production	1,760 units	1,680 units
Time taken	6,600 man-hours	
Standard item allowances (per model)	90 minutes	165 minutes

Assembly department:

Production	1,050 models
Standard time allowances	9 hours
(per model)	
Budget	12,600 hours

[C.M.A.]

7. Give the journal entries as they would appear in a fully integrated system of accounting, for the following figures covering the week ending June 6:

	£
Net wages drawn	2,150
National Insurance: employers	250
employees	250
P.A.Y.E.	400
Graduated pensions: employers	50
employees	50
Hospital Saturday Fund	10
Salaries cheques drawn net	450

The wages and salaries analysis is as follows:

Direct labour	1,920
Overhead: production	910
administration	480
selling and distribution	300

The deductions from wages and salaries are not paid over to the respective authority until the end of the month.

[C.A.A.]

CHAPTER SEVEN

MANUFACTURING OVERHEAD

A perusal of current accounting literature reveals that one of the problems in accountancy lies in the large number of synonymous terms in current use, especially 'overhead' which is variously referred to as burden, oncost, loading, and so on. Most authors display a preference for one term, usually for reasons which fail to satisfy the supporters of alternative terminology. Nowadays, there is a general acceptance of the idea that indirect costs are equally as valid and as necessary as prime costs, so that the selected term should avoid giving an impression that such costs are something of an unnecessary addition to the product cost. Thus, **unproductive costs** and **burden** are particularly eschewed. In the present work *overhead* is adopted according to customary usage throughout the United Kingdom mainly due to the *Terminology of Cost Accounting* published by the Institute of Cost and Management Accountants.

Overhead is categorized into the principal activity groups of manufacturing, administration, selling, distribution, and research, because the incidence of cost will usually vary from one activity to another. The present chapter is devoted to a study of manufacturing overhead and the other categories are covered in Chapters Eleven and Twelve.

Common Costs

Every business has certain items of cost which are common to several products or services and these **common costs** arise in two well-defined situations—overhead and joint products. The latter is usually the easier situation to deal with for two reasons. It is primarily concerned with direct costs and it is capable of a single stage apportionment (*see* Chapter Ten). Overhead, however, is comprised of the indirect elements of cost—the materials, labour, and expenses which are not passed on to the customer but are used up in providing the goods and services required by the customer. Therefore, overhead represents the revenue expenditure incurred in the provision of facilities for producing goods or services.

Problem of Common Costs

Overhead costs are obviously not only common to several products but, in many cases, are common to several functions or activities, too. The accountant is, therefore, faced with problems in making an equitable apportionment of the common cost between the relevant products, functions, or activities. The difficulty lies in finding common features in the relevant categories to provide an acceptable basis of apportionment, which is recognized as equitable to the recipients. The careful selection of the bases of apportionment for common costs is important because any apportionment introduces a measure of arbitrariness into the costs, and the ultimate accuracy of the result will be diminished relative to the degree of arbitrariness involved. Since there are frequently several stages of apportionment required for overhead costs, this 'loss' of accuracy can be serious unless very great care is taken to find and to use appropriate bases of apportionment.

Product Costs

The ascertainment of product costs is the subject of Chapters Eight to Twelve, but it is also appropriate to the present chapter as overhead forms an integral part of product cost. When examining the opportunities for identifying overhead with the company's products, it is apparent that the various departments of a factory fall into two distinct groups—production departments and service departments. The production departments are those directly engaged on the products, and the service departments render particular services for the benefit of other departments, but do not work directly on the products. Since the products do not pass through service departments, it is not possible to directly identify service activities with the products. However, it is not difficult to find common ground between the products and the overhead of production departments. The service department costs are, therefore, charged against the production departments at the **secondary apportionment stage**. Thus, *all* overhead is ultimately charged to the production departments so that it can be allocated to the products.

Cost Centres

Factory departments are usually convenient administrative groupings which may embrace several operations or activities. The machine shop is a good example of a production department with several differing activities such as milling, grinding, turning, drilling, planing, and so on. Even within these principal activities there may be further variations arising from different types or sizes of machine. Amongst the service departments a good example is the maintenance department with the builders, electricians, and fitters. There may well be further sub-divisions of these trade groups as in dividing the builders into bricklayers, plumbers, carpenters, painters, etc. These sub-divisions of a department are referred to as **cost centres**, and the fundamental criterion for their establishment is that of cost incidence. Clearly, the incidence of overhead is likely to vary between machines of different types or sizes—in the usage of power; floor space; rate of depreciation; and so on. Accurate costing demands a recognition of this varying cost incidence as the overhead relevant to a particular product will depend on the particular machines used in its manufacture. This will only be possible where cost centres are properly established.

Cost centres are either **locational** or **functional**. The locational (or spatial or geographical) cost centre is a defined place within the factory, examples of which are the foundry, the machine shop, and the packing room. Functional (or activity) cost centres, on the other hand, are concerned with some particular activity throughout the factory, such as planning, inspection, or internal transport. It is important to realize that each cost centre must be a homogeneous unit engaged in a single form of activity if overhead is to be allocated to products accurately and meaningfully. Often a cost centre will consist of a single machine, but it may also be a group of *similar* machines.

Overhead Analysis

There are two distinct objectives in the analysis of overhead costs, to facilitate cost control and to ascertain product costs. These objectives are achieved through three successive stages of analysis known as **allocation**, **apportionment**, and **absorption**, respectively. Each factory is organized on the basis of administrative departments (or groups of departments) usually referred to as **budget centres** (or responsibility centres) as denoting points of managerial responsibility where cost control can be exercised. The factory as a whole forms a single budget centre which is sub-divided into other budget centres (the administrative divisions and departments). It is at these points that cost control is exercised by the managers or foremen in decision-making. (A topic fully covered in Chapters Thirteen to Eighteen.)

Overhead Allocation

In the first instance every item of overhead expenditure is directly identified with one particular budget centre and analysed (or allocated) thereto. This is known as **overhead allocation** and the identification of costs with the officials responsible for them is an essential part of the accounting contribution to cost control. The following examples illustrate the allocation of overhead costs. The salary paid to a works manager is allocated to that budget centre which is the whole factory and, as a common cost of all the factory departments and cost centres, it will need to be apportioned. The salary paid to a departmental manager or foreman will be allocated to that department, but apportioned between the cost centres in the department. There are several other overhead costs which can be allocated to a department, such as indirect materials and small tools identified from stores requisitions; departmental indirect labour and waiting time of the direct workers; the depreciation of machinery and plant; power consumption where it is separately metered, etc.

It is essential to allocate costs wherever possible to ensure the utmost accuracy in analysis as, generally, overhead allocation is a straightforward exercise with no complications and none of the arbitrariness found in both apportionment and absorption.

Overhead Apportionment

It is necessary for the overhead allocated to budget centres to be apportioned to subordinate budget centres and then cost centres. This apportionment of common overhead costs is referred to as **primary apportionment**. A **secondary apportionment** (discussed later in this chapter) will also be required when the service department costs are charged to the various departments using the services provided. It is vital to the compilation of reliable cost data that the bases of apportionment should be realistic and within reasonable limits of accuracy, so as to minimize the effects of arbitrariness present in all forms of apportionment. The choice of a basis for apportionment should observe the 'Golden Rule' that, as far as possible, **the basis of apportionment should be the same as the basis of cost incidence**. This may not be possible, so it is then essential to find a **related basis** as a near-substitute for the incidence of cost, that is, to find a basis of apportionment which will correlate with the basis of incidence. In general, variable costs will be apportioned on activity-related bases, whereas fixed costs will be apportioned on capacity-related bases.

Apportionment Related to Activity

Technical Estimate

Where it is not practicable to meter the consumption of electricity, gas, water, steam, compressed air, and so on, the cost of these items can be apportioned on the basis of a technically estimated consumption. These estimates are normally derived from the theoretical hourly consumption multiplied by the number of hours of operation. This should always be used in manufacturing operations to estimate the consumption of electricity, gas, steam, compressed air, and water, not to find the **actual consumption** but a satisfactory basis of apportionment for the total expenditure. Suppose a factory is charged £600 for electrical power used during a given period. This particular factory has only five distinct cost centres for which the estimated consumption is shown in Table 6, together with the apportionment of cost.

Table 6. Cost Apportionment by Technical Estimate

Dept.	Units/Hr	Operating hours	Estimated consumption (units)	Percentage of total	Apportioned cost £
'A'	20·0	600	12,000	16·7	100
'B'	37·5	480	18,000	25·0	150
'C'	18·0	500	9,000	12·5	75
'D'	30·0	900	27,000	37·5	225
'E'	20·0	300	6,000	8·3	50
			720,000	100·0	£600

The actual metered consumption for the factory will invariably be more or less than the total estimated consumption, although the discrepancy should be fairly small. The point to realize is that the estimated consumption figures indicate the **relative consumption** in the various departments and so provide the 'sharing ratio' of the total expenditure. (This also applies to every other basis of apportionment.)

Lighting and/or space heating costs may also be apportioned on the basis of technical estimates. In these cases the operating hours are likely to be the same for all departments and so the apportionment is made on the basis of the single variable factor—hourly consumption. In the case of lighting this would be the total wattage of each department and for space heating it could be surface area of steam radiators, kilowatts per hour of electric heaters, or therms per hour for gas heaters.

Direct Labour Hours

The number of direct labour hours in a given period is related to the output activity of that period and so provides a reasonable basis for the apportionment of variable costs. It is particularly appropriate for the apportionment of departmental variable costs between cost centres, but less satisfactory for apportioning costs between departments or budget centres. A particular cost item may have varying degrees of incidence in individual departments which would call for a technical estimate to be used or some form of departmental weighting to be applied to the direct labour hours. This basis is generally acceptable for indirect materials, inspection and quality control, indirect labour, holiday pay, internal transport, and sometimes supervision and works management expenses.

Direct Wages

Occasionally, examples will be found in practice of variable costs being apportioned on the basis of direct wages as an alternative to direct labour hours. This is done solely as a matter of convenience and is rarely satisfactory because of the variations in wage rates between cost centres.

Total Departmental Wages

This basis, too, is generally unsatisfactory except for employer's liability insurance and employer's pension fund contributions where the premiums are based on average earnings.

Apportionment Related to Capacity

Number of Employees

There are several expenses which tend to vary more or less directly with the size of the labour force and such expenses are apportioned on the basis of the number of employees in each department. These are the costs of the various personnel services, such as canteen facilities, education and training, medical and welfare services, sports and social activities, wages and time-keeping departments. Generally, therefore, the number of employees is usually a basis of secondary apportionments. Supervision and works management expenses as fixed costs can often be apportioned satisfactorily on this basis.

Floor Area

This is the only satisfactory basis for apportioning the rent and rates of buildings, but it is also useful for various expenses which are related to buildings. It is suitable for lighting costs where all departments require the same intensity of illumination otherwise lighting should be apportioned on the basis of a technical estimate. Heating, too, may be apportioned on this basis where the conditions are suitable. Floor area is appropriate as a basis for apportioning costs such as cleaning, sweeping, decorating and, sometimes, for building maintenance, building depreciation, and fire prevention.

Cubic Capacity

This basis is generally more suitable than floor area for space heating costs and sometimes for interior decorating.

Value of Plant and/or Buildings

Depreciation of plant and plant repairs are apportioned on this basis where it is not practicable to allocate these costs directly to cost centres or budget centres. Building depreciation and building maintenance are normally apportioned on the value of premises only when separate buildings can be identified —thereafter, floor area is usually the only available basis. Fire insurance premiums and fire prevention costs can be satisfactorily apportioned on the basis of plant and building values, although it is often necessary to include some form of weighting to allow for varying degrees of fire risk.

Secondary Apportionment

When the allocation of direct departmental overhead has been followed by the primary apportionment of common costs to all production and service cost centres, the service department costs must be re-charged to the user departments. In general, user departments are charged in proportion to the use made of the services provided, so that the most satisfactory basis will be a rate per unit of service. In the case of plant or building repairs, there is usually a direct charge for each job (*see* Chapter Eleven) but there may be some general maintenance which needs to be arbitrarily apportioned using a technical estimate or plant values. Personnel services will usually be apportioned in the ratio of workers employed in each department; power supplies will be apportioned on the technical estimate of consumption; and so on. Most service departments, however, are caught up in a circle through their services being used by other service departments. The maintenance staff repair and maintain the buildings and equipment of the canteen, the social club, the works hospital, the power generation plant, etc., and, at the same time, these services are provided for and used by the maintenance personnel. Reciprocal services thus create something of a vicious circle for re-charging service department costs, which must be broken.

There are three methods commonly found in practice for breaking the circularity of reciprocal service costs which are illustrated by reference to the following simple example.

The Serotine Engineering Company Limited comprises three production departments and two service departments. The overhead costs for January were £29,000 and after completing the stages of allocation and primary apportionment the departmental costs were:

> Production depts. 'A', £6,000; 'B', £7,200; 'C', £8,600
> Service depts. 'X', £2,800; 'Y', £4,400.

The cost of service department 'X' is apportioned on the basis of estimated units of service consumed, while service department 'Y' is apportioned on the basis of total wages paid in departments.

	Dept. 'A'	Dept. 'B'	Dept. 'C'	Dept. 'X'	Dept. 'Y'
Consumption of					
'X' (units)	2,160	720	1,440	—	2,880
Total wages paid	£3,600	£4,800	£1,200	£2,400	£2,800

Before beginning to solve this problem, it is desirable to simplify the bases of apportionment by converting them to percentages as follows:

	Dept. 'A'	Dept. 'B'	Dept. 'C'	Dept. 'X'	Dept. 'Y'
Proportion of 'X' (%)	30	10	20	—	40
Proportion of 'Y' (%)	30	40	10	20	—

Algebraic Method

The use of simultaneous equations provides an accurate basis for apportioning reciprocal service costs, but each service department represents an unknown so that the solution becomes increasingly complex for more than two services. Certainly, with more than three service departments providing reciprocal services it is better to use the continuation method unless a computer is available. In the above example:

Let a be the total cost of 'X' after apportioning 'Y', and let b be the total cost of 'Y' after apportioning 'X'. Then

$$a = £2,800 + 0.2b; \quad \text{so, } a - 0.2b = £2,800 \quad (1)$$
$$b = £4,400 + 0.4a; \quad \text{so, } b - 0.4a = £4,400 \quad (2)$$

Solving (1) × 5: $\quad 5.0a - b = £14,000$
(2) × 1: $-0.4a + b = \quad £4,400$

$$4.6a \quad\quad = £18,400$$

$$\therefore a = £\ 4,000$$

Substituting in (2):

$$b - 0.4a = £\ 4,400$$
$$\therefore b = £\ 4,400 + £1,600$$
$$\therefore b = £\ 6,000$$

The appropriate proportions of a and b can be apportioned to the production departments to complete the overhead schedule as shown in Table 7.

Table 7. Algebraic Apportionment of Reciprocal Services

	Dept. 'A' £	Dept. 'B' £	Dept. 'C' £	Total £
Departmental costs	6,000	7,200	8,600	21,800
Apportionment a (30%, 10%, 20%)	1,200	400	800	2,400
Apportionment b (30%, 40%, 10%)	1,800	2,400	600	4,800
TOTAL:	£9,000	£10,000	£10,000	£29,000

Continuation Method

The first service department account is 'closed off' by apportioning its costs between user departments. Then the second service department is apportioned, and so on until all services have been apportioned. On completion of this first round, reciprocal service department accounts will have been 're-opened' by apportionments from other departments after the initial apportionment. Thus, a second round of apportionment begins, and a third one, and so on until the amounts remaining are insignificant and arbitrarily transferred to production departments. Using the above example, the overhead schedule (Table 8) would appear as follows:

Table 8. Continuation Apportionment of Reciprocal Services

	Total £	Dept. 'A' £	Dept. 'B' £	Dept. 'C' £	Dept. 'X' £	Dept. 'Y' £
Departmental costs	29,000	6,000	7,200	8,600	2,800	4,400
Apportion 'X'	—	840	280	560	(2,800)	1,120
'Y'	—	1,656	2,208	552	1,104	(5,520)
'X'	—	331	110	221	(1,104)	442
'Y'	—	133	177	44	88	(442)
'X'	—	26	9	18	(88)	35
'Y'	—	17	6	12	—	(35)
TOTAL	£29,000	£9,003	£9,990	£10,007		

Generally, there will be only a small margin of error in the final result arising from approximation in using this method of apportioning reciprocal services. Such a small error is well worth the convenience compared with the algebraic method.

Elimination Method

Each service department is apportioned in turn amongst the users, but once a department has been apportioned it is eliminated from any subsequent apportionments of other service departments. In this way, the services are eliminated in turn and the problem of reciprocal services disappears. It is advisable to take first that department serving the greater number of other service departments. Alternatively, the service department carrying the greater amount of cost could be apportioned first (Table 9) and the other departments being taken in declining order of amounts.

Table 9. Elimination Apportionment of Reciprocal Services

	Total £	Dept. 'A' £	Dept. 'B' £	Dept. 'C' £	Dept. 'X' £	Dept. 'Y' £
Departmental costs	29,000	6,000	7,200	8,600	2,800	4,400
Apportion 'Y'	—	1,320	1,760	440	880	(4,400)
'X'	—	1,840	613	1,227	(3,680)	—
TOTAL	£29,000	£9,160	£9,573	£10,267		

Although delightfully simple in use, this method introduces a margin of error which is generally unacceptable. Its unreliability is emphasized in the following re-working of the problem apportioning 'X' first (Table 10).

Table 10. Elimination Apportionment of Reciprocal Services

	Total £	Dept. 'A' £	Dept. 'B' £	Dept. 'C' £	Dept. 'X' £	Dept. 'Y' £
Departmental costs	29,000	6,000	7,200	8,600	2,800	4,400
Apportion 'X'	—	840	280	560	(2,800)	1,120
'Y'	—	2,070	2,760	690	—	(5,520)
TOTAL	£29,000	£8,910	£10,240	£9,850		

Overhead Absorption

Blanket Rates

Absorption rates are established for each cost centre within the factory to enable an equitable charge for overhead to be made against each product. The alternative to cost centre rates would be to use **blanket rates** either for the factory as a whole or for departments embracing several cost centres. The incidence of overhead cost varies considerably between the differing activities within the factory—hand labour and machine labour are obviously contrasting situations in this respect, but it is also true that machines differ greatly from each other in both capital cost and operating cost. Thus, blanket rates are invariably unreliable and should never be used unless the circumstances are wholly exceptional and, consequently, separate overhead absorption rates are computed for each cost centre.

Time Basis

The many varied items of expenditure which make up the aggregate overhead for a given cost centre preclude any possibility of using bases of absorption which are the same as the incidence of these costs. Practical politics demands a single rate to embrace all items of overhead cost rather than several rates. Fortunately, there is a common factor for all overhead expenditure, namely, **time**. Rent is payable for an agreed period of time; depreciation depends on the life (time) of an asset; power consumption varies directly with operating time; wages and salaries are paid per hour, per week, per month. It is therefore necessary to absorb overheads on a time (or time-related) basis if the results are to be equitable as between one product and another.

Pre-determined Rates

Overhead is almost invariably absorbed by means of absorption rates which have been determined in advance of production. The primary reason for doing so is to avoid delays in the completion of product costs which might otherwise arise through waiting until *actual* overhead expenditure has been ascertained. To use actual rates would usually mean waiting until after the end of the financial year before completing product costs which is quite unacceptable. The overhead absorption rates can be **pre-determined** by reference to the actual results for earlier periods, but it is preferable that the overhead expenditure and the volume of expected activity are forecast for the ensuing financial year, in other words, some form of **budget** is required.

At the end of the financial year, the overhead absorbed into costs will be different from the actual expenditure and also from the budget. This over-absorption or under-absorption of overhead consists mainly of fixed costs and represents a 'budget variance' arising from either a changed volume of activity from that forecast or the actual expenditure being more or less than that budgeted.

Methods of Absorption

Percentage of Value of Direct Materials

There is patently no connection between time and the value of materials so that this method is completely unsuitable for the absorption of overhead. Even materials storage and handling costs are seldom related to the cost of materials, and such expenses cannot be satisfactorily absorbed on this basis. It is difficult to think of one situation where this basis would be acceptable.

Percentage of Prime Cost

Although prime cost includes direct wages which are time related, this method is also unsuitable because of the influence on it of materials cost.

Percentage of Direct Wages

Direct wages are quite obviously time related whatever the method of remuneration in use. Where 'time' wages are paid, earnings will vary directly with hours worked, so that direct wages are equally useful with direct labour hours. Under output-related remuneration schemes, time and earnings will not have this close relationship although they still tend to move in mutual sympathy. Even so, piecework earnings are generally unsatisfactory as a basis for overhead absorption. On the other hand, workers rewarded by a premium bonus scheme receive time wages plus a bonus and, even despite wide fluctuations in their hourly earnings, overheads can be absorbed on the time wages alone.

Contrary to the opinions expressed in certain textbooks, this method has much to commend it as a means of absorbing overhead where the conditions permit. It is quite dishonest to reject this basis of absorption on the grounds of differences between workers in skills, age and sex. These are, of course, arguments against blanket rates, but they cannot generally be sustained against **cost centre absorption rates**. A cost centre, by definition, is a **homogeneous unit engaged in a single form of activity**, and it follows, therefore, that within a single cost centre there will normally be only one class of labour and one rate of pay. Naturally, this method could not be adopted where time wages are known to vary from man to man in a given cost centre, but this position will be very much an exception. Research in both the U.K. and the U.S.A. has shown that this is still the most widely used method of absorption and as such it deserves intelligent consideration. Also, it has the advantage that the relationship between overhead and time wages tends to remain constant over periods of several years under inflationary conditions, whereas hourly rates need frequent revision to correct for changes in price levels.

Rate per Direct Labour Hour

As a 'time-based' method of absorption, this basis is generally preferred to the direct wages method, which is only time related, and in some circumstances it will certainly yield more accurate results. It has the possible disadvantage of requiring the collection of additional data—the hours worked—but in most factories this is unlikely since the direct labour hours are recorded anyway. During periods of inflation the rate needs regular up-dating to keep pace with the price rises in overhead expenditures. It is sometimes suggested that a rate per direct labour hour is particularly suited to the absorption of overhead in labour-intensive situations. This may be so, but it would be in spite of (rather than because of) the labour-intensive production. It would, however, be appropriate to use this method where the incidence of overhead is influenced by the labour force in terms of numbers of personnel or hours worked.

Rate per Machine Hour

The incidence of most indirect costs is time based and some, such as power, are only incurred while machines are running. In many instances, therefore, the only satisfactory basis for the absorption of overhead is a machine hour rate. This method is generally recognized as being the most reliable and the most sophisticated of all the bases of absorption. Clearly, it can only be introduced where production is machine based, but with the mechanization of processes still gathering momentum towards a more capital-intensive production, the incidence of overhead will be influenced increasingly by machine usage.

In many cases the direct labour hour rate will yield the same result as the machine hour rate—that is, where there is a constant ratio between the two as, for example, in the case of one man to one machine and direct labour hours are congruent with machine hours. Where the crew complement of a machine may change from time to time, and the incidence of overhead is machine related, a machine hour rate is the only possible method of absorption. There may be some difficulty in those situations requiring considerable 'setting-up' prior to a production run. During these times the machine is not running, but it is 'in use'. Provided that the ratio of running time to setting time is reasonably constant this will not really matter, otherwise it is probably better to use a direct labour hour rate during setting, and a machine hour rate for running time.

Rate per Departmental Production Hour

This method is normally found only in process industries, but it can be used for flow-line production in engineering factories. Although there is a certain blanket rate characteristic about this method, it is perfectly valid where all products entering the department receive identical processing. It would certainly be unacceptable in a department providing alternative operations for the various products. It is analogous to the machine hour rate in that the various operations within the process are linked so that, for this purpose, all are seen as a single operation.

Rate per Unit of Product

This is an easily applied basis of absorption but can only be adopted in the very rare examples of a **single product** output. Even in such cases, there must be little or no variation in the production time per unit or the results will be distorted by the fact that this method is neither time based nor time related. It is, consequently, generally unsuitable for factory overhead absorption.

Illustration of Absorption Bases

The following details are taken from a jobbing company's annual budget for a factory in which there are three manufacturing departments:

	Total £'000	Dept. 'A' £'000	Dept. 'B' £'000	Dept. 'C' £'000
Direct materials	500	200	120	180
Direct wages—time	300	100	150	50
—bonus	120	30	70	20
Overhead expenses	450	120	300	30
Total costs	£1,370	£450	£640	£280

	Hours	Hours	Hours	Hours
Direct labour	575,000	200,000	250,000	125,000
Machine time	400,000	125,000	250,000	25,000
Departmental activity	6,000	2,000	2,000	2,000

	Cost Centre Rates		
	'A'	'B'	'C'
Percentage on direct wages	120%	200%	60%
Rate per direct labour hour	£0·60	£1·20	£0·24
Rate per machine hour	£0·96	£1·20	£1·20
Rate per departmental hour	£60·00	£150·00	£15·00

During the year the completed jobs included the following:

Job Number 374/E	Dept. 'A'	Dept. 'B'	Dept. 'C'
Direct materials (£)	850	120	65
Direct labour (hr)	525	620	240
Direct wages—time (£)	240	400	90
—bonus (£)	60	220	30
Machine time (hr)	350	680	50
Departmental time (hr)	4·6	5·2	4·2

Solutions:

	Dept. 'A' £	Dept. 'B' £	Dept. 'C' £	Total £
(1) Percentage of direct wages				
Prime costs	1,150	740	185	2,075
Overhead absorbed	288	800	54	1,142
Factory cost	£1,438	£1,540	£239	£3,217
(2) Rate per direct labour hour				
Prime costs	1,150	740	185	2,075
Overhead absorbed	315	744	58	1,117
Factory cost	£1,465	£1,484	£243	£3,192
(3) Rate per machine hour				
Prime costs	1,150	740	185	2,075
Overhead absorbed	336	816	60	1,212
Factory cost	£1,486	£1,556	£245	£3,287
(4) Rate per department hour				
Prime costs	1,150	740	185	2,075
Overhead absorbed	276	780	63	1,119
Factory cost	£1,426	£1,520	£248	£3,194

It is often wrongly assumed that the various method of absorption are mutually exclusive and that, consequently management has to select one basis and apply it in all cost centres (the individual cost centres would have the same **basis** but not the same **rate**). In practice, the cost accountant considers each cost centre individually and adopts for it that method which is most appropriate to its circumstances. The overhead of a hand assembly department could not be absorbed by using a machine hour rate for there are no machine hours. For that reason, it would be silly to absorb the machine shop overhead other than through machine hours. In the above example, it may be decided that the most appropriate bases of overhead absorption are:

    Department 'A'—percentage on direct wages.
    Department 'B'—rate per machine hour.
    Department 'C'—rate per direct labour hour.

In which case the factory cost Job 374/E would be:

	£
Prime cost	2,075
Overhead—Department 'A'	288
—Department 'B'	816
—Department 'C'	58
Factory cost	£3,237

Thus it is that the really efficient costing system will use several different bases of absorption at any one time depending on the prevailing conditions

Exercises

1. A small manufacturer produces his product in various sizes. All components are produced in the machine shop where the plant varies considerably as does the type and grade of labour. Products are then transferred to the assembly department.

Overhead is absorbed as a percentage of direct labour and the management claim that this is justified since all components are assembled into a similar type of product.

Discuss the suitability of the present method of absorbing overhead in an organization of this nature. [C.M.A.]

2. A manufacturer who has hitherto been selling all his output to a variety of customers takes on a contract to provide thirty per cent of his output to a multiple retailer. Part of the contract is that the multiple retailer will provide as a free issue the materials required to be used on the contract.

You are required to: (*a*) discuss what effects this new contract is likely to have on the level and nature of the manufacturer's overhead; (*b*) describe the circumstances in which the free issue of materials would justify a change in the manufacturer's method of absorption of overhead into the product. [C.M.A.]

3. Briefly describe two ways of dealing with the problem of apportioning service department costs amongst service departments which, in addition to doing work for the main operational departments also serve one another. [C.M.A.]

4. A firm which manufactures special engineering assemblies to customers' orders, has the practice of adding a fixed percentage to prime costs, in order to recover its overhead costs.

This percentage is fixed from the previous year's annual accounts.

In one year each job undertaken showed a satisfactory profit, but the year's results showed a deficit on the profit and loss account.

The total overhead incurred was not substantially different from the previous year's figure.

(*a*) Give an explanation of this position.

(*b*) In view of the poor results obtained for the year, what alteration to the system would you suggest? [A.C.A.]

5. Give a critical appraisal of the various methods in use for the absorption of manufacturing overheads. Your answer should make reference to production methods and any other non-overhead factors which may influence the choice of a basis for absorption. [C.A.A.]

6. A company manufactures two products, each of which passes through several departments.

	Departments			
	Cutting	*Machine*	*Finishing*	*Assembly*
Production budget (in units)				
Product 'A'	3,000	2,560	2,500	—
Product 'B'	1,200	—	2,500	16,000
Overhead budget	£12,000	£4,800	£5,000	£6,000
Standard hours (per unit)				
Product 'A'	4 hr	5 hr	2 hr	—
Product 'B'	6 hr	—	1 hr	30 min
Direct wages budget	£9,000	£6,000	£4,000	£8,000

You are required to:
(*a*) Name two methods of calculating overhead cost rates based on labour.
(*b*) Using the above information calculate:
  (i) the overhead cost rate for each method for each department;
  (ii) the total costs of product 'A' under each of the methods given in (*a*).
  [C.M.A.]

7. The following information is taken from the budget for year ending June 30, of Mordor Fabrication Limited:

Departments	Overheads allocated and apportioned £	Floor area (Sq. ft)	Plant value £	Effective total H.P.	Total machine hours	Direct labour hours
Production:						
Foundry	20,000	5,000	20,000	200	—	6,000
Machine shop	30,000	20,000	120,000	1,000	20,000	26,000
Heavy press shop	18,000	15,000	60,000	400	10,000	15,000
Assembly dept.	10,000	10,000	10,000	100	—	8,000
Services:						
Plant maintenance	18,000	5,000	10,000	300		
Power generation	16,000	10,000	20,000	300		
Building services	6,000	5,000	10,000	100		

Required:

(*a*) Apportion the service department costs on appropriate bases.
(*b*) Calculate overhead absorption rates on suitable bases for **each** of the production departments.
  [C.A.A.]

8. The XYZ Washing Machine Manufacturing Company has three production departments (machining, assembly and finishing) and two service departments (materials handling and production control).

The estimates of costs for the forthcoming year during which the planned production is 2,500 washing machines, are as follows:

Material:
  Machine shop £60,000; assembly £40,000; finishing £10,000; materials handling £1,000.

Labour:
  Machining—10,000 hr at £0·50; 8,000 hr at £0·45; 2,000 hr at £0·35.
  Assembly—6,000 hr at £0·40; 4,000 hr at £0·30.
  Finishing—5,000 hr at £0·40; 2,000 hr at £0·35.
  Materials handling—£2,000.
  Production control—£2,800.

Other costs:
  Machine shop £20,960; assembly £6,480; finishing £3,960; materials handling £4,000; production control £1,200.

It is estimated that the benefit derived from the service departments is as follows:
  Materials handling—machine shop 60%; assembly 30%; finishing 10%.
  Production control—machine shop 40%; assembly 30%; finishing 20%; materials handling 10%.

You are required to:
(*a*) prepare a statement showing the overhead to be absorbed by each of the production departments; and
(*b*) calculate the overhead absorption rates, using the following bases:
  Machine shop—direct labour hour.
  Assembly—percentage on direct wages.
  Finishing—production unit.
  [A.C.A.]

9. During November the following production costs were incurred in a manufacturing company:

		Indirect material costs £	Indirect wages £	Indirect expense £
Allocated to:				
Production department:	'A'	600	3,000	—
	'B'	1,200	2,000	—
	'C'	800	4,000	—
Service department:	'Y'	400	1,000	—
	'Z'	600	2,000	—
Not allocated		600	4,000	12,500
		£4,200	£16,000	£12,500

The basis of apportionment of costs to departments is:

To:	Department 'A' %	Department 'B' %	Department 'C' %	Total %
Service department:				
'Y' costs	30	25	45	100
'Z' costs	20	40	40	100
Production costs not allocated	40	15	45	100

Transfers of overhead during the month to work-in-progress account were:

	£
From: department 'A'	11,700
'B'	6,920
'C'	13,975

You are required to prepare for November:

(a) an overhead analysis sheet for the production departments;

(b) a production overhead expense control account for the whole company;

(c) an overhead control account for each production department and the whole company. [C.M.A.]

CHAPTER EIGHT

COST ASCERTAINMENT

Product Costs

Managers, students, and even some accountants are sometimes misled into believing that a sound costing system will provide the **true cost** of a product. In the sense of absolute accuracy this is quite illusory! No matter how sophisticated the costing system may be, nor how efficiently it is operated, there will always be some items of cost which will be dealt with on a more or less arbitrary basis. As pointed out at the beginning of Chapter Seven, whenever costs are treated arbitrarily there must necessarily be some impairment of the ultimate accuracy and, since obviously every multi-product situation requires the arbitrary apportionment of common costs between the various products, there will be some inaccuracy in product costs to the detriment of compiling **true product costs**.

This is the normal situation for most businesses as single product output is very rare indeed. Many firms produce a single type of product, but variations in colour, size, materials, quality, and so on create a multi-product situation, since every change in the specification results in a separate product. Even in the rare examples of a single-product industry, there will not be any true product costs because of the many arbitrary decisions that need to be taken. Depreciation is a notable example, as the annual provision is calculated on an arbitrary life period modified by an arbitrary allowance for early obsolescence. Then, again, materials issued from stores are priced by arbitrary methods such as L.I.F.O. and F.I.F.O. It is impossible to conceive that the *absolute true cost* of any product can at all be obtained in an ongoing business.

Historical Costing

The evolvement of sophisticated techniques in management accounting has led some popular writers to the view that the ascertainment of product costs is an out-dated exercise, having little or no relevance to the needs of modern management. This view stems largely from the fact that product cost is generally compiled in arrears, that is, it is essentially **historical costing**.

Historical costing is criticized because it simply reports past events and the time-lag between the event and its reporting makes the information out of date and, therefore, irrelevant to current decision-making and, because of this delay, it is valueless in aiding cost control. It is probable, however, that any inordinate delay in the presentation of information arises from an inefficient system of cost accounting, rather than from the historical basis of cost ascertainment. Furthermore, budgetary control depends on actual (that is, historical) performance for variance analysis and is seldom criticized in that respect even though any time-lag can make variances just as obsolete as other historical costs. At the same time, a really efficient system of job costing can keep costs 'up to date' and provide help in cost control—albeit rather less satisfactorily than is possible under standard costs and budgets.

Uses of Product Costs

Product costs are required for three purposes: profitability comparisons between products; consideration of selling price policy; and stock valuation. There are, however, three distinct bases for the determination of product costs: **absorption cost** forms the subject of Chapters Eight to Twelve; **standard cost** is dealt with in Chapters Thirteen to Eighteen; **marginal cost** forms the basis of Chapters Nineteen and Twenty. Each has its advantages and limitations for reflecting product costs and the adoption of one basis rather than another is generally a matter of policy and, to some extent, a matter of opinion amongst management regarding the significance of product costs obtained by alternative methods.

Profitability

Profit may be defined simply as the **margin between costs and revenue**. The profit yielded by a given product can be compared with that of other products but, to be really significant, the profit needs to be reduced to a relative basis for comparison between products, such as a percentage of selling value; an amount per unit of limiting factor; per £ of total cost; and so on. Management is then able to decide on the most profitable mix of products to manufacture; or to direct attention towards expanding the sales of the more profitable lines; or to discourage salesmen from 'pushing' a particular product, etc. Naturally, it is essential to use these ratios (as indeed all ratios) with some care and certainly not in isolation from other factors relevant to the particular decision. For instance, the use of profit as a percentage of sales without also considering the volume could lead to serious losses.

Selling Price Policies

All businesses have the problem of setting their product pricing policy. In this the cost of manufacture is a fundamental factor for, if the company is to remain in business, it must make profits by selling its products at prices in excess of costs. It is quite common for businesses to **set a price** for their product which is **based on cost**, which often leads them to declare that selling price is determined by cost. Against this, the economist claims that a selling price is determined by the interaction of supply and demand, in other words, 'by what the market is prepared to pay', without any consideration arising of the cost involved. Certainly, as the economist says, a customer (the market) will not pay more for a product than he feels it is worth to him in terms of the satisfaction obtained. However, the producer must obtain a price which exceeds his cost, at least in the long run.

The incompatibility of these two attitudes is, however, more apparent than real. The price of an article is the sum actually paid for it, so to speak of the 'price' for an article which is never sold is to utter a contradiction in terms. Consequently, when a manufacturer looks at his costs and then 'fixes a selling price', he is really saying 'since my cost is £x, I am only prepared to make and sell this item *if the price is at least £y*'. The customer then decides whether or not that is the price by his acceptance or rejection of the offer.

Stock Valuation

It is a precept of accountancy that stocks should be valued at the lower of cost or market value, but this presupposes some knowledge of both these values. In a manufacturing business the valuation at cost of finished goods and of work in progress is dependent on the existence of some form of cost ascertainment. The valuation of stocks is an essential exercise in an assessment of the profit performance of a business, especially where there are differences of volume or product mix between the opening and closing stocks. A reliable system of cost ascertainment is essential if the period's profit is to be computed with confidence.

Methods of Cost Ascertainment

Basically, it is possible to identify two fundamental groups of costing methods in the ascertainment of product costs, specific order costing and process costing. In the provision of services rather than tangible products the same distinction applies—specific order costing is used for *ad hoc* services, whereas operating costing is used for continuing services.

Specific Order Costing

The principles of cost ascertainment are the same for contract costing, factory job costing, or batch costing. In each case the objective is to determine the cost of producing for a single order, that is, specific order costing. There are points of difference between these 'methods' but such variations arise from the nature of the production situation rather than the principles of cost ascertainment. The direct elements of cost are collected for each separate order and the addition of overhead provides the total cost of production (*see* Chapter Nine).

Jobbing Production. Specific order costing is found in two quite different situations. First, as one would expect, it is used in jobbing and contracting businesses. Here, there would be no production at all without first receiving a firm order from the customer. There will be little or no repetition in design of the previous orders, and thus materials are often special purchases also and, therefore, easily debited to the relevant job account in the work-in-progress ledger. Manufacturing or construction activities stem from the execution of the particular order, thus enabling direct labour and direct expenses to be readily identified with the respective jobs.

Production for Stock. Alternatively, many manufacturers produce goods for stock in anticipation of receiving future orders from their customers. This is, in no sense whatever, a *jobbing situation*; indeed, production may be repetitive to the point of standardization. However, output stems from a series of manufacturing orders for given quantities of stated products. Since the factory activities are initiated by specific orders, the situation is analagous to jobbing production. The costs incurred by a specific order are debited to the appropriate job cost account; in this case, not for one or two units but often for quite large quantities, or a batch of units, hence the use commonly of the term 'batch costing' as an alternative to 'job costing'.

Process Costing

Process costing differs from specific order costing in a quite fundamental manner (*see* Chapter Ten). The emphasis in process costing is on the accumulation of costs arising in a department during a given period of time, in other words, process costing is essentially departmental costing rather than order costing. Unit costs are averages derived from all the units processed during the given period of time. In general, two distinct forms of process costs are recognizable—the **accumulation method** and the **operation method**.

The Accumulation Method. The total costs of the first process are transferred to the second process, the cumulative costs of processes one and two are transferred to process three, and so on. The total cost of the final process is thus also the aggregate cost of the products. The principal deficiency of this method lies in the difficulty of making comparisons with previous performances of processes beyond the first, because any gains or losses at one stage of production will automatically be reflected in the costs of all subsequent processes.

The Operation Method. Costs are ascertained separately for each process and no cost is transferred from one process to another. This overcomes the objection to the previous method and enables the current performance for each process or operation to be usefully compared with previous or standard performance. The total cost of the product is obtained by aggregating the costs for the relevant processes used in manufacturing the product.

Operating Costing

This term applies to the ascertainment of cost in the provision of services, as distinct from producing tangible products (*see* Chapters Eleven and Twelve). Despite this, the costing method required will not call for any application of principles different from those already discussed.

In this context, too, it is possible to identify two separate sets of circumstances—the provision of *ad hoc* services and the provision of general or repetitive services. *Ad hoc* services will usually be dependent upon the specific brief given by a client, such as the geological survey of a given area; the study of a company's management structure by consultants; or the hire of a special piece of equipment to perform a single task. The costing of *ad hoc* services will, therefore, normally be done on a job-costing basis since the fact that there is no tangible product at the end is really quite irrelevant. Costing for repetitive services is analagous to process costing since it will be necessary to cost the service over periods of time and, in many cases, to ascertain the cost of each element or part in the total service rather as operation (or activity) costing is used to determine the elemental (individual process) costs of products.

Material Losses

It is a phenomenon of all kinds of manufacturing that material losses occur at some stage in the production sequence. These losses arise from two general causes—the **operating method** and/or the **operating inefficiency**. The losses which arise from the nature of the operating method are usually unavoidable and, being uncontrollable, are accepted as being normal losses. Losses which result from operating inefficiency are, however, seen to be preventable or avoidable and, being susceptible to control, are considered to be abnormal losses.

All materials losses (both normal and abnormal) may be re-grouped into two categories—input losses and product losses, or spoilage. Input losses relate to materials which have been issued to production but do not form part of the finished products. They are represented by materials which are discarded during the course of manufacturing and those which 'disappear' during processing and are generally known as scrap, or waste, depending on whether any part of the input cost is recoverable.

Scrap is defined as a 'saleable residue discarded from a manufacturing process'. This term also includes residual materials which are not in fact sold but re-processed with (and as) good material and so has a value equal to the cost of outside purchase.

The two characteristics of scrap to be noted are that it is tangible and possesses a value in re-use or re-sale. Examples of scrap include machining swarf, foundry trimmings, and unvulcanized rubber. Scrap materials which are to be re-processed will usually be valued at the same price as that at which they were issued from stores. Where there is a mixture of two or more ingredients in the discarded material, as with non-ferrous metals, the scrap is valued at the average price of the material content. Scrap materials which are sold, instead of being retained for re-use, will be valued at the current market price obtainable on the sale irrespective of the issued value.

Waste is defined as having no value: either a valueless residue or material which 'disappears' during the course of processing. The difference between scrap and waste (as a residue) is thus entirely a matter of recoverable value. It is by no means exceptional for industrial waste to have a *negative value* in the sense that there may be expenditure incurred in disposing of the unwanted material. Such disposal costs are likely to become increasingly significant in the future as anti-pollution regulations impose constraints on the tipping of toxic waste or the discharging of untreated factory effluents. 'Disappearing' waste arises from combustion, evaporation, or dust particles emitted into the atmosphere which, too, are likely to be increasingly subject to anti-pollution controls.

Spoilage (or product losses) is defined as sub-standard units of product, that is, units of product which fail to satisfy the company's quality control standards. These faulty products are of two kinds: those which can be rectified and so brought up to the required standard or quality; and those beyond correction. In the first case, the work of rectification is put in hand by the issue of a works rectification order. When the spoiled unit is beyond rectification it is disposed of in one or other of the following three ways.

(*a*) The faulty unit may be functionally sound, and so sold as a sub-standard product at a price below the normal selling value.

(*b*) Where the unit is not functionally acceptable, it may be treated as scrap where the value of the material content is recoverable in whole or in part.

(*c*) Where there is no possibility of recovering part of the unit's value as sub-standard or as scrap, there is no alternative but to treat the spoiled work as waste.

The different forms of materials losses are illustrated diagrammatically in Fig. 24. There is a danger of confusion, in practice, regarding materials losses, as the terms scrap, waste, and spoilage are frequently used in senses different from those given here. The most common difference is found in the Engineering Industry where the term 'scrap' is applied to 'spoilage', because much spoilage is non-rectifiable, but is sold to scrap dealers for the value of the metal content. It is much more important to understand the underlying

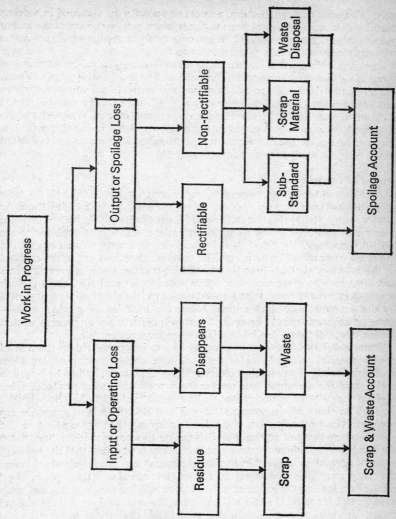

Fig 24. Diagram of materials losses in production

concepts than to learn the definition of particular terms—the meaning of any term can then be readily discerned if it is properly taken within the context of its use.

Accounting for Input Losses

Normal Scrap and Waste

Since all forms of normal loss are unavoidable and thus uncontrollable, they represent a necessary part of the cost of producing good (or saleable) units. The costs of normal scrap, waste, and spoilage are included in product costs by debiting total input costs to the relevant job or process cost account in the work-in-progress ledger. This account will be credited with any value recoverable from the sale of normal scrap so the good production will bear the net cost of the scrap created in its manufacture. The estimated value of scrap is debited to scrap account and credited to work-in-progress account. With regard to waste, there will be no value credited to the work-in-progress account, but the physical quantity of waste will normally be credited to the account so as to leave the actual quantity of good output. Where the waste discarded from production incurs additional expense in its disposal, this becomes an added cost of manufacturing the saleable products and is debited to the relevant work-in-progress account.

Abnormal Input Losses

All abnormal losses are avoidable, and so controllable, and should not arise in the normal course of production. As such, abnormal losses of all kinds do not form any part of the cost of the good units produced. In the first instance the cost of materials losses are included in the costs of inputs debited to the work-in-progress ledger and so it is necessary to segregate such costs from the valid costs of the good units. The costs of abnormal losses are credited to the relevant work-in-progress account on transfer to an appropriate loss account, namely, scrap account, waste account, or spoilage account. Such accounts invariably relate to **abnormal losses**, even though this is not suggested by the account title, since **normal losses** are included in product costs—separate accounts should be opened for each department or process so that the incidence of losses can be localized to encourage control.

Abnormal Scrap. The cost of abnormal scrap is represented by the cost of issued material in the 'saleable residue' from manufacturing arising from **avoidable causes**. It means that either additional material had to be issued to make good the abnormal loss or else fewer good units were produced from a given quantity of issued material. The issued value of the scrap is thus credited to the work-in-progress account and debited to the process scrap account. The proceeds from the sale of scrap material are credited to the process scrap account so that any balance on this account is the 'loss' from abnormal scrap. When discussing normal scrap it was said that the **recovery value** of normal scrap is debited to scrap account and this is indeed so! When the scrap material is sold, the scrap account is credited with the value received on the sale, leaving the balance on the account relating only to abnormal scrap as the debit for normal scrap is the same as the credit for the sale of normal scrap. This is more convenient and more sensible than trying to keep the two kinds of scrap completely separate from each other. The year-end balance on a scrap account is finally written off to the profit and loss account.

Abnormal Waste. Abnormal waste is represented by the issued value of materials in avoidable losses from disappearance in process or from the discarding of a valueless residue. This value is credited to the appropriate work-in-progress account and debited to the process waste account. At the close of the accounting year, any balance on this account is transferred to the profit and loss account. Any disposal costs for abnormal waste will also be debited to the process waste account to give the full cost of controllable waste.

Scrap and Waste Account

Both scrap and waste are input losses in that they relate to materials which have been issued to production but do not form part of the finished products. It is important to distinguish them in this way as an aid to identifying the incidence and causes of abnormal materials losses and so seek ways of controlling such losses. Nevertheless, from a purely accounting point of view there would appear to be little or no benefit in opening separate accounts for what is really a single category of abnormal materials loss. There may be some difficulty in finding a suitable title for such an account—**materials input losses account** appears to be apt—but common usage of the terms scrap and waste suggests that, in most companies, practical politics will more likely favour **scrap and waste account.** From a book-keeping point of view, therefore, there is no virtue in making this nice distinction between scrap and waste and the following journal entries summarize the procedure which is illustrated in Fig. 25.

(1) Dr. Scrap and waste account.
    Cr. Work-in-progress account.
    Being the transfer of materials input losses for the period concerned.
(2) Dr. Cash (or dealer) account.
    Cr. Scrap and waste account.
    Being the value recovered from the sale of scrap materials.
(3) Dr. Departmental scrap and waste account.
    Cr. Cash (or contractor) account.
    Being the cost of disposal of waste materials.
(4) Dr. Departmental scrap and waste account.
    Cr. Work-in-progress account.
    Being the recovery value of normal process scrap.

Accounting for Spoilage

Normal Spoilage

Spoilage should not really occur since it represents a failure to achieve the required standards of quality. Consequently, to speak of **normal spoilage** is really a contradiction in terms since poor workmanship *is* controllable and need not be accepted. Even so, there are occasions in practice, especially in factories using sophisticated production techniques, where an agreed level of spoilage may be recognized as being unavoidable and, therefore, accepted as normal. For example, a factory may install an automatic power press for blanking circles from coils of steel strip. The press may have two or more separate speed settings and it may be supposed that, at the slower speed, the incidence of spoilage is negligible. At the higher speed, however, various vibrations are set up within the machine which every now and again cause a slight 'hiccup' in the feed mechanism. This 'hiccup' leads to the stamping of imperfect circles so that the incidence of spoilage is, say, five per cent at the higher speed.

This is a situation where the spoilage is avoidable by running the machine at the slower speed but, if the average cost per unit (including five per cent spoilage) at the higher speed is less than the average unit cost at the slower speed, it is clearly the least cost alternative to operate the press at the higher speed. Operating at the higher speed about five per cent spoilage will occur

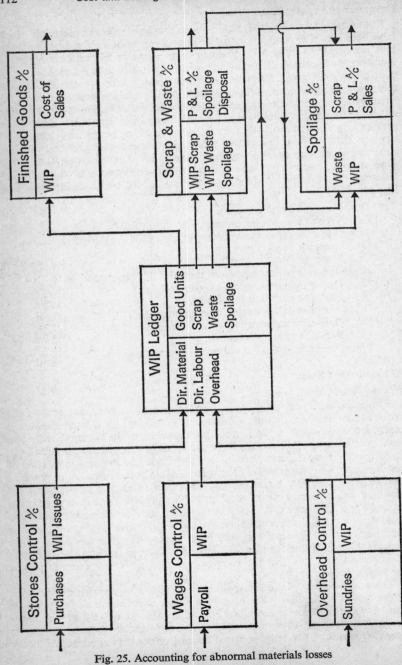

Fig. 25. Accounting for abnormal materials losses

but, since this arises from the nature of the operation (the higher speed), it will be **unavoidable** within this context and so **normal**. The imperfect circles blanked out by this power press will not be capable of rectification but will be sold as scrap metal and the recovered value will be credited to the work-in-progress account to offset the cost of normal spoilage.

Spoilage Rectification

There are some forms of spoilage which are physically beyond rectification such as circles with a 'bite' out of them; holes which are drilled oversize; and suit lengths which are cut too short. There are also examples of spoilage which can be corrected such as scratches which can be 'polished out'; surplus material which can be 'trimmed-off'; and undersize holes which can be 'drilled-out'. Obvious additional expense will be incurred in rectification from the application of labour and overhead (and, occasionally, material also), so the criterion of spoilage rectification is not the physical opportunity for correction but, once again, the least cost alternative. This is illustrated by the following two examples:

Example 1

Product XB307 failed to satisfy the quality control standard and was rejected but is considered to be capable of rectification. The following data applies:

		£
Cost incurred up to point of spoilage		2·53
Recovery value (sale as 'sub-standard')		2·00
Cost of rectification (to first quality)		1·15
	£	£
If rectified, the additional cost		1·15
If replaced, the additional cost	2·53	
Less sale as 'seconds'	2·00	0·53
GAIN from replacement (non-rectification)		£0·62

Example 2

Product QA142 was found to be faulty by the inspection staff and recommended for rectification. The following data applies:

		£
Cost incurred up to point of spoilage		136·20
Recovery value (sale as 'scrap metal')		12·16
Cost of rectification		48·50
	£	£
If rectified, the additional cost		48·50
If replaced, the additional cost	136·20	
Less sale as 'scrap'	12·16	124·04
GAIN from rectification (non-replacement)		£76·54

Where normal spoilage is capable of rectification, to satisfy the company's quality control standards, it is only justifiable to do so where this is the least cost alternative. The cost of such rectification (as in Example 2) will be debited to the relevant work-in-progress account as part of the cost of good output. Where rectification is not undertaken (as in Example 1) then any recovered value is credited to the relevant work-in-progress account and the cost of replacement is debited to the same account.

Rectification Costs

In accounting for spoilage it is sometimes difficult to identify the **cost of spoilage**, but it is necessary to do so despite any attendant difficulties. The problem is easier when each category of spoilage is considered separately. The costs of rectifying spoilage are those expenses incurred in restoring the product or component to its desired standard or quality. This will invariably require the application of labour and overhead with, occasionally, some additional material. As no work of any kind should be carried out unless authorized by the issue of a work order, the rectification work is only undertaken against an official **rectification order**. The rectification order may be issued by the production control department (the progress department) or by the inspector who rejected the piece. All labour spent in rectification will be 'booked' against the relevant order number, as will all stores requisitions for additional materials withdrawn from the stores. Overhead will also be absorbed by the rectification order, usually with the labour posting. On completion of the rectification to the inspector's satisfaction, the total cost of rectification is charged to the work-in-progress account for normal spoilage (*see* Fig. 25 on page 112). The relevant journal entries for rectification costs are:

(1) Dr. Rectification order.
Cr. Stores account.
Cr. Wages account.
Cr. Overhead account.
Being the costs of rectifying spoilage.
(2) Dr. Work-in-progress account.
Cr. Rectification order.
Being costs of rectifying normal spoilage.
(3) Dr. Spoilage account.
Cr. Rectification account.
Being costs of rectifying abnormal spoilage.

Non-rectifiable Spoilage

Spoiled units will be disposed of which are beyond rectification, or for which the cost of rectification is greater than the margin between the full selling value and the non-rectified receiver value. In general, there are three disposal methods—sale as sub-standard products, sale as scrap metal, and disposal as waste (*see* Figs. 24 and 25 on pages 100 and 112 respectively).

Sub-standard Products

A product may be perfectly functional yet fail to satisfy the company's quality control standards and becomes spoilage on the inspector's rejection. Examples of this are manifold throughout most manufacturing industries and include: coats with the lining imperfectly sewn in; woollen garments showing a tiny knot where two pieces of wool are joined, saucepans with the handle lug very slightly askew, and refrigerators with a chipped surface. Potential customers will be unwilling to buy an imperfect product except at a price below the normal selling price. Indeed, many people will be willing to accept the imperfection and think it worth while where they see a significant price-saving opportunity.

These 'faulty' products are variously known as seconds, imperfects, sub-standards, and so on and this fact is usually printed on the product or its label to preserve the manufacturer's reputation for quality. In this instance, the cost of spoilage is the amount by which the selling price is reduced. The value at which the item is held in stock until sold will be the cost of manufacture reduced by this loss from spoilage. The following journal entry gives effect to this:

Dr. Spoilage account.
Cr. Work-in-progress account (or finished stock account).
Being the loss in value from spoilage.

Scrap or Waste Products

Those units of output which are non-rectifiable nor suitable for sale as sub-standard products will be disposed of as scrap or waste. In these cases, the cost incurred in manufacturing up to the rejection point will be transferred to the spoilage account:

Dr. Spoilage account.
Cr. Work-in-progress account.
Being the manufacturing cost of spoiled goods.

Where the value of the material content is recoverable through the sale as scrap of the faulty units, this value should be transferred through the scrap and waste account:

Dr. Scrap and waste account.
Cr. Spoilage account.
Being the recovery value of spoiled units sold as scrap materials.

In those cases where the spoiled units are completely valueless and expense is incurred in their disposal, the expected cost of disposal is debited to the spoilage account and credited to the scrap and waste account:

Dr. Spoilage account.
Cr. Scrap and waste account.
Being the cost of disposal as waste of spoiled units of output.

Exercises

1. Basically, we can identify two fundamental groups of costing methods used in the ascertainment of product costs although most costing textbooks provide an impressive list which—at first sight—seems to belie this simple division.

Required:

Discuss this quotation carefully and fully.   [C.A.A.]

2. Explain what is meant by: (*a*) normal, and (*b*) abnormal scrap and waste of materials during the process of manufacture. What treatment would you give them in the cost accounts?   [A.C.A.]

3. A food company produces a wide range of products under its brand name.

Included in its costs is a considerable amount of setting up cost concerned with cleaning the mixing machines and preparing the equipment for the manufacture of new batches. This is independent of the length of the run which is determined by the popularity of the particular product, the amount of stock the company will carry and the production plan.

(a) Explain what methods are available to the company to deal with these setting up costs in calculating their product costs. Explain the relative advantages of each method.

(b) Occasionally the product is not of the required standard and is scrapped. Discuss the methods of dealing with the cost of this scrapped product.

[C.M.A.]

4. Blue Sludge Limited is an old-established business which manufactures a wide range of domestic holloware for both home and export markets. It has built-up an enviable reputation for quality and operates an efficient system of inspection and quality control. Experience shows that twelve and a half per cent of the company's output fails to reach the high standard of quality demanded on first inspection. The factory's inspection team uses three grades of rejection for spoilage—rectifiable; seconds; scrap.

Required:

Describe the administrative procedures suitable for dealing with this spoilage and explain the cost accounting routine.

[C.A.A.]

5. You are required for a manufacturing company to:

(a) calculate unit cost of production and the unit cost of rework for product 'X' and product 'Y'.

(b) prepare a total profit and loss statement for the current position as budgeted.

(c) prepare a profit and loss statement showing the position if the re-work department were eliminated and the rejected items sold for scrap.

Two products are produced whose prime costs, excluding the cost of re-work, have been given as follows:

	Product 'X' £	Product 'Y' £
Direct materials	3	4
Direct labour:		
Department 1 (40p per hr wage rate)	2	4
Department 2 (50p per hr wage rate)	3	2
Prime cost	8	10
Selling price	17	20

The work in Department 2 is extremely delicate, and ten per cent of the items produced require re-working. For administrative convenience, a separate re-work department has recently been established. The wage rate here is twenty per cent higher than in department 2 and the time taken per unit reworked is half of that taken on the original production in department 2.

The budget for the coming year includes the following:

Production	8,000 units of 'X'	
	10,000 units of 'Y'	
Variable overhead	twenty per cent of direct wages in departments 1 and 2 only	£
Fixed overhead	department 1	28,000
	department 2	44,000
	re-work department	6,600

Fixed overhead is absorbed on a direct labour hours basis.

The company now has the opportunity of selling for scrap those items which at present go to the re-work department. It would receive £2 for each unit of 'X' and £3 for each unit of 'Y'. Eliminating the re-work department would involve a reduction of £1,500 of its fixed overhead.

[C.M.A.]

CHAPTER NINE

SPECIFIC ORDER COSTING

Nature and Application

Specific order costing is essentially historical costing in that it is cost ascertainment *ex post facto*, but as discussed in Chapter Eight, that is no reason for an outright condemnation of cost ascertainment in general nor of specific order costing in particular. A specific order costing system is one which collects separately the elements of cost for each job or order manufactured. In effect, the purpose of specific order costing is to determine the cost of producing one unit. A single unit in this context may be one item such as a ship, a batch of similar items, or a particular order or contract. There are three types of businesses using some form of specific order costing:

(1) **Jobbing Production**—these are companies which manufacture only to the specific requirements of their customers against firm orders or contracts and so produce a wide variety of work; although there is some tendency to specialize within a particular industrial field, they may never produce two jobs alike. Examples of these are: the manufacture of foundry patterns and other tool-making; steel fabrications and heavy engineering plant; special-purpose machine tools; buildings and bridges; roads and railways; printing and publishing.

(2) **Multi-product Situations**—where there is a wide range of products manufactured under batch conditions and the various factory departments are not sufficiently specialized to permit the introduction of flow-line processing. Products which may be manufactured in batches include furniture and soft furnishings; clothing and textiles; canned and frozen foods; toiletries and cosmetics; kitchen utensils; toys, games, and sporting equipment.

(3) **Small Manufacturers**—having a limited market for their products which prevents the introduction of intensive methods of production, but who adopt a system of batch production with frequent change-overs. Products in this category include jewellery; specialized printing; decorative metalware and domestic fittings.

Factory Job Costing

Many manufacturers produce goods 'for stock' in anticipation of future orders from their customers (that is, batch production) and also fulfil a 'jobbing' role by making special orders to a customer's own specifications. In either case, a **job costing system** demands the prerequisite of a **job order system**, that is, production (or manufacturing) orders. In other words, there is no continuous flow of output but a state of 'interrupted' production flows undertaken only against specific orders, so it is irrelevant whether the business is manufacturing *standard* products to be sold 'ex stock' or, alternatively, only issuing manufacturing orders after a firm order to supply is received from customers, or even both.

Naturally, where at least part of the company's output is dependent on receiving the customer's orders to supply, there will tend to be a job order system in operation. This in turn will frequently, though not necessarily, prompt the adoption of job costing.

Job costing may be more appropriate for certain sections of a business while other sections are more suited to process costing or operating costing. An example of this is in the manufacture of special-purpose machine tools produced to customers' requirements, hence a basic system of job costing. Nevertheless, certain standard components may be produced under flow-line conditions which calls for process costing while a system of operating costing may be adopted for the transport department.

The Production Order

The production (or manufacturing) order will normally originate in the production control department, or in whichever works department exercises the production control function such as the planning department or the progress department. Whilst a general authority to issue production orders resides in the production control department, it lies dormant until activated by some external force, usually in this context the stock replenishment order, on reaching re-order level, or an **internal sales order** issued by the sales department. The internal sales order is a notification to all concerned of a firm order received from a customer. Unless the ordered goods can be delivered from the finished goods warehouse stock, they must be specially manufactured in the works and so, on receiving a copy of the internal sales order, the production control department issues a production order for the manufacture of the ordered goods. There are four basic requirements of a production order:

(1) It must be in writing and have a serial number for identification purposes.

(2) It must state exactly what is to be made. This means a full technical description including the relevant catalogue numbers or drawing numbers or quotation references. The importance of this clear specification cannot be over-stressed.

(3) The manufacturing order should call for a **definite** quantity of like units. Both cost control and production control are likely to be vitiated by the ordering of vague quantities such as 'about ten tons', 'say, 1,000 gallons', or 'approximately fifty dozen'. The availability of adequate materials and the planning of machine loading depend on knowing definite quantities.

(4) The order should be issued for a single production run only. There are two situations in which orders could be issued to cover more than one production run. First, for long-run contracts with widely spaced deliveries (say, every six months) where the production time is much shorter than the delivery period. In this situation a separate run will be made every six months. Secondly, orders to manufacture for stock are issued to keep workers employed during slack periods.

As these slack periods may be intermittent and, in order to avoid the necessity of repeatedly issuing fresh orders, a 'blanket' order may be issued either for no stated quantity or for a ridiculously high quantity. (In effect, this latter position is really a **standing order**.) From the accounting viewpoint, this is really several jobs under a single reference number and will result in meaningless costs where various machines are used for different runs; where varying quantities are produced by separate runs and where the period of time in completing the full order is so lengthy that significant cost changes occur in materials, labour, and overhead.

Job Cost Accounts

A copy of the manufacturing (or production) order is sent to the accounts department where a job cost account is opened for the order in the work-in-progress ledger. The folio number of a job cost account for filing, identification, and reference purposes should be the serial number of the relevant manufacturing order as this avoids confusion and facilitates the charging of costs to the appropriate jobs. The work-in-progress ledger is thus composed of all the accounts of uncompleted jobs at various stages of completion. The work-in-progress ledger contains a ledger control account, to facilitate ledger balancing, which is a summary of all the individual job accounts and it is the balance on this control account which is shown in the balance sheet as work-in-progress. Since the work-in-progress ledger includes a separate cost account for each job, the final balance on the job cost account clearly represents the total cost of manufacturing the customer's order. Therefore, the job cost system really reduces itself to the organization of collecting, collating, and analysing all the cost data which are relevant to the various jobs undertaken by the company. Initially, this demands a consideration of the source of cost data for each of the elements of cost in turn.

Direct Materials Costs
Materials Schedule

The production order includes a list of all the materials which are required to manufacture the goods specified. The details of fairly simple jobs will be entered in a suitable box on the face of the production order. This will, however, only be practicable where the job requires few different items of materials, say, up to six. A greater number of items may be conveniently listed on the reverse side of the production order and a printed ruling may be needed for this purpose. For complex jobs requiring, perhaps, several hundred different items of materials, it is customary to issue an appendix to the manufacturing order known variously as a **bill of materials**; a **materials schedule**; a **parts list**; or as a **materials sanction**. This list of materials (whether it is a few items included in the production order or a schedule appended thereto) fulfils several useful functions. It indicates the quantities of each item which will be demanded from the stores and, therefore, it enables the **materials stock control department** to 'allocate' items to the job from the **free balance** (*see* Chapter Fourteen). It also provides a useful control against which actual usage can be compared, although its value in this context will obviously depend on the reliability of the schedule itself.

Materials Usage

The basic document for recording the usage of materials is the stores requisition (*see* Chapter Four) which is passed from the stores through materials stock control to the accounts department. The stores requisitions are priced and extended in the accounts department and posted to the appropriate job cost accounts. The journal entry for each requisition will be:

Dr.   Work-in-progress control account.
Dr.   Job cost account.
Cr.   Stores control account.
Cr.   Material item account.

In practice, the requisitions are posted in 'blocks' for which only a single entry is needed in each of the two control accounts. Where machine posting is in operation, individual requisitions are posted to the relevant cost accounts and then the machine's *register* is 'cleared' to the ledger control account. There is much to commend the practice of postings to the ledger being made directly from the requisitions but this tends to introduce a considerable volume of detailed entries in the various job accounts. One method which is frequently suggested for overcoming this is to use the **raw materials abstract** (a columnar analysis book) for summarizing all the issues for a period so that a single posting can be made to each job cost account (*see* Fig. 26). It is now

Raw Materials Abstract													Period Ended.................................
Job No.		Job No.		Job No.		Job No.		Job No.		Job No.		Job No.	
Reqn.	Value	Reqn.	Value	Reqn.	Value	Reqn.	Value	Reqn.	Value	Reqn.	Value	Reqn.	Value
	£ p		£ p		£ p		£ p		£ p		£ p		£ p

Fig. 26. Raw materials abstract

generally recognized that the raw materials abstract is quite unnecessary with all forms of mechanized book-keeping, but even for manual posting methods it is subject to the following criticisms.

(1) There will usually be an increase in the volume of clerical work generated by the materials requisitions from the use of a raw materials abstract. Each requisition must be recorded in the abstract, then each job is totalled and the period total is posted to the work-in-progress ledger. Although an individual job may require a large number of items, it is unlikely that all these materials will be issued within a single accounting period so that the extra work load for each period of the job's duration may well become significant.

(2) The absence from the job account of any description of the materials used makes it difficult to effect any realistic comparison of the actual results with the materials schedule, or with the estimate compiled as a basis for

making a quotation to the customer. Significant variances are not, therefore, available so that waste and inefficiency may go undisclosed. To attempt any summary of materials by type within the abstract would create an impossibly cumbersome situation and lead to further increases in the volume of clerical work.

(3) It is not sufficient to know materials wastage in total for a particular job, the causes should be located and investigated. This will be relatively easy where the details are posted to the job cost account direct from the requisition. It is much less straightforward to investigate variances when the raw materials abstract is in use, for each posting to the job must be checked back to the raw materials abstract. Even then, the abstract only gives the requisition serial number and its value and, further reference back to the individual requisitions is needed.

Job Account Appendix

A more satisfactory alternative—if it really is necessary to reduce the detailed information shown in the job cost account—would be to use the materials schedule (or bill of materials) for the purpose. Just as the materials schedule is issued by the production control department as an appendix to the manufacturing order, so the accounts copy of the materials schedule becomes an appendix to the job cost account. To do this the materials schedule requires columns (or column space) at the right-hand side, so that against each item on the schedule may be recorded the details of actual issues obtained from the stores requisitions. This has the added benefit that actual issues are readily compared with the scheduled items and an analysis of 'variances' encourages the exercise of cost control—an important advantage. Finally, the materials schedule is totalled for the issue values of materials, and this total is debited to the job cost account.

Sectionalized Materials Schedule

It may be desirable for a very long materials schedule to be sectionalized on a departmental basis so that the cost of completing the various stages of production may be readily obtained. This sectionalization also facilitates the keeping of 'running totals' for materials costs as the job progresses, so that a reliable valuation of work in progress is available in the preparation of short-term accounts. When the materials schedule is sectionalized to provide a list of the materials required in production by each department, it also becomes possible to use the departmental copies as **pre-printed stores requisitions**. It would be necessary for this purpose, of course, for each department's schedule of materials to be given on separate pages of the full schedule. It would be further desirable for all the materials required by a department to be issued at one time, or problems of 'part-issues' may arise. Nevertheless, part-issues may be unavoidable and then individual stores requisitions should be used as usual unless all the issues will be completed within a single accounting period.

Excess Job Materials

It is frequently necessary to issue to jobs rather more materials than are required in the finished product. This may be due to the nature of the productive processes, for example, extra material may be issued to enable the material to be held in a machine such as steel bar in automatic lathes or yarn on bobbins in a twisting frame. In such circumstances it is essential that arrangements are made for the surplus materials to be returned into the stores and also to ensure that this return is properly documented.

On materials being returned to the stores, the storekeeper should raise a **materials returns note** (in effect, a credit requisition) which is passed to the materials control section for up-dating the stock records. The materials returns note is then passed to the cost department for pricing, extension, and posting to the accounts, for which the journal entry is:

Dr. Stores control account.
Dr. Materials item account.
Cr. Work-in-progress control account.
Cr. Job cost account.

Any failure to follow this procedure will give rise to inaccurate job costs as well as to the possible creation of stock discrepancies.

Inter-job Transfers

Materials which are surplus to one job are sometimes transferred to another job within the same department. From the shop-floor viewpoint this is obvious common sense as the alternative would be for the surplus materials to be returned to the stores and then requisitioned out again. Nevertheless, most accountants see a very real danger in that the physical transfer will be completed without any supporting documentation and so fear for the accuracy of their records. Shop-floor personnel are likely to consider any documentation as unnecessary (the stores requisition has already been issued for the original withdrawal from stores) and simply another example of the bureaucratic mentality of accountants.

Little imagination is required, however, to appreciate the effect of not recording these transfers! All the materials originally withdrawn from stores will have been debited to the job cost account for which they were issued, so that the accounts will overstate the materials cost of the transferor job and consequently undercost the transferee job. Furthermore, the stock control records may require up-dating to give effect to this transfer, particularly in respect of the allocations made against the manufacturing order for the transferee job and also to adjust the free balance in stock (*see* Chapter Fourteen). The problem may be solved in either of two ways.

(1) For the foreman of the production department concerned to issue a **materials transfer note** indicating the transferor job number and the transferee job number together with the full description of the materials involved and the quantity concerned (*see* Fig. 27). In factories having sophisticated systems of production control the materials transfer note may be issued by the progress department or the production controller instead of by the shop foreman.

(2) To issue a **materials return note** for the transferor job together with a **stores requisition** for the same material in respect of the transferee job. This second procedure is generally preferred for accounting purposes as each of the two documents concerned relates to a single job cost account, whereas the transfer note affects two separate ones.

With both these methods there may be no need for the stock control record of the particular materials to record the transfer as the physical stock balance is unaffected thereby, apart from the allocations and the free balance.

Materials Transfer Note			From Job no..........................		
Department...			To Job no............................		
Please note that the following materials have been transferred between the jobs stated above:			For Office Use		
Quantity	Code No.	Description	Price	Per (unit)	Value £ p
Foreman's Signature		Date	Material Control		Cost Dept.

Fig. 27. Materials transfer note

Nevertheless the transaction is sometimes fully recorded for the sake of completeness. The full documentation of materials transfers between jobs is essential to ensure the accuracy and reliability of both job costs and stores records. It is, therefore, essential that the accountant not only establishes the right procedure but also takes steps to ensure that it is observed.

Materials Losses

Generally, materials losses of one kind or another arise under most manufacturing conditions (*see* Chapter Eight) and may be categorized into two main groups—normal and abnormal. Normal materials losses arise from the nature of the materials or from the nature of the manufacturing process involved. They are, therefore, unavoidable and so largely uncontrollable. As such they form a part of the production cost and are, consequently, **left in the job**. Abnormal losses, however, arise from the use of unsuitable materials, inefficient labour, inadequate facilities, poor organization, maladjusted plant, and similar causes. Since such losses arise from **unacceptable causes**, they are recognized as being avoidable and, therefore, as **controllable**. These abnormal losses are not considered to be valid production costs and are credited to the relevant job cost account and debited to the appropriate departmental account.

Conversion Costs

The two elements of conversion cost, wages and overhead, tend to be incurred simultaneously and the incidence of each is also time related. Thus, in most methods of cost ascertainment, it is normal practice to use the basic labour records in the computation of the overhead absorbed by the product. Since the overhead absorption rate will normally be pre-determined in advance of the production (*see* Chapter Seven), attention here can, therefore, be concentrated on dealing with the direct labour cost.

Time Sheets

It is essential that the wages earned by the workers are analysed between prime cost and overhead and that the direct wages in turn are analysed between jobs. In the main there are two forms of labour record suitable for recording job time—time sheets and operation cards (*see* Chapter Six). The time sheet provides a record of the worker's activities during the time he has been in attendance, usually on a daily or weekly period. The length of time spent on individual tasks is obtained from the recorded starting and finishing times for each job. The labour cost depends upon the operator's earnings which in turn depends on the method of remuneration. Under premium bonus plans, the time sheet usually provides the information needed to calculate the bonus as it shows both the time taken and the work done. The overhead to be absorbed can then be computed from the information on the time sheet and entered thereon against the respective job numbers. The wages and overhead cost are then posted from the time sheets to the work-in-progress ledger, the necessary credits to complete the double entry being made in the wages account and the overhead account.

Where an operation is spread over more than one day, the use of daily time sheets creates a separate posting for each day of operation. In these circumstances it may be desirable to prepare **operation summaries** from all the relevant time sheets to enable a single posting to be made in the work-in-progress ledger for the complete operation.

Operation Cards (or Job Tickets)

The operator is issued with separate operation cards for each job or task he performs which, like stores requisitions, relate to a single manufacturing order. As explained in Chapter Six, the use of operation cards has certain advantages over time sheets. They are frequently 'pre-printed' with the task details and so are both more reliable and more legible. Furthermore, the starting and finishing times of each job can be recorded by mechanical time recorders. The time spent on the job is obtained from the starting and finishing times given on the operation card. The operator's earnings, calculated according to his rate of pay and the method of remuneration in force, will be entered on to the operation card. The overhead absorbed by the job is calculated at the relevant pre-determined absorption rate for the particular cost centre and also entered on the operation card. Operation cards avoid any necessity to prepare operation summaries before debiting the conversion costs to the relevant job cost account in the work-in-progress ledger.

Lost Time

The arrangements for accounting for lost time are similar to those already described for materials losses, with the exception that lost time is invariably *abnormal* relative to the job itself. Labour losses are analysed as lost or **idle time** on the time sheet or operation card. The wages cost of idle time is debited to the idle time account and credited to the wages control account, so that it never appears in the job cost account at all. A weekly departmental analysis of idle time by causes is a useful aid to the control of labour costs.

Design of the Factory Job Account

The job cost account records the details of direct materials, direct labour, direct expenses, and factory overhead for the complete manufacturing order.

The cost data is gradually compiled as the job proceeds through the various stages of manufacture and suitable analysis provides the opportunity for the actual results to be compared with the various sections of the quotation estimate as an aid to cost control. When job costing is applied to the production under batch conditions of standard products for stock, the job cost account sheet may subsequently do service as the finished goods stock account, too. The layout of job account sheets varies widely from the traditional form of ledger account, to quite elaborate rulings, to provide a detailed analysis of data. Nevertheless, the traditional ledger format is seldom found in practice with job costing except for the simplest design of product and, even then, it is rarely adopted as usually there will be many debits but very few credit entries posted to the job account.

Analysis of Cost Elements

The design of a job sheet depends, therefore, on the amount of detailed information required by the management of the business. Some analysis by the elements of cost is usually desirable to locate wastage and inefficiency, as a basis for their elimination through investigation and executive action. A

Job Cost	Customer's ref............................		Job No............................			
Description			Quantity			
Date	Ref.	Details	£	p	£	p
		Direct Material				
		Total Material				
		Direct Labour				
		Total Labour				
		Direct Expense				
		Total Dir. Exp.				
		Works Overhead				
		Total Wks. OHD				
		Works Cost				
		Administration Overhead				
		Selling Overhead				
		Carriage & Distribution				
		Total A, S & D				
		Total Cost		£		

Summary of Estimate No............................ Dated					
Direct Material	Direct Labour	Direct Expenses	Works Overhead	A. S. & D. Overhead	Total Estimate
£	£	£	£	£	£

Fig. 28. Simple design of a job cost sheet

simple design of a job cost is shown in Fig. 28. The first feature of this particular layout is the segregation of the elements of cost, but the small amount of space for postings makes it suitable for only small jobs. The second feature is seen in the comparison of the actual costs with the estimated cost on which the quotation is based to pinpoint any significant deviations. This comparison has the twofold objective of encouraging cost consciousness and control at the decision points of the business and of improving the estimating techniques, so that realistic selling prices are given in the quotations requested by potential customers.

Three-dimensional Design

An alternative design of cost sheet is given in Fig. 29. This three-dimensional layout not only provides for the elements of cost to be separately

Job Cost Sheet						Job Order No..........	
Description						Customer's Ref..........	
Date	Dept A £	Dept B £	Dept C £	Dept D £	Dept E £	Dept F £	Total £
Direct Materials							
	£	£	£	£	£	£	£
Direct Labour							
	£	£	£	£	£	£	£
Factory Overhead							
	£	£	£	£	£	£	£
Totals:	£	£	£	£	£	£	£
Number of units made			Estimated Cost				£
Unit Cost		£	Variance from Estimate				£

Fig. 29. Departmentalized job cost sheet

compiled but also includes an analysis by departments. This departmental analysis would be particularly useful where it is the practice to calculate the departmental overhead as a percentage of the direct wages on the cost sheet. As with Fig. 28 this cost sheet has relatively little space for separate postings and will only be practicable for simple jobs. In contrast to Fig. 28, this design not only provides a comparison between actual and estimate, but the **variance** (or difference) is shown too. It is doubtful that any real benefit is gained from the use of the departmental analysis columns for two reasons. The overhead absorption is probably more conveniently applied to the direct labour document (time sheet or operation card) and posted at the same time as direct wages, especially as there are not likely to be many separate labour items in each department. Secondly, the opportunity has been missed to compare the actual cost against the estimate on a departmental basis (this comparison is merely done in total) which would yield the greatest benefits from the control aspect (*see* Chapter Thirteen). Another obvious deficiency in the design of this cost sheet is the lack of information on the nature of each transaction recorded, as all that is shown is the date and the amount! It can only be presumed that the cost sheet is intended for use with 'abstracts', with their attendant inconveniences. Although this design appears to be quite sound at first sight, on closer inspection its weaknesses prevent a wide general application in job cost systems.

Horizontal Analysis of Job Costs

Most jobbing businesses, and particular non-jobbing businesses using a job cost system of cost ascertainment, require a more appropriate design possessing greater flexibility in use. A suggested alternative is given in Fig. 30,

Job Cost Sheet		Sales Dept Ref:		Job No............................									
Description:...				Quantity:									
Customer:				Customer's ref:									

Date	Ref	Details	Materials		Labour		Overhead		Direct Expense £	Total Cost £	F.G. Issues			
			Qty	Value £	Hrs	Wages £	Variable £	Fixed £			Date	Ref	Qty	Value £
Total Costs														
Estimate														
Variances														

Fig. 30. Job cost and finished goods sheet

			Materials			Labour			Overhead		Direct Expense £	Total Cost £
Date	Ref	Details	Qty.	Raw Mtls £	Fittings £	Hrs	Time Wages £	Bonus £	Variable £	Fixed £		
Total Costs												
Estimate												
Variances												

Job Cost Sheet   Sales Dept Ref:................ Job No...........................
Description:... Quantity: ....
Customer: .... Customer's ref: ....

Fig. 31. Analysed job cost sheet

which provides a horizontal analysis by elements of cost in contrast to the vertical analysis adopted in Figs. 28 and 29. An additional feature is seen in the 'rulings' for recording the issues from finished goods stock of the units manufactured against the relevant job order number. This feature enables the job cost sheet to be converted to a finished goods stock account on its transfer from work in progress when the job has been completed. The job cost sheet will be physically transferred, the work-in-progress control account is credited and the finished goods ledger control account is debited to complete the double entry. The finished goods requisitions received from the warehouse will be priced, extended, and posted to the credit side of this account and the corresponding debits will appear in either the cost of sales account or in the trading account. This practice is only necessary where goods manufactured for stock are costed under a job costing system. Goods made specially to customer's specifications will normally be dispatched immediately on completion when the journal entry would be:

Dr.   Cost of sales account.
Cr.   Work-in-progress control account.

In this latter case there would be no need to provide facilities for recording the part-issues from the warehouse stocks.

The design of a job cost sheet (or factory job account) is essentially an individualistic matter. General principles of wide application have been discussed in this chapter, but they need to be adapted to the particular requirements of each individual business. For example, there may be no need to include the column for direct expense shown in Fig. 30, nor to have separate columns for fixed and variable overhead, but additional columns for a more detailed analysis may be required as shown in Fig. 31. Here there are additional columns for both materials and labour to yield a more detailed analysis. The limit to the number of analysis columns is set by the width of the sheet and, perhaps, the ingenuity of the designer, but too many columns become self-defeating where the final result shows only one or two items per column. The F. G. ISSUES columns have been omitted from Fig. 31 and, if required, they can just as conveniently be accommodated on the reverse side or even at the foot of the sheet. Both Figs. 30 and 31 are readily applicable to very large or very small jobs since there is no printing or analysis below the column captions and a single sheet can be used for small jobs while continuation sheets can be introduced for the larger jobs.

Contract Costing

Contract costing is that form of specific order costing which is adopted by firms engaged in civil engineering and building construction and to some extent by manufacturers of heavy engineering equipment. The latter group really use contract costing within a factory environment and experience similar conditions to those already described, so this section is devoted to a consideration of costing for construction contracts. Each contract is given a distinguishing number for reference purposes and this same number is applied to the contract account.

One notable feature of contract costing is the very high proportion of direct cost in contrast to factory job costing. It is easy to identify many expenses directly with particular contracts which would be overhead in a factory. Supervision and some managers' salaries, such as the site agent and foreman, are allotted to a particular contract and devote all their efforts thereto so that they become 'direct costs'. Another example is found in the use of plant and machinery on the site, much of which may be wholly consumed on the contract and, therefore, also becomes a direct cost.

Plant Depreciation

There are two common methods of charging plant costs to a contract. In the first method, plant and equipment sent to a construction site are charged to the contract at original cost for newly purchased items, or at book value for items transferred from other contracts. On completion of the contract, or when the item is no longer needed for the contract and so returned to the plant yard, the plant is valued and that value is credited to the contract. The contract is charged with the plant depreciation occasioned by its use of the particular plant, that is, the diminution in value from wear and tear. Any repair and maintenance of plant is normally done on site and so charged direct to the contract.

Modern practice seeks to attain a closer control of all activities in a business and this is particularly true of the costly items of plant used in the construction industry. It is now usual for the larger companies to establish plant-hire departments (or even subsidiary companies) and to charge contracts on a time basis for the use of plant. This second method provides an incentive for the contract manager to make the best use and utilization of plant by eliminating idle plant which must be 'paid for'. The company's earnings may also be increased by leasing plant to smaller businesses which cannot afford to buy specialist equipment of their own. The hourly rental charge is based on the costs of depreciation, repairs, fuel, operators' wages, transportation between sites, and 'plant-hire overhead' divided by the expected operating hours. Under a system such as this it also becomes possible to measure the profitability of the plant-hire activities.

Materials Control

The control of materials on construction sites is traditionally weak, despite the fact that profit performance can be significantly improved by relatively small savings in materials costs. There are two particular areas of materials management which call for attention. First, buying discipline is essential to ensure that economic quantities are purchased at favourable prices, so the purchasing function should be centralized and site personnel should be strictly limited in their authority to order from suppliers. Secondly, materials on site should be carefully stored and placed in the charge of an efficient storekeeper. There are considerable problems in accounting for bulk materials such as bricks, timber, sand, and cement, but careful checking of delivered quantities and good store-keeping can minimize losses. Fittings of various kinds should be strictly controlled and placed in a lock-up stores compound. Excessive quantities should not be sent to the site as this encourages waste and surpluses may be expensive to return. The site storekeeper should also be responsible for the proper documentation of materials, especially in regard to stores requisitions, purchase requisitions, deliveries by suppliers, and stores records generally. Actual materials usage should be compared with the original estimate as a check on both the estimating department and the contract management.

Labour Cost

On large contracts there will be a resident timekeeper responsible for recording the attendance time of workers, for preparation of the payroll, and for paying out wages. On smaller sites these functions will be exercised by the site clerk. It is now customary to introduce a mechanical time-recorder for attendance time. Workers are usually paid at an hourly rate supplemented by some form of premium bonus based on a set task. A wages analysis in the same form as the labour element in the estimate will provide a useful comparison for control purposes.

Sub-contracting

Most contracts include a considerable amount of sub-contract work. This is treated as a purchase and debited to the contract account as direct cost. It is essential for sub-contract work to be properly supervised on the site and the invoices from sub-contractors should be carefully checked against the order and the actual work done.

Overhead

The overhead for contract work is usually confined to the provision of centralized services and is customarily recovered as a percentage of the prime cost or of the contract price. In larger organizations a more sophisticated system of functional cost centres may be introduced, each with its own pre-determined absorption rate. Purchasing costs may be absorbed as a percentage of materials and sub-contracting; personnel and training costs may be absorbed as a percentage of direct wages; estimating and planning may be a percentage of prime cost; administration overhead may be absorbed as a percentage of the contract price.

Progress Payments

In large contracts it is usual for the client to make progress payments as the work proceeds. This is desirable and necessary to assist the contractor in financing the work by reducing his investment in work in progress. The amount of the progress payment is based on the contract price of defined stages of construction. It is customary for the client's architect or surveyor to issue a certificate denoting the satisfactory completion of a given stage of the work to justify a progress payment. The terms of the contract usually permit the client to withhold part of the contract value of the certified work and pay a lesser sum. This **retention money** is held as security against possible penalties for late completion or claims for subsequent faulty work and forms an agreed proportion (about twenty per cent) of the work certified. The contractor will normally only take credit for part of the profit contained in the invoiced work (say, two-thirds) as a provision against possible future losses on the remainder of the contract.

Design of the Contract Account

There are many variations in practice for dealing with contract accounts, mostly arising from the treatment of progress payments. The simplest and most straightforward system is to open two accounts for each contract—the contract cost account and the contract certified work account.

The design of the contract cost account is similar to Fig. 31, although there may be some modification to the column headings and perhaps additional columns to provide a more detailed analysis. The columnar analysis should accord with the 'estimate' sections to facilitate a detailed comparison of the actual costs with the estimated costs.

Certified Work Account

The contract certified work account is simple in design and usually conforms to the traditional ledger account. The amounts invoiced are credited to this account and debited to the client's account. The imputed profit in invoiced work is debited to the contract certified work account and credited to profit and loss account. The journal entries for progress payments are thus:
  (1) Dr. Client's account.
      Cr. Contract certified work account.
      Being the contract value of invoiced work.
  (2) Dr. Contract certified work account.
      Cr. Profit and loss account.
      Being imputed profit in invoiced work.
The contract certified work account will have a credit balance which represents the imputed cost of the work invoiced and will be deducted from the

contract cost account in the balance sheet to give the value of work in progress. On completion of the contract, the final balance on the contract cost account is transferred to the contract certified account. When the final invoice is sent to the client it is credited to the contract certified work account so that the balance on this account is the residual profit or loss on the contract and is transferred to the profit and loss account.

Exercises

1. XY Constructors Limited manufactures special-purpose machines against customers' specifications, the average production time for such machines being three months. Quotations to customers are based on carefully prepared estimates of costs. Describe a system which will enable the management to be made aware of excess usage of material and operatives' times and comment *briefly* upon the way in which information should be used.   [A.C.A.]

2. Give details of the methods which can be used to charge for the use of plant and machinery in contract costing, and state the circumstances in which you would use each method.   [C.A.A.]

3. You have recently been appointed as cost accountant of Angler Castings Limited which produces non-ferrous castings to customers' specifications and maintains an efficient job costing system.

You discover that most of the jobs done in No. 3 Foundry are so small that the cost of preparing job costs for individual orders is quite uneconomical—in some cases almost half the conversion cost. The trade is highly competitive so that only very small price increases are at all possible as a means of covering these costs.

Write a report to the chief accountant suggesting an alternative to the present job costing system for No. 3 Foundry. Your report should also make reference to the effects (if any) which might be expected on the costing methods used for other departments in the factory.   [C.A.A.]

4. As management accountant for a company in the constructional engineering industry engaged mostly on long-term bridge-building and steel-framed building contracts involving periodic progress payments from customers, you are required to prepare a report for your managing director on methods of valuing work in progress for the purpose of the company's accounts.

The report should deal with the following:
   (a) work in progress and completed work held in workshops awaiting delivery to site;
   (b) work in progress (erection) on site;
and the possible effects of the different approaches to the problem of dealing with their valuation.   [C.M.A.]

5. The factory of a jobbing engineer consists of three workshops, viz. machine shop, assembly shop, and paint shop. The estimated number of direct labour hours to be worked in the workshops during the current year are 9,000, 11,000, and 5,000 respectively.

Factory fixed overheads are estimated at £5,000 for the year and variable overheads as follows:

	£
Machine shop	9,000
Assembly shop	8,250
Paint shop	4,000

The hourly wage rates are:

	£
Machine shop	0·60
Assembly shop	0·50
Paint shop	0·40

You are required to use the foregoing information, and that which follows, to prepare a detailed estimate of cost for a piece of equipment, and to provide for a profit of fifteen per cent on the price to be quoted.

		£
Materials from own stores		460
Components to be bought in specially		117
Direct labour:		
Machine shop	40 hrs	
Assembly shop	60 hrs	
Paint shop	10 hrs	
Packing and delivery		15

Administration costs are absorbed by adding ten per cent to the total of the costs already referred to.   [A.C.A.]

6. Libra Publishers Limited undertakes jobbing printing and job A256 for 10,000 advertising leaflets was issued to the works on May 5. The following details were taken from the works records for the month of May:

> Materials: Requisition 1324 dated May 12—£84
>   Requisition 1329 dated May 13—£11.
> Direct Labour for week ended May 17:
>   Dept. 'A'—10 hours at £0·80 per hour
>   'B'—20 hours at £0·70
> Direct Labour for week ended May 24:
>   Dept. 'C'—4 hours at £0·50 per hour
>   'D'—6 hours at £0·60
> Overheads:
>   Department 'A'—150% of direct wages
>   Department 'B'—£2·50 per labour hour
>   Department 'C'—£1·00 per labour hour
>   Department 'D'—250% of direct wages

The job was completed and dispatched on May 23.

You are required to show the completed job account at May 31.

[C.A.A.]

CHAPTER TEN

PROCESS COSTING

Process cost systems are usually simpler than job cost systems since most businesses will have fewer departments, or processes, than production orders, but there are problems in process costing which are quite unknown in specific order costing systems. One general proposition applicable to all process cost systems is that process costs per unit are essentially **average costs for a defined period of time**. Most process costs are averaged weekly and monthly, although quarterly averages are sometimes required to smooth out short-term fluctuations and, in some circumstances, a close control of costs may even require daily average unit costs.

The determination of average unit costs requires information regarding both costs and output quantities for the period. The costs incurred are readily obtainable from the accounting records, whereas the output data, especially for intermediate processes, has to be culled from the factory records. The cost accountant must satisfy himself that the production records are reliable and that satisfactory methods are used for measuring output by counting, weighing, meter readings, and so on, otherwise the whole costing exercise is suspect.

Conditions for Process Costing

In the main, process costing is only applicable to the single product situation because of its averaging characteristic. Nevertheless, this is more apparent than real, since in practice multi-product businesses can usually be arranged so that individual sections produce a single product or perform a single operation. Process costing is, therefore, applicable under the following conditions:

(a) Where the factory is arranged so that departments or sections manufacture a single product—as under flow-line production.

(b) Where batch production with reasonably long runs is adopted so that single products are made for up to, say, three months.

(c) Where separate production centres perform standard operations on a variety of different products.

(d) Where operations or processes are common to several products which are only distinguishable from each other by their material content.

Departmentalization

A process cost account is opened in the work-in-progress ledger for each separate operation or process. The proper classification of production activities within a factory is thus an important prelude to the design of a process costing system. The factory may be divided into 'processes' which embrace several linked operations and form administrative departments (the terms process and department are frequently synonymous) or, alternatively, an administration department may include several cost centres performing separately measurable processes.

Since process costs are **period averages** it is clearly desirable that they should not also be averaged over too many activities which would vitiate inter-period comparisons and hamper the location of inefficiencies or wastage. Separate process accounts are only possible where it is practicable and economic to measure the output from a given operation, and also where the benefits of closer control will justify the expense of the analysis.

Types of Process Accounts

There are four ways in which process costs may be compiled, from a pairing of two sets of alternatives. First, there is a choice between total costs and conversion costs. Under a total cost system all the materials issued, direct wages and overhead are debited to the process accounts. Whereas, under a conversion cost system, only direct wages and overhead are debited to the process account and materials are included solely on the basis of physical quantities. Conversion costs are widely used in practice, especially where the raw material prices are subject to price fluctuations as with non-ferrous metals or where the processes are common to several products which differ only in the materials used.

Cumulative Process Accounts

Secondly, there is a choice between cumulative accounts and operation accounts. With cumulative accounts, the costs of the first process are transferred to the next process, and so on. In this way the costs debited to the final process represent the total cost of manufacture.

This method is quite unrealistic even though it is the only method featured in some textbooks, and can be faulted on three counts. All products are unlikely to spend the same proportion of time in a given process or, indeed, to go through all the same processes. Then, the production time cycle introduces a time-lag between processes. Suppose that products pass through four separate processes each of which takes one week, then the costs debited to Process Four relate, say, to week four.

However, the units being worked in Process Four came through Process One *three* weeks ago, Process Two a fortnight earlier, and Process Three in the previous week. The whole thing is clearly nonsense, however short the production cycle is in each process. The intervention of inter-process stocks would make matters even worse. Finally, the cumulative method can be criticized for hazarding the opportunity to control costs through inter-period comparisons for each process. Any excess cost or cost reduction in one process is automatically transferred to all subsequent process accounts, thus increasingly obscuring the performances in those following processes.

Operation Accounts

The alternative to cumulative accounts lies in operation accounts, where each process is debited only with the costs which are added in *that* process. Each process account is thus independent of all the other process accounts and carries only those costs applicable to the process for which the foreman or manager can generally be made responsible for their control. The final product cost is obtained by aggregating the individual process costs, although the incidence of process losses tends to complicate matters as explained later in this chapter.

It is not necessary, however, to compile product costs as a matter of routine in each accounting period, but only as and when required. Provided that process costs are carefully controlled and significant cost changes do not occur, such as general wage increases, the product costs need only be revised about every six months and then just for representative products. Process costs, on the other hand, need to be prepared frequently and regularly to locate operating efficiencies and inefficiencies.

Process Losses
Foundry Costing

Materials losses, both normal and abnormal, occur at some processing stage in all process industries, as either processing losses or as spoilage. Strictly speaking, all such losses are part of the conversion cost but, in practice, the materials loss element is excluded from the conversion cost and included in the finished product cost by inflating the materials value. This feature is well illustrated by reference to the production of castings in an iron foundry where all the types of materials losses may arise.

Example

The metal charged to a cupola in the iron foundry of Neoplant Limited during April was as follows:

Pig Iron 'A'	30 tons at £48·00 per ton.
Pig Iron 'B'	20 tons at £43·50 per ton.
Steel Scrap	10 tons at £28·00 per ton.
Ferrous Alloy	5 tons at £54·00 per ton.
Home Scrap	35 tons at 'average cost'.

This yielded sixty tons of good castings and thirty-two tons of scrap work, runners, heads, etc., which were returned to the metal stores for re-use. (These results are shown in Table 11.)

Table 11. Ironfoundry Cost Statement for April

Metal	Tons	£ per ton	£
Pig Iron 'A'	30	48·00	1,440
Pig Iron 'B'	20	43·50	870
Steel scrap	10	28·00	280
Ferrous alloy	5	54·00	270
Home scrap	35	44·00	1,540
METAL CHARGED	100	44·00	4,400
Loss in melt	8	—	—
METAL POURED	92	47·83	4,400
Scrap metal	32	44·00	1,408
GOOD CASTINGS	60	49·87	2,992

Notes: (*a*) Loss in melt is **waste** and has no recoverable value.
(*b*) Scrap metal is returned to stores at average issued value.

This example has been worked on the assumption that all materials losses are normal, which may not be so. Suppose that the normal loss in melt is five per cent of the input and normal scrap is forty per cent of the metal poured. The revised cost statement for April would then be as Table 12.

Table 12. Revised Ironfoundry Cost Statement

Metal	Tons	£ per ton	£
METAL CHARGED	100	44·00	4,400
Normal melting loss	−5	—	—
STANDARD YIELD	95	46·32	4,400
Abnormal melting loss	−3	46·32	−139
METAL POURED	92	46·32	4,261
Normal scrap (40%)	−37	44·00	−1,628
STANDARD OUTPUT	55	47·87	2,633
Abnormal scrap (GAIN)	+5	44·00	+220
GOOD CASTINGS	60	47·55	2,853

Metal Charged

Many foundries adopt standard formulae or recipes and produce all castings to one or another of these unless a customer specifies otherwise. This is sound practice for it ensures a standardized metal quality in the company's products and builds up customers' goodwill, through reliability. To ensure adherence to the recipes it is necessary to weigh all the ingredients at the cupola. This cannot be over-stressed as otherwise variations in the metal-mix will occur, resulting in either poorer-quality products leading to customers' complaints or better-quality products, which will reduce profitability. A simple record should be kept of the materials charged each day (*see* Fig. 32). This daily charge sheet also forms a useful basis of stock control by providing details of material issues. There should also be space to record the charges of coke and limestone.

Melting costs comprise the cupola wages, overhead, and fuel costs. This conversion cost is expressed as a cost per ton of output, that is, metal poured. Since the melting costs should not be affected by the metal-mix, the conversion cost is usually kept separate from the metal costs.

Metal Poured

It is essential to know the weight of metal poured from the cupola, but this is difficult to obtain accurately in many foundries. There are three methods of ascertaining the poured weight which are commonly found in practice.

Weighing at the Spout. This is the most accurate method and so the more desirable, but not always practicable as it requires the installation of a weighing machine at the cupola. The ladle for transporting the molten metal from the cupola is placed on the weighing machine beneath the cupola spout, and its weight (the **tare**) is taken and recorded on a ladles poured sheet. The ladle is then filled from the cupola after which the gross weight is taken and recorded. The weight of metal poured is then obtained by deducting the tare weight from the gross weight.

Recipe	Formula			Times Charged	Total Usage			
	cwt	qr	lb		ton	cwt	qr	lb
Cupola Charge Sheet Date								
Soft Mixture Pig Iron no. 1 Pig Iron no. 2 Ferrous Alloy Bought Scrap Own Scrap (soft mix)								
Hard Mixture Pig Iron no. 3 Pig Iron no. 4 Steel Scrap Own Scrap (hard mix) Ferrous Alloy								
Special Mixture								
Total Charged for day								
Melting Bed coke Charge coke Total Coke Limestone								

Fig. 32. Daily cupola charge sheet

Computed Weight. The weight of metal poured is obtained by the formula:

Weight of good castings produced + weight of faulty castings
+ weight of runners, risers, etc.

This is a reasonable method of computing the weight of metal poured, providing that a careful control is exercised over the prompt return to stores of scrap metal. It is also necessary to have reliable weights of good castings and scrap metal.

Deduced Weights. This is the least accurate method of obtaining the weight of metal poured but in some cases it may be the only practicable one, particularly in those foundries attached to large engineering works. The exercise is to calculate the metal loss by finding the difference between the net consumption of metal and the weight of good castings produced—the metal charged, *less* the melting loss, gives the metal poured. However, the two primary figures, themselves, may have to be deduced in turn.

(*a*) Opening stock of pig iron and scrap
    Add purchases and sales returns
    Less closing stock of pig iron and scrap

= net consumption of metal.
(b) Weight of castings sold during the period
Add closing stock of good castings
Less opening stock of good castings
= weight of good castings produced.

Production Ratios

Most process industries have less difficulty than do foundries in determining output quantities at intermediate stages of processing, but they often find the situation complicated by losses arising at all or several stages of production. The materials element in process losses is easily allowed for by taking the initial input quantity for a given final output quantity—the losses at intermediate stages can be ignored. The problem with conversion costs is, however, quite different since unit costs are calculated on the output of each process. Losses arising in subsequent processes include the conversion cost of earlier processes, so that the unit costs of earlier processes are increased in terms of the **final** output. Individual process unit costs are converted into final output unit costs by means of the **production ratio** or **chained scrap factor**. The production ratio of a given operation or process is defined as the input for that process needed to yield one unit of finished output.

Process Waste Analysis

The production ratios for the various processes are derived from the expected losses at each stage of processing. In the absence of standard or normal process losses, the production ratio could be based on average losses as shown in Table 13.

Table 13. Process Waste Analysis

Process	Input (lb)	Output (lb)	Waste (lb)	Loss % of output	Production ratio
'A'	5,000	4,750	250	5·26	1·667
'B'	4,750	4,200	550	13·10	1·583
'C'	4,200	3,600	600	16·67	1·400
'D'	3,600	3,200	400	12·50	1·200
'E'	3,200	3,000	200	6·67	1·067
Total	5,000	3,000	2,000	66·67	1·000

In the process waste analysis, the waste is expressed as a percentage of the **output** because this simplifies the calculation of the production ratio. Nevertheless, the same answer can be reached by taking the waste as a percentage of the input and modifying the calculations accordingly. The calculation of the production ratio is made as follows—starting with Process 'E' and working upwards.

(a) Final output is taken as being one unit.
(b) To produce one unit in Process 'E', since waste equals 6·67% of the output, requires an input of 1·067 units.

(c) To produce one unit in Process 'E', Process 'D' must yield 1·067 lb ('E' input); but 'D' input is 1·067 lb × 1·125 = 1·200 lb.

(d) For an input to 'D' of 1·200 lb, Process 'C' must yield 1·200 lb; but waste in 'C' equals 16·67% of output, so 'C' input is 1·200 lb × 1·167 = 1·400 lb.

(e) For a final output of 1 lb, Process 'B' must yield 1·400 lb; but waste in 'B' equals 13·10% of output, so 'B' input is 1·400 lb × 1·131 = 1·583 lb.

(f) For a final output of 1 lb, Process 'A' must yield 1·583 lb; but waste in 'A' equals 5·26% of output, so 'A' input is 1·583 lb × 1·053 = 1·667 lb.

The reader, by now looking for a short cut in all this arithmetic, will realize that the same production ratio figures can be obtained by expressing the input quantities for each process as a ratio of the final output of 3,000 lb. Unfortunately for simplicity, this will not be so in practice as the data in Table 13 has been over-simplified for ease of illustration. In practice, the input of any process will not usually be exactly the same as the output of the preceding process, for two very good reasons. All products emerging from a given process will not enter each of the subsequent processes, as many of them may be alternatives such as plating or polishing, copping or balling. It is usual also to hold stocks between processes so that more or less than the output of one process enters the next process through inter-process stock changes. The practical situation will be similar to that shown in Table 14.

Table 14. Revised Process Waste Analysis

Process	Input (lb)	Output (lb)	Waste (lb)	Loss % of output	Production ratio
'A'	5,063	4,810	253	5·26	1·667
'B'	4,524	4,000	524	13·10	1·583
'C'	4,200	3,600	600	16·67	1·400
'D'	1,800	1,600	200	12·50	1·200
'E'	2,560	2,400	160	6·67	1·067

The production ratio for Process 'A' (1·667) determines the total materials input to yield a single finished unit from Process 'E', but for conversion costs the production ratio is used on an individual process basis. Table 15 illustrates this principle in columns five and six.

Table 15. Direct Labour Cost Analysis

Process	Process output (lb)	Process wages £	Process cost per 100 lb £	Production ratio	Per 100 lb finished £
'A'	4,810	32·23	0·670	1·583	1·061
'B'	4,000	36·72	0·918	1·400	1·285
'C'	3,600	28·26	0·781	1·200	0·937
'D'	1,600	30·48	1·905	1·067	2·033
'E'	2,400	10·44	0·435	1·000	0·435
Total					£5·751

Since the process unit costs are calculated on the **output**, they are expressed in terms of the production ratio for the following process. In the case of Process 'A' in Table 15, it is necessary to produce 1·583 lb to yield 1 lb of finished product. Since 1·583 lb produced at 'A' will be only 1·000 lb finished, the finished cost per lb of 'A' is: £0·670 × 1·583 = £1·061 per lb.

Multi-product Processing

In multi-product situations, all products are unlikely to pass through all processes, particularly as certain processes will be alternatives. Here, each product will have its own unique production ratio since it is determined by the relevant processes involved and the level of loss at each process. The following example illustrates the application of the production ratio to multi-product situations:

The Breakwell Co. Ltd. manufactures three separate products marketed under the names Bingo, Bango, and Burko. The following details have been extracted from the factory records for October.

Process	Input (cwt)	Output (cwt)	Wages £	Labour (hr)	Overhead absorption
1	125	100	264	528	200% on direct wages
2	90	75	144	360	150% on direct wages
3	100	75	240	400	£1·250 per labour hour
4	84	60	420	600	£0·625 per labour hour
5	50	30	125	250	£1·000 per labour hour
6	24	20	205	345	180% on direct wages

Product data:

	Bingo %	Bango %	Burko %
Material 'P' at £13·50 cwt	80	20	60
Material 'Q' at £18·00 cwt	—	75	40
Material 'R' at £6·00 cwt	20	5	—
Processes involved	1, 2, 5, 6	1, 2, 3, 4, 6,	1, 2, 3, 4

Workings

(a) Process Waste Analysis

Process	Input (cwt)	Output (cwt)	Process losses (cwt)	Process losses (% output)	Production ratios Bingo	Bango	Burko
1	125	100	25	25	3·000	3·360	2·800
2	90	75	15	20	2·400	2·690	2·240
3	100	75	25	33⅓	—	2·240	1·870
4	84	60	24	40	—	1·680	1·400
5	50	30	20	66⅔	2·000	—	—
6	24	20	4	20	1·200	1·200	—

(b) Process Conversion Costs

Process	Output (cwt)	Labour (hr)	Wages £	Overhead £	Conversion cost Total £	Per cwt £
1	100	528	264	528	792	7·920
2	75	360	144	216	360	4·800
3	75	400	240	500	740	9·867
4	60	600	420	375	795	13·250
5	30	250	125	250	375	12·500
6	20	345	205	369	574	28·700

(c) Materials Mixtures

	Bingo £	Bango £	Burko £
'P' at £13·50 cwt	80% = 10·800	20% = 2·700	60% = 8·100
'Q' at £18·00 cwt	—	75% = 13·500	40% = 7·200
'R' at £6·00 cwt	20% = 1·200	5% = 0·300	—
Mixture per cwt	£12·000	£16·500	£15·300

(d) Product Costs

	Process costs (per cwt) £	Bingo PR	Bingo Per cwt finished £	Bango PR	Bango Per cwt finished £	Burko PR	Burko Per cwt finished £
Process 1	7·920	2·40	19·008	2·69	21·305	2·24	17·741
2	4·800	2·00	9·600	2·24	10·752	1·87	8·976
3	9·867	—	—	1·68	16·577	1·40	13·814
4	13·250	—	—	1·20	15·900	1·00	13·250
5	12·500	1·20	15·000	—	—	—	—
6	28·700	1·00	28·700	1·00	28·700	—	—
CONVERSION COSTS			£72·308		£93·234		£53·781
Materials—							
Bingo	12·000	3·00	36·000				
Bango	16·500			3·36	55·440		
Burko	15·300					2·80	42·840
TOTAL COSTS			£108·308		£148·674		£96·621

Valuation of Output

As with most businesses, process industries will always have some work in progress; that is, work will have been commenced on some units but not completed. It follows, therefore, that the process costs relate partly to the finished units transferred to the next stage and partly to those units in a semi-finished state. The cost accountant's problem is to find an appropriate basis for apportioning the period costs between the completed units and the incomplete units. Consider Latentworth Chemicals Limited, which, on August 1, commenced the operation of Process 'D', and the following relates to the first month's operations.

Introduced into Process 'D'	880 units
Transferred to Process 'E'	720 units
Materials issued	£4,074
Conversion costs	£6,426

Calculations

$$\text{Cost per unit} = \frac{\text{process costs}}{\text{units processed}}$$

$$= \frac{£10,500}{880} = £11·932$$

∴ Transfer value = 720 units at £11·932 = £8,591
∴ Work-in-progress value = 160 units at £11·932 = £1,909

880 units at £11·932 = £10,500

Little thought is needed to appreciate the fallacy in the above calculations. The transfers to Process 'E' are **completed units**, whereas the closing work in progress consists of **incomplete units** so that the transfers are under-valued and the work in progress is over-valued. To determine the correct valuations, some means must be found of distinguishing between the two groups of units. Suppose now that the 160 units still in work in progress are considered to be *on average* seventy-five per cent completed, it follows logically that 160 units three-quarters finished are equivalent to 120 units (160 × 0·75) fully finished. Therefore, the work done in Process 'D' during August is equivalent to:

$$\begin{aligned}
\text{Units completed} &= 720 \text{ units} \\
\text{Work in progress (160 units} \times 0·75) &= 120 \text{ units} \\
\text{EFFECTIVE WORK DONE} &= 840 \text{ units}
\end{aligned}$$

$$\begin{aligned}
\text{Then, cost per unit} &= \frac{\text{process period costs}}{\text{effective units}} \\
&= \frac{£10,500}{840} = £12·500
\end{aligned}$$

$$\therefore \text{ Transfer value} = 720 \text{ units at } £12·500 = £9,000$$
$$\therefore \text{ Work-in-progress valuation} = 120 \text{ units at } £12·500 = £1,500$$

The relevant postings for August in Process 'D' Account are shown in Fig. 33. In considering the September data, another feature of the problem is revealed in that the period starts with 160 partly finished units which require an average of only forty equivalent units of work to become fully finished. Suppose that the data for September are as follows:

Additions into process	790 units
Transferred to Process 'E'	825 units
Materials issued	£3,161
Conversion costs	£6,660

Closing work in progress is eighty per cent complete on average.
Calculation of work done in September:

$$\begin{aligned}
\text{Opening work in progress 160 units at } &25\% \text{ incomplete} = 40 \text{ units} \\
\text{Inputs} \qquad\qquad 790 \text{ units at } &100\% \text{ incomplete} = 790 \text{ units} \\
&\qquad\qquad\qquad\qquad\quad 830 \text{ units} \\
\text{Closing work in progress 125 units at } &20\% \text{ incomplete} = 25 \text{ units} \\
&\qquad\quad\text{EFFECTIVE WORK} = 805 \text{ units}
\end{aligned}$$

$$\begin{aligned}
\text{Period cost per unit} &= \frac{\text{process period costs}}{\text{period effective units}} \\
&= \frac{£9,821}{805} = £12·200
\end{aligned}$$

Work-in-progress valuation = 100 units at £12·200 = £1,220.
The transfer valuation is obtained by taking the 'difference' or balance on the account (*see* Fig. 33) of £10,101. This figure is made up of the opening work-in-progress valuation, *plus* the period costs in completing opening work in progress, *plus* the units started and completed during September.

Opening work in progress	120 units at £12·500 =	£1,500
	40 units at £12·200 =	488
Inputs	665 units at £12·200 =	8,113
	825 units	= £10,101

Average Unit Cost Valuation

In the above example, the closing work in progress is valued on the first-in first-out basis at the current period cost rates. A similar practice is used for abnormal losses later in the chapter. However, as an alternative to the unit costs of the current period, it is suggested by some authorities that *average unit costs* can be used which are calculated on the aggregate of opening work-in-progress valuation plus the period costs. Despite its popularity, this method can be criticized as not reflecting accurately the current operating conditions.

This 'average' method distorts the process unit costs, which become averages of the current period costs plus those costs brought forward from an earlier period. This distortion vitiates the comparison of current performance with previous periods or standards as well as imparting some distortion to the valuation of closing work in progress, completed output and process losses. It is noticeable that the people who suggest that both F.I.F.O. and average method are acceptable, also define the conditions under which this is so. A

Process 'D' Account

Date	Details	Units	£	Date	Details	Units	£
Aug 31	Materials	880	4074	Aug 31	Balance c/d	160	1500
" "	Direct wages		2856	" "	Transferred to		
" "	Overhead		3570		Process 'E'	720	9,000
		880	£10,500			880	£10,500
Sep. 1	Balance b/d	160	1500	Sep. 30	Balance c/d	125	1220
" 30	Materials	790	3161	" "	Transferred to		
" "	Direct wages		2960		Process 'E'	825	10,101
" "	Overhead		3700		(by difference)		
		950	£11,321			950	£11,321

Fig. 33. Process 'D' cost account

careful study of these conditions shows that they are saying, 'where the result is likely to be similar under both methods, then the average method may be adopted from expediency'. The average method, therefore, is unacceptable on the grounds of principle because it distorts the results, but for convenience it could be used instead of F.I.F.O. provided that it yields the same result.

Varying Degrees of Completion

In some processing there may be varying degrees of completion between materials and conversion cost, particularly where all additional materials are introduced at the start of the process, or all added at a late stage in processing. Where this occurs, it becomes necessary to calculate the effective units, or equivalent units, separately for materials and for conversion. This is illustrated by the following data relating to Process 'Q'.

Work in progress at March 31 consisted of 180 units valued £568
80% of the materials had been issued
60% of the conversion was completed.
During April, 2,000 additional units were started
2,100 units were completed and transferred
Work in progress at April 30 was 75% complete as to materials and 40% complete as to conversion.

Period costs—direct materials	£4,032
—direct wages	£2,024
—overhead absorbed	£3,036

Workings

(a) *Calculation of Effective Units*

	Physical units	Materials Degree incomplete (%)	Materials Effective units	Conversion Degree incomplete (%)	Conversion Effective units
Opening work in progress	180	20	36	40	72
Into process	2,000	100	2,000	100	2,000
	2,180		2,036		2,072
Closing work in progress	80	25	20	60	48
Output	2,100		2,016		2,024

(b) *Calculation of Period Unit Costs*

$$\text{Materials} \quad \frac{£4,032}{2,016} = £2 \cdot 00 \text{ per unit}$$

$$\text{Conversion} \frac{£5,060}{2,024} = £2 \cdot 50 \text{ per unit}$$

(c) *Valuation of Closing Work in Progress*

Materials	60 units at £2·00	= £120
Conversion	32 units at £2·50	= £80
Total	80 units	= £200

(*d*) *Valuation of Completed Output*

Opening work in progress	£568
Period costs	£9,092
	£9,660
Less closing work in progress	£200
Completed output	£9,460

Valuation of Process Losses

As usual, normal materials losses form part of the cost of the good production. This is readily done in process costing as unit costs are calculated on the output quantity, but it is necessary to credit the process account with the physical quantity of normal losses at no value for waste, or at recovered value for scrap. The valuation of abnormal losses, on the other hand, will depend on the degree of completion in the affected units. The following example of Process 'H' provides a comprehensive illustration of both normal and abnormal losses.

Data for Process 'H' in January

	Physical units	Materials completion %	Conversion completion %
Opening work in progress (value=£372)	100	100	60
New units put into process	1,600		
Process scrap material	170		
Spoilage in process	150	80	30
Completed output to stock	1,145		
Closing work in progress	150	70	40
Normal waste is 5% of the input			
Normal scrap is 10% of the input			
Scrap recovery value is £1·00 per unit			
Period costs for January:			
Materials issued	£2,987		
Direct wages paid	£1,104		
Overhead absorbed	£2,270		

Calculations for January of Process 'H'

(*a*) *Effective Units*

	Physical units	Materials Degree incomplete (%)	Materials Effective units	Conversion Degree incomplete (%)	Conversion Effective units
Opening work in progress	100	0	—	40	40
Into process	1,600	100	1,600	100	1,600
(i)	1,700		1,600		1,640

Less

Normal waste (5%)	80	100	80	100	80
Normal scrap (10%)	160	100	160	100	160
Abnormal waste	5	0	—	0	—
Abnormal scrap	10	0	—	0	—
Spoilage (abnormal)	150	20	30	70	105
Closing work in progress	150	30	45	60	90
(ii)	555		315		435
Completed output (i–ii)	1,145		1,285		1,205

(b) Unit Costs

	£			£
Material issued	2,987	Direct wages		1,104
Less normal scrap	160	Overhead		2,270
Net materials	2,827	Conversion cost		3,374

$$\frac{£2,827}{1,285} = £2 \cdot 200 \text{ per unit} \qquad \frac{£3,374}{1,205} = £2 \cdot 800 \text{ per unit}$$

(c) Valuations

Element	Per unit	Abnormal Waste eff. units	£	Abnormal scrap eff. units	£	Spoilage eff. units	£	Closing W.I.P. eff. units	£
Materials	2·20	5	11	10	22	120	264	105	231
Conversion	2·80	5	14	10	28	45	126	60	168
TOTAL	5·00		£25		£50		£390		£399

(d) Process 'H' Account

	Units	£		Units	£
Balance b/f	100	372	Normal waste	80	—
Materials issued	1,600	2,987	Normal scrap	160	160
Direct wages		1,104	Abnormal waste	5	25
Overhead absorbed		2,270	Abnormal scrap	10	50
			Spoilage	150	390
			Transfers to stock	1,145	5,709
			W.I.P. balance c/d	150	399
	1,700	6,733		1,700	6,733

Joint Costs

In any multi-product industry there are always instances where certain items of cost are common to several products. This creates a somewhat difficult problem for the accountant in determining the amounts which are properly attributable to each product. **Common costs** fall into two distinct groups—direct costs and overhead. (Chapter Seven is devoted to a study of factory overhead, which is the cost of providing the facilities for production.) Overhead is an inevitable phenomenon of all multi-product manufacturing and is generally identified with products through a common factor of time.

Common direct costs, on the other hand, relate to **joint products**, and in this context are referred to as being **joint costs**—a term which is often taken to also include the overhead of joint products.

Definition of Joint Products

Joint products are two or more products separated during the analytical processing of either a single raw material or an agreed mixture of input materials. There are two main production situations leading to joint products. The first group embraces **complementary products** which must of necessity be produced together, the relative proportions being more or less fixed. Complementary products include gas and coke from coal; meat and hides from animal carcasses; and pig iron and slag from a blast furnace. The second group comprises **alternative products** where, for a given input, an increase in the output of one product may be obtained by decreasing the quantity of another, although not necessarily in the same ratio. Alternative products are obtained from materials such as crude oil, pig iron, and timber.

Pre-separation Costs

Joint costs are those costs which relate to the common processing of joint products up to the point of separation. Beyond this 'split-off' point the products become separately identifiable and thus capable of being separately processed, so that post-separation costs are readily attributable to individual products. The pre-separation costs, however, are common to all the products emerging at the 'split-off' point, and the joint costs must be apportioned between the various products if product costs are to be obtained.

Relevance of Product Costs

It is sometimes argued that the apportionment of joint costs is an unnecessary exercise since it does not aid cost control. This is quite true, but then cost and management accounting has two fundamental objectives—cost control and decision-making—and the latter requires product cost information.

The management decisions for which product costs are relevant include:

(a) Valuation of stocks and work in progress.
(b) Determination of product profitability.
(c) Setting selling prices and price structures for product ranges.
(d) Pricing 'cost-plus' contracts and other price 'justification'.
(e) Product mix and output variations.

Joint Cost Apportionment

The ascertainment of product costs for decision-making necessitates the apportionment of the joint costs between the joint products. Whatever the circumstances, the crucial factor in cost apportionment is the choice of a suitable basis. In Chapter Seven (page 91) it was suggested that the basis for apportionment should be that of the cost incidence or one which correlates with the basis of incidence. This is not usually a problem with overhead, where time provides a common basis for apportionment, but with joint costs it is less easy because units may become changed during manufacture or, at separation, the joint products may emerge in *different units*. It is, therefore, often difficult to identify costs with particular products or to find any common relationship between costs and individual products. The problem can frequently be eased by considering separately the materials cost and the conversion cost. Conversion cost tends to be related to output quantities whereas materials cost is related to input quantities.

Bases of Apportionment for Joint Costs

Cost tends to vary with the volume of units processed and with the relative prices of the inputs of materials, labour, and services. Thus, joint costs tend to be apportioned on the basis of physical units and/or on some value basis.

Physical Units. In the most simple cases joint cost is apportioned on the basis of the physical output quantities of each product at the 'split-off' point. This is easy to use and has a measure of logic to support it. The units of measurement must, of course, be the same for all products; that is, tons, or gallons, or feet, or else it becomes nonsense. Clearly, under this method, each product has the same unit cost at separation so that this basis is often referred to as the **average unit cost** method of apportionment.

In those industries, where joint products emerge in different physical states, they are measured in differing physical units, examples of which are: solids in tons, liquids in gallons, and gases in cubic feet, and to attempt any apportionment on the basis of these respective physical quantities would be absurd. It is, however, probably not difficult to convert the various output quantities into a common unit or physical coefficient such as weight: the weight of gas, for example, is easily calculated given the volume, temperature, and pressure.

Value Theory in Joint Costs. Despite the logic of apportioning costs on a physical units basis, there is much criticism of such methods arising mainly from an almost instinctive feeling that different products should have differing unit costs. Illogical as this is, it undoubtedly has a significant influence in an area of considerable uncertainty. A stronger objection to the use of physical units for apportioning joint costs is that the purchase price of the raw material is really an amalgam of the varying prices of the constituent elements in that raw material and that the costs of the joint products are the elemental prices, plus the conversion cost, and these differential values should be recognized in apportioning joint costs. The theory is really logically irrefutable, but the practice is like a 'will o' the wisp' which we are all chasing but never quite catch.

Purchase Values. The most satisfactory value method to use would be the purchase values on the open market of the separated products at 'split-off' point. The drawback here is that such prices are rarely available because the manufacturer who processes the raw material to obtain the joint products seldom offers them on the open market, but further processes them for sale in a more finished condition. The quantities that do come on to the open market will be so small as to distort the price structure and render it useless as an apportionment basis.

Weighted Unit Cost. As a substitute for purchase values it is possible to assign arbitrary weights to output quantities which has the effect of 'pricing' the various joint products. Ideally, such weights should be derived from purchase prices, but these are unlikely to be available and some arbitrary assessment may be made by what is termed 'intuitive judgement'. Even so, this may provide more realistic apportionments than a strictly physical basis where the joint products are known to possess differing intrinsic values. The use of weighting is illustrated thus:

Product	Output (units)	Weights	Weighted (units)	Joint cost £	Unit cost £
'X'	5,000	8	40,000	12,000	2·400
'Y'	2,500	5	12,500	3,750	1·500
'Z'	3,750	2	7,500	2,250	0·600
TOTAL	11,250		60,000	£18,000	

Clearly, the cost is apportioned on both the output and the weight. It is also obvious that the unit costs are proportional to the assigned 'weights' thus emphasizing the price or value characteristic of weights.

Standard Values. The use of standard values for joint products is sometimes recommended as providing a more reliable and realistic basis for apportioning joint costs. This has something of the mystical air about it, which tends to surround standard costs with the implication that it is impious to criticize it. Whereas it is only the product of someone's judgment and as such it is merely another name for 'weighting' since the standard value per unit is the weight.

Sales Values. The justification of using selling values for the apportionment of joint costs lies in the argument that, in the long run, selling prices are governed by, and ultimately reflect, costs. This is really saying that selling price is determined by cost, which it is not! It is also saying that all products earn the same margin of profit, which they do not! Although this basis is widely used it is difficult to accept it as other than a convenient way of charging what the traffic will bear.

Despite the apparent popularity of sales value as a basis for apportioning joint costs it is possible to discern differing applications of this method in practice. The final selling values of the joint products may be used but is generally criticized because it will lead to blatant distortions where the different products incur varying amounts of cost in further processing beyond the 'split-off' point as shown in Table 16.

Table 16. Joint Cost Apportioned on Final Sales Value

Product	Output (units)	Value weight (price £)	Sales value £	Joint cost £	Post-separation costs £	Profit £
'P'	3,000	2·00	6,000	2,400	1,000	2,600
'Q'	8,000	3·00	24,000	9,600	7,000	7,400
'R'	2,000	10·00	20,000	8,000	12,000	Nil
			50,000	20,000	20,000	10,000

The saleable value of each product is enhanced by the post-separation processing and thus the profit figures are distorted, as is the apportionment of joint cost. It would be more equitable, before making the apportionment, to deduct the subsequent costs from the sales values as shown in Table 17.

Table 17. Joint Cost Apportioned on Net Sales Value

Product	Sales value £	Post-separation costs £	Net S.V. £	Joint cost £	Profit £
'P'	6,000	1,000	5,000	3,333	1,667
'Q'	24,000	7,000	17,000	11,333	5,333
'R'	20,000	12,000	8,000	5,333	2,667
	50,000	20,000	30,000	20,000	10,000

Although an improvement on the first method, this is still not satisfactory as it takes no cognizance of the profit which must be earned by the subsequent processing. Rather than deducting the subsequent costs, it would be preferable to deduct the **added value**. The result is shown in Table 18 where it is assumed that the same level of profit (twenty per cent of sales value) is earned by all products in all processes.

Table 18. Joint Cost Apportioned on Separation Sales Value

Product	Final S.V. £	Subsequent added value £	Separation S.V. £	Joint cost £	Profit £
'P'	6,000	1,250	4,750	3,800	1,200
'Q'	24,000	8,750	15,250	12,200	4,800
'R'	20,000	15,000	5,000	4,000	4,000
	£50,000	£25,000	£25,000	£20,000	£10,000

Objections to Sales Value for Apportionment

The use of sales value to apportion joint costs is open to several criticisms from points of principle:

(1) Selling price is not determined by cost but by the interaction of the forces of supply and demand in the market. It cannot be assumed, therefore, that selling values reflect costs.

(2) Fluctuations in selling prices generated by market influences upset the relationship between products. For example, if the results shown in Table 18 were repeated exactly in another period, with the single exception that the price of 'Q' had risen to £4·00 per unit, then 'P' and 'R' would receive less and 'Q' would be given more of the joint cost, even though the total joint cost is the same and the output quantities are unchanged.

(3) Product costs determined by reference to selling price are only of use for inventory valuation. All sales value methods are **circular** for pricing and profitability decisions (*see* page 148, items (*b*) to (*e*)) and so are generally unusable.

(4) The use of selling value evades the issue as far as **cost ascertainment** is

concerned and simply becomes a matter of convenience. It may be argued that the problem is so difficult that sales value is no worse than any other basis, but this is a counsel of despair which should lie beyond both professional and academic thinking among accountants.

By-product Costs

By-products are defined as saleable products obtained from the manufacture of some major product, or recovered from material discarded during processing. It is generally accepted that the distinction between joint products, and main and by-products, is one of relative values. Two products of near equal value emerging from a process would be joint products but, if one had several times the value of another, then there would be a main and by-product relationship between them. Strictly speaking, scrap (having a saleable value) is really a by-product and indeed it is just as difficult to draw a line between by-products and scrap as it is between joint products and by-products. A good distinction is that by-products are subject to further processing and/or marketing strategy before being sold, whereas scrap is sold without further treatment.

Treatment of By-product Costs

The joint cost may be apportioned between main products and by-products by one of the bases discussed for joint products. Alternatively, the value of the by-product may be considered too small to justify the formal apportionment of cost to it. Where the by-product is relatively insignificant one of the following procedures may be adopted.

Standard Value. The by-product is given a standard value or nominal cost which is credited to the process cost account. The cost of the main product is thereby reduced. The use of standard values has the advantage of price changes in the by-product being isolated from the main product.

Sales Revenue. The sales revenue from the by-product is credited in full to the process cost account and thereby reduces the cost of the main product. There are no profits or losses identified with by-products and fluctuations in by-product prices may slightly distort main product costs depending on their relative importance.

Other Income. Where the value of the by-product is relatively insignificant, any revenue from its sale is credited to the profit and loss account as sundry income. In this case the whole of the cost is borne by the main product.

Exercises

1. 'In the treatment of joint costs, as in many other fields, the accountant is quite unconsciously a source of error. He all too often insists on setting off a particular cost against a particular revenue in some subordinate or departmental account, instead of boldly carrying forward joint . . . costs into a consolidated account, there to be met out of general revenue.' (*Economist*)

'The allocation of joint costs among joint products is essential if we are to know just how profitable each of our products is.' (*Salesman*)

Comment on the above quotations making particular reference to the reasons why most organizations allocate common costs to joint products.   [A.C.A.]

2. 'The costs incurred up to the point where the different products are separately identifiable will be common to all products and—as with other forms of common costs—must be apportioned between all the products so separated if their respective product costs are to be ascertained.'

Required:

Discuss critically the various methods of dealing with costs incurred up to the point of separation when compiling product costs for joint products and for by-products. [C.A.A.]

3. Define each of the terms given below, when used in connection with materials, in a business operating on a process cost basis:

(a) (i) normal losses and gains; (ii) abnormal losses and gains;

(b) (i) by-products; (ii) joint products.

How would you evaluate and deal in the process accounts with each of these items? [C.M.A.]

4. Gloriana Limited produces components for the motor industry under a system of batch production and the Cost Department operates a system of batch costing. Negotiation with various motor manufacturers has led to some degree of standardization for these components and the management of Gloriana Limited is now preparing to introduce 'flow-line' production with five separate 'lines'.

Required:

Write a report to the managing director of Gloriana Limited explaining the changes necessary in the costing system consequent on a change to 'flow-line' conditions. Give a clear indication of any resultant changes in the cost data being provided to management and their significance. [C.A.A.]

5. In certain continuous process industries such as meat packing and chemicals, the problem of accounting for by-products often occurs.

Explain two methods which might be used in accounting for the cost of by-products, in the following cases:

Sales of main product	10,000 at £10	
Total production cost	12,000 at £6	
Selling and administration expenses		£20,000
Sales of by-product		£4,800 [A.C.A.]

6. Glowcake Limited passes a single raw material through two processes—at the end of which, two products emerge (B2 and N4) together with residual waste. The waste material costs £8 per ton to process before it can be discharged into a nearby river—this cost is borne by the good production of B2 and N4.

It would be possible to turn this waste into a saleable by-product by suitable processing with added chemicals, when it would sell for £75 per ton. The cost of obtaining one ton of by-product G8 from one ton of waste would be:

Additional chemicals	£26
Process labour	£18
Process overheads	£36

Required:

Write a report to the works manager giving your views on the proposal to produce the by-product G8. [C.A.A.]

7. The PQ Company Limited, is considering an order for an additional 2,000 lb per month of Beta Powder at a price of £1·37 per lb.

On the basis of the following cost information—the only information available—prepare a process account and a report advising management as to whether or not it should accept this order.

Beta Powder—Final Process Account for November, 1972

	lb	£
Opening work in process	1,800	1,772
Transferred from previous process	19,000	18,050
Direct process costs—labour	—	6,000
Direct process costs—expenses	—	2,200
Transferred to finished goods store	16,500	—
Closing work in process	2,400	—

Note:

(1) Normal process loss is estimated at five per cent of input from the previous process—no value for this is credited to the process account but excessive losses are charged to the account. Losses are only identified when the goods are complete and then have no scrap value.

(2) Opening and closing work in process can be assumed to be fifty per cent complete as to labour and expenses whilst material is complete. [A.C.A.]

8. Using the information summarized below for the half year ended November 30, 1972:

(a) tabulate a cost analysis statement to give the unit cost for products P and Q separately, for each cost element and in total;

(b) submit journal entries to record the transactions for the half year.

The process is operated to produce first product 'P'. Fifty per cent of the output of product 'P' is then embodied with other materials and processed to produce product 'Q'. Nine-tenths of the remaining output of product 'P' and three-fifths of the output of product 'Q' have been despatched to customers during the half-year.

One work-in-progress account is maintained for product 'P' and another for product 'Q'. The progress overhead, amounting to £45,500 is absorbed by the products on the basis of the hours the process is utilized.

Data:	Product 'P'	Product 'Q'
Direct material cost (£)	26,460	17,500
Direct wages (£)	21,840	15,750
Hours process is utilized	600	400
Output, in units	42,000	35,000 [C.M.A.]

9. Starmaker Cycles Limited produces a certain component on a flow-line composed of five separate operations. The following data refer to the output during the month of June 1972:

Operation	Input (units)	Defective (units)	Operation costs £
1	25,000	2,000	345
2	21,000	3,000	630
3	20,000	2,500	680
4	13,500	1,500	360
5	16,000	1,000	300

You are required to calculate the cost per 100 units for each operation *and* for the final output. [C.A.A.]

10. From the following details extracted from the books of a pig-iron manufacturer, prepare a cost statement showing the manufacturing costs for the year ended December 31, 1972. Also, from the data available, include any other information which you consider would be useful to management, and state your reason for thinking so.

	Stock at January 1, 1972 £	Stock at December 31, 1972 £
Limestone	900	405
Coal and coke	7,200	5,100
Iron ore	4,200	5,070

	£
Purchases during the year:	
Limestone	12,000
Coal and coke	117,000
Iron ore	51,000
Wages	48,000
Carriage inwards	6,300
Repairs, renewals and depreciation of plant	12,600

Input 12,245 tons. Wastage during manufacture amounted to two per cent of the total input. This loss resulted during the melting process.

The stock of pig iron at January 1 was £20,000 and at December 31 was £32,500, the sales during the year being £305,000. [A.C.A.]

11. The following data relate to an intermediate process in the manufacture of patent medicine.

			Degree complete	
	Physical units	Value	Materials	Labour and overhead
		£	%	%
Opening work in progress	300	1,305	75	50
Transferred from the previous process	1,600	4,800		
Spoilage in process	50		70	30
Closing work in progress	350		80	60

Costs for the period:

Additional materials issued	£954
Direct wages paid to operators	£1,890
Overhead absorbed into output	£2,520

Required:

(a) A tabulation showing the calculation of the effective units of work done for the period.
(b) A statement showing the calculation of unit costs for each element of cost.
(c) Schedules setting out the valuation for the period of:
  (i) the spoilage in process;
  (ii) the closing work in progress;
  (iii) the finished output transferred. [C.A.A.]

12. From the information given below relating to process 'X' for a certain period, you are required to prepare:
  (a) a statement of equivalent whole units of production;
  (b) an account of the process showing the total and units costs with other relevant information.

Work in progress at beginning of period:

        Units   500

Costs:	£
Transfers from previous process and material 'A'	6,250
Material 'B'	1,500
Material 'C'	300
Labour and overhead	2,700
	£10,750

Costs incurred during the period:	£
Transfers from previous process,	
3,600 units	32,750

		£	
Material: 'A'		9,000	
'B'		16,500	
'C'		6,300	
		———	31,800
Labour and overhead			28,710

Units completed during the period	2,950
Units scrapped during the period:	
Normal	100
Abnormal	50

The units scrapped were:
100% complete for materials, and
80% complete, labour and overhead

Work in progress at end of period:
Units   1,000

	% complete
Material: 'A'	100
'B'	60
'C'	30
Labour and overhead	50

[C.M.A.]

CHAPTER ELEVEN

COSTING FOR FACTORY SERVICES

Characteristics of Service Costs

The provision of services rather than tangible goods requires methods of cost ascertainment which are no different in essence from those already described for saleable products. The two major differences from product manufacture, which characterize service industries, are seen in the lack of materials losses in production and in the consumption of the service simultaneously with its provision. This latter characteristic also means that stocks of finished goods and work in progress will not be present. Therefore, cost systems for service activities tend to be rather more simple than is the case with product manufacturing.

Unfortunately, experience shows that there is a widely prevalent attitude that service activities do not require the same degree of control or sophistication which is applied to products. This stems partly from a belief that such activities are relatively insignificant in amount and so do not merit more than crude accounting procedures. It also originates in the attitude that all service activities in a factory are overhead costs and will be arbitrarily dealt with anyway. In three particular factory services—plant maintenance, power supply, road transport—this attitude has led to considerable neglect of good accounting practice with a consequent lack of reliable data both for control and for decision-making.

The Least-cost Alternative

In most factories the costs of service departments are ascertained only by a means of determining the global sum (total) which is to be arbitrarily apportioned amongst the departments using that service. Where this is so, it is a pity that such little use is made of valuable accounting data. The service department costs provide information which will assist management to control the costs of providing the service within, or apart from, a formal system of standards and/or budgets. Cost control is obtained by selecting the least-cost alternative in each situation, all other things being equal. In a simple system of cost ascertainment for a service department it may be assumed that the previously recorded cost of a particular task is the alternative to the current cost of performing that task. A comparison between the two sets of data will reveal the least-cost alternative and, where that is not the current performance, then senior management should call for an explanation and insist on the choice of least-cost alternatives in the future. In this way, service department foremen are encouraged to be cost conscious and so exercise cost control. The subject of control is developed fully in Chapters Thirteen to Eighteen, but is also referred to later in this chapter.

Decision-making

The costs of factory services ultimately become part of the costs of the production departments and to that extent are likely to be included in cost data used for decision-making in respect of the production activities. Nevertheless, in this context, little significance is attached to service costs as they are normally seen as an outcome of the utmost arbitrariness and so are hardly better than crude approximations. Unfortunately, this is frequently all too true in practice but there is no real reason for it, since service costs can and should be based on sound principles of cost accounting. Not only would this yield more reliable data on service costs for inclusion in other departmental costs, but would provide significant data for decision-making in respect of the services themselves. This is especially true of plant replacement decisions, make or buy decisions, and capacity decisions.

Costing Methods for Services

As with product manufacture, there are basically two methods of cost ascertainment for services. Determination of the cost of providing one particular special service requires a system of job costing as each service is a 'one-off' job. This is true especially of plant repairs following a breakdown, or the transportation of special jobs. Under these conditions, cost will be accumulated by jobs in just the same way as for product jobbing manufacture. Materials issued from stores to the job and the direct wages paid to the workers are analysed against the relevant service job order number.

Alternatively, a regular routine or continuous service may be provided such as power generation and supply, or preventive maintenance, or a regular delivery service. The operation of this continuous service is costed similarly to factory process costing and is generally referred to as **operating costing**. Thus operating costing relates to the operation of a service, whereas operation costing refers to the operation of a particular manufacturing process. Apart from this rather nice distinction, however, operating costing for services is analogous to operation costing for products.

Cost Units

Operating costs, like process costs, relate to a defined period of time and consequently will be average costs per unit of service for that period. The calculation of unit costs presupposes the existence of suitable cost units, but the recognition or definition of appropriate cost units for services is often thought to be a matter of some difficulty. It is, however, really a matter of identifying the **independent variable** in each situation and adopting that as the unit of service. In transporting goods, for example, there are really two independent variables influencing cost—the distance and the load carried—so that a **composite unit** (the ton/mile is usually adopted). Pressure units also use composite units such as foot/lb and 'lb per square inch'. Most services, however, rarely bear any relationship to such physical units of output and consequently will use **time units**. The characteristic of a service, whereby it is consumed as it is provided, leads to the notion that the amount of service is directly related to the length of time during which it is provided. Therefore, the most practical cost unit for many service activities is a time unit and this is usually the direct labour hour.

Cost Elements

There is an unhappy tendency to dismiss the costs of factory services as being merely overhead and, as a consequence, to pay them scant attention. A constructive attitude towards service costs recognizes that all the elements of cost (material, labour, expense) can be present in both direct and indirect forms. In other words, a service generates its own direct costs and its own overhead. The fact that factory services ultimately become the overhead of production departments is irrelevant in the service department context and should be ignored for the sake of objectivity in costing.

Cost Centres

An objective approach to factory services reveals that the service department is partly a functional grouping and partly a matter of administrative convenience. Within the service department there will normally be several subordinate activities contributing to, or complementing, the principal function. Each subordinate activity has its own cost characteristics and should be treated as a separate cost centre for cost analysis. Many such cost centres will be functional cost centres while others will be locational cost centres.

The maintenance department provides a good example of service cost centres. It will customarily have at least one locational cost centre in the fitting shop which, in large factories, may itself be sub-divided into cost centres for each type of machine tool. Most maintenance work for both production and service departments, however, is largely performed in the user departments by peripatetic personnel. The maintenance department, therefore, is organized on a specialist or functional basis according to skills or trades. Each trade group is supervised by a specialist foreman and so forms a functional cost centre operating throughout the entire factory. Typical maintenance functional cost centres include mechanical fitters, electricians, carpenters and builders.

The number of cost centres is dependent on the size of the factory and the corresponding size of the maintenance department. For example, there may be three principal divisions each in charge of a professional engineer—mechanical, electrical, building—which are further grouped under foremen. Thus the building section may have cost centres under individual foremen for bricklayers, plumbers, carpenters, painters, and so on. With all service departments it can be generally accepted that each foreman or supervisor will usually represent a separate cost centre, and this is particularly relevant for control since cost centres are thereby also responsibility or budget centres.

Charging User Departments

As mentioned on page 157, cost ascertainment for factory services is no more than the determination of a global sum to be arbitrarily apportioned amongst the users of the service itself. In other words, the total cost of providing the service is divided in one way or another amongst the customers. It will be recalled that such a system was also assumed in Chapter Seven when considering the three methods of secondary apportionment for re-charging service department costs (*see* page 94 onwards). This is the simplest method of dealing with service costs whereby the total cost for a period of providing the service is apportioned amongst the user departments according to their estimated use of the service during that period. This practice has several drawbacks because of its crudeness and should be avoided where a more sophisticated treatment is possible.

Drawbacks of Secondary Apportionment

In the first place, a service department may provide several different services for the benefit of the user departments. It is most unlikely in practice that each individual form of service will have the same unit cost as all the other services. Therefore, unless all user departments require the same ratio of these services, the re-charging must be inequitable.

Secondly, the rate per unit of service may well vary from one period to another because of changes in the operating efficiency of a service department, but the gains and losses on operating cost are automatically 'passed-on' to all the customer departments. Clearly such a practice is often likely to be inequitable to the users, while the service department responsible escapes from the effects of its own misdeeds or loses the credit for improved efficiency.

A third drawback to the secondary apportionment methods for re-charging service department cost lies in the usage of the service, especially where there is an occasional fluctuating demand. It is possible that a given department may have a steady demand for a particular service for period after period. Other departments using this service, however, may have widely fluctuating demands, so that their actual usage varies from one period to another. When everything else remains stable in this situation, the unit cost of the service also fluctuates from period to period and, consequently, so does the charge to the department with a steady demand, even though the department's actual consumption of the service is virtually at a constant level. This is not only inequitable but absurd!

Fixed Rate per Unit of Service

Obviously a more acceptable basis must be found, if the service department costs are to be charged equitably to the consumer departments. This can simply be achieved by determining a cost (or charge) per unit of service supplied and by then avoiding any fluctuation in the unit price of the service caused by factors outside the influence of customers' departments. This fixed price per unit of service must take account of all costs normally covered in the long run (which would embrace the full normal cycle of demand) and be charged to all users without distinction.

A pre-determined rate must be established and this can be derived from budgeted costs for an estimated level of activity. The cost accountant, therefore, needs to forecast the probable demand for the service during the full period of the normal demand cycle. From his knowledge of the cost-behaviour patterns in this department he can predict the expected cost of the service at 'normal' activity. It is then a relatively simple exercise to compute a unit rate for re-charging other departments.

Maximum Demand Situations

In some instances there may be the added complication of having to provide sufficient capacity to meet a potential maximum demand load. For example, all forms of power (electric, hydraulic, pneumatic, steam, and so on) may be subject to fluctuating demand but the productive capacity must be capable of meeting this maximum demand load at any one time. To install sufficient capacity to meet no more than the average demand will mean that demand will only be met for about half the time which may seriously disrupt production. Therefore, if the demand for a particular power has a peak, sufficient capacity is needed to satisfy that demand even if it is only for, say, five per cent of the time. This is the perennial problem of peak loading.

Influence of Cost Behaviour

Clearly, the costs of the service really fall into two groups—the fixed costs of providing the capacity to produce and the variable costs of the actual consumption of the service. The separation of these costs is essential for equitable charging of the service to users, especially where the user departments display differing demand patterns. The following example illustrates this principle of peak charging for factory services.

Manacle Fabrications Limited has five production departments and three service departments ('A', 'B', 'C'). Service department 'B' produces an average of 50,000 units per month at a total cost of £7,500 of which one-third is the cost of providing the capacity to meet a maximum demand output of 500 units per hour. It has been the company's practice to average total service costs over the actual consumption as a basis for charging the user departments. A recent policy change now requires separate charging for capacity and consumption at pre-determined rates and the following information has been prepared to do this.

Dept.	Units per hour maximum	Units per hour minimum	Average usage (units per month)
1	200	50	14,000
2	50	40	4,000
3	10	8	2,000
4	100	72	11,000
5	60	30	5,000
'A'	30	20	6,000
'C'	50	30	8,000
Total	500	250	50,000

Cost rates:

(a) Overall average $\dfrac{£7,500}{50,000} = 0.15$ per unit.

(b) Per unit of max. demand $\dfrac{£2,500}{500} = 5.00$ per unit.

(c) Per unit of consumption $\dfrac{£5,000}{50,000} = 0.10$ per unit.

Dept.	Capacity £	Consumption £	Total £	Average* £	Difference £
1	1,000	1,400	2,400	2,100	+300
2	250	400	650	600	+ 50
3	50	200	250	300	− 50
4	500	1,100	1,600	1,650	− 50
5	300	500	800	750	+ 50
'A'	150	600	750	900	−150
'C'	250	800	1,050	1,200	−150
Total	£2,500	£5,000	£7,500	£7,500	Nil

*The average is the average usage from the first table at the overall cost rate of £0.15 per unit.

This clear recognition of the characteristics of cost behaviour enables the cost accountant to achieve a realistic approach to both cost ascertainment and apportionment. It is also invaluable for emphasizing the cost of capacity which is fully utilized for only a small proportion of time. Department 1 in the above example incurs additional costs of £300 (an increase of fourteen per cent) under the revised scheme. In future this department is to be charged with £1,000 per month whether it consumes any or none of service department 'B'. This is rather more realistic and equitable to both department 'B' and to all the other departments.

Peak Avoidance

It should also prompt the manager of department 1 to consider the level of maximum potential demand in his department. He could reduce his service costs by a more even or regular use of service department 'B'. This might be possible through more efficient production planning and co-ordination of the various manufacturing processes but if not, because of the nature of the processes concerned, it must just be accepted. It does, however, also beg the question of the desirability of attempting to meet the maximum demand.

Use of Probability Ratings

A statistical analysis of the demand pattern for the user departments may show that the maximum is only required at widely spaced intervals, say, on no more than one day in thirty. By the use of probability ratings it may be possible to accept some lower capacity level which will be adequate on, say, 95 days in every 100. It then becomes a matter of balancing the costs of the extra capacity for one hundred per cent coverage against the cost incurred through production interruptions on perhaps five per cent of all days. The degree of statistical confidence acceptable in setting the realistic capacity level for a department depends on the circumstances and each case is decided on its merits. It should be possible, however, to operate effectively at some acceptable capacity level below the total maximum demand potential and so reduce capacity costs overall.

In the illustration for Manacle Fabrications Limited, department 1 showed a maximum demand of 200 units per hour and a minimum demand of 50 units per hour. Table 19 (on page 163) shows the hypothetical consumption over a period of 100 hours by department 1, from which it can be seen that the maximum demand is likely to be made for only one per cent of the time. Capacity of 150 units per hour (three-quarters of maximum potential demand) would be adequate for ninety per cent of the time so that the extra capacity of fifty units per hour is very expensive if only needed for ten per cent of the time. The departmental demand may be met by **spreading its load**, accepting some interruption in production. Nevertheless, it may be necessary to have the full demand potential available where the nature of the manufacturing processes requires this capacity for particular tasks, unless the difference can be met from spare capacity provided for other departments.

In theory, service departments should be equipped with adequate capacity to meet the maximum demand from all consumer departments simultaneously. However, apart from making some allowance for this for each individual department as just explained, some additional reduction in capacity may also

Table 19. Hypothetical Distribution of Service Usage in department 1

Units per hour	Number of hours	Cumulative usage	
50	3	3	
60	5	8	
70	8	16	
80	11	27	
90	14	41	
100	16	57	Median = 95·6 hrs
110	12	69	Mean = 105·1 hrs
120	9	78	
130	6	84	
140	4	88	
150	3	91	
160	3	94	
170	2	96	
180	2	98	
190	1	99	
200	1	100	
	100		

be accepted. Further statistical analysis may reveal the small degree of probability that all departments would make their maximum demands simultaneously. This is analogous to banks holding sufficient cash to cover only a small proportion of total deposits on the assumption that all depositors are unlikely to withdraw their deposits simultaneously. By the same token, whilst it is possible for all departments to simultaneously make their maximum demand for a service, the probability is quite low. Thus it becomes feasible to calculate the amount of capacity needed to maintain the service at an acceptable level of probability. This not only reduces the initial capital cost of providing capacity, but the plant utilization factor will also be much higher, thus inducing lower costs per unit of service.

Departmental Cost Control

The use of pre-determined rates for charging consumers with the service provided has clear benefits in being equitable between all user departments and in the stability of the rate. Pre-determined rates, however, also yield considerable cost control advantages to the service department itself. The use of a fixed rate for the service prevents the 'passing-on' to customers of any abnormal losses or cost increases, which is particularly important should they arise from service department inefficiency or, alternatively, that consumers do not gratuitously receive the benefits of improved efficiency.

Over/Under Absorption of Costs

The service department is debited with all actual costs incurred in performing its service, but credited at the pre-determined rate for the 'sales' to other departments. Inevitably, there will be an over/under absorption of the service costs and the amount over/under absorbed for a given accounting period provides an indication of departmental performance and efficiency. This interpretation arises from the fact that the amount over/under absorbed represents differences of actual from budgeted or estimated or forecast conditions.

Activity Changes

The pre-determined cost rate for charging user departments with the service is derived from the estimated, or budgeted, cost of the service for the estimated level of activity during a given accounting period. Actual unit costs for the period will differ from the pre-determined rate if the actual level of activity (consumer demand) is more or less than the forecast activity. Any difference in activity leads to the over/under absorption of the fixed costs and may be the result of internal or external influences. The user departments may make higher or lower demands for the service (external), or the service department (internal) may produce more or fewer units of service with given resources. Thus, greater activity arising from improved service department efficiency results in an over-absorption of fixed costs—the amount over-absorbed providing a measure of the improved performance.

Performance Variables

Similarly, the costs incurred by the service department may be more or less than the expected, or budgeted, costs for the actual activity level. The issue of dearer or cheaper materials; the usage of lower or smaller quantities; higher or lower wages; increased or reduced time performance; all lead to cost differences from the budget and so to an under/over absorption. Such differences are a reflection of the departmental performance within the period and particularly of the service management or supervision.

The over/under absorption of costs is not merely a *difference* but a highly significant indicator of managerial performance. Of course, to be really useful in this context the over/under absorption has to be carefully analysed to identify the various causes, or decisions, which have given rise to the particular result. This can be done through an analysed comparison between actual and estimate to locate the points of difference. This exercise stimulates cost control on the part of the supervisor as well as encouraging management to seek improvements in departmental operating performance. The details of costs and re-charging can be summarized in a monthly operating account. The balance of the account represents the overall efficiency of the service for the period and is transferred to the profit and loss account as an increase or erosion of profit.

Wider Considerations

The principles discussed in this chapter are of far wider application than for service department costs solely. In many ways, the present chapter may be taken as a summary of the ideas developed so far, as well as providing an introduction to the remainder of the book. The function of accounting is to create a management information system which provides financial data as a basis for decision-making and control. A little thought on this function shows that the accounting system must satisfy both criteria so that ascertainment and control are not alternatives but **complements**.

It is, however, not unusual to see a conflict between cost ascertainment and cost control, or between accounting data used for decision-making and that used for control. The result is the creation of a virtually unbridgeable gulf between ascertainment and control, which is quite ridiculous! This conflict is usually more apparent than real and often arises from ill-formed concepts based on prejudice rather than logic. Cost data is so vitally important for both managerial control and decision-making that it should be seen to fulfil both requirements. In the context of this chapter, this means that the oft-denigrated historical costs can and should be used to encourage cost control in all activities of the business, as well as providing decision data. Standard costing is not something apart from product costing, but a natural evolution through the intelligent use of historical data, combined with an appreciation of cost behaviour and linked to the interpretation of past performance. Cost control, through pre-determined rates derived from up-dated historical performance, stimulates a search for more reliable and objective criteria for setting standards which will yield more significant variances. Standard costing provides this enhanced sophistication and will be discussed in Chapters Thirteen to Eighteen.

The Decision Points

Nevertheless, cost control is possible and practical without standard costing or indeed budgets. The point to appreciate is that cost control does not mean rigidly conforming to some agreed policy but **choosing the least cost alternative** —all other things being equal. Costs are *controlled* when at a *minimum* for a given level of activity. Cost control, therefore, is exercised at the **decision points** of the business when a choice is made between alternatives. It is a function of management at all levels and, consequently, not an accounting function. The contribution of accounting to cost control lies in structuring the system to disclose those decisions or choices which have not been least-cost ones. Thus, a pre-determined cost or an earlier performance provides a datum or reference point (which is tacitly recognized as being a least-cost alternative) against which current performance can be measured and evaluated. Managers are thereby persuaded to exercise cost control as the accounting system reveals their cost performance to superiors, to whom they are accountable for their actions.

Factory Maintenance Costs

Maintenance cost will now be considered in closer detail and, since the principles are of wide application, the following will also serve as an illustration of costing for factory services in general.

Materials

The maintenance department will keep its own stores for the various materials it needs. The materials carried in stock range from consumable items (such as oils, greases, cleaning materials, paints, small tools, nails, and screws, etc.) through raw materials (including steel bar and rod, sheet metal, bricks, glass, and timber) to spare parts for machinery and equipment. Additionally, there will sometimes be a need to purchase certain special items such as major components and sub-assemblies for plant repairs or special-purpose fittings for building repairs. It is clearly necessary to recognize the importance of materials control in the maintenance department—just as it is for production materials. The principles of procurement and storage explained in Chapter Four are equally valid for the maintenance stores. There is, too, the question of what method is to be used for pricing issues from the stores. Standard items held in stock will usually be priced on a F.I.F.O. basis, but consideration should be given to the alternative bases so that the most suitable method for the circumstances can be adopted. The special items purchased fór particular jobs will, of course, usually be priced as invoiced by the supplier.

Maintenance Stores Control

The application of stock control to the maintenance stores is sometimes a thorny problem. At the outset it should be said that stock control techniques should be introduced only where there is a clear advantage to be gained. There is no merit in stock control (or any other accounting technique) being introduced for its own sake. On the other hand, stocks represent a considerable investment of capital and careful control can yield significant cost savings. Stock control methods are discussed in Chapter Fourteen, and the maintenance stores may well benefit from some of these in improved efficiency and reduced costs. There is, however, one aspect of stores control which is essential, namely that all issues from the maintenance stores should only be made against properly authorized requisitions.

Labour Costs

Maintenance staff will normally use weekly time sheets for recording activity time, but occasionally it will be possible to use daily time sheets. In large factories it may be practicable to introduce operation cards for major repair work and for plant construction. The time sheet provides the basis for the analysis of activity time into direct and indirect tasks and for the analysis of gross wages.

One of the common features of maintenance work is the very high proportion of overtime and night or weekend work. Overtime premium, therefore, tends to form a significant proportion of gross wages. There are two ways of dealing with this situation so that costs between different jobs are equitable. The first is to average the overtime premium over all the work done by apportioning the worker's gross wages amongst his various jobs at a rate derived from dividing the gross wages by the total hours attended. The alternative is to analyse all overtime premium as cost centre overhead so that all tasks bear an equitable share through the cost centre absorption rate.

Maintenance Direct Costs

The greater proportion of maintenance costs will be direct and only a small proportion forms maintenance overhead. In the main, direct costs are those which can be readily identified with tasks performed for other departments —both production and service departments. Thus, maintenance materials used outside the maintenance department itself represent direct materials consumed in providing the maintenance service and will be debited to the appropriate cost account. Similarly, direct labour is any maintenance labour employed on work for other departments. Therefore, the replacement parts and the fitters' wages in repairing a machine are direct costs to that job and, similarly, a fitter engaged week after week on preventive routine maintenance, such as going through one or more production departments to check, clean, and lubricate machinery, is direct labour and the stores items he uses are direct materials.

Maintenance Overhead

Earlier in this chapter the maintenance department was quoted as an illustration of functional cost centres. Each cost centre will incur its own indirect labour and materials costs, such as supervision, general labour and clerical labour, and additionally there will be general maintenance overhead such as management costs, stores expenses, and office administration, which will be supplemented by the maintenance share of general factory overhead. These general overhead expenses will need to be apportioned on realistic bases between the various maintenance cost centres. Maintenance work, by its very nature, tends to be labour intensive so that bases of apportionment and bases of absorption tend to be labour related—using either time or wages. All overhead relating to the maintenance department is thus analysed and apportioned between the various cost centres, and each cost centre will have its own unique rate of absorption.

Maintenance Costing Methods

Maintenance activities are either repair (or breakdown) work, or preventive work. Each breakdown calls for a special one-off repair job which is usually subject to a high degree of urgency to minimize the delay or interruption to output. This is clearly a jobbing situation and the repair order is the basis of both the work and the cost accounting. A job account is opened in the maintenance ledger for each repair order to which is debited the materials drawn from stores and any special purchases of replacement parts. In both cases the duly authorized stores requisition is the journal voucher and posting medium.

The direct labour cost is derived from the time sheets of the fitters engaged on the repair, and posted to the job account. At the same time, the cost centre overhead will be absorbed by debiting the job account at the appropriate rate. It is thus quite straightforward to compile the job cost for the repair.

On completion of the repair the customer department is charged for the repair by being debited with the appropriate amount which is then credited to the maintenance department. The easiest system would be one where the amount charged was the balance on the repair job account. There are, however, advantages in using a standard rate for work done as discussed earlier in this chapter. For breakdown work there are two alternatives to the actual cost method. Under the first method the 'customer' is charged for materials at cost plus the actual labour time at the pre-determined (or standard) wage rate and overhead rate. The other method envisages a sophisticated system of cost estimating which determines the standard charge for the job, and the maintenance department bears any excess cost or enjoys any cost saving. Thus, the difference between the actual cost and the amount charged is a measure of maintenance performance. Such a system will be a form of standard costing and has much to commend it, although there may be considerable problems in setting the standards or budgets (*see* Chapter Sixteen).

Operating Costing

Proper care and attention given to fixed assets minimizes the risk of break-downs and preventive (or routine) maintenance is now an accepted practice in most factories. Prevention is not only better than cure but usually much less costly. Routine maintenance is a continuing exercise and undertaken under standing orders issued annually. A cost account is opened in the maintenance ledger for each standing order. This account is debited with the materials drawn from stores, the direct labour of fitters engaged in the task, and the overhead absorbed. The continuing nature of the work makes it analogous to process manufacturing and it is possible to calculate a unit cost weekly and/or monthly. The customer departments can be charged for the service on a monthly basis at either the actual period cost or at pre-determined rates.

Monthly Operating Statement

The use of pre-determined or standard rates enables a monthly operating statement to be prepared for the maintenance department. In a sense this is a *quasi* profit and loss account. The balance on the summary represents the difference between the charges made for the maintenance services and the actual cost of providing those services. The operating statement should be prepared so as to indicate the surplus or deficit from each cost centre which had contributed to the overall result. Senior management will thus have a useful guide to the performance of individual supervisors.

Exercises

1. A company manufacturing special-purpose equipment has a toolroom which undertakes the following activities:
   makes loose tools in large batch quantities for the manufacturing departments;
   makes special jigs and tools to facilitate the execution of individual production orders for special-purpose equipment;
   manufactures jigs and tools for other engineering concerns;
   machines components required by the company's maintenance department for maintenance, exceptional revenue and capital expenditure work.

Required:

Design the cost ascertainment and cost control procedures for this toolroom.
[C.M.A.]

2. The Croft Tool and Engineering Company Limited has three separate factories in the same town. Two years ago, a plant engineer was appointed to take charge of a single maintenance department formed from the individual maintenance sections in each factory. During these two years the maintenance function has been re-organized on a 'group' basis and its management and administration has been improved.

Required:

Submit a report to the plant engineer outlining a suitable costing system for the maintenance department including the basis for re-charging maintenance services to user departments.
[C.A.A.]

3. The AB Company Limited produces the chemical Plus II at a rate of 200 gallons per hour from equipment which operates for eighteen hours per day seven days per week. The standard selling price and cost per gallon of Plus II is as follows:

	£	
Standard selling price		1·00
Standard cost:	£	
Material	0·50	
Labour	0·20	
Variable expenses	0·05	
Fixed expenses	0·10	
		0·85
		£0·15

Although a system of preventive maintenance is in operation costing £500 per week (included in the fixed expenses in the standard cost), over the last few months the average productive time lost from breakdowns has been fifteen hours per week. The direct repair costs of these breakdowns, which were not allowed for in the standard costs, averaged £600 per week. At a meeting called to discuss this problem, the maintenance manager produces the schedule detailed below. This schedule indicates that by increasing the amount and cost of preventive maintenance done in the present maintenance time, the productive time lost with its attendant emergency repair costs would be reduced.

PREVENTIVE MAINTENANCE COST SCHEDULE:

Weekly maintenance cost (accurate only to within ± 10%)	*Breakdown hours*
£	
3,000	0
1,800	5
1,100	10
500	15
100	20

Required:

(a) Compute from the above information the combined cost of breakdowns and preventive maintenance for the various levels of breakdown hours shown in the schedule, and show the optimum level of preventive maintenance, and

(b) comment on the additional information you require before a final decision on the optimum maintenance level could be made. [A.C.A.]

4. Discuss ways in which the cost accountant may assist management in the control and reduction of power costs. [C.A.A.]

5. One of the budget centres of the XY Manufacturing Company is the boiler house, which raises and supplies steam for all manufacturing budget centres in the company.

The foreman of one of the manufacturing budget centres has complained to the works manager that in his accounts he is charged at different rates each month per lb of steam used. The highest rates have been as much as twenty per cent above the lowest.

Required:

Explain in a report to the works manager:

(a) How such different rates per lb of steam can be incurred in the boiler house.

(b) Why being charged at different rates should present a difficulty to the foreman of the manufacturing budget centre.

(c) What procedure, as management accountant of the XY Manufacturing Company, you would propose to install to remedy this position. [C.M.A.]

CHAPTER TWELVE

COSTING COMMERCIAL ACTIVITIES

Production is defined in economics as the provision of goods and services which will satisfy human wants. Thus, any activity to satisfy a human want which is undertaken for reward is 'productive'. It is a pity that much carelessness in terminology often attaches the term production solely to manufacturing and labels all other economic activities as 'unproductive'. Bad is often made worse in those businesses where even indirect factory labour is deemed to be 'unproductive'. This is not just an exercise in semantics for the misuse of these terms creates an attitude of mind which uncritically accepts the so-called productive costs and endeavours to eliminate the unproductive items. Sufficient has already been said about both direct costs and overhead to demonstrate the fallacy of this thinking.

Production at its simplest is a change of material form (manufacturing) and also a change of place and/or ownership (commerce). Commerical activities do not induce any change in the material form of the goods but satisfy human wants in making goods and services available to the consumer. Thus, commercial activities are primarily concerned with **marketing**; secondly, with **administrative** procedures; thirdly, with **research and development**. There is considerable justification for the classification of research as a commercial activity, although many people would dispute such a claim. Nevertheless, it is convenient to include it as such in the present work.

Marketing Costs

Criticism was made in Chapter One of the common practice of treating all marketing costs as overhead expenditure, whereas it is usually possible to analyse them into direct and indirect categories. In most businesses, too, it will be necessary to establish cost centres for the marketing activities so that marketing overhead can be properly analysed and absorbed.

Marketing activities can be divided into the two broad areas of selling and distribution. As explained in Chaper One, the incidence of product cost in usually quite different in these two areas, and so demands their separate treatment. It is not merely convenient to make this distinction, but usually essential for accurate cost ascertainment and control as well as for reliable decision-making.

Marketing activities are many and varied, even within a single industry or company, so that marketing costs create problems of considerable complexity. Much of the difficulty stems from influences external to the business and outside its control. Changes in fashion, government action, new discoveries, the supply of money, general state of the company, competitors, political activity, and so on, all have their effect. The real problem in marketing cost analysis, though, is that the customer is the controlling factor. In a free enterprise economy, the customer has an absolute right to buy or not as he chooses.

Selling Cost Centres

The selling function exists to create and stimulate demand for the company's products or services and to provide the means for securing the orders to satisfy that demand. This definition embraces a whole spectrum of different activities which contribute to the overall objective. Cost accounting recognizes this fact by establishing various **cost centres** within the selling function to facilitate meaningful cost analysis, to aid effective cost control, and to supply significant data for decision-making.

The number of selling cost centres will clearly depend on the size of an organization—small businesses may simply have but one, whereas a large national company may have at least fifty. Significant increases in the size of a business lead to functional fragmentation which creates additional cost centres. Typically, functional cost centres are identifiable with the responsibilities of executives, managers or supervisors, although diverse responsibilities invested in a single person may require the establishment of cost centres for each separate activity.

Variables in Sales Accounting

There is, however, a conflict (which soon becomes apparent) in the creation of selling cost centres. The incidence of cost arises from the expenditure incurred by the various activities of sales promotion. The results of these activities, however, are reflected in the volume of orders received from customers. It is virtually impossible to clearly identify any particular sales order with one specific promotional activity, but it may be readily identified with a geographical area or sales territory. This is further complicated by the existence of distinct product groups which are effectively separate markets within a given territory. In other words, there are really three independent variables in sales accounting—products, geographical areas, promotional activities—which need to be reconciled.

Promotional activities can probably be safely eliminated from this triangular conflict as the object of the exercise is to win orders; and orders are readily identifiable with products (or product groups) and customers (or territories). A company selling several distinct product groups which form independent markets and where each product group requires a specialized sales force, will organize primarily on a product basis with sub-division by territories. Another company may have separate but related product groups, all of which are collectively promoted. In this instance the company will probably have a territorial structure with product sub-divisions. This is really a re-statement of the postulate that functional cost centres are identified with the areas of managerial responsibility.

Sales Promotion Costs

Some selling costs will be directly related to cost centres for products or areas and analysed thereto. Others, collected by activities, will be common to several primary cost centres and require apportionment between them on suitable bases. This situation is analogous to the factory where there are primary cost centres (production departments) and activity or service cost centres.

Advertising

Advertising forms the primary group of selling activities (chronologically if not principally) since it serves to create and stimulate demand for the company's products or services. Cost effectiveness in advertising is always a problem to evaluate objectively for several reasons.

Advertising is rather a matter of 'casting one's bread on the waters' and it is often difficult to identify a particular order with some specific advertisement —especially for general or reminder advertising. The use of clip coupons in press advertising provides some measure of positive response, but it usually fails to reveal any 'spin-off' in orders for the company's products generally or for orders placed directly with retailers or distributors. Again, the extent of competitors' advertising affects the effectiveness of one's own publicity. Competitive advertising is like 'running to stay in one place' and its benefit is measured by that share of the market which might otherwise have gone to competitors—very much a matter of subjective judgement. Furthermore, orders from customers seldom arise directly from a single advertisement or medium. There is usually a cumulative effect from a company's whole marketing strategy over a period of time which results in a positive response to some particular sales promotion. Exhibiting at trade shows, for example, may generate a flattering response in firm orders, but it is not at all unusual for some customers to deliberately place orders on such occasions which would have been given anyway.

Advertising Cost Centres

Nevertheless, in spite of the limitations, it is desirable to make some effort to measure the cost effectiveness of advertising. The first step is to arrange a suitable analysis of costs through the institution of advertising cost centres. Whilst advertising as a whole will be a functional cost centre, a recognition of the various advertising media leads to the establishment of several subordinate cost centres. For example, the following cost centres may be needed: press, television, posters, catalogues, direct mail, and trade shows. There is no problem in ascertaining the cost of particular advertising activities since this is readily available from invoices, and so on, which can be analysed by media. It is much less simple to analyse the orders received in this way.

Assessing Market Response

This is essentially a marketing exercise rather than an accounting one, but the accountant may need to seek the data by inductive reasoning. This may be done by **differential analysis** in noting the effect on the order flow generated by a change in advertising. For instance, the result of using a new medium or the discontinuance of an existing one. Care is necessary to avoid attaching too much significance to any changes revealed as it is not possible to isolate all the relevant influences. Nevertheless, it is possible to detect a movement in sales by comparing the results after the event with those which preceded it. The difference may be assumed to be mainly influenced by the event. This is crude but it may be useful in the absence of more reliable data.

The market response may also be tested by noting the incidence of **customer inquiries** before and after the event; or the effect of advertising may be seen in changed **order patterns**. In some cases it may be possible to obtain market response data with a high level of reliability through market research techniques, although this is very expensive to obtain. Whatever method is adopted, there is a need for it to be properly evaluated and with a clear recognition of the limits of error.

Evaluation of Market Response

The evaluation of market response should not be made in terms of the selling value of orders. Although changes in sales volume are useful indicators of market response, they are unsuitable for comparison with promotional costs. The revenue received from the sale of an additional unit is partly offset by the variable (or out-of-pocket) cost of producing and marketing that unit. The significant factor is the difference between variable cost and revenue known as **contribution** (*see* Chapters Nineteen and Twenty). Thus it is that the proper evaluation of market response lies in the changed contribution which is compared with the advertising cost change. Profit has risen where the extra contribution exceeds additional cost or where lost contribution is less than cost savings from discontinuing some advertising.

Salesmen

It will be seen that salesmen generally fulfil two functions in marketing—sales promotion (creating and stimulating demand) and obtaining orders for the company's products. It is probably impossible, and usually unnecessary, to separate these two functions. Unlike advertising, the costs of salesmen can be readily identified with the relevant cost centres usually on a territorial basis, and sales commission relates to specific orders and can be charged to special orders, or to product groups as a direct cost. Other costs of salesmen are selling overhead and analysed to the cost centres—these include salary, company car, entertainment expenses, and so on.

Like advertising, it is not easy to evaluate the cost effectiveness of salesmen, even where orders for company products are obtained by salesmen. It is impossible to say how much the order depended on the salesman personally and the extent to which it was influenced by advertising, reputation, or price or delivery—it is obviously some combination of all these factors. Again, some products are easier to sell than others and some territories are more difficult than others. It is also noteworthy that consumer goods may be sold on a single visit while capital goods sales may depend on a long series of visits spread over two or three years.

Sales Commission

The payment of commission to salesmen fulfils a dual function: it acts as an incentive to the salesman in winning orders, but it also diminishes the employer's cost risk. Sales commission is a variable cost and is avoided if no order is taken; however, it does represent an effective deduction from sales revenue. Although commission is usually calculated as a percentage of selling value, it should be based on the contribution since high variable manufacturing cost seldom permits a generous commission and relatively low variable cost allows room for strong incentives. (This topic is developed more fully in Chapter Twenty.) Alternatively, commission could be calculated on added value, especially where materials form a significant proportion of total cost. Greater profits are not necessarily gained from increased sales volume but cause and effect are less easily discernible in selling than in manufacturing and this calls for considerable care.

Accounting for Selling Cost

As explained previously, the sales territory is the natural selling cost centre since this accords with the normal organization structure. It also provides a convenient point for the absorption of selling overhead into the product as sales are made in territories. Direct product costs and direct territory costs (selling overhead) analysed to the territorial cost centres are generally recognized as being controllable by the area manager. Under standard costing, actual is compared with standard and the variances are analysed by causes (*see* Chapter Seventeen). Where standards are not available the actual result is compared with an average or previous performance. In this context, unit costs are essential for significant comparisons.

The selection of an appropriate unit is vital for this purpose. As in other situations, this calls for a recognition of the independent variable. Sales volume is the only available basis even though it is not entirely satisfactory since some selling costs (such as advertising, sometimes) may vary inversely with sales. A further difficulty is that the relationship may even change from time to time. In adopting sales volume as the independent variable it is preferable to use sales value or added value for multi-product situations, although sales units may be satisfactory for single products.

Apportionment of Selling Cost

Selling overhead which is common to two or more territories will need to be apportioned on a suitable basis. Sales value as a variable item is quite unsuitable for this purpose since selling overhead is generally a fixed cost and should be apportioned on a constant basis. Head office sales department is probably best apportioned in the ratio of territorial costs which are analysed direct to cost centres. Advertising should be apportioned on some arbitrary assessment of the benefits to each territory from general advertising. Local advertising will naturally be allocated direct to cost centres. Product advertising should be treated initially as deferred revenue expenditure and then prorated directly to products. Sales invoicing can be apportioned on the number of orders dispatched; while credit control costs may be prorated on the number of customers per area.

Absorption of Selling Overhead

Since selling overhead is composed of disparate elements, none of which are properly related to product variables, the selection of an absorption basis is largely an arbitrary exercise. In practice, sales value is most commonly used despite its general unsuitability. It is particularly inapt where material cost is significant and especially if materials prices fluctuate as in the non-ferrous industry. In most cases a ratio of added value will provide the more satisfactory basis for absorption. This is appropriate because the company is really selling the value added to the raw materials.

Distribution Costs

Distribution completes the marketing exercise and comprises three separate activities—warehousing (finished goods stock), packing, carriage. Compared with the selling function, distribution cost analysis is quite simple and straightforward. The cost centres are functional and unambiguous, the costs are generally direct product (or job or order) costs or direct departmental (or cost centre) costs.

Warehousing Costs

Holding stocks of finished goods might be seen as a selling function since the opportunity to obtain immediate delivery may predispose a customer not to trade with a competitor. However, the distinction between selling and distribution is not significant in this context and common practice recognizes warehousing as a distribution cost. The costs of stockholding are discussed in Chapter Fourteen, but for our purposes here they can be seen to vary with the value of the goods, their size or bulk, their 'shelf-life', and the average storage period. These factors vary considerably between themselves so that it is not easy to discern a mutual cost variable, which hinders the choice of a basis for absorbing warehouse costs. However, it will usually be found that within a given product group, that warehousing costs vary with sales value. It is necessary then to find separate rates of absorption for each product group based on sales values. This is relatively easy where the warehouse is appropriately sectionalized, otherwise it is best done by some form of sampling or controlled test runs.

Many companies establish depots or warehouses in strategic sales areas to improve the service to customers. In such cases, the depot costs are allocated to the relevant sales area. A proportion of the central warehouse cost will also be apportioned to the depots in respect of the service given by the central warehouse to the depots. The depot costs will then be absorbed at the relevant depot rate on all dispatches from that depot. Dispatches from the central warehouse will be charged at the central absorption rate, even if made to customers in an area having a depot of its own.

Packing Costs

Packing goods for dispatch to customers and arranging for delivery is usually a function of the warehouse. The cost incidence for the packing and dispatch function may, however, differ significantly from that of warehousing. On the whole it is more influenced by the number of orders than sales value or size. Nevertheless, large orders attract higher costs than small ones and allowance must be made for this. The most satisfactory procedure is to arrange a scale of charges which bears more heavily on small orders and diminishes as the order size increases. This can be done by analysing packing and dispatch costs into two categories—those which are 'order-related' (such as documentation) and those which are related to the size or sales value of orders (such as containers). It should be possible in most instances to frame a scale of charges to include both warehousing and packing costs. Separate scales based on invoice value would be prepared for each product group. This would appear to be an unnecessarily complex procedure, but the scales are surprisingly simple to compile in practice and easy to apply.

Carriage Outwards

The cost of carriage outwards depends on the method of transportation used, on the distance covered and also on the weight/bulk of the goods concerned. The use of public carriers or haulage contractors for delivering the company's products to customers will normally be charged per consignment. Thus, the charge becomes a direct expense of the job or order carried. The journal entries for this would be:

(1) Dr. Carriage outwards account.
     Cr. Carrier's personal account.
(2) Dr. Job account (or cost of sales account).
     Cr. Carriage outwards account.

Where there are a large number of small orders it is usually more convenient to charge the cost of sales account at an average rate for these items in bulk. This will result in an over/under recovery on the carriage outwards account which should be relatively small and written off to the profit and loss account at the close of the financial year. Carriage outwards for goods sent from the central warehouse to depots are chargeable to the depot or sales area cost centre instead of to a job account. These costs then form part of the distribution overhead for that depot. In most cases this is equitable since sales from a depot will normally be local deliveries with weight/bulk being the only significant variable. Furthermore, this is likely to be reflected in the sales value (or added value) of the goods since local depots tend to carry a restricted range of the company's products.

Own Transport Costs

Many companies operate their own fleet of vehicles for delivering all or part of their products. The size of fleet will vary from a few vehicles used for local deliveries, to very large fleets of different types of vehicles serving a complex web of deliveries on a nationwide basis. It is normal for the fleet capacity to fall short of the total requirement, to ensure maximum utilization of vehicles, and outside transport firms then provide the balance of the requirement. A careful appraisal of transport needs will reveal that some journeys can be undertaken more economically by public carriers and this should be done. It can only be worth while for a manufacturer to invest capital in road fleets where there is a real cost advantage from doing so.

From the accountant's viewpoint, there are two problems to be solved with one's own transport. In the first place, he must establish a suitable costing system for the transport department and, secondly, he has to find a suitable method of re-charging the transport service. These two problems are clearly interlinked and interdependent. The only satisfactory way to deal with this is by treating the transport department as an independent unit selling its services within the company, in much the same way as that suggested for the maintenance department in Chapter Eleven.

Transport Cost Centres

The first step in installing a transport costing system is to establish suitable cost centres. In theory, each vehicle is a separate cost centre, but in practice it is possible to group similar vehicles into a single cost centre. There is one proviso to this cost centre grouping which is that all the vehicles in a given cost centre are engaged in similar work. For example, a company may have a fleet of ten identical trucks: four trucks are used for local deliveries, three trucks make bulk deliveries to distribution depots, and three trucks are used for long-distance deliveries direct to customers. Although all ten trucks are identical, they would form three cost centres because of the differences in operating conditions.

Cost Analysis

All costs incurred in operating the fleet will be analysed to cost centres—making a distinction between fixed costs (or standing charges) and variable costs (or operating expenses). The basic document in transport costing is the vehicle log sheet (Fig. 34) which is kept for each vehicle on a daily basis. The

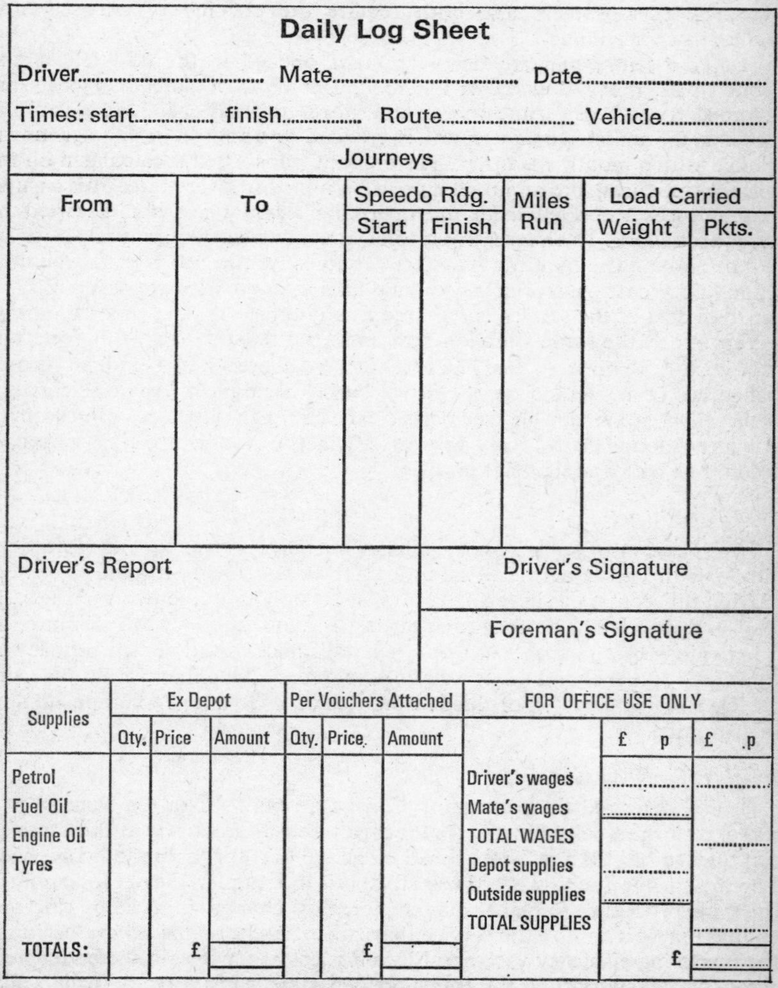

Daily Log Sheet

Driver........................ Mate........................ Date........................

Times: start.............. finish.............. Route.................... Vehicle...............

Journeys						
From	To	Speedo Rdg.		Miles Run	Load Carried	
		Start	Finish		Weight	Pkts.

Driver's Report	Driver's Signature
	Foreman's Signature

Supplies	Ex Depot			Per Vouchers Attached			FOR OFFICE USE ONLY		
	Qty.	Price	Amount	Qty.	Price	Amount		£ p	£ p
Petrol							Driver's wages	....	....
Fuel Oil							Mate's wages	....	
Engine Oil							TOTAL WAGES		....
Tyres							Depot supplies	....	
							Outside supplies	....	
							TOTAL SUPPLIES		....
TOTALS:		£			£			£	....

Fig. 34. Vehicle daily log sheet

daily log sheet provides details of the inputs (time and wages; fuel consumed; oils and greases; etc.) and the outputs in terms of load and distance. An operating account is opened for each cost centre which is debited with all the relevant direct expenses and quantities, plus a proportion of transport overhead.

The various maintenance costs for vehicles include tyres, repairs, overhauls, and servicing. These costs are variable with mileage but do not occur every week—or indeed every month in some cases. To raise debits when they occur vitiates performance comparisons between one period and another and diminishes cost control opportunities. There are two possible methods to overcome this problem and both require the opening of a cost centre maintenance account.

The cost centre maintenance account is opened in the cost ledger and debited with the various costs incurred. Details of maintenance costs are obtained from fitters' time sheets and stores requisitions. Under the first method, the maintenance account is credited and the operating account is debited with a monthly transfer. The amount transferred is calculated on the mileage run during the month at a pre-determined recovery rate. This ensures that unit costs derived from the operating account are not distorted by infrequent debits. The alternative is to keep the two accounts entirely separate by not making the monthly transfers. There is no need to transfer monthly amounts for cost control purposes, and *ad hoc* summaries are easily made if the total cost of the service is required at any time.

Very much the same situation applies to the fixed costs of the fleet. The fixed costs arise on an annual basis and include depreciation (though this may sometimes be computed on a mileage basis), insurance, road tax, carrier's licence, and garaging. The fixed costs can be charged to the operating account at a pre-determined recovery rate or left in the cost centre fixed expenses account as with maintenance costs.

Transport Cost Units

The selection of suitable cost units is not always easy in transportation, although the general rule of adopting the independent variable is equally valid in this context as in others. In transport operation the two variables are load and distance. The operating costs will tend to vary with distance, all other things being equal, but (for a given distance) a fully laden vehicle will consume more fuel and oil as well as taking more time than would the same vehicle running empty. For this reason, it is usual to adopt a composite unit the ton/mile.

Re-charging Transport Costs

Orders delivered by a company's own transport should be charged at a standard, or pre-determined, rate for carriage or alternatively at the commercial rate, rather than at a rate based on actual cost for the period concerned. The arguments for this are those advanced in Chapter Eleven for applying the same procedure to plant maintenance. Cost changes induced by efficiency changes are carried by the service department and provide an evaluation of the operating efficiency variance. Since it is easy to ascertain the commercial rates for transportation, the transport department has a ready-made selling (or transfer) value for its services. Not only does this permit the calculation of an operating profit, but it is possible to show a return on the capital invested in the fleet. From this it may be seen whether or not the company has invested wisely or could obtain a higher return from an alternative investment.

Research and Development Costs

The scope of research activity varies so greatly in both content and scale that it is quite impossible to devise any costing system for research which is of universal application. Another problem with research costs is that of discerning a realistic output factor to measure the cost effectiveness of research activity. Furthermore, in most business situations, activity generates cost; but in research, activity is often a response to an agreed level of expenditure. All this tends to create an atmosphere of vagueness and arbitrariness in which few of the recognized rules are applicable.

Nature of Research Activity

(1) **Pure Research** is directed towards general problems which have no particular connection with a company's current production, but it is aimed at increasing the general body of knowledge. There is not really a great deal of pure research in business organizations and most of it is undertaken by universities and research foundations.

(2) **Applied Research** is directed towards the development of new products or new equipment which have not been previously manufactured. Not all the work done will lead to commercial opportunities for much of it will be abortive. However, even abortive work often yields a 'spin-off' benefit in some other area.

(3) **Product Development** is aimed at improving existing products or manufacturing processes by better design, reduced waste, higher performance, lower cost, and so on. Quite often significant progress in this area has to wait for breakthroughs in pure or applied research to solve inherent technological constraints.

Importance of Industrial Research

The value of industrial research lies in the commercial advantages gained at the expense of competitors. In highly competitive industries this can represent significantly higher profits, even for a short-term lead. This is also true of the sophisticated technologies such as electronics where research can lead to cost reduction on a grand scale.

However, all businesses can benefit from some research activity leading to better products or better ways of producing them and so improving their competitive position. In recent years there have been signs of a growing awareness in many companies of the need to introduce or expand research and development activity. In the larger companies this may mean recruiting specialist staff and providing expensive equipment, in the small firms this may simply be thoughtful inquiry by the technical or design staff with the 'what happens if . . .' approach.

Cost Analysis for Research

Research and development costs may be analysed in a variety of ways such as nature of expense, research function or responsibility, project or activity. This will largely be determined by the criteria adopted by management in the allocation of resources for research, and by the organizational structure of the research department. In small research sections a single cost centre will suffice and a single research cost account will be opened. Larger research departments will be organized into functions which form separate cost centres such as pure research, new product development, product improvement, manufacturing technology, and environmental betterment; or else organized by projects or activities for which separate cost accounts are opened.

Each item of expenditure on research or development will be debited to the appropriate account. The source of these postings will be stores requisitions or suppliers' invoices for materials and equipment. Expensive capital items will usually be amortized arbitrarily over the expected useful life of the asset. Staff salaries and wages can sometimes be analysed from the payroll where they are permanently allotted to functions, although the accuracy of the analysis would be impaired where it is common practice for one function to 'borrow' staff from another function for short periods. The alternative is to require staff to complete time sheets recording their various activities during a month. Staff resent this chore as in some way demeaning their status and as unnecessary—probably with some justification in the latter case as the analysis of research costs is often of limited value for either control or decision-making.

Disposal of Research Costs

There is no disputing that research and development expenditure is a valid cost of the business activities and is indirectly a part of the cost of the company's products. There is, however, considerable controversy about the way in which these costs should be attached to particular products and, even, whether or not they should be allocated to products at all. Those companies which pursue the pure *marginal* approach whereby only variable costs are attached to products, write-off all fixed costs within the accounting year in which they are incurred. As fixed costs, research costs would be similarly treated. Other companies which adopt absorption costing as a whole, may in fact write-off research costs to the profit and loss account rather than allot them to products. These practices are perfectly sound provided it is recognized that the revenue from sales should be sufficient to cover all costs and yield an acceptable return on capital employed.

Capitalization of Research Costs

The crucial factor with the costs of research and development is that the benefits of research are usually received in a financial period subsequent to that in which the costs are incurred. Thus, research is a cost of future output and so, it is argued, research costs should be capitalized for amortization against future output benefiting from the research.

There are two problems in doing this, however. First, it is difficult to identify particular research with specific future products. Even where this relationship is discernible there may be trouble in deciding the total future quantity on which to base the amortization. This creates a risk of significant over/under charging to the products. Secondly, much research proves unsuccessful in outcome and has no bearing on the company's future output. Sometimes an abortive project may have been pursued for two or three years so that the cumulative costs brought forward year by year give rise to a very heavy write-off when it is abandoned. This has an embarrassing effect on that year's profits.

Nevertheless, research failures often contribute to later and successful research projects; indeed, much research which succeeds would have been impossible without the knowledge gained in earlier abortive exercises. The losses incurred on unsuccessful research, it can be argued, are, therefore, a cost of subsequent research projects. That being so, it would seem logical not to write-off the costs of abandoned projects but to carry them forward to be amortized amongst future research projects. The logic quickly becomes an illusion when the practicalities are considered. No criteria are available to determine the 'life period'; it is purely subjective judgment (or guesswork). Nor are there any objective means of deciding which future research has benefited, let alone the extent of that benefit.

Investigations in both the U.K. and U.S.A. indicate that the far greater majority of companies recognize research and development expenditure as a period cost and charge such costs to the period in which they are incurred. The manner of doing so, however, varies widely. Many firms treat them as general factory overhead so that research and development costs are absorbed into products through the production cost centres. Other companies charge them against sales by the use of an absorption rate which is a percentage of works cost, conversion cost, or added value, whichever is preferred. Some companies, with a nice sense of distinction, arbitrarily apportion the annual research cost between general factory overhead and marketing overhead.

In conclusion, there is little if any benefit in cost accuracy to be gained from the capitalization of research costs. Admittedly, to charge current research against current sales is to make the sales bear a cost for a benefit they have not received. However, current sales have benefited from earlier research for which they are not charged. On balance, therefore, current sales have profited by research and are being charged for research. The difference in the total cost of sales from capitalization or current write-off of research will normally be so small in most cases as to be insignificant and does not merit the clumsy book-keeping required by capitalization and its subsequent amortization.

Administration Costs

In the *I.C.M.A. Terminology of Management and Financial Accountancy*, general administration cost is defined as:

> The sum of those costs of general management, and of secretarial, accounting and administrative services, which cannot be directly related to the production, marketing, research or development functions of the enterprise.

In other words, administration cost is a residual—something which is not anything else. Nevertheless, administration cost may well be significant in amount and relates to those activities which are common to production, marketing and research. The managing director and his staff provide the prime example of this. Accounting is another clear illustration, although some specialized aspects of the accounting function may be easily allocated to other functions such as: charging sales ledger costs to marketing; transferring wages department costs to the factory; debiting bought ledger cost to purchasing. The buying office, too, is an activity common to all functions but is mainly concerned with factory requirements; as are the personnel department, welfare services, and company financing.

Administration as a Separate Function

Despite the tacit recognition of administration as a separately identifiable cost grouping in the *I.C.M.A. Terminology*, over the years there has been a continuing dispute concerning the validity of this assumption. The general criticism of the separate classification is based on the argument that there are only two principal functions in any business—production (or manufacturing) and marketing—so that all other activities are subordinate to, and contribute to, these primary functions. As an accountant, it is difficult to feel that this has any significance one way or the other, except slightly for the manner of disposal for administration cost.

Whatever one's opinion of this matter, the activities which comprise administration are clearly defined cost centres to which the relevant costs can be analysed in the first instance. This is esssential for control purposes, too, as each cost centre is also a responsibility (or budget) centre and the official in charge can be expected to justify any significant variances which arise.

Disposal of Administration Cost

The choice here is really quite simple, either charge the administration cost against sales, or apportion the cost between the two primary functions of production and marketing. Those who support the production/marketing argument will probably wish to make an arbitrary apportionment between production and marketing. Those who champion the right of administration to stand alone will claim the privilege of an independent absorption.

From an accounting standpoint, it is hard to accept that greater accuracy in product cost ascertainment is served by the arbitrary apportionment between production and marketing, even supposing this could be achieved objectively. A second accounting criticism of this practice is that it means including some administration cost in the valuations of work in progress and of finished stock. It is generally accepted that work in progress and finished goods should be valued at works cost only and that administration cost is a fixed 'commercial' cost which should be charged against period sales. It is really a matter of opinion whether the actual administration cost is charged against sales in recognition of its fixed nature; or else absorbed at a predetermined percentage of works cost, or conversion cost, or added value, or selling value. They are both acceptable and each is found in practice—a percentage of works cost is the most common but not necessarily the most suitable in all cases.

Exercises

1. Cyclostats Limited manufactures a wide range of equipment from very small sensitive instruments to large robust machines. Standard items are delivered 'ex-stock' from warehouses in different parts of the country, special jobs are delivered direct from the factory to the customer. Distribution to customers is partly by the company's vans, partly by external transport firms, partly by customers' own vehicles. Orders are obtained through agents (on a commission basis); by the company's salesmen (remunerated by salary plus small commission); and direct from customers through extensive advertising in trade journals.

Required:

Give a full description of the costing system you would use for dealing with the selling and distribution expenses. [C.A.A.]

2. You are the cost accountant in a business manufacturing a wide range of electrical domestic appliances sold through several channels of distribution, servicing these on return direct from customers and from the electricity boards and retailers, and supplying spares. In addition, you offer assembly facilities for certain other manufacturers of similar goods and, on a smaller scale, for certain manufacturers of electronic instruments. This latter activity was introduced originally to assist an associate company, but has been expanded because of its outstanding profitability. The appliance design function in the company is a large one, as is the division which deals with selling and distribution. A common administrative department serves all activities.

Required:

What do you see as: (*a*) the purposes; and (*b*) the main problems; of overhead classification, allocation, apportionment and absorption in such a business?

[C.M.A.]

3. A company maintains a fleet of ten lorries, delivering tins of biscuits to retailers, and bringing back empty tins.

Required:

What factors should be taken into account in a system of cost control to embrace the cost of running, maintenance and depreciation? Recommend a suitable unit of measurement to be applied. [A.C.A.]

4. You have recently been appointed as cost accountant of a large manufacturer of durable consumer goods. The company operates its own fleet of vehicles for delivering the company's products throughout the country. Management is anxious to institute a proper costing system for the transport department which will reveal the efficiency and competitiveness of its operations.

Required:

Outline your proposals in a report to the general manager. [C.A.A.]

5. P. Products Limited maintains a research department which until now has been relatively small, operating on a cost budget of approximately £10,000 per annum. This represents one per cent of total cost. There is to be a considerable extension of research activities during the budget year commencing on August 1, and research projects already under consideration are of the following types:

(*a*) two projects for the development of new products;
(*b*) one project for the improvement of a product already being manufactured, where the emphasis is on both functional aspects and cost reduction;
(*c*) three projects for the improvement of manufacturing methods.

The industrial engineer of the company, who is responsible for the research department along with all other engineering activities, expects to increase annual spending on research up to a total of £50,000. He is asking you, as the management accountant, to present your ideas on the cost ascertainment and cost control arrangements which should be applied to this function. Set out your ideas in the form of a report to the industrial engineer. [C.M.A.]

6. A costing system can be used both as a means of controlling a research and development department as well as being a tool for future plans by that department. Set out the type of information you consider would be produced by a costing system in order to assist a research and development department of a large engineering company. [A.C.A.]

7. Describe fully the system you would introduce for dealing with the administration costs of a manufacturing business employing 5,000 people. [C.A.A.]

CHAPTER THIRTEEN

PRINCIPLES OF CONTROL SYSTEMS

Formal Control Systems

The *Concise Oxford Dictionary* defines a **control** as 'the power of directing or command; a means of restraint or check; a standard of comparison for checking inference deduced from experiment'. In other words, **control is the process by which actual performance is directed to conform to plans or expectations.** Fundamentally, control is a 'stimulus-response' situation, whereby a given stimulus provokes a desired response. In this context, any activity which deviates from an expected performance provides the stimulus to which the response is a modified activity. This holds true for both mechanical and human control systems, so that it is possible to identify three separate phases in any formal control system.

1. **The Setting Phase.** Defining the objective of some activity and establishing specific standards (or expectations) of performance for each act necessary to attain that objective. This is the really vital phase of control for the results will only be as good as the care and precision with which the objectives and standards are set.

2. **The Operating Phase.** The standards established in the setting phase are communicated to the 'control unit' (for example, a person or a machine or a servo-mechanism) and followed by the actual performance of the required activity in conformity with the established standard. In this way, the first aspect of control is achieved by directing the actual performance towards the agreed objective.

3. **The Feedback Phase.** The actual performance results of the particular activity are measured and compared against the standard or expectation and any deviation from the norm is determined. This deviation is then the stimulus which generates corrective action through a feedback to the 'control unit' or to the setting phase.

In the **closed-loop system** (Fig. 35) the variance or deviation from standard is reported back to the control unit and so leads to a performance correction in order to conform to the established norm. The closed-loop system assumes that the set standard represents optimum performance and so requires the control unit to automatically correct the operational performance in response to any reported deviation from the standard. Feedback to the setting phase, on the other hand, constitutes an **open-loop system** (Fig. 36) since it recognizes the need, under dynamic conditions, to revise standards where conditions change, or even to modify objectives where these are shown to be unrealistic. It also questions whether the standard itself indicates the optimum performance. The open-loop system is, therefore, much more flexible than a closed loop which it usually embraces and ensures that current performance conforms to the current standard.

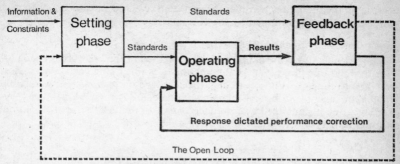

Fig. 35. Formal control systems—closed loop

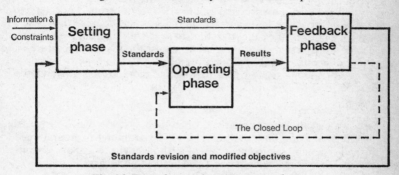

Fig. 36. Formal control systems—open loop

Functioning of Control Systems

The functioning of a formal control system is illustrated by the following examples of both mechanical and human controls.

Simple Closed-loop Mechanical Control

In the normal lavatory cistern the water level is controlled by a ball valve (the control unit) at the inlet pipe. The objective is to ensure that the cistern holds the desired quantity of water but is not over-filled. The ball floats on the water and determines the angle of the valve arm to which it is attached. The other end of the valve arm is attached to the inlet valve near the top of the cistern so that the valve is closed when the arm is horizontal. When the cistern is emptied, the ball falls to the bottom, thus opening the inlet valve. As the water enters the cistern through the inlet valve, the ball floats and rises with the water level until the arm is horizontal and closes the valve.

Simple Closed-loop Human Control

The turnstile at the entrance to an exhibition or sports stadium has the objective of admitting only those who meet the 'standard' by paying the admission charge. The turnstile attendant (the control unit) releases the lock when the entrance fee is paid. This exercise may also embrace an accountancy control where a meter records the number of people passing through the turnstile as the attendant will then be expected to hand in cash equal to the numbers admitted, multiplied by the entrance fee.

Simple Open-loop Mechanical Control

Traffic signals (the control unit) may be installed at the busy cross-roads to regulate the traffic flows. Where the volume of traffic along each road varies from time to time or from day to day, the standard pattern of signals may be modified to accord with the changing volume. This may be achieved by installing rubber pads in the approach roads to measure the traffic volume and then modify the standard time intervals between signal changes.

Simple Open-loop Human Control

When a housewife has prepared her cake mixture and put it into the baking tin, she will make ready to cook it in the oven. The housewife is the control unit for this operation and will have in mind certain basic standards such as the desired oven temperature and the expected cooking time. She will check the progress of the cake from time to time and her intuitive assessment of the cake's progress may prompt her to adjust the oven temperature or to vary the cooking time so as to achieve her objective of a properly baked cake. This is an open-loop system which permits the modification of standards in response to the stimulus of progress assessment.

Complex Mechanical Control Systems

These are essentially computerized open-loop systems which range from automated production lines to space ships. The computer is programmed to monitor all the many related activities of a whole environment and to initiate changes in subordinate activities as these become necessary.

Complex Human Control Systems

These arise in any large organization where there subsists a whole hierarchy of responsibilities for human activities—this is essentially management. Standards of performance are set according to the overall objectives and the expected performance from subordinates. Deviations from standard are fed back to subordinates who should 'automatically' take corrective action to conform to the standard. Deviations are also fed back to superiors who then either encourage their subordinates to modify their behaviour or else re-appraise the standards and adjust them as necessary.

Delegation of Authority

In the small undertaking it is still possible for one man (the proprietor) to fulfil the entrepreneurial function known as management. The very size of larger organizations, however, requires a delegation of authority to subordinates at varying levels, so that the responsibility for making operating decisions and for achieving performance levels becomes diffused throughout the organization. There will be, of course, a general policy laid down to guide the subordinate managers in optimal decision-making, but much is still left to their discretion and initiative. The problem of management control is essentially one of controlling subordinates so that 'control' is often defined as the process by which management ensures that the performances of operating personnel will conform to corporate plans and expectations.

Profit Responsibility

Each decision or action taken by the various members of an organization has its effect upon the costs or revenues of the business and, consequently, on the company's overall profit performance. The aggregate costs and revenues of business are, therefore, the financial quantification of the myriad decisions made by all those employed in the business from the managing director down to the most humble employee. The decisions of people, however, have an effect which tends to be proportional to their responsibilities, and the decisions of certain individuals are much more significant within the context of profit performance than are the actions of those in less responsible positions. So it is really the diverse decisions taken at the various levels of management which result in profits or losses being made.

Responsibility Accounting

The flow of accounting data has to be organized so that each transaction becomes identifiable with a particular decision point and, therefore, with the decision-maker. Each item of revenue or cost in a business is a financial expression of some decision or other and provides, consequently, an evaluation of that decision. It becomes possible, then, to determine the responsibility for each accounting entry by identifying the person who made the relevant decision. Thus, the accounting system can be seen as a management evaluation exercise which measures the effect on profits of each decision (or lack of decision) and which locates the responsibility for any such change in the company's fortunes. Responsibility accounting is the accountant's attempt to measure managerial effectiveness by analysing the corporate results according to decision points or responsibility centres.

The Organization Chart

The accounting system, then, needs to be structured round the spheres of responsibility within the business because these represent the various decision points within the organization. In other words, the company's organization chart forms the starting-point in the design of a management accounting system. Generally, there are two distinct types of responsibility centre—the **physical location**, such as a machine shop or a warehouse, and the **function**, such as sales promotion or production planning. The precise arrangement of responsibility centres varies markedly from one firm to another depending upon the nature of the particular business, the delegation of authority to subordinate managers, and the accompanying organizational structure. Thus, the accountant accepts the organization chart as it stands, for it is no part of the accounting function to design the management structure, nor even, for that matter, to influence its design in accord with some preconceived notion of the accounting system.

Management Control

It has already been emphasized that management controls are necessary where authority is delegated. Responsibility accounting has encouraged the development of accountancy-based management control systems, designed to relate management performance to profit performance. The accounting system continuously monitors managerial decisions in recording costs and revenues by responsibility centres. Actual results are compared with the planned or standard performance and any difference or variance from standard indicates the effect on planned profit performance occasioned by a particular decision. Thus, the analysis of variances by responsibility centres indicates the effectiveness of individual managers, by measuring and reporting the degree to which they have added to, or reduced, corporate profits in their day to day operational decision-making.

Management by Exception

The accounting system is, then, a management control information system which evaluates and reports managerial performance in decision-making. Senior executives are thereby provided with performance analyses for each of their subordinates which guide them in taking executive action against sub-optimal performance. Since these reports highlight the deviations from standard (or optimal) performance on the part of individual subordinates, senior executives can economize their efforts and improve their control by directing their attention exclusively towards the exceptions from standard performance. In practice, of course, attention is given to the adverse or unfavourable variances only, as any betterment of performance is to be applauded not corrected. **Management by exception** enables senior executives to control their subordinate managers with economy of effort and time.

Significance of Standards

The introduction of accountancy-based systems of management control naturally focuses attention on costs and profit. Nevertheless, it is unfortunate that cost control has become confused with management control in much accounting literature, because their close inter-relationship blurs the lines of demarcation. Furthermore, the 'exceptions principle' of concentrating on the variances tends to overrate the significance *per se* of a standard or budget. This leads frequently to an attitude of exaggerated esteem bordering on the mystical where the standard is accepted without question as an inviolable truth. This is nonsense for any standard cost or budget, however carefully and scientifically prepared, is no more than an estimate of a future cost within estimated future conditions. As such, a standard may be just as wrong as any other figure through human errors of judgment or carelessness.

This attitude also encourages the operation of management control through a closed-loop system. The emphasis on variances stimulates subordinates to achieve standard performance which, again, is essentially a closed-loop control. In practice, therefore, the operating results are fed back to the control unit (say, a shop foreman) who is expected to conform to the established standard by taking the appropriate action to eliminate any adverse variances.

The Profit Gap

The whole of economic activity is directed towards the satisfaction of wants, and every business undertaking endeavours to fulfil this purpose by the provision of goods and services. However, no business undertaking is simply a philanthropic organization but is motivated by the incentive of gain (or profit). Indeed, in the self-adjusting competitive economy which is a feature of Western society, unless profits are made, a business must eventually collapse. Put simply, profit may be defined as the difference between total revenues and total costs. Maximum profit, therefore, occurs when the widest possible gap can be achieved between these two factors by increasing selling prices and/or reducing unit costs.

Market-determined Selling Prices

On the whole, there is little that any business can do in the way of setting arbitrary selling prices since price is determined externally by the market through the interaction of supply and demand. In other words, the selling price of any commodity is only that which the consumer is willing to pay. The purchaser is only prepared to offer more for one article than for another when it possesses some feature or characteristic which increases his satisfaction and for which he is prepared to pay extra. It is true that price increases tend to follow higher costs during periods of inflation, but this only means that as the market has accepted a price increase that the price could have risen anyway.

Cost-based Price Setting

It is a common fallacy, even amongst accountants, that the concept of the market determination of selling price is simply economic theorizing with little relevance to the practical world of every-day business. This attitude arises from a complete misunderstanding of the role of cost in price setting which is particularly noticeable in jobbing situations. The basis for the preparation of tenders or quotations is undoubtedly the predicted cost plus the expected profit in supplying the goods required. The acceptance of the quotation by the customer turns the quoted price into the selling price so that it would seem that the chain of events confirms the idea that the selling price is determined by the cost.

However, the customer has little more than a purely academic interest in the supplier's cost of production. He makes his decision to buy usually on the basis of the quoted price and will only accept a quotation which is commensurate with his expected benefit or satisfaction from the goods. Where the quoted price is considered to be too high, he will not place an order so there is no sale and no selling price either. Experience in jobbing industries shows that even those manufacturers who claim to fix selling prices on a cost-related basis are just as sensitive to market conditions as any other supplier, so that production cost is really only used to locate the pricing area and the *cost plus price* is often amended upwards or downwards in sympathy with prevailing market conditions.

Since the supplier's selling prices are not determined by his costs of production, this begs the question of the role of costs in the context of selling prices. Certainly, costs do not determine selling prices, but rather indicate whether or not it is worth while to produce at the prevailing selling prices. The manufacturer who sets 'selling prices' for his products on the basis of cost is really saying *as my costs are x, I am only willing to produce these goods when the selling price is at least y*. It is the customer's decision to buy or not to buy which determines whether or not y is the selling price.

Cost Control

As the manufacturer has little influence and no control over the selling prices for his products, the optimization of profits must depend largely on his ability to minimize costs. All costs are more or less controllable because they arise from internal decisions, so that effective cost control is the major contributor to profit-making in business. Cost control may be defined as choosing the **least-cost alternative**, all other things being equal. Thus, the continuous exercise of cost control must result in minimum costs within the prevailing conditions. Cost will be one of the criteria in every business decision: sometimes the least important factor, often the most critical factor, but always to be considered.

Cost Control Points

Cost control is exercised, when making decisions, by consciously and deliberately considering the cost effects of alternative courses of action, with a view to adopting the least-cost alternative within the constraints imposed by the problem. It is clearly a management function and, paradoxically, not an accounting function, because it is exercised in decision-making and, consequently, the decision points in a company are also the cost-control points. Cost control, as an attitude of mind which seeks the least-cost choice in every alternative, should be reflected throughout all levels of the management team. This idea of cost control may be generally accepted in most businesses, but its application in practice is not so readily found. Quite often the least-cost solution may also be the least convenient or even unpopular amongst workers, so there tends to be a contra-incentive to forgo the least-cost alternative. Hence the need for a management control to direct subordinates in their decision-making as an aid to cost control.

Influence of Management Style

Under an accountancy-based management control system, the budget or standard will be accepted *prima facie* as the least-cost alternative. Hence the adverse variances indicate decisions which were not least-cost alternatives—in other words, the subordinate manager was not exercising cost control. Senior executives should call for an explanation of this from the responsible manager and any subordinate who has been 'carpeted' a few times becomes cost conscious in his decision-making, so as to avoid the disfavour of his superior. However, his idea of cost control tends to be equated with the budgeted or standard cost rather than with the *least-cost decision within the actual operating conditions*. The feedback of actual performance, therefore, leads to corrective action towards the standard so that cost control through standards is often a closed-loop system. This is invariably a feature of autocratic management styles, but it is also found where senior executives, through an undue confidence in the reliability of the standard, demand conformity from their subordinates.

Management Information for Cost Control

If the various members of the management team are to control the costs for which they are responsible, they will require cost data to assist them in reaching their decisions. In Chapter One it was pointed out that 'decisions can only be made sensibly when the person making the decision is aware of the probable consequences from the possible alternatives'. In exercising cost control, the least-cost alternative is unlikely to be chosen unless the decision-maker knows the respective costs of each alternative.

It is a function of accountancy to provide that cost and operating information upon which intelligent cost control must depend. Miscellaneous unrelated statistics may reveal some facts and lead to limited benefits, but they are much more likely to cause confusion and even indifference amongst those who should use them. Costs are unlikely to be controlled by managers unless those same managers can easily understand the costs for which they are responsible and also appreciate their significance for decision-making. To be used effectively, cost information presented to management should satisfy three necessary conditions: it must be punctual; it must be relevant; and it must be comparative.

Punctual Information

The executive who depends on information in his endeavours to control costs requires it as early as possible. The whole purpose of the exercise will be frustrated when the decision must be taken prior to receiving the information or where the decision is delayed until the necessary data is available. Under normal operating conditions, any undue time-lag between the happening of an event and its reporting (the feedback to the control unit) can easily vitiate any corrective action. Unless a manager is made aware at an early stage of a particular situation developing in his department, it may become impossible to find a remedy. Conversely, he may go on to over-correct a fault unless he is promptly notified of the effects from corrective action already taken. Late information not only frustrates cost control but in a real sense also diminishes managerial responsibility.

Relevant Information

It is vital for the accountant to understand and appreciate the information needs of individual managers so that they are given data which is relevant to their decisions. The accountant must discuss their needs with executives and have a thorough understanding of the company's production and marketing activities so that performance results can be reported accurately and significant features emphasized. Furthermore, to be relevant for a particular manager, control information must relate to the decisions within his responsibility and control. Accountants are sometimes so preoccupied with compiling, collating, and computing data that it all becomes an end in itself and information provided for other departments is looked on either as a gracious favour or as a plain nuisance. Accounting is a service which is provided for the benefit of all other functions in a business and this fundamental principle should not be lost to sight.

On occasions this bureaucratic attitude goes even further, when accountants insist on providing each executive with the information which is good for him, rather than with that he needs. Much of the development in management-control techniques owes its origin to the realization amongst accountants of the value for this purpose of accounting data, but the controls devised by accountants are sometimes influenced more by their own interpretation of the significance of accounting data than by the needs of the decision-makers. Recent research by Professor Dew and Dr. Gee supports this view. They found that investigations in seven large companies showed that nearly half the control information being produced was not used by management. The most important reason for non-use was that managers were given information concerning aspects outside their control. There is no purpose in any information service when its information is not used, and this is just as true of accountancy as of any other service. Accountancy is an expensive service and can only be justified by its contribution to profit performance through the provision of information leading to sound decision-making. Otherwise, profits can be best increased by the savings from discontinuing the accounts department which produces non-relevant information.

Comparative Data

Throughout Chapters Eight to Twelve it was emphasized that the significance of cost figures can only be seen from making a comparison with some other known data and that this is especially true in the context of cost control. Any cost viewed in splendid isolation is almost meaningless and, consequently, completely useless for decision-making of any kind. To say that a hydrostatic pentometer has cost £210 to manufacture is a statement of fact and may even be of some interest, but to be useful its significance must be manifest. If the selling price of this article is £250, there is some meaning to a cost of £210 for it is readily apparent that the profit is £40, although this then begs the question of whether or not sixteen per cent of selling value is a good, bad, or indifferent profit margin. Even more, perhaps, it questions the acceptability of £210 as the cost of manufacture, hence the need for a realistic cost comparison to be made.

Past Performance Data

Under systems of historical costing, past performance provides a basis of comparison for current performance. For example, the knowledge that two months ago a hydrostatic pentometer cost £218 adds a new dimension to the current cost of £210. There are obvious risks in the use of a single example for comparative purposes as it may be unrepresentative for a variety of reasons. Several years' experience, however, will usually provide averages which can be useful as a basis for comparison with current performances. Values can and do vary considerably from time to time, but physical performances (such as hours or weights) are much more stable. Consequently, average hours per unit or average weight per unit, when up-dated at current prices, provide reasonable bases for the comparison of current performances. An intelligent use of historical costs leads to the establishment of average or normal costs, and the comparison of current performance against the 'normal' cost will disclose the 'abnormal' deviations. The disclosure of these variances then stimulates corrective action leading to cost control.

Control Weaknesses of Historical Data

The first serious weakness inherent in the use of historical data for cost control lies in the emphasis on past performance. The control of today's costs calls for a comparison with today's standards. Good management looks forward rather than backwards, and this is particularly true in the ever-changing conditions of a dynamic business environment.

Secondly, some past performances contain 'abnormal' items for one reason or another which tend to distort any averages which include them. The more obviously unrepresentative items can be eliminated from the average but some must remain. Historical costs, therefore, are unsuitable for comparison purposes as there is really no way of knowing how reliable or accurate they are. This naturally diminishes the significance of any variance from the average. The deviations as such are plain, but it is virtually impossible to know *whether* the differences should have arisen because there is no way of knowing which of the two sets of data is the more correct. In these circumstances it is even more difficult to decide *why* the variation has occurred, whilst unreliability of the 'yardstick' renders impossible the calculation of *how much* they should have changed.

Standard Cost Data

A consideration of these drawbacks in the use of historical records as a basis for evaluating current performances leads to a search for a more reliable 'yardstick'. In other words, the establishment of theoretical norms or standards of performance and cost against which to measure actual achievement. A standard cost has been defined as:

A predetermined cost calculated in relation to a prescribed set of working conditions, correlating technical specifications and scientific measurements of materials and labour to the prices and wage rates expected to apply during the period to which the standard cost is expected to relate, with an addition of an appropriate share of budgeted overhead.

(*I.C.M.A. Terminology of Management and Financial Accountancy*)

Therefore, being confident of the accuracy of the 'yardstick', the significance of any variances from a standard—which represents what the cost should be—can be readily assessed.

Standard Costing

Standard costing is a form of responsibility accounting since it aims to determine the managerial responsibility for deviations from standard as an incentive to cost control. The need to identify particular managers with the responsibility for costs calls for the accounting system to be structured on the management organization chart. Therefore, standard costing is essentially departmental costing whereas historical cost systems are fundamentally product costing. This is an important distinction for it is really a contradiction in terms to refer to a *standard job costing system* as, although standard product costs are compiled, they are not used for control through variance analysis. Comparing actual and standard on a job or product basis would erode the value of standards for control purposes by obscuring cost responsibility.

The Planning Principle

The introduction of either budgetary control or standard costing usually yields cost benefits even before it is actually in operation. Accountancy-based systems of management control require the application to accounting of the principles of planning, whereby future actions and their alternatives are carefully considered. In establishing standards of performance, a consideration of the factors which are likely to influence performance and cost will frequently disclose possible sources of economy, more efficient methods of production, or improved plant layout. This is an exercise which in itself contributes to cost control in suggesting least-cost alternatives from reductions in production costs and increased productivity.

Conclusion

Management is the function of procuring and utilizing all the factors of production in the most suitable proportions to achieve the optimum profit performance of a business. Accountancy systems are designed to aid management to fulfil its function through the preparation of data to aid decision-making and control throughout the whole chain of command from top to bottom of the organization.

Exercises

1. A manufacturing company is operating a system of cost-finding for products. What changes are necessary to establish a comprehensive system of budgetary control and standard costing? [C.M.A.]

2. 'It has been said that the sign of a good manager is his ability to delegate responsibility and this is especially true of expenditure control. If control of expenditure is delegated, as it should be, the means to enable those responsible to exercise control must be provided. The means is the **budget.**'
Discuss the implications of the above statement in relation to the procedure you would adopt when called on to install a budgeting system in an organization.

[A.C.A.]

3. 'The fundamental idea that individuals should be charged only with costs subject to their control is conceptually appealing.' Comment on this statement outlining the guide lines you would employ for charging costs to individuals.

[A.C.A.]

4. One of the criticisms frequently levelled at industrial management is that although control systems are introduced into manufacturing units, these controls are rarely integrated with one another. If one accepts that the main controls required are of output, its quality and cost, what contributions would you, as management accountant, make towards integration of cost control techniques with production control and quality control? [C.M.A.]

5. It has been claimed that 'comparison is the essence of control', do you agree with this claim? Give also the usual bases of comparison used in costing, stating their advantages and disadvantages. [C.A.A.]

CHAPTER FOURTEEN

STOCK CONTROL

The maintenance of stocks is an expensive matter for it represents a considerable investment of capital. In many ways these are also **idle funds** since the items stocked do not **appreciate** in value through storage—apart from those exceptional cases of **maturation** when storage is really analogous to **processing**. The materials themselves must be paid for and further funds are needed to finance the storage facilities such as buildings, equipment, fittings, lighting, heating, staffing, and so on. This leads to two contra-directional forces influencing the size of inventory. Since the **investment** in stocks tends to vary more or less directly with the size of the inventory, there is pressure to keep stocks at a minimum. On the other hand, the risk of delays to production through non-availability of materials (and the costs thereof) tends to vary inversely with the size of inventory and creates a pressure towards maximum stock levels. The optimum inventory level will be found at some point between these two extremes; but its determination is a matter of some complexity because stores movements create a dynamic situation of constantly changing stock levels. The problem is overcome in practice through the setting of fairly wide stock limits known as **maximum stock level** and **minimum stock level**. The former limits the investment in stocks while the latter ensures that stocks are sufficient for normal demands.

Minimum Stock Level

Each item held in stock has its own minimum stock level (M.N.L.) and the actual quantity held in stock should not fall below it under normal business conditions. Opinions differ on the nature of minimum stock, but if one accepts that inventory control aims to ensure adequate stocks to keep production running, then minimum stock is seen as a **buffer stock**. That is, M.N.L. is a precaution against either unexpected delays in delivery or exceptionally high consumption during the lead time (or delivery period). The minimum stock level thus depends on the rate of consumption during an emergency period, the duration of which may be set by accepting some purely arbitrary period such as three working days or five working days, and so on. Alternatively it could be related to the **normal lead time**, say one-fifth, on the assumption that the probable period of delayed delivery is likely to be correlated to the lead time. A normal delivery period of five days is unlikely to be more than one or two days late, but in five weeks the delay could be one or two weeks, and one month in five months is not improbable. Experience shows that a twenty per cent delay factor needs some modification in the establishment of *minima* and *maxima* within the general principle. Prudence suggests that buffer stocks should be based on a minimum of three days' consumption, while stock investment restraint suggests an upper limit of, say, three weeks usage. This is reasonable because, under normal conditions, delivery will be made *before* minimum stock is reached and also because three weeks' usage relates to a lead time of fifteen or more weeks which is often long enough to provide **advance warning** of potential delays.

Calculating M.N.L.

The basis of calculation can be either the supplier's quoted delivery period or the average lead time derived from the company's past experience. Stock levels determined by reference to average past performance can be corrected statistically to improve their reliability. This is illustrated in Tables 20 and 21 by using a hypothetical situation for five different items of stock where the desired statistical confidence level is assumed to be ninety-five per cent on a single-ended test. (The subscript p indicates the estimated population mean in each case.)

Table 20. Lead Time and Usage from Past Performance

Stock items	Delivery period (weeks)			Weekly usage (units)		
	N_1	$\bar{x}$	σ	N_2	$\bar{y}$	σ
'A'	30	0·5	0·2	10	500	20
'B'	26	1·5	0·4	10	400	14
'C'	20	3·0	0·6	10	200	9
'D'	15	7·0	0·8	10	40	5
'E'	10	12·0	1·0	10	10	2

N_1 = number of orders analysed; N_2 = number of weeks covered. The crude averages ($\bar{x}$ and $\bar{y}$) can be corrected statistically to improve their reliability by using the **standard error** at the desired confidence level. The corrected means shown in Table 21 are obtained by using the following formulae:

$$\text{Lead time } (\bar{x}_p) = x + \frac{1·67\sigma}{\sqrt{(N-1)}} \quad \text{Usage } (\bar{y}_p) = y + \frac{1·67\sigma}{\sqrt{(N-1)}}$$

From normal distribution tables, $1·67\sigma = 0·4525$ which means that 95·25 per cent of all items will be found to have a value of less than *the mean* + $1·67\sigma$. It is thus possible to be certain that ninety-five per cent of all lead times will be less than (a) in Table 21 and also that weekly usage will not be greater than (b) in Table 21.

Table 21. Calculation of Minimum Stock Levels

Stock items	Lead time (weeks)		Weekly usage (units)		Usage during delivery period	Minimum stock quantity
	$\bar{x}_p$	$\bar{x}_p + 1·67\sigma$ (a)	$\bar{y}_p$	$y_p + 1·67\sigma$ (b)	(c)	(d)
'A'	0·562	0·895	511	544	487	272 (e)
'B'	1·633	2·300	408	431	991	216 (e)
'C'	3·229	4·229	205	220	930	186
'D'	7·356	8·689	43	51	442	89
'E'	12·557	14·224	11	14	199	40

(a) 95 per cent of all deliveries will be made within this period.
(b) 95 per cent of all weeks will not exceed this usage quantity.
(c) Maximum usage at 95 per cent confidence level from (a)×(b).
(d) One-fifth of the usage during the delivery period (c).
(e) One-half of the weekly usage (b) is absolute minimum.

Re-order Level

Purchase orders are issued from time to time to replenish stocks and, as production continues to consume materials, the material stocks will fall during the time taken for the suppliers to execute the order. It is, therefore, essential to establish that stock level which acts as the signal for a replenishment order to be issued. The point usually chosen is the lead-time usage plus the minimum stock quantity; in this way the buffer stock will not be called on during normal conditions but is available for emergencies. Using the data given in the example for the M.N.L. calculation, the **re-order level** (R.O.L.) for each of the five items is shown in Table 22.

Table 22. Calculation of Re-order Stock Levels

Item	Usage		M.N.L.		R.O.L.
'A'	487	+	272	=	759
'B'	991	+	216		1,207
'C'	930	+	186		1,116
'D'	443	+	89		532
'E'	199	+	40		239

On this basis there is only an 0·05 probability of having to use 'buffer' stocks, and normally the minimum stock level will not be reached.

Maximum Stock Level

The maximum stock level (M.X.L.) is set after a consideration of the storage capacity available and its cost; the supply of capital; risks of deterioration and obsolescence; and economic purchasing quantities. The best starting-point for this exercise is the **economic order quantity** (E.O.Q.) for each item held in the stores. Once known (on the assumption that this E.O.Q. is adopted), it becomes possible to compute the probable maximum stock holding. At the ninety-five per cent confidence level it is possible to calculate the **minimum** usage during the shortest delivery period which—if deducted from the re-order level—will indicate the stock level when the goods are received from the supplier under these conditions. This stock level added to the E.O.Q. will establish the maximum stock of this item at that confidence level. In other words, there would only be an 0·05 probability that stocks would ever exceed that quantity. In the case of item 'A' (from the illustration already used) the minimum usage would be:

$$(\bar{x}_p - 1 \cdot 67\sigma)(y_p - 1 \cdot 67\sigma) = (0 \cdot 229)(478) = 109 \text{ units}$$

As the re-order level is 759 units, delivery would be made with the stock at 759 less 109 = 650 units. On the assumption of an E.O.Q. = 1,000 units, then M.X.L. for 'A' is 1,650 units.

The **average stock level** (A.S.L.) will be 972 units; that is, the re-order level, *less* the average usage during the average delivery period (511 units × 0·562 weeks) plus half the E.O.Q. (759−287 + 500).

Economic Order Quantity

The economic order quantity (E.O.Q.) is that size of order yielding the lowest cost per unit purchased. The E.O.Q. is a matter of some complexity, but clearly it is a considerable advantage to management in choosing a least-cost alternative. Generally speaking, there are four factors which influence the E.O.Q.:

(1) **The supplier's price**, as most manufacturers and factors reduce prices for large quantities on a single order. There is, therefore, usually a clear price benefit from larger quantities.

(2) **Storage costs**, since the provision of storage facilities tends to vary more or less directly with the size of stocks held, which in turn is dependent on the E.O.Q. Larger E.O.Q. will raise the M.X.L. and call for greater facilities which incur higher costs. However, because of the 'fixed' element (average stock size when delivery is made) the cost per unit of E.O.Q. tends to fall as E.O.Q increases.

(3) Materials in store have to be paid for and are (in a sense) idle—that is, earning no income—but the capital invested in buying those materials could have been used to finance some other activity. The capital tied up in stocks has, therefore, an **opportunity cost** equal to the income forfeited by not seeking an alternative investment. In practice this is usually an arbitrary interest rate calculated on the A.S.L. for the **average time** (A.T.) that materials are held in stock before use.

(4) **The risk of deterioration** in storage will increase with the length of time the materials are kept in store. It follows that as the E.O.Q. rises so does the A.T. and, therefore, the risk of deterioration, too.

The supplier encourages his customers to buy in large quantities by offering reduced prices, and the costs of storage tend to diminish per unit of E.O.Q. as E.O.Q. increases. The other two factors, however, will tend to raise the cost per unit as E.O.Q. increases. There is an additional factor which could be considered—the cost of the administration per purchase order issued. This will, generally, be the same fixed sum whatever the E.O.Q., but it will normally be insignificant relative to the value of the order itself, unless the average order is for a small quantity. Where it is known to be significant then some allowance for it will be included in the E.O.Q. computation, otherwise it can safely be ignored.

The calculation of E.O.Q. is illustrated by reference to item 'E', in the previous example for which the following data are available.

(a) Supplier's price:
   £8·00 per unit for 250 units and over in multiples of 50 units.
   £7·60 per unit for 500 units and over in multiples of 100 units.
   £7·00 per unit for 1000 units and over in multiples of 500 units.

(b) Storage costs are £0·40 per unit of maximum stock.

(c) Interest on stocks is included at eight per cent per annum.

(d) The **deterioration factor** is $1 + (A.T./S.T.)^2$, where S.T. is the maximum storage time for the material to remain at all usable. This factor is used to multiply the sum unit price of E.O.Q. from $(a) + (b) + (c)$. (For material 'E', S.T. = 10 years.)

Table 23. Storage Costs for Material 'E'

E.O.Q.	M.X.L.	Storage costs £ Total	Per E.O.Q. unit
250	402	160·8	0·643
300	452	180·8	0·603
350	502	200·8	0·574
400	552	220·8	0·552
450	602	240·8	0·535
500	652	260·8	0·522
600	752	300·8	0·501
700	852	340·8	0·487
800	952	380·8	0·476
900	1,052	420·8	0·468
1,000	1,152	460·8	0·461
1,500	1,652	660·8	0·441
2,000	2,152	860·8	0·430

Table 24. Interest Charges and Deterioration Factor for 'E'

E.O.Q.	A.S.L.	A.T. (weeks)	Price £	Interest* per E.O.Q. unit £	Deterioration Factor
250	226	22·7	8·0	0·253	1·002
300	251	27·3	8·0	0·281	1·003
350	276	31·7	8·0	0·308	1·004
400	301	36·4	8·0	0·337	1·005
450	326	40·1	8·0	0·358	1·006
500	351	45·5	7·6	0·373	1·008
600	401	54·5	7·6	0·426	1·011
700	451	63·6	7·6	0·479	1·015
800	501	72·7	7·6	0·532	1·020
900	551	81·7	7·6	0·585	1·025
1,000	601	90·9	7·0	0·589	1·031
1,500	851	136·4	7·0	0·833	1·069
2,000	1,101	181·7	7·0	1·077	1·122

* The interest per E.O.Q. unit is obtained from the formula
$$\frac{A.S.L.}{E.O.Q.} \times \frac{A.T.}{52} \times \frac{8}{100} \times price$$

Table 25. Summary of Cost per Unit Purchased

E.O.Q.	Price £	Storage £	Interest £	Total £	Det. factor	Overall £
250	8·000	0·643	0·253	8·896	1·002	8·914
300	8·000	0·603	0·281	8·884	1·003	8·911
350	8·000	0·574	0·308	8·882	1·004	8·918
400	8·000	0·552	0·337	8·889	1·005	8·933
450	8·000	0·535	0·358	8·893	1·006	8·946
500	7·600	0·522	0·373	8·495	1·008	8·563
600	7·600	0·501	0·426	8·527	1·011	8·621
700	7·600	0·487	0·479	8·566	1·015	8·695
800	7·600	0·476	0·532	8·608	1·020	8·780
900	7·600	0·468	0·585	8·653	1·025	8·867
1,000	7·000	0·461	0·589	8·050	1·031	8·300
1,500	7·000	0·441	0·833	8·274	1·069	8·845
2,000	7·000	0·430	1·077	8·507	1·122	9·545

Thus, for material 'E' the E.O.Q. is 1,000 units since this gives the lowest overall cost per unit purchased.

Stock Control Record

The establishment of **control limits** will not of itself provide stock control. Control systems are designed to so regulate movements or activities that they conform to a pre-determined plan or pattern or policy which implies some form of corrective action being taken when deviations occur—whether the functioning of the system is manual, mechanical, or electronic. The actual situation must be reported and compared with the expected or desired situation; corrective action then following as necessary. A simple illustration of control can be seen in a 'temperature-controlled' room. When the desired temperature is reached this is *reported* to a thermostat control in the room; the actual temperature is compared with the pre-determined level; the thermostat activates a switch to cut off the supply of further heat; and *vice versa*. The introduction of stock control also demands these three features:

(a) The setting of norms, or limits, or policies: **setting phase.**
(b) A system of reporting actual results: **control phase.**
(c) Signals which initiate corrective action: **feedback phase.**

The control operation for stock is generally to be found in a stock record designed to record stock movements; to provide a comparison between actual and desired conditions; to initiate any necessary corrective action. The setting of the stock 'norms' has already been discussed above, namely M.N.L., M.X.L., R.O.L., and E.O.Q. The *actual* result for comparison with these norms is the balance in stock (or inventory) at any one time so that action may be taken to keep it within M.N.L. and M.X.L.

The Bin Card

It is quite common to find several stores records being kept simultaneously in many manufacturing businesses. First, there would be the storekeeper's record (customarily referred to as the **bin card**) which records the quantities only of stock receipts, issues, and balances together with some reference number relating to each transaction. It is commonly supposed that the bin card is always kept with the materials and up-dated by the stores-hand at the time of each transaction, but although true in many cases, it is more likely nowadays to be kept in the stores office and posted by a stores clerk. Many firms have now dispensed with this record as being superfluous, especially with the introduction of computers (or even punched cards) for recording stores movements.

The Stock Control Card

The other two records met in practice are the **stock control card** and the **stores ledger.** Modern practice eschews the avoidable duplication of records for any purpose, so that these two requirements are normally combined into a single comprehensive record. The stock control card (Fig. 37) is divided into two distinct parts. The left-hand side is used to record the physical movements of stores items; while the right-hand side contains control memoranda to complete the full picture of stocks. The details given at the head of Fig. 37 are those most likely to be needed in practice but each business adapts these

Stock Control Card

Location........................ **Stock Control Card** Folio ....
Title............................ Description................... Code No. ....
Unit............................ Max. Stock.................... Min. Stock.....................
Re-order level.................. Re-order Qty. ....Delivery Period.............

Received				Issued				Balance		Allocated			Free Blce. Qty.	Ordered		
Date	G.R. Note	Qty.	Price	Date	Job No.	Qty.	Price	Qty.	Price	Date	Job No.	Qty.		Date	Purch. Order	Qty.

Fig. 37. Stock control record

to its own requirements. Some companies may not need all these details, for example, 'location', while others may find it necessary to include additional information.

The Stores Ledger

The physical record shows the materials received into stock, the issues made from the stores, and the quantity retained in stock. The ledger section of the stock record is found in the price columns and, especially, under the physical balance. In practice, it is seldom necessary to extend the quantity and price on a day-to-day basis to show the **stock value**. This is rarely needed for other than the preparation of year-end accounts, but it is a simple enough exercise should it be required at any other time. For short-term accounts, it is usually sufficient to take opening stock plus purchases less issues to find the stock value.

A single record combining the stores ledger with the stock control record may lead to administrative difficulties when dealing with rival claims to maintain this record. On the one hand, stock control is part of the production control function which requires the stock record to be kept in the factory offices; while, on the other hand, the stores ledger is an accounting function. Experience does not support the view that only accounts clerks are capable of compiling accurate records; and so there does not seem to be any valid objection to the stores ledger being kept outside the accounts department as part of the stock control system.

The Control Memoranda

The recorded balance in stock is the **control figure** and provides the signal for control action, especially the issue of replenishment orders to the suppliers.

However, issues from stores are made against production orders; but there is normally a time-lag between the issue of a production order to the works and the commencement of manufacture. In jobbing production, especially, dependence on the physical balance may create problems of supply should orders in the 'pipe-line' require unusually large quantities of a certain item. The inclusion of the **allocation columns** on the stock control card permits the anticipation of issues in the near future and also the calculation of the **free balance** (that is, the physical quantity in stock for which there is not an early requirement in production).

Prudence suggests that the re-order signal should be taken on the free balance rather than on the physical balance, but this can be modified according to the length of the time-lag between the issue of a production order and the commencement of its manufacture. In capital goods industries there is sometimes a delay of several months before an order goes into production; in such situations, stocks are likely to be excessive if the allocations of stores materials are made at the outset. There are two possible ways of making allowance for lengthy time-lags in this context. These are to make the allocation either during the month preceding the expected start-date, or at a point in advance of the start date which is equal to the normal delivery period of the materials to be first issued.

The remaining section records the detail of replenishment orders outstanding and is wholly for memorandum purposes since it does not affect any other item. The simplest treatment of this data is to enter details of orders placed with suppliers and *cross out* the information as deliveries are made. Some companies make these entries in pencil so that part-order deliveries can be easily dealt with by erasing the original quantity and inserting the new balance outstanding.

Perpetual Inventory System

A stores inventory may be defined as a detailed list of all the items held in the stores at any one time. Such a list may be compiled by **taking stock** (a physical count) or by **balancing-off** all the accounts in the stores ledger and then listing these balances to provide the inventory. If it is assumed that the second course is adopted, then it becomes possible to re-define the stores inventory (in this context) as *the detailed list of balances contained in the stores ledger*. Effective stock control requires inventory data to be available on a day-to-day basis and this has led to the balance in stock of each item being recorded after each receipt or issue is made. In this way the stock balance (or inventory) is continuously maintained up to date and the practice has become known as the **perpetual inventory system**. Students should take careful note that all that is required for the operation of the perpetual inventory system is that the stock balance is recorded after each movement of material into or out of stores—nothing more and nothing less. The reporting of stock balances is an essential part of materials control and the perpetual inventory system thus becomes a major feature of the stock control record.

Stock Discrepancies

Many discrepancies may arise in stock recording or in counting issue quantities or in placing receipts in the various storage positions and so on, so that the **recorded stock balance** differs from the **physical stock balance** from time to time. The causes of stock descrepancies fall into three distinct groups:

(*a*) **Clerical errors**
    (i) *Miscalculating* issue, receipt, or balance quantities.
    (ii) *Omitting* to record transactions on the record card.
    (iii) Posting transactions to the *wrong* record card.
    (iv) *Loss of documents* such as requisitions and goods received notes.
(*b*) **Physical errors**
    (i) *Short or over issues* relative to the requisition.
    (ii) Placing items in the *wrong storage* position.
    (iii) Issue of unreported *alternatives or substitutes*.
(*c*) **Physical losses**
    (i) Breaking bulk (or the 'turn of the scales').
    (ii) Shrinkage, evaporation, and deterioration.
    (iii) Breakages and pilferage.

Clearly, the benefits of stock control will be vitiated where the inventory figure is unreliable, therefore, the control must be extended to embrace the **verification of feedback data**. In this context it requires a reconciliation between the recorded stock and the physical stock with an investigation into the causes of discrepancies so that the controllable losses may be eliminated.

Continuous Stocktaking

The traditional custom of an annual stocktaking is too infrequent for modern requirements. Over the period of twelve months a considerable number of discrepancies can arise, and the length of time between successive checks in itself increases the difficulties of investigation into the causes of these discrepancies. Needless to say, this in turn will inevitably exacerbate the problems of stock control. Modern practice leans towards a system of **continuous stocktaking** (also known as **stores audit**). Under this method some of the items held in stock are checked each day, for example, a daily check of one per cent of all items will mean that the whole stores is checked through about two and a half times each year on average; a two per cent daily check will give an average of five checks per annum for all items (approximately once every ten weeks). The daily selection of items for checking should be done entirely at random. For this purpose, a **table of random numbers** will be invaluable in ensuring perfect randomness as well as making the selection an easier task.

Stores Audit Responsibility

The organization of a stores audit requires careful preparation and a detailed consideration of the stores environmental factors. The 'auditors' should prepare a daily report of their check indicating the stock differences revealed and, where possible, the causes of the discrepancies. A suitable form for this purpose is illustrated in Fig. 38. The audit team should be quite independent of the stores and of the stock control. Otherwise, where a single executive has responsibility for both the audit and the stock function, there may be a tendency to conceal the discrepancies revealed. Nevertheless, there can be no universal rule on where the responsibility *should* lie as this depends on the administrative structure of the company concerned. Where an internal

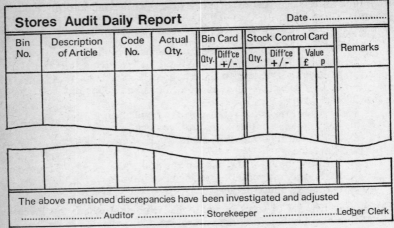

Stores Audit Daily Report									Date ....
Bin No.	Description of Article	Code No.	Actual Qty.	Bin Card		Stock Control Card			Remarks
				Qty.	Diff'ce +/-	Qty.	Diff'ce +/-	Value £　p	

The above mentioned discrepancies have been investigated and adjusted
.... Auditor .... Storekeeper ....Ledger Clerk

Fig. 38. Stores audit report

audit department exists, it would be natural for the stores audit to be one of its activities. Alternatively, it may be undertaken by the cost department which has a clear interest in the reliability of stores records; or by the organization and methods section, which is concerned with the proper functioning of systems as well as with their design.

System Audit

The opportunity should be taken to extend the scope of the stores audit beyond stocktaking. The checkers' terms of reference should be defined to include a re-appraisal of the 'control limits' on which they should make recommendations for their revision if deemed desirable. Stores movements are part of the dynamic business situation and from time to time the maximum and minimum stock levels will call for modifications to be made, as indeed will the re-order level. Effective control demands that this review is undertaken as a regular exercise and common sense indicates that continuous stocktaking provides the opportunity. In every progressive business there will be items held in stock which have become obsolete as a result of modified designs, introduction of new materials, or changes in consumer demand. The continued storage of obsolete items is a waste of space, money, time, and effort; thus the stores auditors should also report all slow-moving and idle stocks so that redundant items can be disposed of.

Stores Audit Frequency

The frequency of checking is a matter of management policy but it is suggested that an average of one per cent daily is a desirable minimum. More frequent checking of items will yield improved benefits in control through the early disclosure of weaknesses, but is more expensive to operate. A balance needs to be struck between improved information and higher costs. In this context it should be noted that each item does not require equality of treatment: slow moving stocks could be checked less often than the average, whereas items with a high rate of turnover demand a more frequent checking.

Furthermore, low value items could be safely left for longer intervals than would be prudent for expensive materials. The daily average of (say) one per cent thus needs to be adjusted for its application to individual items of stock by allowing for both their rate of usage and their value.

The Audit Frequency Formula

In practice, the frequency at which individual items will be checked is determined by any one of a number of methods ranging from the purely arbitrary (informal judgement) to the application of a complex scientifically derived formula. The following method is given as an illustration of the weighting given to stock items by allowing for the rate of turnover and stock value within the context of the desired overall checking frequency. It is certainly not intended to imply that this is the only possible method, let alone the most suitable under all conditions. The individual checking frequencies are derived from the formula:

$$f = {}^{p}\sqrt{(2TV)}$$

where f = the number of times per year that the item should be scrutinized by the stores audit clerks;

T = the annual rate of turnover of the stock item;

V = the average stock value of the item as a ratio of the overall average stock value per item;

p = the reciprocal of the daily average frequency of checking for twenty days (assuming 250 days p.a.).

Daily check	1% (0·010)	1½% (0·015)	2% (0·020)	2½% (0·025)
p =	5·00	3·33	2·50	2·00

Illustration

The following five items are included in a manufacturer's raw materials store where the average stock value is £250 for each separate item stored. (This average value relates to the average quantity held in stock for all items—not to unit prices.)

Table 26. Calculation of Stock Audit Frequencies

Stock item	Average value £	Rate of turnover	Value factor	2TV	f 0·010	0·015	f 0·020	f 0·025
'A'	50	6	0·2	2·4	1·19	1·30	1·42	1·55
'B'	200	1	0·8	1·6	1·10	1·15	1·20	1·26
'C'	500	12	2·0	48·0	2·17	3·20	4·71	6·93
'D'	1,000	3	4·0	24·0	1·89	2·60	3·56	4·90
'E'	5,000	8	20·0	320·0	3·17	5·65	10·00	17·89

Alternatively, f may be expressed in weeks as an interval between successive checks in the following manner for a fifty-week year:

Stock item	f 0·010	f 0·015	f 0·020	f 0·025
'A'	42 weeks	38 weeks	35 weeks	32 weeks
'B'	45 weeks	43 weeks	41 weeks	39 weeks
'C'	23 weeks	16 weeks	11 weeks	7 weeks
'D'	26 weeks	19 weeks	14 weeks	10 weeks
'E'	16 weeks	9 weeks	5 weeks	3 weeks

For items with a low rate of turnover *and* a low value factor, f may have a value less than unity, but very near to it It should be accepted that **every** item in the stores will be checked at least **once** in each financial year, so that f will be presumed to have a minimum value of 1.

The ABC Plan

The ABC plan of selective stores control classifies all the stock items into one of three groups ('A', 'B', 'C') and establishes a separate system of control for each group. Group 'A' comprises all the more expensive materials, whereas group 'C' includes all the small value items. The dividing lines between groups are chosen arbitrarily, but a useful guide is that 'A' covers roughly the top fifty per cent of total stockholding turnover value and 'C' comprises the top fifty per cent of the turnover in units. The procedure is demonstrated in the following simple example.

Stock code	Annual usage (units)	Unit costs £	Annual turnover £
201	1,400	20·00	28,000
202	25,000	0·90	22,500
203	3,000	11·80	35,400
204	6,500	0·80	5,200
205	600	68·00	40,800
206	4,000	3·00	12,000
207	10,000	0·22	2,200
208	500	57·60	28,800
209	10,000	1·75	17,500
210	40,000	0·19	7,600
	100,000		200,000

The first step is to array the data in descending order of turnover. At the same time expressing the individual turnover figures as a percentage of the total turnover and the individual usage figures expressed as a percentage of the total usage.

Stock code	Units	Units %	Turnover	Turnover %
205	600	0·6	40,800	20·4
203	3,000	3·0	35,400	17·7
208	500	0·5	28,800	14·4
201	1,400	1·4	28,000	14·0
202	25,000	25·0	22,500	11·25
209	10,000	10·0	17,500	8·75
206	4,000	4·0	12,000	6·0
210	40,000	40·0	7,600	3·8
204	6,500	6·5	5,200	2·6
207	10,000	10·0	2,200	1·1

The first three items cumulatively represent 52·5 per cent of the turnover but only 4·1 per cent of the physical usage and would form group 'A'. The last three items in aggregate represent only 7·5 per cent of the turnover, but 56·5 per cent of the physical usage and would form group 'C'. The remaining four items then comprise group 'B' and represent 40·4 per cent of physical usage and 40 per cent of the turnover.

Group 'A' Materials

The items in group 'A' are very closely controlled through carefully set *control limits* which are regularly reviewed. The E.O.Q. for each item will also be scientifically determined after considering all the relevant factors. Group 'A' items are also subject to frequent stores audit—say, within an overall daily check averaging at least two and a half per cent of all the items in the group.

Group 'B' Materials

Control of 'B' items is exercised through the establishment of E.O.Q., together with a safe re-order level for each stock item. The stores audit would check group 'B' materials at an overall daily average of one and a half to two per cent of all items in the group.

Group 'C' Materials

The simplest physical controls are introduced for group 'C' items and subject to about 0·5 per cent daily check. Stock levels may be controlled through the **two-bin system** under which new deliveries of materials are divided into two parts. The first part is the quantity equal to the re-order level and is sealed or locked away or separately wrapped. The balance is the second part and is made available for issue on demand. When the 'open' stock has been issued, the second part becomes available for issue and a replacement order is sent to the supplier. The **two-bin system** enables the business to dispense with the stock record, but it will still be necessary to maintain the *stock ledger account* for each item. Ordering supplies of high-usage, low-value materials will frequently be done on the basis of annual contracts which require the suppliers to make regular deliveries of materials on a monthly or weekly basis. The period's delivery being equal to the period's average budgeted usage, consequently there may be no need to establish either an E.O.Q. or a re-order level.

Annual Stocktaking

Traditions die hard, so it is not really surprising that there are still many businesses where the annual stocktaking is a normal feature. Naturally, those businesses, which for one reason or another have not introduced a system of continuous stocktaking, will be obliged to undertake this annual exercise; but there are many businesses with reliable systems of stores audit which still cling to this year-end 'spring clean'. The cost of mounting a full physical stocktaking is very high in terms of the numbers of personnel involved, the great volume of paperwork and calculating required, and in most circumstances the two or three days of lost production whilst the check is being made, unless it can be done during a holiday period shut-down. The size and complexity of a full stocktaking demands careful planning and control if it is to be done in the most efficient and economical manner.

Preparation for Stocktaking

Initially, it must be the overall responsibility of a single official, usually the accountant, to ensure a properly co-ordinated and comprehensive programme which avoids duplication and overlapping. The broad picture must be considered in detail so that individual work loads can be assessed as a basis for estimating the number of personnel required for all the various tasks. Small teams of two, three, or four men may be necessary for dealing with some items, and it may be prudent for the checkers to work in pairs, at least, so that they provide a check on each other's work. Some days before the actual stocktaking is done, it is essential to hold a briefing conference for all participants and to issue printed detailed instructions of their tasks. A briefing conference has the benefit of informing everyone of the overall strategy as well as explaining each individual's contribution to the corporate effort. It is also an opportunity for the 'controller' to satisfy himself that every participant understands his own instructions and to answer any remaining doubts or difficulties.

Stock Recording

During the stocktaking every single item in the raw materials stores, work in progress, and finished stock must be counted, weighed, or measured to determine the physical quantity on hand. This quantity must then be recorded on the stock sheets together with a full description, including any relevant code numbers or other references, of the materials concerned. All the stock sheets should be prepared in advance of the stocktaking, including the entry of the appropriate particulars with the sole exceptions of the quantity and the price. This practice achieves considerable economy of time for the checkers, who are then required to enter only the quantity for each item. It should also result in a neater and more legible document as stocktakers are frequently recruited from amongst manual workers rather than the clerical staff. As stock sheets are completed by the checkers, they should be forwarded to the accounts department for pricing and extension to maintain a steady work-flow. The controller should give careful attention to the inclusion in the stock sheet of items stored in the open or with sub-contractors and to the exclusion of customer's materials.

Conclusion

Materials control is a necessary requirement in all businesses to avoid the risk of quite substantial losses which is inherent in holding stocks. Throughout this chapter the controls have been related to stocks of raw materials and other production materials, but apply equally to the holding of finished goods against the acceptance of customers' orders. **Inventory control** is achieved through the application of the **planning principle** to the setting of control limits and a **study of costs** in the determination of the economic order quantity. The controls devised are then supported by the stores audit which checks both the physical balances and the functioning of the control system itself. In this way a comprehensive system of control is established which satisfies the two fundamental criteria of limiting investment in stocks while holding adequate supplies for normal requirements.

Exercises

1. To determine the optimum inventory level it is necessary to compare the costs of holding the inventory with the cost of ordering and setting up production facilities. Give examples of the types of costs which can fall under each category and the problems likely to arise in determining these.   [A.C.A.]

2. As cost accountant of a manufacturing concern of medium size, you have proposed to the directors that the stores control system should be improved. Your proposals are to be discussed by the directors at their next board meeting. To enable them to appreciate the basic requirements of an up-to-date system the directors have asked you to present a report concentrating on certain definite aspects.

Prepare a report to the directors dealing particularly with the following:

(a) the steps to be taken to introduce maximum, minimum and re-order stock levels, enumerating the factors to be considered in setting each level and stating the advantages to be gained by their use;

(b) the importance of stores turnover as a measure in considering requirements for working capital. [C.M.A.]

3. It has been suggested that when money tied up in stocks is going down, there is satisfactory stock control—give your views. [C.A.A.]

4. (a). There may be a danger that stores requisitions do not give a clear description of what is required or that the storekeeper may wrongly identify an item. As a result incorrect materials or parts may be issued, with consequent delay in production. Also there is the danger that the wrong account in the stores ledger may be credited.

Set out the essential features of a stores accounting system which would help to overcome these difficulties.

(b) What is meant by the terms 'perpetual inventory' and 'continuous stock-taking'? [A.C.A.]

5. Kingmakers Limited is a medium-sized jobbing business in the engineering industry. The company uses a wide range of raw materials which are retained in stock as well as many 'special' materials for particular jobs. Many of the orders require sub-assemblies which can be made from standard components although it is sometimes necessary to buy 'special' components. The company operates two separate stores—one for raw materials and the other for components. In addition, there is a tool store for moulds, dies, patterns, and so on.

Required:

Describe carefully a suitable system of stores control which will ensure a satisfactory level of stocks to avoid production delays but which, at the same time, minimizes investment in stocks. [C.A.A.]

6. The physical stock of material D.7 is different from the quantity shown as stock on the bin card and also that shown as stock in the stock ledger account.

You are required to: (a) give possible reasons as to how the differences may have been caused; and (b) describe how you would deal with such differences in the stock ledger accounts and how you would correct the bin card. [C.M.A.]

7. Describe *fully* the organization and procedures required to undertake a complete physical stocktaking for a large manufacturer of durable consumer goods. Your answer should include the necessary documentation and specimen forms may be included where appropriate. [C.A.A.]

8. The following information is available in respect of component D20:

	Maximum	Minimum
Stock level:	8,400 units	
Budgeted consumption:	1,500 units per month	800 units per month
Estimated delivery period:	4 months	2 months

(a) You are required to calculate: (i) re-order level; (ii) re-order quantity.

(b) Define the re-order level. What factors must be considered in setting this level?

(c) Does the re-order quantity have an effect on the average stock level of a component? Support your answer with a suitable explanation. [C.M.A.]

CHAPTER FIFTEEN

BUDGETARY CONTROL

In Chapter One it was pointed out that 'management will tend to maximize profits (all other things being equal) within the limits and constraints of a given capacity, or given resources; a given economic environment; and a given business policy'. That is to say, that management seeks to optimize both the use of its resource inputs and the outputs derived from those same resources. Sufficient has also been said to demonstrate the complexity of the business environment with its many competing claims to scarce resources having alternate uses. Optimization (or even near optimization) is unlikely to be reached without some very careful consideration of the multi-variate factors involved. Also, optimizing each individual decision will not necessarily result in an overall optimization on a company basis. For example, the marketing optimum will probably conflict with the production optimum, so that attempts to optimize each independently of the other will invariably result in the frustration of both.

Optimum performance depends on an appraisal of both inputs and outputs; an appreciation of the interaction and the interdependence of all activities; and the establishment of a corporate policy linked to a recognition of the responsibilities of individual managers. Profit optimization is achieved only by the properly planned use of available resources when the different activities are efficiently co-ordinated and the various decisions are policy oriented or controlled. Indeed, these are the generally recognized **objectives of budgets** —planning, co-ordination, control.

The Budget Concept

In the *I.C.M.A. Terminology* a **budget** is defined as:

A financial and/or quantitative statement, prepared and approved prior to a defined period of time, of the policy to be pursued during that period for the purpose of attaining a given objective.

Budgeting is a familiar activity to each of us in our private lives as well as in business, government, and voluntary groups. Common sense suggests that we are better able to maximize our satisfaction by considering available alternatives, future opportunities, potential hazards, and targets or aspirations before making our decision or choice. The simplest domestic budget calls for **planning and forecasting** (for example, saving for an annual holiday, or for a new motor, or for major clothing items). **Co-ordination** of the various domestic activities is also needed to avoid overlapping or waste—the right hand should know what the left hand is doing. Finally, **control** (or self-discipline) is needed to keep to the agreed policy for the family finances— extravagance on clothing may mean spending less on food. Careful and sensible domestic budgeting optimizes total satisfaction.

The Business Environment

In business the choices are much more difficult and the outcomes far less certain. Nevertheless, a budget should always be a realistic expectation and not merely a pious hope. Just as it would be foolish for the average person to budget for a luxury yacht, so it would be absurd for a manufacturer to budget for what he cannot make or to produce what he cannot sell. In forecasting future profits it is essential to use realistic values for the inputs and the outputs. Intelligent budgeting requires executives to carefully consider their roles and problems within the future defined period of time. They must accept the discipline of a rigorous analysis of their past performance to be combined with a forecast of the probable influences on the business in the future. They must also recognize the probable consequences for their own activities of the decisions being made in other sectors of the company and hence the need for co-operation and co-ordination.

The Planning Objective

The *planning* aspect of budgeting first-of-all enables management to determine those policies needed to achieve the desired goals. A knowledge of the costs of the resource inputs together with the predicted incomes forms the basis for profit forecasting. This will, of course, depend on planned output levels and product mix which in turn are dependent upon the cost/income behaviour patterns. Adjustments to output mix or output quantities will induce changes in planned profit performance, and a knowledge of cost/income behaviour enables management to determine the optimum within the expected constraints.

Resource Availability

Planning sales and production compels a consideration of the availability of the required resources. This is particularly true for raw materials, supplies, and labour which must be purchased and made available when required for production. It also calls for a close look at stocks and inventory models; labour recruitment and training; plant facilities and premises. Above all, budgets provide forecasts of **cash movements**—which is often the most critical area of business.

The fact that profits are expected from planned activities does not mean that there will naturally follow a correspondingly sustained net inflow of cash. Especially in the short run the most common problem facing growth industries is a lack of liquidity, despite high profits. This is partly due to the time-lag between paying for labour and raw materials consumed in production and receiving the cash flows generated by sales on credit. It is also influenced by the irregularity of many cash flows arising from differing periods of credit, from capital expenditures, and from varying lengths of the production cycles for differing products.

Problem Anticipation

The planning objective of budgeting thus enables management to anticipate future problems and difficulties and so take corrective action at an early stage. The company is better placed to arrange overdrafts or other forms of temporary finance when the need is anticipated instead of negotiating under the duress of an unexpected emergency. Similarly, an anticipated shortage of capacity or materials or labour may be avoided through seeking alternatives or substitutes. On the other hand, surplus resources such as cash, facilities, materials, or labour may be put to some other use.

The Co-ordinating Objective

It is essential to co-ordinate the disparate activities of a business if optimum performance is to become a realistic goal. Production and marketing activities must be co-ordinated for it is absurd to manufacture goods with little or no sales potential, however brilliant the quality or underlying technology may be. It is equally disastrous for the company to develop markets for goods beyond the capacity or skill of the production facilities. Again, it may be technically possible to manufacture a given product for which a ready market exists and yet be foolish to do so where production costs are high, but selling prices are so low that no profit is earned. Budgets stimulate co-ordination between these two major activities of a business and encourage the marketing function to promote the sales of what can be made whilst encouraging the production of what can be sold.

Subordinate Activities

To a lesser degree, budgets also lead to the co-ordination of the various subordinate activities in the different departments of the organization. Without this co-ordination, departmental managers may make decisions solely within the context of their particular responsibilities and this will frequently lead to unsatisfactory decisions from the corporate viewpoint. In any large organization the delegation of authority to subordinate managers requires a co-ordination of activities to ensure that corporate objectives are reached. Budgets do this by relating all decision-making to corporate profit performance.

The Control Objective

Setting budgets provides targets for managers against which actual performance can be measured, thus providing a management control system. In fact, although budgets are normally seen as an accounting control, the preparation of budgets is only the **setting phase** of a formal control system. Effective control from the use of budgets only follows from the addition of the **operating phase** and the **feedback phase** supported by corrective action where necessary. Budgetary control, therefore, demands rather more than the establishment of budgets—it requires that the budgets be *used*. In the *I.C.M.A. Terminology*:

Budgetary control is the establishment of budgets relating the responsibilities of executives to the requirements of a policy, and the continuous comparison of actual with budgeted results either to secure by individual action the objective of that policy or to provide a basis for its revision.

The effectiveness of budgetary control depends initially on the setting phase and, therefore, on the planning and co-ordinating objectives. Secondly, it rests on an efficient accounting system for recording actual results and comparing them with the budgets. Finally, it depends on the enthusiasm of management and the willingness of executives to correct unsatisfactory performances.

The Budget Committee

The responsibility for preparing the budget is usually given to a budget committee composed of representatives from the various major functions of the company. The exact membership of the budget committee varies widely in practice from one business to another, but some form of collective responsibility is desirable to ensure realistic planning, proper co-ordination, and effective control. In some companies the management committee will also function as the budget committee; sometimes the senior executives, forming the management committee, will nominate their respective deputies to form the budget committee as a management sub-committee; in smaller companies the budget committee may have an advisory (rather than executive) function with the decisions being made by the managing director and the accountant.

Preparation of the Budget
The Budget Officer

The administration of the budget is the responsibility of a budget officer (or budget director or budget accountant). His duties will include:

(1) Calling for budget estimates from each budget centre.
(2) Providing information on past performance to assist executives in preparing new budgets.
(3) Resolving any difficulties experienced by individual managers.
(4) Receiving and checking departmental budget estimates.
(5) Submitting budget estimates to the committee and discussing them collectively with the committee in preparing the master budget.
(6) Notifying departmental heads of any revisions to their estimates, resulting from committee action.
(7) Preparing and issuing variance analysis reports on a daily or weekly or monthly basis.
(8) Acting as co-ordinator for all budget activities.

Opinions differ as to the status of the budget officer within the organization. Some authorities argue that he should be responsible directly to the company's chief executive and independent of the accounting function. On the other hand, budgetary control is more usually recognized as an accounting function since it depends on accounting data. It is, therefore, more usual for the budget officer to be either the chief accountant or a senior accountant reporting directly to him, hence the common use of the title budget accountant.

The Budget Period

A budget refers to **a defined period of time**, and indeed it is impossible to prepare any budgets free from the constraint of time. Therefore, before any budget estimate is made, it is necessary to define the length of the budget period. In practice, different budgets may be prepared for differing periods. However, one year is a natural period as it spans a full seasonal cycle, and it also accords with the conventional accounting period for reporting to shareholders and for government taxation assessment. Initially, then, the budget period will coincide with the accounting year and annual budgets will be prepared.

Short-term Budgets

The annual budget is supplemented by budgets for shorter periods of, say, one month, or three months, or six months as necessary. The determining factor in deciding the length of these shorter periods will be the expected degree of variation in operating conditions. Cash flows might fluctuate considerably from one month to another through irregular receipts and payments. This is particularly noticeable in seasonal trades and especially when accompanied by unusual credit periods; for example, in marketing horticultural equipment all sales made after March 31 may be due for settlement on the first day of October following. Capital expenditure, sales of fixed assets, dividend payments, and investment interest are common examples of irregular cash flows. The importance of maintaining adequate cash balances demands that monthly cash budgets are prepared to supplement the annual one. The control function in budgets will normally require monthly (or four-weekly) budgets to be prepared so that adverse trends can be detected early and corrected promptly.

Long-term Budgets

Modern management has become increasingly aware of the need to look well ahead in business matters and to prepare long-term forecasts. This is particularly important in matters of capital expenditure for capital plans typically take several years to mature. Furthermore, the large sums involved for major capital projects call for an intelligent anticipation of the probable amounts and times if difficulties are to be avoided. Thus, the annual budgets are further supplemented by long-range forecasts of three to five years; and occasionally up to ten years or even longer. Long-term plans are not stated in the precise terms of annual budgets, but rather as probability statements of diminishing definition as the relevant time-scale is extended. (This topic is developed more fully in Chapter Twenty-one.)

Types of Budgets

Appropriation Budgets

In those cases where the effectiveness of an expense is difficult to measure, or the need for it is largely a matter of judgement, it is desirable to control such expenditure by deciding in advance just how much should be allowed. The purpose of an appropriation (or allowance) budget, therefore, is to establish an upper limit on expenditure for a given activity. Thus, the allowance is the **maximum which cannot be exceeded**. The Government's Budget and most local authority budgeting is an appropriation budget. Examples of appropriation budgets in industry and commerce are seen in capital expenditure, research and development, advertising and (sometimes) administration costs.

Fixed Budgets

The *I.C.M.A. Terminology* defines a fixed budget as one which is designed to remain unchanged irrespective of the output or turnover actually attained. The purpose of a fixed (or forecast) budget is to provide a basis for planning and for co-ordinating activities. As such it represents a forecast or plan which has been prepared in advance of the budget period to provide a fixed point of reference from which actual results can be measured. Fixed budgets are not *fixed* in the sense of being *unalterable*, or of setting a maximum expenditure level as in appropriation budgets, but rather that they cannot be adjusted for changes in volume or activity.

Fixed Budget Variances for Variable Costs

The problem of using fixed budgets arises with variable costs since they are activity related. This can be demonstrated by using a simple illustration.

A certain factory department manufactures a single product and the annual fixed budget for raw material is £24,000 (8,000 units at £3 each). Higher output levels give rise to adverse variances while lower outputs show favourable variances since actual expenditure fluctuates directly with output, all other things being equal.

Output (units)	Actual at £3 each £	Budget at £3 each £	Variance £	
6,000	18,000	24,000	6,000	(favourable)
7,000	21,000	24,000	3,000	(favourable)
8,000	24,000	24,000	—	
9,000	27,000	24,000	3,000	(adverse)
10,000	30,000	24,000	6,000	(adverse)

In reality, there are no variances at all in the above five cases since 6,000 units should only incur £18,000 expenditure; and so on for other activity levels. Suppose further that 7,000 units were manufactured by using materials costing £22,000. Compared with a fixed budget of £24,000 there is a favourable variance of £2,000 when in fact there has been over-spending of £1,000 for an output of 7,000 units. From the viewpoint of controlling subordinate managers, such variances are a nonsense and would speedily bring the whole system into disrepute.

Flexible Budgets

The effective control of variable costs is only attainable through flexible (or control) budgets where the actual expenditure can be compared with what the expense should be for the actual volume of activity experienced. In the *I.C.M.A. Terminology* **a flexible budget is one which, by recognizing the difference in behaviour between fixed and variable costs in relation to fluctuations in output or turnover, is designed to change appropriately with such fluctuations.** In other words, the purpose of flexible budgets is to provide a set of standards which can be used in the measurement of executive performance.

Forms of Flexible Budgets

Flexible budgets may be prepared in either of two forms. The columnar form (Fig. 39) is really a series of budgets which have been prepared for several different levels of activity. From this it is possible to obtain the budget (or expected) expenditure for any given level of activity. Where the actual activity falls between any two of the given output levels the budget is obtained by interpolation. For example, an activity level of 1,700 hours would have a total budget allowance of £485. An alternative form of flexible budget is seen in Fig. 40. If the actual activity in a given period was 8,600 hours, then the budget allowance would be obtained as follows:

Variable cost	$£6,800 \times \dfrac{8,600}{8,000} =$	7,310
Fixed cost	=	3,400
Budget allowance	=	£10,710

Therefore, the departmental expenses would be expected to rise by £510 because of the additional variable cost incurred by working an extra 600 hours.

Works Overhead Budget (4 weeks) Period..............................

Department.............................. Foreman..............................

Activity (Direct hours)	1000	1200	1400	1600	1800	2000	2200
Activity (% of capacity)	50%	60%	70%	80%	90%	100%	110%
Electrical power	60	72	84	96	108	120	132
Water rate	10	12	14	16	18	20	22
Consumable stores	15	15	18	18	21	21	24
Small tools	20	23	26	28	30	32	33
Internal transport	47	54	59	66	71	80	85
Shop clerks	45	48	51	54	57	60	65
Sweeping & cleaning	24	27	30	33	36	39	42
Oilers & beltmen	15	18	21	24	27	30	33
Totals:	£350	£395	£435	£470	£500	£525	£545

Fig. 39. Columnar flexible budget

Manufacturing Expense Budget Period..............................

Department.............................. Capacity..........8000 hrs..........

Foreman/Manager.............................. Activity..........80%..........

Expense item	Type of Expense	Variable £'000	Fixed £'000	Total £'000
Electrical power	V	1·25	—	1·25
Coal and fuel oil	SV	·75	·60	1·35
Insurance	SV	·30	·62	·92
Consumable stores	V	·12	—	·12
Indirect wages	SV	2·40	·60	3·00
Supervision salaries	F	—	·25	·25
Totals:		6·80	3·40	10·20

Fig. 40. Tabular flexible budget

Basic and Current Budgets

A **basic budget** is established for use unaltered over a long period of time. It may be either fixed or flexible in use, but the budget data are not up-dated as conditions change. Any revision of wage rates or materials price changes would not lead to changes in the basic budget. Changed conditions will immediately give rise to variances from the basic budget which consequently tend to obsure **operating variances**. For control purposes, therefore, it is necessary to isolate the operating variances by using current budgets. A **current budget**, on the other hand, is established for use over a short period of time and is related to current conditions. (This aspect is further discussed under standard costing in the following chapter.) The variances from a flexible current budget are, therefore, the really significant performance variances and provide the basis for an effective management control system.

Setting Budgets
Limiting Factors

It requires but little thought to recognize that there are limits to the setting of budgets. For example, the sales budget is restricted by the size of the market; plant capacity will limit the factory output; available capital controls the rate of expansion. In any business there may be several different limiting factors present at any one time, and each product may be subject to a different limiting factor from all the other products. Furthermore, the limiting factor is essentially a short-term phenomenon so that it changes from time to time for a particular product. There will always be a limiting factor of one kind or another—at one time it could be plant capacity which is overcome by buying additional plant; then a shortage of labour to operate the plant which is overcome by recruiting more workers; then the market becomes the limiting factor which may be overcome by advertising, and so on.

The Principal Budget Factor

Each function or department of the company will have its own limiting factor which must be given special consideration when establishing budgets. Since all the functional budgets are integrated into the master budget, they must be interdependent also. Therefore, the limiting factor in any one functional budget may become a limiting factor in other budgets too. It is for this reason that the preparation of the master budget usually requires revisions to the various functional budgets. Overall, there will be at any one time a single factor which limits several functional budgets or even the master budget. This is the factor known as the **principal budget factor**, and the extent of its influence must first be assessed to ensure that the functional budgets are reasonably capable of fulfilment.

However, having identified a principal budget factor (P.B.F.), it is not sufficient to simply accept it, for consideration must be given to extending the limiting factor. This is particularly important where there is a significant margin between the P.B.F. and all other limiting factors. For example, the product Newgeld is subject to the following limiting factors:

Market demand	16,000 units
Plant capacity	18,000 units
Skilled labour	15,000 units
Raw materials	5,000 units

In this instance the raw materials are the P.B.F. for Newgeld, but the gap between the P.B.F. and other limiting factors is so wide that strenuous efforts are required to improve the situation. Efforts need to be directed towards new sources of supply, a careful consideration of substitute materials and product design changes to reduce materials usage.

Staff Involvement

The primary responsibility for the preparation of budgets must rest with the managers or supervisors who will be expected to achieve them. Initially, each budget centre executive should be asked to prepare his budget since he will be familiar with all the operating conditions and aware of the local problems, pitfalls and strengths. Unfortunately, it is all too common in practice for budgets to be prepared by one or two key persons in the accounts department. Although the use of accounting data make this understandable, it is likely to undermine the effectiveness of budgeting. It is by no means unknown for the accounts staff to submit budget estimates direct to top management without any prior consultation with the operating executives concerned. Such thoughtless action generates considerable resentment and frustration amongst executives, who are expected to achieve performance objectives imposed by budgets developed by others. This will be particularly noticeable where they are unsympathetic to the budget plan and have had no opportunity to influence its development. It is unlikely that optimum results will be attained without the full involvement of those responsible for exercising budgetary control.

Confidentiality

It is essential that every member of the management team, from senior executives down to the shop-floor foremen, understands the budget as a prediction of his performance and accepts it as a realistic and attainable objective; recognizing it as aiding him in his managerial role and as a guide in his decision-making. This is not likely to be evident where the budget remains a carefully guarded secret in the accounts department for whatever reason. The most usual excuse for the non-disclosure of information is the preservation of confidentiality, or that it is likely to be misunderstood and so misused. Generally speaking, this is arrant nonsense! Misguided attempts to maintain confidentiality probably cause more trouble, frustration, misunderstanding, ill-feeling, and ruptured human relations than any other single factor—apart from the fact that usually it is totally unnecessary anyway. Everyone in an organization has something to contribute to the budgeting process. When budgeting is first introduced to a company, a foreman's lack of budget experience will make his contribution small. Consultation will earn his co-operation and, as the foreman becomes more familiar with budgeting, his contribution will increase accordingly.

Role of the Budget Committee

All that has been said about staff involvement in setting budgets does not imply that the budget committee has a purely nominal function. It is the responsibility of the budget committee to co-ordinate and integrate the preliminary departmental budgets into the corporate budget plan. This will often mean making modifications to individual forecasts and their reference back to the relevant executive for his comments before consolidation into the master budget. The preparation of budgets is essentially a team exercise and the best results are gained where everyone concerned is involved at all stages and kept fully informed throughout.

Functional Budgets

An organization consists of a wide spectrum of activities or functions for which budgets are prepared. The sectors for which individual budgets are prepared are known as budget centres and normally correspond to the management structure since budget responsibility is related to managerial responsibility. It follows, therefore, that there will be a whole hierarchy of budgets reflecting the organizational pattern of the business, starting with the major functions which are sub-divided down to departmental levels. A functional budget is one which comprises the income or expenditure appropriate to, or the responsibility of, a particular function.

The number of functional budgets will vary from one business to another, depending on its size, the product range, the manufacturing and marketing techniques, and the form of management structure adopted. Nevertheless it is usual to find the following principal functional budgets being prepared for the major areas of activity:

(1) The Marketing Budget
(2) The Manufacturing Budget
(3) The Administration Budget
(4) The Research and Development Budget
(5) The Capital Expenditure Budget
(6) The Cash Budget

The Marketing Budget

This is probably the most difficult budget to prepare because of the manifold uncertainties in marketing. It is usually also the most important major functional budget, as profits only accrue through sales and consequently all other activities are really subordinate to marketing. The marketing budget is subjected to a dual sub-division into areas of activity and responsibility. First, the marketing budget comprises the sales budget, the selling budget, and the distribution budget. Secondly, the marketing budget is sub-divided into functional budgets for each administrative section within the marketing area. For example, it is common practice to organize the marketing function into territories—each of which is a budget centre as the responsibility of the area manager. In the United Kingdom a company may establish eight such marketing territories on the following basis:

(1) South-east England
(2) South-west England
(3) Wales and West Midlands
(4) East Anglia and East Midlands
(5) North-west England
(6) North-east England
(7) Scotland
(8) Northern Ireland

The Marketing Budget Matrix

Each territory would have its own marketing budget which would be aggregated to form the company marketing budget. The individual territory budgets, however, will be sub-divided into their respective sales budget, selling budget, and distribution budget, thus providing a marketing budget matrix (Fig. 41). It is often helpful to prepare an analysis of the marketing budget by types of customer. The classification of customers would be by types of sales outlet such as retailers, wholesalers, manufacturers, public authorities, and so on. This is particularly important where special terms or discounts are offered to certain classes of customer and will often indicate desirable changes in marketing policy. An analysis by average order size will also be useful in showing the minimum order quantity that should be accepted to yield a profit.

Territory	Sales Budget	Selling Budget	Dist'n Budget
	£'000	£'000	£'000
South-east England	2,500	360	150
South-west England	1,250	200	120
Wales & West Midlands	2,100	310	100
East Anglia & East Midlands	1,400	220	120
North-west England	1,800	260	135
North-east England	650	100	60
Scotland	900	150	90
Northern Ireland	400	60	45
Totals:	11,000	1,660	820

Fig. 41. Marketing budget matrix

Sales Budget

The sales budget is derived from a forecast of the physical sales volume evaluated at anticipated selling prices. The best starting-point for sales prediction is usually past performance—not only the current year, but earlier years too for trend-spotting. Trends enable past performance to be extrapolated to predict future performance, but such trends need to be viewed in the context of changing conditions arising from both external and internal influences. External influences include general business conditions and state of the economy; governmental policies; the activities of competitors; changes in population, living standards, and buying habits and availability of material and labour. Internal influences on sales forecasting include new product development; plant capacities; sales promotion policies; revised marketing strategies; and the desired return on capital employed. Many companies rely on field estimates from salesman as a basis for the sales budget, which is still a useful basis provided that it is recognized that most salesmen tend to be optimistic in their expectation of future sales and allowances are made for probable external influences.

Selling Budget

The selling budget is a forecast of the activities, resources, and costs of sales promotion. It includes direct selling expenses such as salesmen's salaries, sales commission, travelling, and car expenses, and the cost of providing sales office facilities including rent and rates of premises, staff salaries, postage, and telephone. Advertising and publicity in its various forms in the different media is also part of the selling budget. This budget depends largely upon the sales budget and is, therefore, rather easier to prepare since all the difficult decisions will have been made in the sales forecasting.

Distribution Budget

This budget covers those activities involved in delivering the goods to the customers and comprises the expected costs of warehousing, packing, and transportation. Here again the budget is based on past experience up-dated by the sales budget for the period. It includes: the rent and rates of warehouses and distribution depots; wages paid to packers, warehousemen, and drivers; salaries paid to managers, foremen, and clerks; insurance of goods, premises, and vehicles; depreciation of buildings, vehicles, and equipment.

The Manufacturing Budget

This shows the quantity of products to be manufactured during the budget period and the budgeted costs of that output. Quite often it is merely the sales budget duly adjusted for changes in finished stock levels, although it is important to remember that the sales budget will have been influenced by the productive capacity of the factory. It cannot be over-stressed that the sales and production budgets must be properly balanced and co-ordinated. Like the marketing budget, the manufacturing budget will have a dual sub-analysis. The manufacturing budget is the summation of the production budget, the direct materials budget, the direct labour budget, the direct expenses budget, and the factory overhead budget. It is also sub-divided into the factory departmental budgets which are the control or responsibility budgets related to the various factory budget centres. Each departmental budget is in effect a **mini-manufacturing budget** covering the output, materials, labour, and overhead relevant to that budget centre.

Production Budget

This shows the physical units of products to be made during the budget period. Like other budgets, the annual production budget will be broken down into monthly (or four-weekly) budgets for control purposes. Jobbing businesses, and those where a high proportion of the output is made to customers' specifications, face considerable problems in scheduling future production unless orders are received well in advance of manufacturing. This can be a difficult problem, although most such firms find that the use of labour hours or machine hours instead of product units resolves the difficulty and facilitates the preparation of the production budget. In its turn, the production budget forms the basis of the other subordinate budgets within the manufacturing budget.

Direct Materials Budget

Derived from the production budget, the direct materials budget indicates the quantities and costs of the sundry materials needed to fulfil the forecast of output. In companies manufacturing standard products, use is made of bills of materials or of standard parts lists but, in jobbing situations, the direct materials budget will be rather more tentative. The monthly budgets for direct materials will also contribute to the purchase budget and the cash budget, emphasizing once again the interdependence of all budgeting activity. Also, the direct materials budget will be closely connected to the stock control routine for raw materials especially within the context of the minimum, maximum, and re-order stock levels.

Direct Labour Budget

Once the production budget is prepared it is a relatively easy task to draft the direct labour budget, whether in a jobbing business or a repetition industry. The production control or works planning department will have compiled standard operation schedules detailing the types of machine, grade of labour, rates of pay, and allowed time for each task. With the aid of these, it is easy to convert the production budget into a direct labour budget for each factory department and then for the factory as a whole. The direct labour budget also contributes in its turn to the cash budget.

Direct Expenses Budget

The forecasting of direct expenses, too, is easily done from the production budget. The direct expenses budget involves cash expenditure and in its turn will be included in the cash budget.

Factory Overhead Budget

The preparation of any expense budget should be based on the principle that every item of expenditure is chargeable to one budget centre or another so that the manager, supervisor, or foreman of the department can be held responsible for all incurred expenditure. This is particularly true for all overhead expense. The preparation of the overhead budget will, therefore, be compiled by budget centres rather than by types of expense for the factory as a whole. Here, too, is an ideal opportunity for staff participation in the setting of budgets. The most satisfactory method of setting factory overhead budgets is to provide each departmental supervisor with his production (or output) budget from which he will be asked to prepare an estimate of his overhead expenditure.

Cost Department Co-operation. The foreman will need the active help and co-operation of the cost department to tell him the levels of expenditure in previous periods, the degree of costs variability and the probable cost movements in the budget period. He also requires assistance from the cost department in preparing the monthly control budgets. It is vitally important that the role of the cost department in preparing departmental overhead budgets is recognized as being **advisory** and not one of imposing in some subtle manner the accountant's idea of what the budget should be. This requires considerable tact and discretion, coupled with a full appreciation of the foreman's position and needs. After all, it is the foreman's budget, it is his performance control, and it is designed to help him to perform his job more effectively. When the foreman sees the budget as his own estimate he is much more likely to accept it as a desirable goal and strive to achieve it.

Service Departments. What has been said of factory overhead budgets relates specifically to the production departments, but it is equally valid for the various service departments. There may be some difficulty in agreeing the 'output' levels for services, but past experience linked to the production budget usually enables satisfactory estimates to be made. Once the 'output' is agreed the budget preparation follows the same procedure as for production departments with the head of department preparing his own estimates in consultation with the cost department and the budget accountant.

The Administration Budget

Generally, this is one of the easiest of budgets to prepare. There is seldom any of the complications from cost variability and activity changes found in preparing other budgets. Administration costs are fixed in character and established for a given capacity or activity level. Consequently, administration budgets are invariably fixed-type budgets and frequently appropriation (or allowance) budgets.

The Research and Development Budget

The importance of this budget depends on the scale of research activity within the company, but in companies with advanced technologies, or in highly competitive industries, the expenditure on research may be very significant. The problems in accounting for research and development expenditure were fully discussed in Chapter Twelve and the budgeting for research is considered within the context of that chapter. The cost accounts contain the records of past expenditure on research, which provide the basis for estimating expenditure in the next budget period. Estimating **research output** is clearly an acute problem, but the experience of the research director will be invaluable in this respect. As an appropriation-type budget, the total allowed expenditure provides a useful limitation which aids the budget preparation. One of the important advantages in budgeting for research and development comes from the planning objective. The research director is compelled to consider his next year's activities and to formulate a balanced programme of work which is likely to yield the maximum contribution to the company's profitability. In a large organization there are several budget centres for which individual budgets are prepared and here too the annual budget will be sub-divided into the monthly control budgets.

The Capital Expenditure Budget

The capital expenditure budget represents the expected expenditure on fixed assets during the budget period and is one of the most important areas of management decision-making. The funds available for capital expenditure are necessarily limited, even though very large sums are involved, and considerable care is needed to ensure that funds are invested in only the more profitable projects. Another important aspect of capital expenditure is that it usually represents a long-term commitment, the benefits of which accrue over an extended period of time. For this reason it is necessary to adopt a long-term approach of up to ten or more years. This topic is more fully developed in Chapters Twenty-two to Twenty-four.

Capital Expenditure Control

In most companies the board of directors authorizes capital expenditures by *appropriation* based on detailed submissions prepared by senior executives seeking the authority to purchase additional assets or to replace existing assets. The main control of capital investment arises in advance of the approval, but agreed expenditures appear in annual budgets and monthly budgets. This is particularly important for inclusion in the cash budget.

The Cash Budget

All budgets are related to the cash budget which is a forecast of the cash flows (or receipts and payments) for the budget period. The importance of preparing a cash forecast cannot be over-stressed for the availability of adequate cash resources is vital to successful business operation. Workers must be paid in cash; taxation liabilities must be settled in cash; suppliers may withhold materials unless paid promptly; and so on. In most cases a monthly cash budget will be found adequate as settlements between debtors and creditors are conventionally made at the end of each calendar month, but occasionally it may be desirable to prepare weekly or even daily cash forecasts.

Time-lag

The preparation of a cash budget is simply a matter of adding the budgeted revenue to the opening cash balance and deducting budgeted cash payments. However, in practice it is not quite so straightforward since the various functional budgets relate to **income and expenditure** while the cash budget summarizes receipts and payments. The difference arises, of course, from the time-lag induced by credit transactions and is further complicated by varying degrees of time-lag for different items of revenue or expenditure. The only satisfactory manner of dealing with this situation is to prepare a cash flow working sheet as a basis for the cash budget. The following problem illustrates the preparation of a cash flow working sheet.

Cash Flow Working Sheet

Problem situation: the Alpha Manufacturing Company Limited has prepared the following forecasts:

		Purchases						
Month	*Sales*	*Raw materials*	*Fuel and power*	*Other*	*Wages*	*Salaries*	*Direct expenses*	*Sundry expenses*
	£	£	£	£	£	£	£	£
July	29,800	14,400	1,305	2,050	3,124	2,010	426	1,876
August	24,600	13,800	1,050	1,860	2,800	1,830	414	1,828
September	27,000	14,400	780	2,020	3,128	1,950	432	1,952
October	32,400	13,500	840	2,250	2,860	1,805	405	1,810
November	36,000	12,600	1,020	2,400	3,550	2,280	378	1,822
December	40,500	15,900	1,035	2,700	3,520	2,430	480	1,960

Notes:

   (*a*) The anticipated cash balance at October 1 will be £5,000 overdrawn.

   (*b*) Eighty per cent of the debtors pay at the end of the month following that in which sales are invoiced, ten per cent pay at the end of two months and the remainder at the end of three months with the exception of one per cent of sales which are bad debts.

   (*c*) Fifty per cent of the raw materials are purchased from one supplier who allows two per cent cash discount for payment in the same month, and it is proposed to take advantage of this.

(*d*) Fuel and power costs are accumulated and paid at the end of every quarter beginning on April 1.

(*e*) All other suppliers of goods and services allow one month's credit.

(*f*) Included in the sundry expenses is a standing charge for depreciation of £1,000 per month.

(*g*) Wages are paid one week in arrears.

August and November are five-week months, the remainder are four weeks. Salaries are paid monthly at the end of the period to which they refer.

(*h*) New plant costing £50,000 is on order and a deposit of twenty per cent is payable on delivery. This delivery is expected during December.

Required:

A detailed cash budget in accordance with the above information in respect of the three months ending December 31. [C.A.A. adapted]

Solution: the cash flow working sheet has two columns for each month—one to record income and expenditure (that is, the raising of each transaction whether for cash or foɪ credit); and a second column for receipts and payments (that is, the entering of cash flows in the period in which they occur).

CASH FLOW WORKING SHEET

	August I & E £	August R & P £	September I & E £	September R & P £	October I & E £	October R & P £	November I & E £	November R & P £	December I & E £	December R & P £
Sales: July (£29,800)		23,640	2,980			2,682				
August	24,600			19,680		2,460		2,214		
September			27,000			21,600		2,700		2,430
October					32,400			25,920		3,240
November							36,000			28,800
TOTAL RECEIPTS:						26,742		30,834		34,470
Raw materials:										
50% (at 2% dis.)	6,900	6,762	7,200	7,056	6,750	6,615	6,300	6,174	7,950	7,791
50% (one month)	6,900	—	7,200	6,900	6,750	7,200	6,300	6,750	7,950	6,300
Fuel and power					840	—	1,020	—	1,035	2,895
Other purchases	1,860	—	2,020	1,860	2,250	2,020	2,400	2,250	2,700	2,400
Wages	2,800		3,128	2,906	2,860	2,927	3,550	3,555	3,520	3,350
Direct expenses	414		432	414	405	432	378	405	480	378
Salaries	1,830	1,830	1,950	1,950	1,805	1,805	2,280	2,280	2,430	2,430
Sundry expenses— excl. depreciation	828		952	828	810	952	822	810	960	822
Capital expenditure									10,000	10,000
TOTAL PAYMENTS:						21,951		22,224		36,366
Opening cash balance:						(5,000)		(209)		8,401
Monthly surplus/deficit:						4,791		8,610		(1,896)
Closing cash balance:						(209)		8,401		6,505

The cash budget is then obtained by taking the figures shown in the relevant receipts and payments columns—in this case for October, November, December.

The Master Budget

When the functional budgets have been prepared they are collated and summarized to provide a summary budget. From the summary budget a forecast can be prepared of the profit and loss account for the budget period, together with the closing balance sheet. These are considered by the board of directors and judged satisfactory or otherwise. Where the expected result fails to satisfy the directors, the whole plan will be reconsidered in seeking ways of improving performance such as changing the product mix, strengthening the sales force, and so on. Any amendment, of course, causes adjustments to the relevant forecast functional budgets and may call for considerable revision to be made. When the forecasts are finally approved they become the period budgets and the summary then becomes known as the master budget and incorporates the budgeted profit and loss account and the budgeted balance sheet. The master budget is an instrument of company policy and the functional budgets represent the sectional goals for the budget period.

Variance Reports

The head of each budget centre receives a monthly report of the performance of his department. This shows his budget for the month alongside the actual expenditures incurred for the period. The difference between the budget and actual is known as a variance which is **favourable** when giving rise to higher profits or **adverse** when reducing profits. Actual revenue which is greater than budget will be favourable, but actual expenditure which exceeds the budget is adverse. The significance of variances is that they indicate the extent to which the supervisor has made decisions which deviate from the budget. Cost variances, especially, indicate the effect on the company's profit performance generated by these departures from the agreed policy in the budget. The departmental variances are, therefore, a measure of the managerial effectiveness of that particular executive.

Significance of Variance

It is important to recognize that variances are to be expected and not seen as something rather undesirable. There is nothing magical about a budget (nor a standard cost) for it is simply an estimated forecast of future income or expenditure. As such it is like all predictions and subject to some margin of error, however small. Furthermore, it is essential to appreciate that actual operating conditions will probably be different from the forecast and the best decisions within the context of the actual situations may still give rise to unfavourable variances. This was the basis of the arguments advanced for adopting flexible rather than fixed budgets. It should be clearly explained to all managers that they are not to be condemned for any and every adverse variance, nor will they be necessarily applauded for a favourable variance. There must be an underlying reason for any variance, and the existence of a variance *per se* is of much less significance than the cause which is responsible for it.

Concluding Summary

Sound budgetary control does not consist of a slavish endeavour to meet the budgets under actual operating conditions. Managers should see the budget as a guide to those decisions which are likely to lead to optimum performance. The reporting of actual results and variances provides a measure of the manager's performance which initially indicates to him whether or not it is satisfactory and pinpoints those areas where he might find improvement.

The reports also aid senior management to assess the efficiency of subordinate managers, especially in calling for explanations of significant variances. The dual-control aspect of budgets, therefore, becomes apparent. Optimum profit performance should come from observing the budget which has been carefully planned and co-ordinated; managerial control is gained through the monthly reporting of variances.

Exercises

1. Your organization has decided to introduce a comprehensive system of budgetary control. As a first step it has been decided to form a budget committee, and you have been requested to prepare a report for your managing director on the functions of such a committee within the system of budgetary control and who should serve on it.
[A.C.A.]

2. It is necessary in evaluating alternative strategies for a business to be able to estimate accurately the cash flows which will take place as a result of each alternative. Only in this way can the strategies be appraised and compared.

You are required to explain:

(a) the role of the management accountant in the estimating of cash flows generally; and

(b) the responsibilities of the management accountant in particular with regard to the estimating of cash outflows for projects which call for an extension of the volume of production for existing products. [C.M.A.]

3. As financial controller you are responsible for the control of all administration costs. Your managing director states that he cannot see why the yardstick of standard costing and budgetary control should not be applied to routine office functions in the same fashion as they are applied on the shop floor. Draft a reply stating whether or not—with reasons—you consider they could be, illustrating your answer with hypothetical figures relative to one function of your own choice. [C.A.A.]

4. (a) Comment in detail on the factors you would observe and the steps you would take in constructing a budget for selling and distribution costs for a manufacturer of a widely distributed household durable product.

Set out your points in brief numbered notes.

(b) Arising from (a) what proposals can you make for setting standards to control these costs? [C.M.A.]

8. The sales budget for the AB Company was £1,032,000 for the year ending December 31, and was built up from the estimates of the sale of four different products as from below:

Products	Quantity	£
'A'	50,000	100,000
'B'	150,000	330,000
'C'	80,000	140,000
'D'	220,000	462,000
	500,000	£1,032,000

The actual results for the year were as follows:

Products	Quantity	£
'A'	60,000	115,000
'B'	140,000	308,000
'C'	80,000	120,000
'D'	140,000	294,000
'E'	80,000	160,000
	500,000	£997,000

From this information prepare a statement showing the company's budgeted and actual receipts and analysing the reasons for any unearned or decrease in income. Also prepare a short report to the management setting out any factors they should take into account when considering the statement. [A.C.A.]

6. Your company manufactures two products 'A' and 'B'. A forecast of the number of units to be sold in the first seven months of 1973 is given below:

	Product 'A'	Product 'B'
January	1,000	2,800
February	1,200	2,800
March	1,600	2,400
April	2,000	2,000
May	2,400	1,600
June	2,400	1,600
July	2,000	1,800

It is anticipated that:
(a) there will be no work in progress at the end of any month;
(b) finished units equal to half the sales for the next month will be in stock at the end of each month (including December 1972).

Budgeted production and production costs for the year ending December 31, 1973 are as follows:

	Product 'A'	Product 'B'
Production (units)	22,000	24,000
	£	£
Direct materials per unit	12·5	19·0
Direct wages per unit	4·5	7·0
Total factory overhead apportioned to each type of product	66,000	96,000

Prepare for the six months' period ending June 30, 1973, a production budget for each month and a summarized production cost budget. [C.M.A.]

7. You have been asked to prepare a cash forecast for the next four periods, each of four full weeks, commencing at the beginning of period No. 4, when the bank balance will be £25,000.

You have collected the following information to assist you:

Period (actual)	Sales £	Materials received £	Wages earned £	Expenses paid £
1	30,000	20,000	6,000	4,000
2	40,000	18,000	9,000	5,000
3	28,000	17,000	8,000	6,000
(Estimated)				
4	36,000	22,000	7,000	4,000
5	28,000	16,000	7,000	6,000
6	30,000	12,000	8,000	5,000
7	34,000	17,000	7,000	5,000
8	40,000	20,000	8,000	6,000

Notes:
(1) Cash is received for sales half in the month following sales and half in the second month following sales.
(2) Materials are paid for two months after being received.
(3) There is a week's waiting time in respect of wages at all times.
Prepare your cash forecast in a form suitable for presentation to management.
[C.A.A.]

CHAPTER SIXTEEN

SETTING STANDARD COSTS

Standard costing takes budgeting to its logical conclusion in the development of an effective system of control. Whilst many benefits will accrue to the use of budgetary control without standard costs, its full potential will be realized only when the budgets are set on standard costs. Standards are usually much more precise than budgets because they are more carefully determined and also because they relate to more clearly defined activities, such as the specific operations to be performed in a particular cost centre, as distinct from a budget centre which may embrace several cost centres performing many different operations. A standard cost is, therefore, a very carefully prepared estimate of the cost of performing a given operation under specified conditions. Having said that, however, there are considerable differences of opinion amongst accountants regarding the basis for setting standards.

Historical Basis of Standards

Cost is the product of quantity and price and standards must be set for both factors to give sensible standard costs. Standard prices or cost rates are easily obtained by up-dating current prices and estimating their magnitude in the next budget period. However, **different types of standard** may apply to the quantity or performance assessment. In the first place, a standard may be determined by **reference to past performance**. In using the experience of past performance for setting standards there are two possible datum points which can be used, either the *average* of historical results or the *best* (that is the lowest cost) individual past performance.

Average of Past Performance

When installing standard costing for the first time, many managements are wary of spending time and money on establishing 'theoretical' costs until they have had the opportunity to taste the fruits of this technique. A further reason, which is often advanced for setting standards on past performance, is a reluctance to wait while the long painstaking process of setting standards is gone through before receiving any benefits. In such cases as these, there is much to be said for setting the initial standards by reference to the averages of historical results.

Weaknesses of Past Averages. Apart from expediency, however, the use of past averages has nothing to recommend it as a standard for it requires but little thought to appreciate the weaknesses inherent in this practice. Firstly, the average may be distorted by unusual items and so be higher or lower than normal. This drawback can be mitigated to some extent through the use of statistical techniques such as standard deviation, the inter-quartile range, or even using the median or the mode instead of the arithmetic mean.

A further consideration of great importance is the length of production run as the average may have been calculated on varying runs which range from very small quantities to exceptionally large orders. In such circumstances as these, the incidence of **setting-up time** can be a potent factor in distorting averages. Where it is decided to establish standards on the average of past performance, then very great care must be exercised in computing the figure to be used if the standard is to be at all reasonable.

Best Historical Performance

There are two principal advantages accruing to this method as compared with the average of past performance. In the first place it is readily determined and requires no statistical manipulation. Secondly, it provides a goal to strive towards in order to repeat this best performance. Against this, however, it can be argued that even the best of past performances is not really a reliable point of reference and should be treated with caution for three reasons.

(1) It might not represent the best possible performance since opportunities may exist for still further improvement.
(2) This best historical performance could be the result of non-recurring influences or freak circumstances.
(3) It could also be the result of a faulty cost analysis at the time the best cost was prepared.

Apart from the manifold uncertainties which surround any record of historical cost, a standard founded on past performance is undesirable because it is concerned with historical conditions. Effective cost control is only possible when standards are determined within the context of present or expected circumstances.

Forecast Standards

Standards should represent not what costs are or have been, but what they **should be** within the prevailing conditions. Standards such as this can be compiled only after a sound technical analysis has been made of all the relevant factors. This is underlined by the I.C.M.A. publication *An Introduction to Budgetary Control, Standard Costing, Material Control and Production Control* which defines a standard cost as:

> **An estimated cost, prepared in advance of production or supply, correlating a technical specification of materials and labour to the prices and wage rates estimated for a selected period of time, with the addition of an apportionment of the overhead expenses estimated for the same period of time within a prescribed set of working conditions.**

The prescribed set of working conditions quoted in the definition is another area of controversy amongst accountants, although all are agreed that the term refers to the physical resources and facilities necessary for production and also to the level of operational activity which is to form the basis of the standard performance. The dispute arises from a consideration of three distinct environmental situations. **Ideal conditions, normal conditions,** and **expected conditions** which, respectively, give rise to ideal standards, normal standards, and expected standards.

Ideal Standards

Ideal standards are set at the highest performance that can be attained under the most favourable conditions possible. Such standards make no allowance for defective materials, accidents, operator fatigue, machine breakdown, external price movements, or any other undesirable and avoidable condition. The fact that it is virtually impossible to reach so high a degree of perfection renders the ideal standard beyond any possible attainment. Its purpose of encouraging an attempt to improve efficiency by striving after the high ideal is, therefore, really rather quixotic.

Disincentive of Ideal Standards. Because the ideal standard is impossible to reach, it always results in adverse variances and this cannot but have a demoralizing effect on all concerned as even the greatest efforts will ever fall short of the goal. The psychological effects of universal failure may deaden the will to strive and so stifle all efforts at cost control that there results a general falling off in efficiency with lower productivity. In any case, it would be unreasonable to hold any person as responsible for these variances since they result largely from assuming unrealistic conditions. Consequently, it follows that cost control is not really helped by setting ideal standards.

Normal Standards

The normal level of activity which forms the basis for setting normal standards is the **average activity** over the full period of a business cycle and so takes in booms and slumps. The primary objective behind the use of normal activity is to ensure the absorption of all fixed overhead throughout the cycle. During the same period it is thereby possible to indicate the effect of operating at activity levels which are above or below normal capacity. It is little use in practice, however, as it is inclined to be unrealistic for most of the time. Furthermore, the normal standard is of little value in achieving effective cost control as the variances inevitably include some portion resulting from working to other than normal capacity. It is difficult for the length of a business cycle to be estimated with any reasonable degree of accuracy and even more hazardous to forecast costs during that period so that confidence is weakened in such standards.

Expected Standards

An expected standard is one which represents what cost should be within the context of conditions as they really are. It acknowledges and accepts that there are certain ineradicable (at least for the time being) inefficiencies present in the organization and the use of expected standards takes into account these shortcomings, but it must be emphasized that the use of expected standards does not condone inefficiency where it can be improved. **The expected standard is an attainable goal** and recognized as such by all concerned, so it becomes an effective instrument of cost control as the variances of actual from standard reflect performances which are either better or poorer than anticipated. Each responsible official knows his target performance and recognizes that any variance represents a gain or loss which is the result of his actions; with the corollary that he can be expected to justify those decisions which have generated variances from standard. Needless to say, expected standards are by far the most common type of standards in use.

Revision of Standards

If the measurement of performance is to be satisfactory at various times, the standard must be consistent otherwise this will vitiate any comparison between the results of different periods—the word 'standard' itself implies constancy. However, to accept a standard or point of reference does not preclude for all time the possibility of amendment, but it does mean that each price movement or change in wage rates will not necessarily be reflected immediately in revised standards. It is true, of course, that a given standard cost may be outdated almost as soon as it is established as the result of external factors, and this begs the question of the length of time for which a standard should be maintained without revision. Amongst accountants there are two principal schools of thought regarding this problem.

Basic Standards

One group argues that standard costs should not be revised unless there is some alteration in the physical or performance standards. Such standards are known as **basic standards** and are intended to remain in force for long periods of time. The main advantage claimed for basic standards is that they reveal long-term trends in much the same way as does an index number. This is particularly so when the actual costs are expressed as a percentage of the standard cost. For example, a certain commodity may have had a standard price of £80 five years ago and in subsequent years the actual prices may have been respectively £84, £78, £86, £92. Then the ratio of actual to standard in each year is shown in Table 27.

Table. 27. Ratio of Actual Prices to the Basic Standard

Year	1	2	3	4	5
Price	£80	£84	£78	£86	£92
Ratio	100	105	$97\frac{1}{2}$	$107\frac{1}{2}$	115

The trend of price movements becomes apparent from a study of the above data and can be useful by extrapolation in forecasting the likely price level in years six and seven.

The use of basic standards does avoid the heavy work load which may be imposed by frequent revisions to standards. It is apparent, however, that as time goes by the basic standard will deviate more and more from current prices and performance. This will give rise to variances in which the controllable aspects are obscured by the changes in conditions. Nowadays, the introduction of new materials, changes in product design, increasing labour productivity, and improved manufacturing methods often make it desirable to revise the standards much earlier than is originally intended. For these reasons the use of basic standards is much less common in practice than is the use of current standards.

Current Standards

The second school of thought on standards revision contends that standards should reflect performances under prevailing conditions. Such standards, known as **current standards**, are intended to be representative of what costs should be in the existing circumstances. Since they relate to prevailing conditions, current standards are established for use over a short period of time—

usually not more than one year. There are some businesses, however, which revise their standards each time there is any change at all in one or other of the elements comprising the standard cost. Apart from the impossibility of registering trends, the great drawback to the use of current standards lies in the volume of clerical work involved in making frequent revisions to standards necessitated by changing conditions. Minor price movements may be ignored for a time to minimize this work, but sooner or later they must be incorporated into the standards. Alternatively, of course, it may be decided to revise the standards annually and when setting standards for a next year budget the possible price movements in that period should be anticipated.

From the point of view of controlling costs, especially at the shop-floor level, there can be little doubt that current standards will be more effective than basic standards. The foreman of a machine shop can in no way influence the purchase price of materials used in his department and consequently cannot be held responsible for variances arising from price changes. On the other hand, the difference between the current standard prices of standard and non-standard materials may well be his responsibility for using the non-standard material. Similar situations may arise with all the elements of cost and the use of current standard costs reveals these day-to-day decisions. Cost control, then, requires the use of current standards and their more widely practised application arises from this fact that current standards provide a realistic guide to operating efficiency.

Choice of Standards

The selection of one or another type of standard naturally depends on the intentions of the company in introducing standard costing. **Ideal standards** give the spur to strive for perfection, but the impossibility of attainment dulls any incentive in all except the most quixotic of persons. **Normal standards** allow an assessment to be made of the effects on costs and profits of working at differing levels of activity but tend to be rather unrealistic. **Expected standards** show what a cost should be so that the variances measure the efficiency of departmental operations and are essential for cost control.

Expected standards, by definition, must also be current standards and indeed if it were otherwise they would lose their effectiveness as a means of cost control. Ideal standards, too, can have no meaning unless they are current ideal standards. Basic standards purpose to disclose trends over long periods and at the time they are established they may be based on either ideal conditions or expected conditions. It is probably better to use expected conditions as the variances of actual costs under actual conditions will be more significant in disclosing trends.

Dual Standards

Some companies use ideal standards in conjunction with either normal or expected standards. Variances between the two standards can then be analysed to indicate how far further improvement in methods is possible. These **methods variances** indicate the extent to which profits are eroded by the use of less efficient methods of production and provide a measure of the effectiveness of, for example, the organization and methods department; or the production control function; or the company's capital expenditure policy; or the accident prevention officer, and so on. When used with other standards, ideal standards may be based on the most modern equipment and facilities which are obtainable, even though it is not considered to be economic to replace the present equipment. One large company using dual standards has adopted a second ideal standard which assumed that all known technological constraints have been overcome. This type of standard provides a goal for the company's research and development team in seeking new research opportunities.

Trend Variances. Basic standards may also be used together with current standards. In this way, long-term trends can be analysed while the advantages are gained of cost control in measuring the day-to-day efficiency of production. Indeed, many accountants contend that only in this way can the full benefits be experienced from using the technique of standard costing. Basic standards are converted to current standards through an analysis of variances resulting from 'uncontrollable' changes in standard cost rates such as wage awards or materials price movements; and from the introduction of new methods or revised materials specifications since setting the basic standard. These **trend variances** are valuable in forecasting future conditions and in evaluating the effect on costs and profits of external influences. They also provide an indication of the degree to which internal economies are offset by outside losses or supplemented by external gains. The variances of actual costs from the current standards are then available as a measure of the efficiency of the various operating activities within the undertaking for which individual

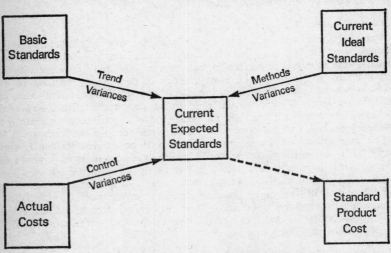

Fig. 42. Relationship of dual standards

members of the management team can be held responsible. The use of dual standards is illustrated diagrammatically in Fig. 42.

Introduction of Dual Standards. It is unlikely when first installing standard costs that a company will be interested in more than one type of standard and that one usually will be a current expected standard. As experience is gained in the operation of standard costing another standard may be added or, when the current expected standards are revised following price or wage rate changes, the original standards may be retained as basic standards. Then long-term trend variances can be analysed as well as the cost control variances. Ideal standards may be introduced at any time after the expected standards are in operation to yield methods research variances.

Motivational Aspects of Standards

It is implicit in the use of standards and budgets that they are expected to provide an incentive for managers and workers to control costs. Until very recently, industry has held the simplistic view of incentives, which is analogous to the donkey's stick or carrot, either negatively as punishments for failure to achieve targets or positively as rewards for achievement. Experience throughout history has shown the fallacy of the punishment approach to incentive, and there is ample evidence in industrial history that such an attitude from management is ultimately self-defeating. Nor has the reward approach been greatly successful because it has assumed that a monetary reward (wages) is the primary, or even sole, motivation for people to work. An effective appraisal of accountancy control systems shows them to be primarily of the 'punishment' type, for example, rebuke, demotion, or dismissal for failure to comply. This attitude is, however, modified to some extent by introducing rewards related to cost savings estimated from a study of cost behaviour.

Human Control Systems

Unfortunately, the mechanistic nature of accounting systems has tended to blind accountants to the human aspects of business. This is also the probable reason why so many accountants favour autocratic management styles. Nevertheless, it is becoming increasingly recognized by accountants that something more is needed than merely setting budgets or standards if effective control is to be found. No human control system can be truly effective unless those being controlled are willing to accept the standards of performance set for them. There is a need, therefore, to recognize the motivational aspects of performance standards and to consider the extent to which these standards are acceptable to the individual as the target towards which he will strive. A standard is much more likely to be met where a person accepts it as his own goal, whereas it is less probable that the standard will be reached where the individual has rejected it.

Conflicting Goals

In general, accounting control systems have emphasized the reactions of individuals to the setting phase and an insistence on consultation with individual managers regarding the items and amounts to be included in their budgets. 'Consultation' is often regarded as an opportunity to induce (willingly or reluctantly) the acceptance by subordinates of a management plan, rather than as the genuine participation of subordinates in the setting of standards. This has frequently meant standards being imposed on the criterion of 'what is best for all concerned'. As expected, this has led to conflicting goals for management and for individuals, often because the individual's reactions were ignored or not appreciated. However, there is unlikely to be any positive participation under an autocratic style of leadership. Nevertheless, it is common sense to create an environment in which the individual's goals are as consistent as possible with those set for him by management.

Behavioural Aspects

During the last twenty years, several studies have been undertaken (especially in the U.S.A.) to determine whether or not the use of budgets, or standards, leads to common goals for the worker and the supervisor. These studies have revealed conflicting goals and emphasized the mutal distrust between management and workers. They also tend to affirm the personality differences between individuals which induce different reactions to variations from standard—an incentive to one is a discouragement to another. This suggests the adoption of dual (or personal) standards and performance reports. It would be administratively possible, if difficult to do this, but it raises many questions not least being the potentially explosive one of equity and justice. So far our understanding of human behaviour within the working environment is very limited and much more intensive research is required before we can begin to formulate general solutions. The management accountant is ideally placed to aid further research in this area and add to the general body of knowledge on the behavioural aspects of accounting systems and control. In the meantime, accountants should be conscious of the problems of motivation and sensitive to the reactions of individuals to budgets and standards.

Setting Cost Standards

Cost is the product of quantity and price, hence there are two factors in each standard cost—the performance (or physical) standard and the price (or value) standard. **Performance standards** are technical specifications set principally by technical specialists such as engineers, chemists, metallurgists, designers, as well as by accountants. A carefully detailed study of the various activities in a business will often yield in itself considerable benefits to the company. Undertaking this exercise objectively, with a view to setting performance standards, more efficient and more economic ways of doing the same things will be discovered which reduce costs and improve profitability. Nevertheless, useful as such exercises must be in cost control by suggesting least-cost alternatives, standard costing is not a 'one-off' exercise but a continuing cost control in the daily operation of a business. It achieves this by evaluating managerial decisions through a comparison of actual performances against standard performance and the analysis into causes of any variances which arise.

Physical Standards for Direct Materials

The technical specification of materials embodies two characteristics—the description of the material itself including grade or quality and the quantity. These are frequently referred to as **engineering standards** or **design standards** when they originate in the design office of an engineering factory or as **laboratory standards** when they are established by the laboratory staff in a chemical works. Through consultation with all the technical people concerned the cost accountant sets quantity standards for materials, that is, the **input needed to obtain a given output**. Once performance standards are set they only require alteration when there is a modification to the specification or processing method. The standard quantity may be estimated through the following sources.

Schedule of Materials

This specifies all the materials and components which are required to make the product, grouped into assemblies and sub-assemblies. Some industries or products have only a small number of items as for example in brewing, whereas the manufacture of motor vehicles or machine tools use several hundred different items. It is desirable at this stage to critically consider the use or function of each item in the schedule, to conduct a **value analysis** by establishing the necessity for all the features of the various materials or parts, such as:

(1) Are six holding screws necessary, or would three be sufficient?

(2) Would mild steel be any less effective than stainless steel?

(3) Is painting necessary for a 'hidden' part of the product?

Drawings

It is necessary to study carefully all the drawings prepared by the design office to estimate the quantity of material to be found in the finished item. Certain parts, components, sub-assembles, or even main assemblies may be purchased, of course, from outside. In this situation, the standard material specification is the finished item itself.

Production Engineering

The production control department in consultation with the planning department decides **how** and **where** each item is to be made. Customarily this will entail several operations or processes for each item, each of which must be defined and detailed. (Further reference to this will be made under **labour standards**.) The nature of each operation largely determines the form of the raw material for processing at each stage of production and, especially, the type and quantity of materials losses occurring. It is necessary to consider the type of loss (e.g. scrap, waste, spoilage) in order to be able to estimate any **recovered cost** from the re-use or sale of scrap materials. The materials content of a product also includes the cost of containers or primary packing.

Estimating Materials Losses

Some allowances for materials losses are obtainable only through test runs or some form of sampling to determine the average weight of material in the product, such as glass jars or bottles. Many losses can be estimated with considerable accuracy, such as cutting, shearing, pressing, drilling, and turning. In these and similar operations there is a required amount of material to be removed in one way or another which can be easily calculated. Circles 'blanked' from steel strip will leave the corners; a slot $6 \times \frac{1}{4} \times \frac{1}{4}$ in. milled from a casting removes three-eighths of a cubic inch of metal; and so on.

Other losses arise from the method of processing as there are many instances where it is necessary to allow some material for holding in the machine. Examples of this include six inches, say, at the end of a steel bar which is the minimum that can be gripped in the chuck of an automatic lathe, or the 'shorts' left on the wire bobbins of a steel rope-making machine. Other materials losses may be caused by evaporation or friction. There may also be certain spoilage expected at the start of a production run known as 'imperfect trial pieces'. Spoilage is strictly controllable, but a defined level of spoilage may be acceptable as the least-cost alternative to a lower rate of output.

Standard Prices for Direct Materials

Raw materials and components purchased from outside the business will necessitate setting standard prices so that it is possible to isolate and evaluate the performance variances by eliminating the disturbing influence of external price changes. Price changes have relatively little significance for management as, being subject to external influences, they are virtually uncontrollable. It is sometimes suggested that they reflect buying efficiency, but as such they are a very imperfect measure for they are usually beyond the buyer's influence, let alone his control.

External Influences

In setting standard prices it is essential to consider all the various related factors which influence buying cost. The opportunity for trade discounts and quantity rebates has a significant influence on unit buying costs; as does the addition of the cost of carriage inwards. Cash discounts if available should always be taken and allowed for in the standard price. Some suppliers make a charge for the containers in which the goods are delivered, such as glass carboys for acids, but will usually allow full credit for those containers returned in good condition. All returnable containers should be returned to the suppliers and their value omitted from the standard price, although any carriage cost for their return is included as carriage inwards. Non-returnable containers may be *re-usable*, or their sale may *recover* part of the supplier's charge and some allowance for this can be made in the standard cost of the materials.

Forecast Purchase Prices

The standard prices may be based on current purchase values which has the merit of revealing significant price variances. However, it is desirable to revise the standard price whenever there is any change in the current purchase price. This is reasonable where the prices are generally stable, but absurd where prices fluctuate widely and frequently when it is more sensible to use the alternative basis of price-setting by adopting the forecast average price for the relevant budget period. This basis has the merit of requiring only annual revisions to standard prices, but the disadvantage of inducing continual price variances as the **average** is unlikely to be an **actual price** apart from the inherent risk in forecasting. Nevertheless, most companies find the forecast average price to be the easier basis to apply in practice.

Standard Operations for Direct Labour

The setting of labour performance standards involves two separate aspects: the specification of each separate manufacturing operation and the machine or process by which it should be performed; and the estimation of time required to perform each defined operation.

A study of the materials schedule, together with the relevant drawings, will indicate the various operations needed to produce the required products. This is essentially the responsibility of the production control department since its function includes *inter alia* planning the most suitable methods, machines, or processes for manufacturing. The production control department will prepare process charts or standard operation lists which specify the standard methods of production.

Operation Times

The basis for standard performance times is the standard hour. There are, however, differences of opinion amongst accountants regarding the definition of a standard hour. Some recognize it as being synonymous with the 'allowed time' under a premium bonus plan, particularly when standard costing is introduced into a factory where wage payment by results is well established. It is more satisfactory (and more widely used in practice) to define the standard hour as '*a hypothetical unit pre-established to represent the amount of work which should be performed in one hour at standard performance*' (*I.C.M.A. Terminology*). This usually relates to the average time, taken by an average worker, to perform a given task under standard conditions. In practice there are several different methods for obtaining the standard hour for each operation. They may be summarized into the following four categories.

Time and Method Study. This is undoubtedly the most reliable method of setting standard times for labour. It involves listing the elemental movements which are necessary to complete a given task or operation combined with a careful 'timing' by stop-watch. Allowances are made in the timing for fatigue, personal factors, tool care, ancillary activities, and so on. It is important to take account of any variations from time to time in the speed of the machine or track. In such cases, separate (or flexible) standards are needed which are related to the actual running speeds. The operation of time and method study is most commonly found where the operatives are remunerated by some form of wage incentive scheme, when the 'allowed times' for wages will provide the labour standards.

Average Past Performance. Surprisingly good results are often obtainable by this method provided that sufficient items are included to give a useful average and that any 'atypical' values are excluded from the calculations. Clearly, this can never be regarded as 'scientific' in the same sense as time and method study, but it can be quite reliable where there is a small standard deviation, say, a coefficient of variation of up to ten per cent.

Test Runs. Setting standards for new production runs must be done without the advantages of both time and method study and previous performances. The use of test runs for setting standards is better than nothing, but it has a serious weakness in the fact that the times taken by the early throughputs of a long production run are likely to be significantly higher than those of later throughputs. The use of standards necessarily implies a linear function but unit times assume a curvilinear function over a long production run (Fig. 43). The reason for this is that operatives **learn by repetition**—in other words, practice makes perfect. Thus, as the run continues, productivity steadily improves until it levels off at the optimum where it assumes a near-linear function. The standard time under such conditions must depend on the length of the production run and where practicable it may be desirable to use the learning curve to obtain the standard for the early batches. In other words, to use slacker standards during the 'learning' period and the levelled-off curve as standard when learning by repetition is complete. Depending upon the

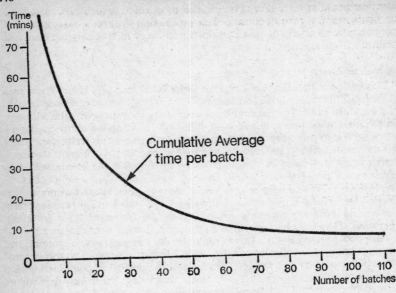

Fig. 43. The learning curve

intricacy and skill required by the operation, it may be possible with experience to estimate the learning curve for new runs.

Forecast Estimates. This method is particularly suitable for jobbing firms in capital goods industries where, by and large, such items are one-off orders with little possibility of a repeat order. Orders of this kind are normally gained through competitive tendering which calls for considerable preparatory work in estimating production costs as a basis for the quotation. Admittedly, cost estimating for tenders is frequently arbitrary and always influenced by marketing considerations, but the object of the exercise, however, is less to estimate the likely production cost than to find a basis for setting the contract price. Nevertheless, the need to set standards for cost control is often sufficient inducement for realistic cost estimates to be prepared which can then be adopted as standards. *In setting the contract price*, any further 'adjustments' made to the cost estimates are then irrelevant from the viewpoint of cost control considerations.

Standard Wage Rates

There are two aspects to be considered in setting standard wage rates—the type or grade of labour required to perform each operation; and the wage rate to be paid for this type or grade of work. Furthermore, the wage rate is influenced by the relevant method of remuneration. The responsibility for setting wage rates is usually a function of the production control department or one of its sections such as planning, time and method study, or ratefixing. Quite frequently (particularly in the smaller companies) it may be done by the cost department in consultation with the ratefixing or time and method study section. Occasionally, standard wage rates are determined by the personnel department on the basis of work-grading or job evaluation.

Time Rates

Where workers are remunerated on an hourly basis, the standard rate is that agreed as the rate for the job. In larger organizations there will be a comprehensive system of labour classification, whereby the various labour activities are assessed for skill and physical effort and grouped into grades for which an appropriate rate is paid. In smaller companies the system is usually less sophisticated and often involves setting personal rates for individuals or small groups of workers. Inevitably, this leads to a proliferation of different rates, many with quite small (and frequently unnecessary) differences. It may be desirable, therefore, to find a few 'typical' rates as standard; but this must give rise to rate variances for all the 'non-typical' actual rates. However, there will normally be only one grade of labour in any given cost centre which would be the standard rate for all operations in that cost centre.

Incentive Plans

Under piecework plans the standard rate is the piece price paid to operators. Usually, there will not be a rate variance and, in those cases where the piece-rate is the sole basis of the worker's earnings, there will be no labour efficiency variance either as the standard wages cost is determined by the number of units produced. Under premium bonus systems, the standard wage rate includes the time wages and the bonus earned at standard efficiency as determined by the standard hour.

Team Work

Certain tasks require the machine or process to be performed by more than one operator. The standard labour rate in such conditions may be a team, or aggregate, rate whereby all the hourly rates of the team or crew are added together to give a combined standard rate per (team) standard hour. The standard cost will then be the product of the standard rate and the team, or departmental, hours. Team standards make it possible to analyse labour-mix variances if desired, but it is arguable whether or not the additional knowledge of variances can justify the extra clerical work involved.

Factory Overhead Standards

The procedure in setting standards for the overhead of production department is precisely that already described in Chapter Seven for calculating the pre-determined overhead absorption rates. Separate rates must be established for each cost centre so that the forecast or budgeted expenditure of overhead needs to be allocated and apportioned amongst the relevant cost centres on one or other of the recognized bases of apportionment. It is essential to separate fixed overhead from variable overhead and to use flexible budgets for realistic and significant variance analysis. This means that *separate* absorption rates are absolutely essential for fixed and variable overhead. Some authorities have attempted to use a single combined overhead rate under flexible budgeting. This is unnecessary and, generally, confusing—and any accounting practice which confuses is bad accounting by any criterion: judged as a management information system it is utter nonsense. The standards (or budgeted) activity levels for the period are set for each cost centre and used to determine the standard overhead absorption rates.

Service Departments

Cost control in service departments was fully discussed in Chapter Eleven, where it was emphasized that a clear distinction must be made between the two aspects of factory services—the provision of the service and the use or consumption of the service. These two aspects must be reflected in the standards set since, for most factory services, there is a joint responsibility for control. The supplier department controls the provision of the service and the consumer department controls the use of the service.

This means forecasting the demand for each service by all the user departments and the estimated usage of services will then form part of the budget for each user department. The total forecast demand for each service forms the basis of that department's budgeted activity. It is then possible to estimate the cost of providing the service and to calculate the standard cost rate per unit of service provided. This will also be the rate at which user departments are charged for their consumption of the service. Factory services, too, have their own direct costs and overhead—a factor which must be considered in setting standards.

Commercial Activities

Standards for commercial activities (*see* Chapter Twelve) are based on budgets prepared for the relevant departments and cost centres. Standard cost rates are obtained from the budgeted cost, divided by the budgeted activity, for a given budget period. Setting standards for commercial activities demands a clear distinction between fixed and variable cost items and the use of flexible budgets. It is also essential to consider carefully all the items to be included in the standard and those factors discussed under direct materials and direct labour which will influence the various cost items of commercial activities. In some cases, notably in the operation of a road transport fleet, a measurable service is provided and the setting of standards must take account of the dual aspect discussed under factory services.

Exercises

1. What information would be required to set a standard manufacturing cost for a completely new machine which an engineering company is to make for sale? From where would this information be obtained?
   Present your answer in brief numbered paragraphs.   [C.M.A.]

2. Specify four different methods of setting standard labour times and write a brief note of explanation on each of them.   [C.M.A.]

3. What do you understand by the term ideal standard? Do you consider that an ideal standard is a satisfactory measure of performance?   [C.M.A.]

4. The Rotary Spandrel Company Limited is an engineering business manufacturing a wide range of components in reasonably large batches. There are five distinct production departments and three service departments. The company is currently considering the adoption of a system of standard costing.
   The principal features of the present accounting system are:
   (1) Monthly profit and loss accounts are prepared from the financial records.
   (2) Job costs are prepared from the costing records by ascertaining the prime cost and adding thereto the overheads recovered as a percentage of the total direct wages included in the job cost.

Required:

Write a report to the managing director explaining the main changes in the present system of accounting which will be needed if standard costing is introduced.

[C.A.A.]

5. For many years there have been suggestions that the preparation of actual product cost information is obsolete, and that the resultant figures are of no use to management.

(*a*) express your views on this;

(*b*) to what extent do you feel that the limitations of actual product costing are removed by the use of pre-determined cost rates?

(*c*) how far, in your opinion, does standard costing further improve the results of product cost ascertainment? [C.M.A.]

6. The benefits from standard costing can be no better than the standards themselves and it is essential, therefore, that such standards are set as accurately as possible.

Required:

Explain carefully how you would set standards for direct material in a manufacturing business. [C.A.A.]

7. List and write a brief note on each of six of the main factors to be taken into consideration in setting direct wage cost standards. [C.M.A.]

8. How would you prepare a material standard cost for products such as bolts and nuts, where production is continuous, and they are costed in lots of one hundred? What information would you need and from whom would you expect to obtain it?

[C.A.A.]

9. It is frequently argued that there cannot be effective cost reduction, organized and carried out to a specific plan, unless there is the involvement of the management in the budgets and in the cost control procedures which form the basis for control.

(*a*) Do you agree with this? Is there, in fact, any part of cost reduction which might be independently stimulated, and how?

(*b*) What cost control procedures are most pertinent to organized cost reduction programmes? [C.M.A.]

CHAPTER SEVENTEEN

OPERATION OF STANDARD COSTING

Causes of Variances

Cost is the product of the two factors, quantity and price, and consequently there can be only two factors which generate (or cause) cost. It follows, therefore, that any variance between standard cost and actual cost can only arise from these two causes—a difference in the quantity and/or a difference in the price. The purpose of **variance analysis** is to analyse any difference between standard and actual by causes. It is important to recognize that the **cause of a variance** is either or both of the quantity and the price. The accounting system is not able to disclose the **reason for a variance**, such as a machine breakdown; the non-availability of standard material; unbalanced machine order loading; and so on. These are typical of the factors which may influence a decision to depart from standard and so give rise to a variance from standard. The difference in quantity or price is really the **proximate cause** of the variance and is as far as the accountant can go. The preparation of variance analysis reports, however, pinpoints the (proximate) causes of variances and prompts senior management to seek the reasons for significant variances.

Classification of Variances

In practice there appears initially to be rather more than these two causes of variances, but this is an illusion stemming from terminology rather than concept. To avoid confusion between similar variances for the different elements of cost, it has become customary practice to adopt terms which identify the element of cost as well as the cause of the variance.

(1) **Materials cost** may differ from the standard cost because more or less materials have been used than the standard quantity specified. Thus it is that the variance caused by a difference in materials usage is known as the **(materials) usage variance**.

(2) **Materials cost** also differs from the standard cost when a higher or lower price has been paid than the standard price specified. Hence, the variance arising from buying or using materials at a different price is known as the **(materials) price variance**.

(3) **Labour costs** differ from the standard cost where more or less labour has been used than the specified standard quantity. However, the 'quantity' of labour is expressed in a measure of time and a difference in the time taken to perform a given task is normally referred to as a difference in efficiency and known as the **(labour) efficiency variance**.

(4) **Labour costs** may also differ from the standard cost because the actual wage rate paid to workers is more or less than the standard wage rate. In this case, the variance caused by the difference in the wage rate is known as the **(labour) rate variance**.

(5) **Overhead costs** differ from the standard cost when a greater or lesser usage of the facilities has been made than the standard level of activity had specified. Therefore, the over/under absorption of overhead reflects a change in the volume of activity and the difference is known as the **(overhead) volume variance.**

(6) **Overhead costs** can differ from the standard cost because the expenditure on services for a given activity volume is different from the standard expenditure for that activity level. Consequently, the difference is known as the **(overhead) expenditure variance.**

These variances may now be suitably summarized as:

Element of cost	*Quantity Variances*	*Price Variances*
Direct materials	Usage	Price
Direct labour	Efficiency	Rate
Overhead	Volume	Expenditure

It will be noted that the six titles represent only the two primary variances of quantity and price, but individual titles identify the cost element with the particular variance.

Elementary Variance Analysis

The analysis by causes of variances from standard is illustrated by reference to a simple practical example.

Materials

During a certain accounting period fifty-five tons of materials were issued from the stores at a price of £9·60 per ton. The standard price of this material is given as £10·00 per ton.

		£
Standard cost	(55 tons at £10·00) =	550
Actual cost	(55 tons at £ 9·60) =	528
Price variance *favourable*	=	22

In the example quoted, the material was used to produce 4,000 articles during the period. The standard schedule specifies an output of eighty units per ton of material. The position for an output of 4,000 units is:

		£
Standard cost	(50 tons at £10·00) =	500
Actual cost	(55 tons at £10·00) =	550
Usage variance *adverse*	=	(50)

The materials position may now be summarized thus: 4,000 units of product were produced from fifty-five tons costing £9·60 per ton. The standard for 4,000 units is fifty tons at £10·00 per ton.

		£
Actual quantity at actual price	(55 tons × £ 9·60) =	528
Price variance *favourable*	(55 tons × £ 0·40) =	22
Actual quantity at standard price	(55 tons × £10·00) =	550
Usage variance *adverse*	(5 tons × £10·00) =	(50)
Standard quantity at standard price	(50 tons × £10·00) =	500

Labour

The 4,000 units produced (above) were made in 280 hours for which the wages paid were £182 although the standard wage rate for the job is £0·60 per hour.

	£
Standard cost (280 hours at £0·60) =	168
Actual cost (280 hours at £0·65) =	182
Rate variance *adverse* =	(14)

The standard allowed time for this work is 5·1 minutes per unit.

	£
Standard cost (340 hours at £0·60) =	204
Actual cost (280 hours at £0·60) =	168
Efficiency variance *favourable* =	36

The labour position may now be summarized thus: 4,000 units were manufactured in 280 hours for £180; the standard cost of 4,000 units is 340 hours at £0·60 per hour.

		£
Actual hours at actual rate	(280 hours at £0·65) =	182
Rate variance *adverse*	(280 hours at £0·05) =	(14)
Actual hours at standard rate	(280 hours at £0·60) =	168
Efficiency variance *favourable*	(60 hours at £0·60) =	36
Standard hours at standard rate	(340 hours at £0·60) =	204

Overhead

The actual expenditure on overhead for this period amounted to £370. The budgeted expenditure was £350 for an output of 3,500 units (that is, £0·10 per unit).

		£
Budgeted expenditure	=	350
Actual expenditure	=	370
Expenditure variance *adverse*	=	(20)
Absorbed expenditure	(4,000 at £0·10) =	400
Budgeted expenditure	(3,500 at £0·10) =	350
Volume variance *favourable*	=	50

The overhead position may be summarized thus: 4,000 units were produced at an actual cost of £370; the standard cost of overhead is £350 for an output of 3,500 units.

			£
Actual expenditure		=	370
Expenditure variance *adverse*		=	(20)
Budgeted expenditure	(3,500 units at £0·10) =		350
Volume variance *favourable*	(500 units at £0·10) =		50
Absorbed expenditure	(4,000 units at £0·10) =		400

Note: in this simple example, all the overhead is assumed to be fixed to emphasize that variances arise from the two causes of price and quantity. The problems of dealing with variable overhead will be dealt with in the next section.

Analysis of Sub-Variances

In practice, it is often possible to make a more detailed analysis of variances which will assist management to control costs. The basic variances already described may be sub-divided to pinpoint more closely the contributory causes of the overall difference between standard and actual. In making this analysis of sub-variances it is essential to be mindful of the two basic causes of variance—differences in price or quantity. These sub-variances are not new or additional variances, but a further breakdown of the basic variances. This is well illustrated by the following example of materials variances.

Materials Variances

A certain dry chemical is produced from the following *standard* mixture:

> 60% of Agron at £50 per ton
> 30% of Bodex at £35 per ton
> 10% of Cruze at £42 per ton

During one month, one hundred tons of chemical were obtained from:

> 67 tons of Agron at £53 per ton
> 28 tons of Bodex at £34 per ton
> 15 tons of Cruze at £40 per ton

In approaching variance analysis for these more sophisticated situations it is important to begin by identifying all the variable factors involved. A glance at the standard prices and the actual prices reveals **price variances** on all three ingredients. The total consumption of materials is one hundred and ten tons for an output of one hundred tons which suggests a **usage variance**: more for agron and cruze, but less for bodex, indicating a different *mixture* of materials. The best approach to this problem is to arrange the data in tabular form as follows:

Key to column headings for materials and labour examples.

S = standard		**Q** = quantity	
A = actual		**M** = mixture	
P = price		**G** = grade	
T = time		**R** = hourly rate	

Material	SQ SM (tons)	AQ SM (tons)	AQ AM (tons)	SP £	AP £	SQ SM SP £	AQ SM SP £	AQ AM SP £	AQ AM AP £	Variances Total £	Price £	Usage £	Sub-usage Mix £	Yield £
Agron	60	66	67	50	53	3,000	3,300	3,350	3,551	(551)	(201)	(350)	(50)	(300
Bodex	30	33	28	35	34	1,050	1,155	980	952	98	28	70	175	(105
Cruze	10	11	15	42	40	420	462	630	600	(180)	30	(210)	(168)	(42
TOTAL	100	110	110			4,470	4,917	4,960	5,103	(633)	(143)	(490)	(43)	(447
	a	b	c	d	e	f axd	g bxd	h cxd	j cxe	k f–j	l h–j	m f–h	n g–h	p f–g

In this example the usage variance has arisen from two causes: a greater total usage (**yield variance**) and a mixture of materials in different proportions from the standard mixture (**mix variance**).

Under the headings for columns f, g, h, j, the three variables (quantity, grade, price) are shown in each case; column f shows all at *standard*; then each variable is changed in turn to *actual* with h showing all variables at actual. Only one variable changes from standard to actual between any two successive columns. Consequently, any cost difference between the two columns is caused by the changed variable thus permitting the isolation of individual variances.

Materials Losses

It is a common phenomenon of manufacturing industries that materials losses arise during the course of production. Often, such losses occur by the very nature of the manufacturing processes concerned and are, therefore, unavoidable and a normal production cost. When setting standards for materials it is necessary to allow for any such losses, in other words to **calculate the standard input for a given output**. Needless to say, perhaps, any difference between the standard input and the actual input is avoidable and constitutes a usage variance. This may be illustrated as follows:

The standard specification for a certain beverage includes a particular liquid costing £2·00 per gallon. During a period of rapid boiling, twenty per cent of the input is expected to be lost through evaporation. In January, 200 gallons were produced from an input of 240 gallons at £2·10 per gallon.

Solution		£
Actual quantity at actual price	(240 galls × £2·10) =	504
Price variance *adverse*	(240 galls × £0·10) =	(24)
Actual quantity at standard price	(240 galls × £2·00) =	480
Usage variance *favourable*	(10 galls × £2·00) =	20
Standard quantity at standard price	(250 galls × £2·00) =	500

It should be noted that a standard loss of twenty per cent requires an input which is twenty-five per cent higher than the output (200 galls × 1·25 = 250 galls).

The calculations for normal materials losses is really no further complicated where two or more materials are mixed together. The really important point to keep in mind is that the standard input is determined by the actual output;

that is, knowing the actual quantity produced it is necessary to calculate the standard input quantity which would yield that output under standard conditions. This is demonstrated in the following problem:

	Standard	*Actual*
Material 'X'	40% at £20 ton	90 tons at £18 ton
Material 'Y'	60% at £30 ton	110 tons at £34 ton
Loss in process	10% of input	(output = 171 tons) [C.M.A.]

Solution

Note: An output of 171 tons requires a standard input of 190 tons (171 × 100% ÷ 90%)

Mat-erial	SQ SM (tons)	AQ SM (tons)	AQ AM (tons)	SP £	AP £	SQ SM SP £	AQ SM SP £	AQ AM SP £	AQ AM AP £	Variances				
										Total £	Price £	Usage £	Sub-usage Mix £	Yield £
'X'	76	80	90	20	18	1,520	1,600	1,800	1,620	(100)	180	(280)	(200)	(80)
'Y'	114	120	110	30	34	3,420	3,600	3,300	3,740	(320)	(440)	120	300	(180)
Total	190	200	200			4,940	5,200	5,100	5,360	(420)	(260)	(160)	100	(260)

Grade Price Variance

In certain industries (notably textiles), different qualities or grades of materials are consumed or at least available for use. In such circumstances it is possible for the actual material to be of a different grade from that contained in the standard specification. Separate grades of materials will normally have individual prices which reflect the quality differences with the result that a price variance may occur when the grade of materials used is different from the standard grade specified. When several such materials are mixed together there will be four variables (quantity, mixture, grade, price) giving rise to four sub-variances. Usage variance may be sub-analysed into mixture and yield; price variance may be sub-analysed into grade price and purchase price. The following problem illustrates this form of variance analysis:

A certain product is made from three different materials and the standard mixture for a finished ton is:

0·4 ton of material 'P' (grade 1)
0·6 ton of material 'Q' (grade 2)
0·2 ton of material 'R' (grade 2)

The standard price schedule provides the following prices per ton:

Material	Grade 1 £	Grade 2 £	Grade 3 £
'P'	56	49	42
'Q'	84	74	64
'R'	220	200	150

The details for one month for an output of 110 tons were:

46 tons of 'P' (grade 2) at £50 ton
62 tons of 'Q' (grade 3) at £60 ton
12 tons of 'R' (grade 1) at £240 ton

[C.A.A.]

Solution

Material	SQ SM (tons)	AQ SM (tons)	AQ AM (tons)	SG SP £	AG SP £	AG AP £	SQ SM SG SP £	AQ SM SG SP £	AQ AM SG SP £	AQ AM AG SP £	AQ AM AG AP £
'P'	44	40	46	56	49	50	2,464	2,240	2,576	2,254	2,300
'Q'	66	60	62	74	64	60	4,884	4,440	4,588	3,968	3,720
'R'	22	20	12	200	220	240	4,400	4,000	2,400	2,640	2,880
Total	132	120	120				11,748	10,680	9,564	8,862	8,900
	a	b	c	d	e	f	g	h	j	k	l

Variance analysis

Materials	Total £	Price £	Usage £	Sub-price Purchase £	Grade £	Sub-usage Mix £	Yield £
'P'	164	276	(112)	(46)	322	(336)	224
'Q'	1,164	868	296	248	620	(148)	444
'R'	1,520	(480)	2,000	(240)	(240)	1,600	400
Total	2,848	664	2,184	(38)	702	1,116	1,068
	g–1	j–1	g–j	k–1	j–k	h–j	g–h

Labour Variances

Wage rates are much less subject to the fluctuations which often beset materials prices as they are really less sensitive to external market factors. Most businesses operating a system of standard costing will have established various labour grades each with its own standard rate of pay. Normally this will also be the actual rate of pay, too, and there will seldom be any sub-variances for labour costs, but only the two basic variances of rate and efficiency. Nevertheless, it is well to consider the possibility of an analysis of labour sub-variances.

Engagement Rate Variance

On the whole, the 'purchase price' of labour tends to be the standard rate for the relevant grade. However, workers may be engaged at a rate which is different from standard. This is most likely to be found in engaging casual labour as the rate paid for casual labour is often subject to local supply and demand conditions at the time.

Grade Rate Variance

Workers of one labour grade are sometimes given tasks specified for a different grade of labour. In factories this may be because no one of the relevant standard grade happens to be available, or sometimes workers standing idle are given non-standard work in preference to paying them to do nothing. In either case, a grade rate variance will occur.

Wages Rate Variance

The analysis of wages rate variance into the sub-variances of engagement rate variance and grade rate variance is made in the same way as the analysis of materials price variance into purchase price and grade price. However, the wages rate variance is normally only a grade rate variance as the engagement rate variance is seldom met in practice.

Labour Yield Variance

This is that part of the labour efficiency variance which occurs when the actual output differs from the standard output for a given labour output. In most cases of a labour efficiency variance this will be the only cause and, therefore, there is no need to analyse it into sub-variances.

Labour Mixture Variance

This type of variance will arise in 'team' situations when the composition of a crew or gang differs from the standard. Generally speaking, there are two reasons for this variance—either the standard team is depleted by absenteeism or the team is composed differently from standard. In the first instance it is not at all unusual for the team to carry on if one member is away provided that the task can be performed by fewer people, albeit somewhat less efficiently than normal.

Labour Efficiency Variance

An analysis of the sub-variances of yield and mixture for the labour efficiency variance follows the same pattern as the yield and mixture sub-variances of materials usage. This is illustrated in the following example:

A certain task requires a team of six men—one worker grade four at £0·60 per hour; three workers grade three at £0·50 per hour; two workers grade two at £0·40 per hour. Their standard output is 500 units in 40 hours. During a given week of 40 hours they produced 450 units despite the absence of a grade three worker.

Solution

Labour grade	ST SM (hr)	AT SM (hr)	AT AM (hr)	SR £	ST SM SR £	AT SM SR £	AT AM SR £	Variances Efficiency £	Sub-variances Mix £	Sub-variances Yield £
4	36	33	40	0·60	21·6	19·8	24·0	(2·4)	(4·2)	1·8
3	108	100	80	0·50	54·0	50·0	40·0	14·0	10·0	4·0
2	72	67	80	0·40	28·8	26·8	32·0	(3·2)	(5·2)	2·0
Total	216	200	200		104·4	96·6	96·0	8·4	0·6	7·8

Variable Overhead Variances

As with materials and labour, there are two primary causes of variances in variable overhead—expenditure and volume (price and quantity). Variable overhead, by definition, tends to vary more or less directly with changes in the level of activity, and it is necessary, therefore, to use flexible budgets for variable overhead as with direct materials and direct labour. The standard cost against which actual cost is to be compared is consequently determined by the **actual level of activity**. At this point, it is desirable to remember the three recognized measures of activity:

(a) Physical units of output.
(b) Number of direct labour hours.
(c) Number of machine hours.

The Standard Hour

It is frequently assumed that all variable costs are directly related to physical units of output, whereas this is a valid assumption only in general terms. The inter-relationship of these three measures is clear: ten per cent more machine hours will require about ten per cent more direct labour and lead to about ten per cent higher output. However, an operator who works more efficiently than standard performance will achieve a higher output than standard in a given time, and *vice versa*. The same is true of the operational efficiency of individual machines. The incidence of overhead expenditure is commonly influenced by time (*see* Chapter Seven), and most variable overhead is correlated to either direct labour or machine time. Hence, the **standard hour**, rather than the physical unit, is adopted as the measure of production activity for the purposes of variance analysis.

Variance Analysis

The analysis of variances for variable overhead is demonstrated by the following example:

The budgeted output for March in a certain department was 160 units of product 'Q'. Variable overhead was budgeted at £240 for 800 direct labour hours. The actual result for March was reported as 150 units produced in 720 hours for an expenditure of £236.

Standard performance is five standard hours for each completed unit at a standard cost of £1·50 (or £0·30 per standard hour). The actual production for March was 150 units which represents an output activity of 750 standard hours. The actual expenditure was £236 which at first sight appears to disclose a favourable variance when compared with the original budget. The use of a flexible budget, however, shows the budget expenditure to be £216 (720 hours at £0·30) which gives rise to an *adverse* variance of £20. The output of 750 standard hours represents an absorbed cost (at £0·30 per hour) of £225 compared with the flexible budget of £216—thus there is a *favourable* volume variance of £9. The whole position may now be summarized as follows:

	Hr	£
Actual expenditure	—	236
Expenditure variance *adverse*	—	(20)
Budget expenditure (actual hr at std. rate)	720	216
Volume variance *favourable*	30	9
Absorbed expenditure (output hr at std. rate)	750	225

Fixed Overhead Variances

The analysis of variances for fixed overhead is rather more troublesome than is the case with variable costs. The difficulty arises from the conflicting concepts of fixed costs and variable absorption. By definition, a fixed cost expenditure will not be influenced by activity changes and tends to be constant for a given production capacity. However, fixed overhead is absorbed at a set rate per unit of activity, consequently there is the paradox that the **absorption of fixed overhead becomes directly variable**. Total fixed overhead variance is, therefore, the difference between the actual expenditure of fixed cost for the period and the amount of fixed cost absorbed into the actual output. As with all other cost elements, there are two primary causes of fixed overhead variance—price and quantity or expenditure and volume.

Fixed Overhead Expenditure Variance

This will be the difference between the standard, or budget, expenditure and the actual expenditure. Since this is a fixed cost, the budget will not be flexed, but remain at a constant expenditure level. Problems arise, however, in deciding the basis of the fixed cost budget when preparing short-term (monthly) budgets. Generally speaking, fixed costs accrue on an annual basis and many items are paid annually; other costs are, however, met by two payments during the year, or quarterly or, like salaries, are paid monthly. The preparation of a monthly budget which includes all the various expense items will necessitate prorating the annual amounts between periods. The annual budget may then be divided by twelve where the short-term accounts are prepared by calendar month, or divided by thirteen for 'four-weekly' accounts, and so on.

The fixed overhead expenditure variance for a given period can be truly meaningful only when the actual expenditure also is recorded on the same basis as the budget. Even so, in an arbitrary apportionment between periods only a part of the fixed expenditure variance for a given period does in fact arise in that period, namely, that variance from budget expenditure which is **in the amounts actually incurred during the relevant period**. Since the items included in an annual fixed budget arise at different times throughout the year, a short-term fixed budget should include *only* those items which accrue during that particular period. Any variance between budget and actual is then truly significant because it has genuinely arisen in that period.

This approach to short-term budgeting results in a fluctuating amount of fixed cost forming the budget for individual periods. This is a matter for concern to some people, who feel that short-term fixed budgets should be equal in amount for each period. There is, of course, no reason at all why that should be so. Again, it may be helpful to recall that a fixed cost need not be constant in amount nor composed of equal increments since it is **not fixed** in either of those meanings, but in the sense of being unaffected in amount by activity changes.

Fixed Cost Calendar Variance

An annual budget is built up from the forecast activity for the particular budget centre, although the forecast activity will vary from one period to another due to seasonal influences and the intervention of public or annual holidays. Consequently, it is unrealistic to divide an annual budget arbitrarily into equal activity periods, since to do so will immediately give rise to variances in each period, although the sum of such variances would be zero in the complete year. Each short-term fixed budget should be related to the forecast activity for that period to provide a realistic analysis of the volume (activity) variance.

It has been postulated that the short-term fixed budget should be based on:

(*a*) the expected incidence of expenditure so that the expenditure variance is realistic; and

(*b*) the forecast level of activity to provide significant volume variances.

Happily, this is a situation where we can eat our cake and still keep it by preparing *both* forms of budget for each period. The monthly differences between the two forms arise from varying behaviour patterns during the year, but for the complete year each will equal the other. This difference between the two budgets is the **fixed overhead calendar variance**, which may be defined as that difference in a short-term budget period between the budgeted expenditure and the standard allowance for the budgeted activity. This variance has to be seen as a short period adjustment variance which, over the complete year, will sum up to zero.

Fixed Overhead Volume Variance

The volume variance for fixed overhead is the difference in standard cost between the budgeted activity (or output) and the actual activity (or output). It represents the over/under absorption of fixed cost in the period concerned. There are two causes of the fixed overhead volume variance—capacity usage and productivity.

Fixed Overhead Capacity Variance

The capacity to produce is determined by the number of hours that the factory can be expected to operate: all other things being equal, the output (capacity) will vary directly with the hours worked. The capacity to produce may be greater than the budget activity through working overtime or an extra shift; it may be reduced by short time, plant breakdown or industrial disputes. A budget centre which operates for less than the budget hours will tend to under-absorb its fixed overhead, while operating above budget activity leads to an over-absorption. The fixed overhead capacity variance may be defined as the difference in standard cost between the budgeted activity and the actual capacity usage.

Fixed Overhead Productivity Variance

Within the actual capacity usage it is possible to operate at more or less than the standard efficiency and so achieve a higher or lower level of productivity. This difference is the fixed overhead productivity variance and defined as that portion of the fixed overhead volume variance which reflects the increased or decreased output arising from an operating efficiency above or below the standard performance. This is defined in *I.C.M.A. Terminology of Management and Financial Accountancy* as that portion of the fixed production overhead volume variance which is the difference between the standard cost absorbed in the production achieved, whether completed or not, and the direct labour hours worked (valued at the standard hourly absorption rate).

Illustration of fixed overhead variance analysis

The budgeted output for March in a certain department was 160 units of product 'Q' in 800 standard hours. The standard fixed overhead rate is £0·50 per hour, and the budgeted expenditure was £312 for the month. The actual result for March was reported as 150 units produced in 720 hours with an actual expenditure of £335.

Solution

	Units	Hr	£
Actual expenditure			335
Expenditure variance *adverse*			(23)
Budget expenditure			312
Calendar variance *favourable*			88
Budget activity	160	800	400
Capacity variance *adverse*	(16)	(80)	(40)
Actual activity	144	720	360
Productivity variance *favourable*	6	30	·15
Absorbed cost	150	750	375

Accounting for Standard Costs

Departmental Costing

Responsibility for costs is dependent on delegated authority within the management structure and is, therefore, synonymous with the departmental management. Standard costing is designed to aid cost control through the determination of responsibility for variances from standard, therefore standard costing is essentially departmental costing. As such it is analogous to process costing and to speak of 'standard job costing' is really to utter a contradiction in terms. Costs must be assembled by departments or by jobs; it is pointless to do both, and since standard costs are responsibility costs they must be assembled on a departmental basis. Under any system of standard costing, we are costing the departments (or budget centres) and not jobs. Consequently, the work in process ledger under standard costing contains an account for each budget centre.

Standard Cost Book-keeping

Considerable variation in the method of book-keeping for standard costs may be seen in practice. As often as not it will be found that a particular procedure is adopted from expediency rather than principle as most standard costing systems are grafted on to an extant accounting system and tend to stay that way. In general, there are two distinct methods of book-keeping with standard costing—usually referred to as the partial plan and the single plan. Other systems are found occasionally, but they are usually designed specifically for local conditions or to meet some special requirement and, therefore, not always suitable for general use.

The Partial Plan

The dominant characteristic of the partial plan of book-keeping for standard cost is that the work in process account is **debited at actual cost** but transfers to finished stock are **credited at standard.** After bringing down the closing work-in-progress valuation at standard cost, the balance remaining on this account represents the net variance for the period. The variances are separately analysed and then transferred from the work-in-progress ledger to the profit and loss account.

The variances from standard for materials and labour are best ascertained from such original posting media as stores requisitions and time sheets. The variances for the period may then be summarized and posted from the work-in-progress account to the profit and loss account. The standard over-head absorption rates will be used for the overhead debits to work in progress as these are synonymous with the pre-determined absorption rates of historical cost ascertainment. Any over/under absorption will then be transferred to the profit and loss account from the various overhead accounts. The relevant journal entries under the partial plan are:

(1) Dr.   Work-in-progress account.
    Cr.   Materials stock account.
    Being the *actual* value of materials issued.
(2) Dr.   Work-in-progress account.
    Cr.   Wages account.
    Being the *actual* wages paid to labour.
(3) Dr.   Work-in-progress account.
    Cr.   Overhead control account.
    Being the *standard* overhead absorbed for the period.
(4) Dr.   Finished stock account.
    Cr.   Work-in-progress account.
    Being the *standard* value of completed output.
(5) Dr.   Work-in-progress account.
    Cr.   Work-in-progress account.
    Being *standard* value of unfinished work.
(6) Dr.   Work-in-progress account.
    Dr.   Overhead control account.
    Cr.   Profit and loss account.
    Being transfer of *favourable variances*.
(7) Dr.   Profit and loss account.
    Cr.   Work-in-progress account.
    Cr.   Overhead control account.
    Being transfer of *adverse variances*.

It is often suggested that it may be necessary to adjust the valuations of finished stock and work in progress to actual cost to satisfy the Inland Revenue. However, in the first place, there does not appear to be any universal requirement on this point. Secondly even if there were, the suggestion is at best naive since the accounting system and the basis of stock valuation is the responsibility of management, not the Inland Revenue. However, in preparing the tax assessment, the Inland Revenue is usually willing to accept accounting data as a basis for agreeing allowances against tax. Even so, there is no need to disturb the accounting system as the data for a tax assessment can be separately compiled and agreed with the company's auditors.

The Single Plan

The principal characteristic of the single plan is the use of **standards throughout the cost accounts through an analysis of variances at source**. The work-in-progress accounts under the single plan are debited and credited at standard cost. Although a few exceptions are found in practice, the raw materials stock account is also kept at standard under the single plan.

Materials

Price variances on materials purchases are analysed in the purchase journal and posted to the materials price variance account. The usage variance is analysed when materials are issued to production and posted to the departmental materials usage variance account. The journal entries for materials are:

(1) Dr.   Materials stock ledger account.
    Cr.   Supplier's personal account.
    Cr. (or Dr.) Materials price variance account.
    Being purchase of raw materials.
(2) Dr.   Departmental work-in-progress account.
    Dr. (or Cr.) Materials usage variance account.
    Cr.   Materials stock ledger account.
    Being materials issued to production.

Labour

In Chapter Six it was pointed out that the payroll and the primary labour records are used as journal vouchers for posting the accounts. This holds good under the single plan of accounting for standard costs. The net wages payable and the various deductions are debited to the wages control account which is cleared by posting labour costs to the work-in-progress ledger and the overhead control account. The journal entry prepared from the time sheets, job cards, and piecework tickets will be:

(3) Dr.   Work-in-progress ledger.
    Dr.   Overhead control account.
    Dr. (or Cr.) Labour efficiency variance accounts.
    Cr. (or Dr.) Wages rate variance accounts.
    Cr.   Wages control account.
    Being wages earned for the period.

Variable Overhead

The expenditure variance will be analysed when the supplier's invoice is being posted to the accounts as explained with raw materials. The volume variance will be analysed at the same time as the overhead absorption is calculated. The journal entries for variable overhead are:

(4) Dr.   Variable overhead control account.
    Dr. (or Cr.) Departmental expenditure variance account.
    Cr.   Supplier's personal account.
    Being payment for variable service.
(5) Dr.   Work-in-progress ledger.
    Cr. (or Dr.) Departmental volume variance account.
    Cr.   Variable overhead control account.
    Being absorption of variable overhead.

Fixed Overhead

The situation for fixed overhead is similar to that explained for variable overhead to give rise to the following journal entries:

(6) Dr.   Fixed overhead control account.
    Cr. (or Dr.) Departmental expenditure variance account.
    Cr.   Supplier's personal account.
    Being fixed overhead incurred for period.
(7) Dr.   Work-in-progress ledger.
    Dr. (or Cr.) Overhead capacity variance account.
    Cr. (or Dr.) Overhead calendar variance account.
    Cr. (or Dr.) Overhead productivity variance account.
    Cr.   Fixed overhead control account.
    Being absorption of fixed overhead.

Performance Reports

The feedback phase of any control system comprises two distinct activities, as explained in Chapter Thirteen. In the first place, the actual performance is measured and compared against the standard and the variance is analysed. Secondly, the variance then becomes the stimulus which generates corrective action through a feedback to the control phase or to the setting phase. The importance of feedback lies in the encouragement it gives to the responsible manager to improve his performance. It is in seeking improvements that an individual manager exercises cost control in the activities for which he is responsible. Feedback is also necessary as a **management control**, by reporting to senior executives those variances which are the responsibility of their subordinates and reflect their performance as managers.

Principles of Variance Reporting

The variance report should be addressed to an individual and contain only those items for which he is responsible and can be expected to control. Additional data may be useful information but it is likely to diminish the impact of the responsibility reporting. **Information reporting** does not require action from the recipient and should always be clearly separated from **responsibility reporting**, which does call for some action to be taken. In reporting to operating managers such as foremen it may be appropriate to state the results in physical units only although money values give real significance to the results by showing the effect on profits. Senior executives, such as the works manager, require both physical and monetary values, whereas top executives normally need only the financial data.

The variance report should be issued regularly (daily, weekly, monthly, according to needs) and always punctually. There can be no excuses for lateness, not even a genuine desire to include other relevant data. Comparative figures are essential for a proper assessment of the significance of reported results, and ratios should also be included. Furthermore, any known reasons for the variances should be stated, such as poor-quality materials or a machine breakdown.

Daily Reports

The great virtue of daily reporting is timeliness, with the consequence that early action can be taken to correct adverse performances. Nevertheless, daily reports can be self-defeating where managers are submerged beneath a flood of paperwork which they have not the time to assimilate. However, provided that daily reports are restricted to vital activities and limited in detail, they can be valuable in aiding control.

Two really significant daily reports can be used for operating departments in most companies. Materials usage and labour efficiency can be reported in physical units on a daily basis for departmental foremen. The value of daily reports in leading to early corrections depends on one day's results being reported on the following day. Unless the accounting system can do this, the report is probably better left undone. Oddly enough, perhaps, next day reporting is usually practicable with manual or semi-mechanized systems but often troublesome with computers.

Daily Materials Usage Report

This report (Fig. 44) is issued to the foreman or departmental manager. A single report covers a week's operations but is up-dated daily and sent to the department each time. Some comparative data is provided to give

Daily Materials Usage Report

Dept.. Foreman........................... Date.......................

Day	Daily Usage				7 days to date		4 weeks to date		Year to date
	Actual Quantity	Standard Quantity	Variance Quantity	Variance %	Standard Quantity	Variance %	Standard Quantity	Variance %	Variance %
Sunday	....	....	....	....	....	....	....	....	....
Monday	....	....	....	....	....	....	....	....	....
Tuesday	....	....	....	....	....	....	....	....	....
Wednesday	....	....	....	....	....	....	....	....	....
Thursday	....	....	....	....	....	....	....	....	....
Friday	....	....	....	....	....	....	....	....	....
Saturday	....	....	....	....	....	....	....	....	....
Total for the week					——	——	——	——	——
Mean weekly variance for this year to date				Mean monthly variance for this year to date					

Fig. 44. Daily materials usage report

perspective to the results. The data is given in physical units only and will usually be suitable for repetitive manufacturing such as continuous process industries, foundries, and flow-line production. It will usually be unsuitable for jobbing situations which use widely differing materials.

Daily Labour Efficiency Report

This report (Fig. 45) also is issued to foremen and provides a performance analysis by cost centres. It compares the actual hours worked against the standard hours produced and shows the efficiency ratio. There may be some

Daily Labour Efficiency Report

Dept.................................. Foreman............................ Date........................

Cost Centre		This Day (Hours)			Efficiency Ratio			
Code	Name	Actual	Standard	Variance	Today	Previous Week	Previous Month	Year to date
Department totals:								

Fig. 45. Daily labour efficiency report

difficulty in obtaining the data for this report unless the factory uses **period-related activity records** (*see* Chapter Six) on a daily basis.

Weekly Reports

In most companies the accounting system is not structured to provide daily reporting so that weekly reporting tends to be the norm. Weekly variance reports for materials and labour may well be similar to Figs. 44 and 45 but provide data for the whole week. Weekly operating reports will usually include costs as well as physical data. Intermediate management will receive weekly summaries of the departmental reports prepared for the foremen and other subordinate managers. The divisional manager of a large organization may receive a weekly divisional operating summary (Fig. 46), which gives a summary of the departmental variances within the division. This particular example does not include the materials price variance as it would be analysed at source so that stocks of materials are held at standard price. The use of **non-standard material** gives rise to an **issue price variance** and, where this might occur, it would be necessary to provide an additional column to include it.

Department	Materials		Labour		Variable OHD		Fixed OHD		Total
	Mix	Yield	Rate	Eff'cy.	Expend.	Volume	Expend.	Volume	
	£	£	£	£	£	£	£	£	£
Totals:									
Weekly average this year to date									

Divisional Operating Summary — Week Ended................

Fig. 46. Divisional operating summary

Monthly Reporting

In general, top management only requires monthly reporting of variances which have been summarized for the company as a whole. The most important report is the monthly profit and loss statement which summarizes the company's profit performance and those factors which have influenced it during the month. This is illustrated in the following example.

BANKSIDE FABRICATIONS LIMITED

Profit and Loss Summary for Period Ended August 28, 1973

	£'000	£'000
Budgeted sales		250
Less Standard cost of sales		200
BUDGETED PROFIT		50
Sales variances		
Sales volume	(20)	
Standard cost in volume variance	16	
Sales volume profit variance	(4)	
Sales price variance	18	
		14
PROFIT IN PERIOD SALES		64

Cost variances

Materials price	..	..	..	(3)
Materials usage	..	..	..	4
Labour wage rate	..	..	..	(2)
Labour efficiency	..	..	..	5
Works variable overhead expenditure		..		1
Works variable overhead volume		..		1
Works fixed overhead expenditure	..	..		(2)
Works fixed overhead capacity		..		3
Works fixed overhead productivity	..	..		4
Administration expenditure		..	..	(2)
Marketing variable expenditure		..	..	2
Marketing fixed expenditure		..	..	(1)
Marketing fixed volume	...	...	...	(4)

6
—

ACTUAL PROFIT FOR PERIOD   70

The monthly profit and loss statement illustrates the **exceptions principle** of management reporting as it concentrates on the variances incurred and avoids reporting information which does not call for managerial action.

Exercises

1. Coalbrook Industries Limited manufactures industrial chemicals. One of its products—'Epsilon 16'—is made from three different raw materials and the standard mixture for a finished ton is as follows:

0·6 ton of 'Dexine' (Grade 1)
0·2 ton of 'Ferron' (Grade 3)
0·4 ton of 'Haddox' (Grade 2)

The company's price schedules provide the following prices per ton:

	Grade 1	Grade 2	Grade 3
	£	£	£
'Dexine'	65	60	55
'Ferron'	42	38	30
'Haddox'	22	20	15

The actual results in November, for an output of 215 tons were:

100 ton 'Dexine' (Grade 2) at £62 per ton
50 ton 'Ferron' (Grade 2) at £40 per ton
90 ton 'Haddox' (Grade 1) at £19 per ton

Required:

Calculate the respective variances for November and present the information in a form suitable for the works manager. [C.A.A.]

2. A company operating a standard costing system uses standard direct wages rates of:

		Per hour
		£
Department:	'A'	0·36
	'B'	0·30
	'C'	0·37

During the month of November there was produced:

		Standard hours allowed
Department:	'A'	180 dozen at 270 per gross
	'B'	30 gross at 26 per dozen
	'C'	9,600 units at 130 per 100 units

There was worked:

	Actual hours		Actual hourly wage rate
			£
Department: 'A'	4,080	at	0·37
'B'	9,900	at	0·33
'C'	11,000	at	0·40

You are required to calculate and present to works management in summary form for each department and in total the standard value of production and the appropriate variances which arise. [C.M.A.]

3. Calculate the various labour variances from the following information:

Standard wage rate	£0·38 per hr
Standard hours per unit	3 hr
Actual hours worked	2,650 hr
Actual wages paid	£1,120
Actual production	900 units

[C.A.A.]

4. The following overhead expenditure and overhead variances were reported for the month of January.

Actual overhead expenditure:

  Dept. 1: £6,200
  Dept. 2: £9,200
  Dept. 3: £3,400

Overhead variances (figures in brackets are unfavourable):

	Dept. 1	Dept. 2	Dept. 3
	£	£	£
Due to a variation in the number of working days in the month	(240)	(340)	(120)
Due to differences between budgeted and actual output	1,600	(600)	1,160
Due to differences between budgeted and actual efficiency	(512)	200	(220)
Due to differences between budgeted and actual expenditure	(48)	(260)	(420)

You are required to prepare overhead control accounts for each department and relevant variance accounts for the month of January. [C.M.A.]

5. The following information has been taken from the books of a manufacturing business for the month of June.

	Budget	Actual
Working days	20	22
Hours worked	16,000	16,800
Output in units	2,400	2,700
Fixed overheads	£8,000	£9,000

Required:
Analyse the respective variances for June and present the results in a form suitable for the chief accountant. [C.A.A.]

6. From the following details determine variances for each of the cost elements, and give the journal entries for the November transactions, including the entries to the appropriate variance accounts.

ABC Company Limited

Standard cost—per unit

Product 'F'

	Material	Units	£ Per unit	£	£
Direct material:	'D'	4	0·75	3·00	
	'E'	2	0·30	0·60	
					3·60
		Hr	Per hour		
Direct wages		8	0·80		6·40
Manufacturing overhead		8	1·50		12·00
					22·00

The manufacturing overhead rate is based upon the budgeted amount of £18,900 and budgeted hours of 12,600.

Data for November:

(*a*) Actual direct costs:

    (i) material: 'D' 6,300 units at £0·73 per unit;

                'E' 3,150 units at £0·50 per unit;

    (ii) wages: 12,000 hours at £0·85 per hour.

(*b*) The manufacturing overhead chargeable to the month's production is £18,120.

(*c*) Output for November consisted of:

    (i) 1,270 units completed and transferred to finished stock;

    (ii) 270 units in progress one-third complete as regards wages and overhead are posted to a work-in-progress inventory account.   [C.M.A.]

CHAPTER EIGHTEEN

PERFORMANCE EVALUATION AND CONTROL

Wealth

Economics has been defined as the **science which studies human behaviour as a relation between ends and scarce means having alternate uses.** Although economics is a behavioural science, it is not concerned with the whole spectrum of human behaviour, but with those aspects which are influenced by scarce means having alternate uses. **Alternate uses** implies some **element of choice**, while **scarce means** suggests a **scale of values.** In other words, economics is concerned with value and with wealth especially (but not entirely), in so far as they can be expressed in money terms. Wealth is a function of production, the creation of goods and services to satisfy human wants, and may be defined as the difference between the **value** set by the community on the goods and services produced and the **cost** of the resources used up in producing those goods and services.

Profit

The creation of wealth is indicated by (accounting) **profit** which, in its turn, is a measure of the success with which the scarce means have been used to meet desired ends. Thus, profit could be defined as **the increase in wealth generated by production** which is analagous to one of the several definitions familiar to accountants that **profit is the increase in net assets (capital) generated by production.** From this it is possible to frame the following definition that:

Accountancy is the science which studies cost/income behaviour as a relationship between ends (or goals) and scarce means, which have alternate uses in order to find a basis for evaluating micro-economic performance.

Ultimately, this means that accountancy measures the profit performance of a business, and that profit (an increase in wealth) is an indicator of the success of a business which may be used to make comparisons of performance.

Inter-process Transfers

Every business activity contributes more or less to the overall corporate profit performance. A recognition of this situation has encouraged some companies to measure each departmental performance by the amount of profit which it contributes to the total result. Consequently, transfers between processes or departments are made at arbitrary selling values determined on a **cost plus basis.** Although this has all the appearance of sound logic, it is quite unsatisfactory in practice.

Shortcomings of Notional Profit

The notional profit under **cost plus transfer pricing** is useless as a performance measure since excess cost attracts additional profit while cost savings diminish the profit. Therefore, the amount of notional profit does not reflect the departmental efficiency and consequently it is worthless as a control signal to management. Another serious fault in this procedure is that the costs of later processes become progressively meaningless. The gains and losses of earlier processes are weighted by the notional profit and transferred to subsequent processes as input costs where they are uncontrollable but influence the profit performance. Furthermore, all the notional profit added at successive stages of manufacture is **unrealized profit** until the goods are finally sold to customers. Year-end valuations of work in progress and finished goods must be reduced to cost by eliminating this unrealized profit, which is a difficult and complicated exercise.

Fixed Cost Transfer Values

The addition of inter-process profits, then, is unsatisfactory, because it creates enormous complications in accounting and fails totally in its objective. An easier and more satisfactory arrangement is to set **pre-determined costs** as transfer prices—in effect, transfers are made at a standard cost. The transfer price could be the notional cost of production based on past performance. Excess costs or cost savings would give rise to variances reflecting departmental performance which would not be transferred to subsequent processes. The costs of transferee departments would not be distorted by the gains or losses of earlier processes as inputs would be charged at a standard (or fixed) cost price.

Control Ratios

The use of ratios (or relative values) is essential in providing reliable bases of comparison, where conditions vary from one period to another. The use of absolute values will often be grossly misleading where, for example, there has been a change in the level of activity between two periods. This was the essence of the argument for adopting flexible budgets in Chaper Fifteen. The study of statistics indicates the necessity of using coefficients (or relative values) for meaningful comparisons of data and, especially, where there are significant differences in conditions such as the scale of operations. The use of accounting ratios has long been practised for performance comparisons with both internal and external 'standards'. Differences in performance ratios suggest possible opportunities for improvement and act as control signals calling for some form of corrective action. In this sense, every current performance ratio is a **control ratio** since it can be compared with a previous period's results; or with a standard or budget; or with some external performance.

Standard Cost Ratios

Standard cost ratios are really the variances in coefficient form and as such they are invaluable in giving perspective to the absolute values of variances which are a vital part of the feedback in the control aspects of standards. The more useful and widely used standard cost variances include the following.

Efficiency Ratio. This is defined as the standard hours produced expressed as a ratio of the actual hours taken to produce the output. An output equivalent to sixty standard hours, which was produced in fifty-six working hours, would give an efficiency ratio of 1·07 indicating a favourable efficiency variance.

Capacity Ratio. This is calculated by expressing the actual working hours of a period as a ratio of the budgeted hours or standard capacity and is analogous to the fixed overhead capacity variance. If the budgeted capacity was sixty-two hours in the previous example, the capacity ratio would be 0·903. This indicates an adverse variance from unused capacity.

Activity Ratio. This is obtained from the standard hours produced expressed as a ratio of the budgeted hours or standard capacity. The activity ratio is analogous to the fixed overhead volume variance. In the previous example, the activity ratio would be 0·968 indicating an adverse variance.

The merits of ratios lie in their qualities as relative measures in comparing disparate results and other standard cost ratios can be calculated for any variance situation—the materials usage ratio may be particularly useful on occasions. For example, suppose that the material usage variance for a given department was £108 adverse in one period, but £120 adverse in the previous one. There thus appears to be a ten per cent improvement in the usage variance. However, if the respective quantities at standard cost were £400 and £800, then the ratios would be 1·27 and 1·15 respectively. These ratios give a new perspective to the department's performance.

Value-added Ratios

These are useful indicators of productivity and show the efficiency with which resources have been used, as well as helping to control business activities by highlighting unsatisfactory performances. The relative efficiency of the factory labour force may be indicated by expressing **value added** as a ratio of the payroll or as a rate per employee. Value added per £ of plant value shows the effective output from the investment in plant and machinery; while value added per £ of management salaries spotlights the contribution from the expenditure on management. The merit of value added is that it excludes the external (uncontrollable) input costs.

Profit Ratios

Profit is the primary criterion for external comparisons of performance since it is a common feature of all businesses in reflecting the money value of increased wealth generated by production activity. However, to be useful, it must be possible to assess the significance of relative profit performances as in the following case. In a given year Bardo Stores Limited reported a profit of £400,000, whereas Munro Supermarkets Limited achieved a profit of £500,000 in the same period. At first sight, Munro Supermarkets Limited appears to have the better performance, but second thoughts on these results beg several questions concerning the *relative* operating conditions in order to assess the underlying significance of these disparate performances. Indeed, profits expressed in absolute terms provide a quite imperfect barometer of business performance unless all other things are equal. Therefore, **profit ratios** are introduced to elicit the underlying significance of a company's financial results.

Profit to Turnover Ratio

There is a need to find a suitable basis of comparison for the results reported by the two companies to evaluate their relative performances. The first basis which is likely to spring to the mind of most accountants is turnover which has been hallowed by many years of tradition. Bardo Stores Limited had a turnover of £2,000,000 in earning its £400,000 profit and, consequently, its profit was twenty per cent of sales. The turnover was £5,000,000 for Munro Supermarkets Limited to give a profit of ten per cent on sales. Therefore, Bardo made £20 profit on every £100 sales, whereas Munro did only half as well with £10 profit for every £100 sales.

Despite its popularity, this 'traditional' ratio is quite unsuitable as an indicator of business performance, even for comparisons between successive years for the same company. This particular ratio is not only largely useless but in some circumstances it may be positively dangerous in leading to faulty decision-making. There are two inter–related factors—pricing policy and volume changes—which provide the basis of the criticism against the ratio of profit to sales.

Pricing Policy

The economic law of demand postulates that greater quantities of a commodity will be demanded at a lower price, all other things being equal. This 'law' is confirmed by common sense and experience. Consequently, it is sound business practice to reduce prices in order to attract additional sales as the 'cut price' shops and supermarkets well know. However, the efficacy of price cutting as a means of increasing profits partly depends on the relevant **elasticity of demand** for the product. Where the elasticity of demand is unity the turnover will remain constant for small price changes, but turnover rises after a price cut for elastic demand and falls when prices are reduced for products whose demand is inelastic. The converse is true of price rises as with inelastic demand there would be increased total revenue, but a reduced revenue would follow price rises where the demand is elastic. Price-cutting, therefore, appears to be justified where, all other things being equal, the elasticity of demand for a product is greater than unity.

Volume Changes

Where the elasticity of demand is unity, a small reduction in selling price leads to an increase in the quantity demanded so that total revenue (or turn-over) is unchanged. Assuming that unit costs remained constant then the profit per unit demanded would fall following a price reduction. For example, 1,000 units of 'Carlox' are currently demanded at a selling price of £10, yielding fifteen per cent profit on sales. The current level of profits is then $(15\% \times 1,000 \times £10)$ £1,500 in total or £1·50 per unit. A price reduction of two and a half per cent (25p) would reduce the profit to £1·25 per unit. To maintain the same total profit of £1,500 the quantity demanded would need to be 1,200 units, an increase in volume of twenty per cent and yielding a total revenue of $(1,200 \text{ at } £9·75) = £11,600$ which is a rise of sixteen per cent. Therefore, it would seem that the demand for a given product must be highly elastic if there is to be any possibility of increasing profits by stimulating demand through price-cutting where units costs remain constant.

Cost Behaviour Influences

Cost behaviour patterns, however, show that aggregate costs will change in the same direction as volume, but **proportionately less**. Fixed costs remain unaffected by volume changes while variable cost items vary more or less directly with volume. Consequently, the unit cost will vary inversely with the volume and more or less restore the reduction in profit per unit from price-cutting with an elastic demand.

In the above example it may be assumed that fixed expenses amount to £4,500 and variable cost is £4·00 per unit. In this case, a price reduction of two and a half per cent which induced an increase of four and a half per cent in the number of units demanded would increase the total profits by nearly £9.

		£
1,045 units of Carlox at £9·75	=	10,188·75
Less variable cost (1,045 at £4) 4,180		
Fixed cost (total) 4,500		8,680·00
Profit (originally £1,500)		£1,508·75

The marginal revenue of £189 is only 1·9 per cent of the original sales income for a price reduction of two and a half per cent, so that the demand is inelastic, yet the profit has risen in total by £9 despite dropping below the original fifteen per cent of turnover to 14·8 per cent.

Contradictory Factors

It is not possible, then, to draw any satisfactory conclusion from a comparison of the profit/sales ratios for Bardo and Munro. The marketing strategy of Munro Supermarkets may be based on an aggressive policy of price-cutting, so that their low profit/sales ratio is a matter for praise rather than blame since it results in higher absolute profits than would be yielded by a more conservative approach. It may be concluded, therefore, that greater profits can be earned by a company which diminishes its profit/sales ratio through reduced selling prices which stimulate demand for its products. At the same time, of course, a low profit/sales ratio is no criterion of excellence for it may arise from high cost inefficiency, a poor pricing policy, or other undesirable cause. The profit/sales ratio is, therefore, quite meaningless as a business performance indicator (except where all other things are equal when it is unnecessary as the absolute profit figures will be just as useful) because it is influenced by contradictory factors.

Return on Capital Employed (R.O.C.E.)

The real criterion in measuring business performance is **the wealth created from the use of scarce resources**. Greater resources can be expected to generate greater wealth and a realistic measure of performance would be obtained by considering the increase in wealth (profits) in relation to the resources available. The shareholders of a company have **provided certain resources** for the use of the directors in achieving their goal of profit-making. Equally, the directors' ability to earn profits will to some extent be circumscribed by the **amount of resources provided** by the shareholders directly or indirectly. The resources of a business are represented by its assets (capital employed) and the profit is a reflection of the use of those resources so that the ratio of profit to capital employed is a more significant indicator of business performance than any other single ratio. The return on capital employed is the relationship between the values produced in excess of the value of resources consumed and the value of the assets employed.

The Nature of Capital Employed

Accountants are generally agreed on the principle of R.O.C.E., but any attempt to define capital employed is fraught with considerable controversy. It is a topic likely to generate more heat than light in debate, but in some published works it is either treated superficially or safely ignored. Nevertheless, the nature of capital employed raises several interesting issues which deserve to be aired as R.O.C.E. really is important. Most authorities in the U.K. seem to suggest that capital employed is equated with net assets and this is certainly the more generally accepted definition. Nevertheless, there are valid reasons for dissenting from this view, which appears to owe more to a preoccupation with the auditor's responsibilities to the shareholders than to the formulation of a measure of management performance. Whether capital employed is taken to be net assets or total assets, there are further problems to be settled first with regard to which assets should be included and the valuations for those assets forming capital employed in a business.

Valuation of Capital Employed

It is necessary to make a clear distinction between the computation of capital employed and the drafting of a conventional balance sheet. These two sets of data are not necessarily identical since they may be prepared for different purposes. This is particularly true when considering the three principally interested parties: the management, the shareholders, and the Inland Revenue, for whom separate sets of final accounts may be prepared. For example, there is no valid reason why the written-down value of an asset for taxation purposes must be used in the published balance sheet—it often is, and then accountants are criticized for issuing accounting reports which fail to give **a true and fair view** of the company. Currently there is considerable debate of this subject on which the Accounting Standards Steering Committee may issue recommendations from time to time. For the moment, it is sufficient to remember that there may be a conflict between published balance-sheet values and the valuation of capital employed as a basis for evaluating managerial performance.

Goodwill

There is much confused thinking on the subject of goodwill which is often further confounded where it has been bought for one reason or another. The nature of goodwill is also sometimes blurred in people's minds because of the bases adopted for its valuation. Goodwill is **capitalized super profits** and as such can hardly be defined as capital employed—even when it is paid for. To include goodwill increases the capital employed and decreases the rate of return for a given level of earnings. It is a ridiculous situation that the acknowledgment of **above average profits** results in a decline in the reported R.O.C.E. and thereby obscures the very point it is desired to emphasize. It is, therefore, generally recognized that goodwill should be excluded from the computation of capital employed. It will follow from this that, in calculating R.O.C.E., the profit figure will be taken *before* writing off goodwill.

Patents and Trade Marks

It is common practice to write off these items soon after they are incurred, but the question here is whether or not they form a part of the capital employed. In most cases, patents and trade marks form such a small part of total assets that there will be little practical difference one way or the other. Sometimes the valuation of patents includes the capitalized costs of research and development and then becomes significant. However, the profit for R.O.C.E. is taken after charging any amounts written off patents when they are included in capital employed and *vice versa* which tends to stabilize the situation either way.

Investments

There are usually two possible bases available for the valuation of investments in the **cost (or purchase) value** and the **market (or realizable) value**. Opinions differ sharply on which is the more appropriate and several large companies have reversed a policy change on this matter in recent years. The opposing arguments may be summed up as follows.

The **original cost** of the securities should be used as it represents the actual amount of resources tied up in the investment. Furthermore, from time to time external factors cause market value fluctuations which could distort R.O.C.E. Any change from cost value is itself an indication of the merits or otherwise of the investment policy and should not be obscured by using the market value. The capital gains or losses from market changes cannot be realized unless the investment is sold and accountancy prudence suggests that profits should not be anticipated.

The **market value** gives an indication of the real value of an investment, and any unrealized appreciation in investments can be clearly identified by taking it to an **investment revaluation reserve**. High current earnings on low original cost may induce complacency by appearing to show a high rate of return, whereas the market value of a security reflects its current yield and may suggest seeking a better alternative use for the funds.

The Two Ratios of R.O.C.E.

The objective in calculating R.O.C.E. is to measure the efficiency with which the company's resources have been used by the management. Investments are necessarily sums invested (employed) **outside the normal activities** of manufacturing or trading. Operating executives are likely to protest that they should not be expected to earn an adequate return on sums invested outside the business since they usually have no influence on such investments. It can be argued that **trade investments** contribute to the earnings of the investor in other ways than dividends and should, therefore, be considered as part of the capital employed. Other investments, however, do not contribute to the normal operations and so, it is argued, they should be excluded.

There is a conflict here which cannot be resolved by a single solution, but only by two separate ratios of R.O.C.E. The directors of a company are entrusted by the shareholders with the total funds available and expected to make the best use of them. The measure of the directors' efficiency in this task is reflected by the total earnings accruing from all sources expressed as a ratio of the total resources available. This rate is referred to as the **utilization** R.O.C.E. and is based on all the resources available including investments. The efficiency of operating executives is measured by the **operating R.O.C.E.** calculated on the earnings from and capital employed in the normal business operations. The calculation of the operating R.O.C.E., therefore, includes neither investments nor investment income. The distinction between these two ratios is important, for recognizing the separate responsibilities of directors and managers and, also, because the **difference between** the two ratios highlights the directors' investment policy.

Cash Balances

Bank balances and cash in hand are other items on which opinions are divided regarding their validity as a part of the capital employed in a business.

For Inclusion in Capital Employed. Cash forms part of the total capital of a business which needs cash to be readily available for its proper functioning. Where cash balances are kept to a minimum, funds are being used to the fullest extent so that to omit cash from the capital employed is to **ignore the importance of funds usage.** The inclusion of cash and bank balances acts as an incentive to maintain such balances at a minimum.

For Exclusion from Capital Employed. The provision of finance is not an operating function but the prerogative of the board of directors. In any case, surplus cash retained in the business should also be omitted. (This is not altogether valid as investments earn a return but idle cash earns nothing.) Cash balances may fluctuate from month to month and distort the ratios of R.O.C.E. This could be overcome by using the monthly average requirement, but in any case fluctuations usually have little influence as cash balances average approximately only five per cent of capital employed.

On the whole, this is a very similar situation to that for investments. In the operating R.O.C.E, the capital employed should include the minimum operating cash balances, but actual cash balances should be included for the utilization R.O.C.E. Loans made to subsidiary or associated companies represent funds employed outside the immediate operations of the company and should be omitted from the operating R.O.C.E.

Trade Debtors

Other things being equal, the business offering more favourable credit facilities will make higher sales and the capital needed to finance credit sales is part of the capital employed. Allowing credit to customers stimulates sales and thereby increases profits. Such additional profit is the return on the capital employed on the debtors and, although it is virtually impossible to analyse it separately, contributes to the overall R.O.C.E.

On the whole, trade debtors should be valued gross as this represents the real investment in trade credit. With gross debtors, the profit is taken *before* making any adjustments to the provision for doubtful debts. The provision for doubtful debts seldom exceeds one per cent of the capital employed which has little effect either way on the valuation of capital employed. Changes in the provision, however, have relatively more influence on the reported profits which can induce distortions in R.O.C.E.

Stocks

Raw materials, works stores, work in progress, fuel stocks, and finished goods represent a considerable investment of funds and are part of the capital employed by a business. Changes in costs and prices from time to time, however, raise questions about the basis of stock valuation. It is an accounting convention that stocks are valued at the lower of cost or market price, but to always follow this rule must impart bias to the R.O.C.E. Any reduction in stock valuation following a fall in market prices also diminishes the profit by the same amount and R.O.C.E. can be seriously distorted by large price falls. The desire to give some consideration to current market values is very real and so also is the prudence of allowing for stock losses, but changes in market values are the result of external (uncontrollable) forces. R.O.C.E. measures the efficiency with which the capital has been employed, and cost is normally preferable in this context irrespective of the movement of external values.

As a general rule, windfall profits or losses arise from purely external sources and as such should be excluded from the R.O.C.E. However, in periods of changing prices, **production costs tend to lag behind purchase prices** unless materials are issued at **replacement prices**. Consequently, manufacturing profits include price gains during periods of rising prices and price losses will reduce profits during periods of falling prices. A crude correction of profits is possible with sophisticated indices developed from price indices weighted for average storage time and the length of the production cycle. In most instances, however, it is not practicable to isolate this 'error' from the operating profit. The methods adopted for pricing materials issues influence both stock valuation and operating profit and, in individual cases, merit consideration when computing R.O.C.E.

Fixed Assets

There are two basic problems in the valuation of fixed assets for the purposes of R.O.C.E. Initially there is the problem of deciding whether the valuation should be at the full asset value or at book value (written-down value). Then there is the further consideration of using either the historical (actual) cost or the replacement value.

Book Value

The valuation of fixed assets at their 'full value' has a certain logic which is conceptually pleasing but deceptive as the arguments for using written-down value are really overwhelming. The provision for depreciation represents that portion of the original investment in an asset which has been **recovered** through the profit and loss account and **re-invested** in other fixed assets or in working capital. Therefore, the book value is the residual capital employed in the fixed asset which should be **relieved of earning a return** to the extent that capital recovery and re-investment has been made. In other words, the use of written-down value prevents double counting in capital employed.

Criticism of book value for asset valuation is often founded on the method of depreciation adopted and the distortion it may introduce to book values. However, in computing the value of capital employed there is no need to take the book value obtained by using one particular method of depreciation. It is perfectly valid to use separate book values for different purposes: such as written-down value for tax purposes based on tax allowances; written-down value for published balance sheets; and written-down value for R.O.C.E.

When computing the R.O.C.E. for a given financial year, there is the further question of whether to take the book value at the beginning of the year, at the end of the year, or at an average for the year? When profit is taken before charging depreciation, the opening book value should be used for fixed assets, but the closing value or average value should be used for profit taken after depreciation. The average book value is more representative of the capital employed in earning the year's profits and is preferable to the closing balances. A simple average may be obtained from the opening and closing balances or a monthly weighted average may be used to give effect to the timing of asset additions and disposals during the year.

Replacement Cost

The use of replacement cost for asset valuation has been hotly debated for many years and there is still no complete measure of agreement on the subject. The A.S.S.C. recommended (*inter alia*) the use of C.P.P. (current purchasing power) for asset valuation in published accounts, but the *Sandilands Report* has now proposed the alternative of C.C.A. (current cost accounting). It is noticeable that this topic has been a live issue only during periods of rapid inflation; at other times it is seldom of more than academic interest. The argument for adopting replacement cost is usually one of showing realistic valuations, but 'realism' depends on one's viewpoint and objective. Popular support for replacement cost (or inflation accounting) in the 1950s sought tax concessions from the Government; in the 1960s it was aimed at warding off the risk of take-overs; now it appears to be seeking both ends.

There can be little doubt that inflation (and deflation) distort money values as measures of purchasing power and so distort the significance of historical accounting data. The effects of inflation are particularly marked over periods of several years so that they are especially relevant in the context of fixed assets. In the case of land and buildings, replacement cost approximates much more closely to the actual value of the asset since real estate tends to show a **net appreciation in value**. Land and buildings should, therefore, be included in capital employed at current values. Plant and machinery, on the other hand, are depreciating assets and it has already been argued that they should be included at written-down values, and profit should be taken after providing depreciation. It is thus apparent that the effects of inflation on the replacement value of older assets is largely compensated by the greater provision of depreciation.

A popular argument in favour of replacement cost is that inflation represents an erosion of capital, because the cost-based depreciation provision will be grossly inadequate to replace the asset at an inflated price. This is really rather naive. Assuming an original investment of £10,000 in a machine which is expected to yield a return of sixteen per cent per annum throughout the ten years of its life. With straight-line depreciation, £1,000 would be recovered and *re-invested* at the end of the first year. The second year profits would be increased by the additional earnings from the £1,000 invested internally at, say, sixteen per cent per annum also. At the end of year two, the recovered capital would be £1,100 for further re-investment, and so on. The earnings from re-invested capital are likely to be far higher than inflation and to do better than simply maintain the original capital invested.

Inflation is a most complex factor in its effect upon the reported results of a business, and the adoption of replacement cost for the valuation of fixed assets is far from being the answer to the problem. It is an area which requires much more research before it is possible to do more than pose the problems, and there are signs that more serious inquiry is being made on an increasing scale by the accounting profession. Meanwhile, the choice between replacement cost and historical cost for valuing fixed assets remains a matter of personal preference in management accounts.

Current Liabilities

Earlier, reference was made to the fact that capital employed is more usually equated with net assets than with total assets, an attitude which stems mainly from attaching undue significance to working capital. Despite its wider popularity, net assets is a less satisfactory basis than total assets for computing the capital employed in a business. As with the assets, each item of current liabilities should be separately considered rather than being taken *en bloc* as working capital.

Trade Creditors

Earlier in this chapter it was claimed that trade debtors form part of the capital employed as a revenue-earning use of resources. It is further argued by many people that trade creditors and trade debtors should be 'netted out' as two aspects of a single phenomenon (trade credit). This is another argument which contains a false logic. Admittedly, each is an aspect of trade credit; but there is a very real and important distinction between creditors and debtors which is emphasized in the *Report on the Working of the Monetary System* (*Radcliffe Report*) published by H.M.S.O. Trade debtors represent a use of funds (**capital employed**), whereas trade creditors are a source of funds (**capital provided**).

In assessing the capital requirements of a business it is customary to make some allowance for expected trade credit from suppliers. Since the company will need less capital from other sources to the extent that its suppliers will allow credit on purchases, trade creditors contribute to the capital employed and should not be deducted from current assets. This is emphasized by considering a company with a policy of paying creditors without delay which must obtain an equivalent amount of capital from other sources. In computing the amount of capital employed it is irrelevant to consider the *sources* from which it is supplied.

Overdrafts and Loans

Similar arguments apply here as for trade creditors. These are sources of capital and should not be deducted from current assets in computing the capital employed. Those who support the idea that capital employed is the same as net assets would not accept that debenture capital should also be deducted, for they do not see the inconsistency of argument. The fallacy in their thinking can be easily seen by considering the 'change' in capital employed where a business pays off a substantial overdraft with the proceeds from a debenture issue. Such a company is not one whit different in assets or liabilities or operating conditions yet, even if the interest on debentures was exactly the same as the rate for the overdraft, the calculated R.O.C.E. would fall. The profit used for R.O.C.E. should be taken before charging any interest on loans or debentures. Such interest is only debited to the profit and loss account as a charge against profits, because of the tax laws and for no other reason.

Accrued Expenses

Accrued expenses are really another form of creditors whether they relate to wages in arrears, insurance premiums, rent and rates, or other type of expense. They should not be deducted from total assets since they too are, in effect, a source of funds.

Proposed Dividends

The company has the use of the sums proposed as dividends until after the annual general meeting when the cash will fall as the dividend warrants are presented for payment. This will be automatically adjusted when calculating the monthly average capital employed. In a simple average it would be more precise to deduct the proposed dividends from the opening balances but not the closing balances, so that the average reflects the funds' usage in proposed dividends for upwards of six months. However, the amounts are relatively so small that any treatment of proposed dividends is unlikely to be significant in R.O.C.E.

Inter-firm Comparisons of Performance

The R.O.C.E. ratio provides a measure of the wealth created by the use of given resources and as such is the best available indicator of business performance. It is particularly suitable for evaluating corporate performance and especially in comparing the results of different accounting periods. Since R.O.C.E. measures the earnings generated by given resources, it is appropriate for comparing the performances of subsidiaries engaged in disparate activities. Large companies, which are organized into **product divisions**, usually keep separate accounts for each division on a similar basis to accounting for subsidiaries and, here too, R.O.C.E. is the appropriate measure of divisional performance. Subordinate units of a group or large company are able to use R.O.C.E. in this way because they can ensure that the ratios are calculated on the same assumptions in each case.

External Cost of Capital

The same assumptions may not apply for comparisons made with performances outside the company. It would be useful to compare the R.O.C.E. for competitors or other companies, but uncertainty regarding the assumptions discussed in this chapter make such a comparison of very limited value. This is especially so if one has to rely on published balance sheet values. The only generally acceptable R.O.C.E. comparison from outside the company in an uncontrolled situation is the **external cost of capital**. However, this is not really significant since most U.K. companies have a R.O.C.E. well above the prevailing interest rates on borrowings.

Centre for Inter-firm Comparisons

British firms can obtain reliable ratios of the performance by other companies through the Centre for Inter-firm Comparisons. Participating firms are provided with simple definitions of terms and guidance on asset valuation including indices for finding the current values of fixed assets. Participants submit to the Centre their own performance statistics prepared to the standard formulae. These figures are checked and, with those from other firms, are used to calculate average performances and individual firm performances. The selected ratios are circulated to all participants but each firm is given a code number to preserve anonymity and confidentiality. The primary ratio used is the R.O.C.E., but this is only the apex of a whole **pyramid of ratios** covering the varying aspects of a business.

Trade Associations

The firms in particular industries often join together to form trade associations for their mutual encouragement and support. The primary purpose of such associations is usually defensive but it is concerned with any aspect of mutual concern and interest. The services offered to member firms usually include the circulation of cost and performance ratios for each member. This service is similar to that given by the Centre for Inter-firm Comparisons, but less sophisticated. Likewise, it is equally confidential since the members of a trade association by definition are also competitors. Nevertheless, this exchange of information provides companies with significant comparisons against which to judge their own performance, and indicates possible areas of improvement in efficiency.

Uniform Costing

A few trade associations have developed quite sophisticated schemes for the exchange of operating data between member firms. The best example of these is operated by the British Federation of Master Printers in which terms are carefully defined as part of a comprehensive system of cost accounting applicable in all the member firms. The performance ratios for individual firms are significant for all members because each is prepared according to a recognized formula. Other trade associations such as the Non-Ferrous Metals Industry and the Ironfounders have issued recommended costing schemes to encourage member firms to improve their costing techniques and to facilitate a general exchange of performance data. In this way, the general efficiency of the industry is improved as well as that of member firms through cost reduction programmes and management control.

Exercises

1. Discuss carefully, the arguments for and against the inclusion of a 'profit element' in the transfer prices adopted for the valuation of inter-process transfers. To what extent do these arguments apply to inter-company transfers in a large group?
[C.A.A.]

2. Discuss the methods of, and the problems which can arise in, establishing prices of transfers of products between autonomous units in a large industrial organization.
[A.C.A.]

3. A parent company manufacturing motor cars takes half of its engine and other castings from a foundry subsidiary company, and the other half from a specialist producer of automotive trade castings. The full capacity of the foundry subsidiary is not being utilized at the moment and the group purchasing agent is concerned that actual costs of the castings made by the subsidiary are exceeding the intra-company transfer price, which is fixed at the competitive price charged by the specialist supplier. The latter, confronted with a similar problem of under-utilization, is now offering the castings at lower prices than previously in an endeavour to attract a larger share of the total requirement.

(a) What advice would you, as management accountant in the foundry subsidiary, give to the group purchasing agent?

(b) Are there any alternative bases for intra-company pricing which are relevant to this particular problem? 　　　　　　　　　　　　　　　　[C.M.A.]

4. 'The use of ratios for reporting accounting results lies in their indication of relative (rather than absolute) movements. Nevertheless, individual ratios can be quite misleading so that business performance can be properly interpreted only when using several ratios together.'

Required:

Discuss this quotation fully. 　　　　　　　　　　　　　　　　　　[C.A.A.]

5. Within a group of companies two factories are making similar (but not identical) products. A decision is to be made to standardize on one product line, to be made in one factory.

　(a) What criteria would you use in reaching the most profitable decision for the group?

　(b) To what extent do you consider that comparisons of 'conversion cost per hour' and 'added value per man' would assist this decision? 　　　　　[C.M.A.]

6. What do you understand by the term 'inter-firm cost comparison'? How would you set about achieving this in a group of companies for which you are the consultant cost accountant? 　　　　　　　　　　　　　　　　　　　　　　[C.A.A.]

7. The AB Holding Company controls over twenty subsidiary companies engaged in various industries. The companies are run on autonomous lines and some of them themselves have their own subsidiary companies. It has been decided by the holding company to set a target return on capital employed for all of its subsidiaries and so that each of the subsidiaries will start off in a similar situation it has been decided that the assets of each company shall be revalued as at October 1. Discuss the problems which will arise in both carrying out this revaluation and also in establishing the desired target rate of return. 　　　　　　　　　　　　　　　　[A.C.A.]

8. (a) Distinguish between (i) production, and (ii) productivity.

　(b) Name and define a cost accounting ratio used in measurement of each of (i) and (ii).

　(c) Illustrate your answer by calculating the appropriate ratio from the following data.

　(d) State the significance and the shortcomings of each.

Machine department:

	Model 'A'	Model 'B'
Production (units)	1,760	1,680
Time taken (man-hr)	6,600	
Standard time allowances (min per model)	90	165
Assembly department:		
Production (models)	1,050	
Standard time allowances (hr)	9	
Budget (hr)	12,600	

　　　　　　　　　　　　　　　　　　　　　　　　　　　　　　　　[C.M.A.]

CHAPTER NINETEEN

MARGINAL COSTING

Concepts of Marginal Cost

For a given level of output within a defined capacity, the total cost of that output is easily determined by taking due account of the fixed (or capacity) costs and the variable (or 'out-of-pocket') costs. Raise that level of output by one unit and the total fixed expenses will remain unchanged while the total variable cost will be increased by the variable cost of that one extra unit. Putting it another way, for a **change of one unit** in the volume of output, the **total costs** will be increased or decreased by the **variable cost per unit**. This will be recognized by economists as **marginal cost**, and accountants have adopted the same term and with it the economist's definition that:

Marginal cost is the amount at any given volume of output by which aggregate costs are changed if the volume of output is increased or decreased by one unit.

Now, although the accountant uses the same definition as the economist, it does not mean precisely the same thing to each.

The Economist's Concept of Marginal Cost

Marginal cost to the economist is essentially the incremental cost of one unit. (One unit may be defined as the minimum quantity change which is practical in the circumstances.) In this sense, one unit may be a dozen tables, one hundred feet of tubing, or fifty motor cars. As output expands, the marginal (incremental) cost falls initially with increasing returns, but then climbs as diminishing returns take effect (this is illustrated in Fig. 47). The average variable cost curve also slopes downwards and then upwards, but less sharply than the marginal cost curve. The average variable cost curve lags behind the marginal cost curve, which intersects it at its lowest point. The price (average revenue) curve slopes downwards from top left to bottom right as does the marginal revenue curve. Profits will be maximized where marginal cost equals marginal revenue which gives an optimum output of ON units. To produce more than ON would reduce profits since the marginal cost of one more unit is greater than the revenue generated by the sale of that unit. The price to be charged is OP as this is the average revenue from the sale of ON units. Thus, the intersection of the marginal revenue curve with the marginal cost curve determines the optimum output level, but the price is determined by the demand (average revenue) curve.

The Accountant's Concept of Marginal Cost

The difference in attitude towards marginal cost between economist and accountant is well illustrated by the approaches to graphing cost curves. It has already been seen (Fig. 47) that the economist plots **unit values**, whereas the accountant plots **aggregate values**. Using the same data as that in Fig. 47,

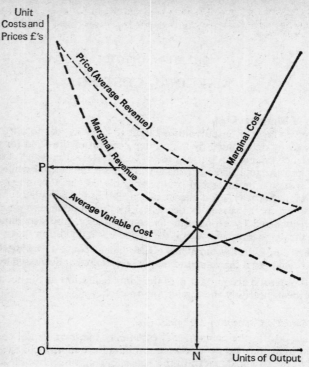

Fig. 47. Unit costs and revenues

the graph of aggregate values is shown in Fig. 48. The fixed costs are OF while FT represents the variable costs. The optimum output level is again seen to be ON which is the point where the gap is widest between costs and revenue. Output beyond ON yields diminishing profits until eventually losses start to occur.

However, in practice, the situation is just a little different from this. The current market price for raw materials can be taken as given and (all other things being equal) will be the same for an individual manufacturer whether his output level is high or low. This is so because his demand *per se* is not sufficient to influence the price against the demands of all the other users of the commodity. Furthermore, Chapter Fourteen on stock control showed that economic order quantity need not change with output fluctuations. Therefore, the price (average unit cost) of raw materials assumes a linear function and so tends to be constant at all output levels for a prescribed set of operating conditions.

The same can be said of wages costs: at any one time there is a market price for labour which tends to be paid for all activity levels, so, as with the other variable costs, labour too has a linear function. For all practical purposes, the average variable cost per unit tends to be a near constant for all output levels within a given capacity to produce. Any change in capacity (*see* Fig. 7 in

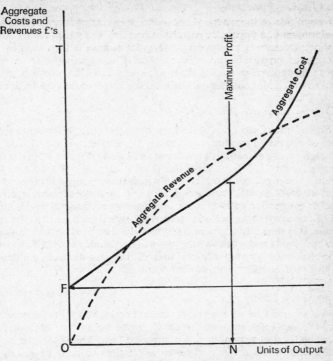

Fig. 48. Aggregate costs and revenues

Chapter Three) will lead to changed operating conditions and probably give rise to different variable unit costs, but within the new conditions the revised variable unit costs will again assume a linear function. Selling prices also (outside a monopoly situation) will be determined by the market as a whole and not by the individual manufacturer. Therefore, the selling price for the manufacturer's product is given and, being the same for all output levels, again has a linear function.

The accountant begins by defining the expected operating conditions for the business, and within these expected conditions he determines the unit costs and prices. Assuming linearity, he is thus able to predict revenues, costs, and profits for any given level of putput. The recognition of fixed and variable costs means that an increase of one unit in the output generates one more unit of variable cost but does not affect the fixed expenditure. The incremental (marginal) cost of that one unit is, therefore, equal to the variable cost per unit within the prescribed operating conditions. The accountant would normally assume linear cost and revenue curves for Fig. 48 within the context of a single company. The economist's curvilinear cost and revenue curves in Figs. 47 and 48 are really applicable to the total output of a given product from all manufacturers (that is, the whole industry) rather than related to the single manufacturer which is the concern of the accountant.

Marginal Costing Philosophy

The recognition of the marginal cost concept in accountancy has stimulated the development of a particular pattern of cost analysis which forms the basis of a distinct accounting philosophy. Marginal costing is thus seen by many accountants as providing the only acceptable basis of costing in contra-distinction to **absorption costing**. It is apparent that the difference between marginal (or variable) cost and absorption (or total) cost is the fixed cost.

Concept of Period Costs

It is argued that fixed costs stem from management policy and represent the costs of providing production capacity for a given period of time. Such costs, therefore, are essentially **period costs** and quite distinct from the output (or marginal) costs. It follows from this that all such period costs are charge-able against the profits of the period in which they occur, with the corollary that period costs cannot be carried forward to a subsequent accounting period. The purpose in valuing work in progress and finished goods stock at the end of one accounting period is to carry forward such costs to the following period. It is thus a fundamental tenet of the marginal costing philosophy that finished goods and work in progress will be valued at marginal cost. This is claimed to be not only more logical in itself, but also discloses a much more meaningful profit performance to management.

The Contribution Theory

Period costs must be paid whether or not production takes place which is why they are also referred to as fixed costs, since the output volume does not influence the level of expenditure for a period cost. Therefore, the earnings from sales must cover the period costs before the company begins to make any profit. At the same time, it should be recognized that the revenue from each unit sold is diminished by the marginal ('out-of-pocket') cost of producing that unit. This net income from sales is referred to as **contribution** since it initially contributes to the fixed costs of the business and subsequently to the profit. Contribution, therefore, is equal to fixed cost plus profit.

Profit Measurement

The adoption of marginal costing also provides the opportunity to re-structure the profit and loss account to show the contribution earned during the period. This form of presentation is more easily assimilated by non-accountants, but its great virtue is that it emphasizes the effect on profits of volume changes.

Stock Level Changes

Where sales volume differs from production volume in a given period, the influence on profits of fixed cost is particularly important. This is illustrated by the following example:

In a certain period, 5,000 tons of 'Torkit' were sold at £5 each. In the same period the output was 6,000 units. Marginal cost was £2·00 per unit and fixed cost was £1·50 per unit based on the normal capacity of 6,000 unit per period. Administration and selling expenses (fixed) amounted to £2,500.

1. *Absorption Method*		2. *Marginal Method*	
	£		£
Sales revenue	25,000	Sales revenue	25,000
Works cost of sales	17,500	Marginal cost	10,000
Gross profit	7,500	Contribution	15,000
Administration and selling		Fixed costs	11,500
expenses	2,500		
		Net profit	3,500
Net profit	5,000		

The difference of £1,500 in the reported profits under these two methods is accounted for by the increase in finished stock of 1,000 units. Under the first method these units are valued at £3·50 per unit, whereas the second method values them at £2·00 per unit. In other words, under the absorption method, £1,500 of the period costs has been carried forward to the next period, and the current period's profit is thereby increased by an equal amount.

If it is assumed that in the following period the sales volume was 7,000 units while production remained at 6,000 units then the results would be as follows:

1. *Absorption Method*		2. *Marginal Method*	
	£		£
Sales revenue	35,000	Sales revenue	35,000
Works cost of sales	24,500	Marginal cost	14,000
Gross profit	10,500	Contribution	21,000
Administration and selling		Fixed costs	11,500
expenses	2,500		
		Net profit	9,500
Net profit	8,000		

This time the absorption method shows a profit which is £1,500 *less* than that disclosed by the marginal method. The reason for this is in the fixed expenses from an earlier period included in the valuation of 1,000 units drawn from stock.

Profit Sensitivity

It is readily apparent from this example that the period profit performance tends to be much more sensitive under the marginal method. The absorption method showed a profit change of £3,000 between the two periods, whereas the inter-period profit change was £6,000 under the marginal method and equal to the contribution change. Under conditions of declining sales but sustained output levels (that is, stockpiling), absorption costing would tend to overstate profits and thereby induce complacency where it is least desirable. Conversely, it diminishes the profit performance when stocks are reduced to meet sales in excess of output.

Volume (or Activity) Changes

Once sufficient contribution has been received to cover the fixed expenses of the business, all further contribution in that period is profit. This means that profit change will be much greater than the activity change which generated it. This is illustrated by the following example of a company which is currently selling 20,000 units per period at £14 each. Fixed costs are £96,000 per period and marginal cost is £8 per unit. These results are summarized in Table 28 together with those for differing activity levels.

Table 28. Relationship Between Volume and Profit

No. of units sold	18,000	20,000	25,000	30,000
	£'000	£'000	£'000	£'000
Sales value at £14	252	280	350	420
Marginal cost at £8	144	160	200	240
Contribution	108	120	150	180
Fixed costs	96	96	96	96
Net profit	12	24	54	84
Ratio: profit/sales	4·8%	8·6%	15·4%	20·0%

An increase of twenty-five per cent in the present level of sales to 25,000 units would lead to a rise of one hundred and twenty-five per cent in profits. In other words, for this situation the profit change is five times as great as the volume change. This 5:1 ratio of profit to volume applies to other *changes from the present sales volume*—30,000 units is fifty per cent higher than the present level of 20,000 units and yields profits which are two hundred and fifty per cent greater. Similarly, a ten per cent reduction in sales to 18,000 units reduces the profit by fifty per cent. The ratio of profit to volume will vary with the datum point. For example, the volume change is twenty per cent from 25,000 units to 30,000 units, but the profit change is about fifty-six per cent; a fall from 30,000 units to 18,000 units is a volume reduction of forty per cent, but the profit falls by eighty-six per cent. Nevertheless, the significant point is that the profit change is always proportionately greater than the corresponding change in volume. This factor is especially important for decision-making and for assessing the significance of past performance. It has special relevance in interpreting published accounts—a point which is often overlooked by the financial pundits.

Application of Marginal Costing

Despite the obvious merits of marginal costing as a management information service, it is not without its critics. There are two major criticisms of marginal costing which have considerable validity. In the first place it is rightly argued that fixed costs must be met 'come what may', but that concentration on the contribution from sales may lead to the acceptance of orders at prices which are below total cost while still yielding some contribution. This is a valid criticism and needs to be kept in mind. Secondly, it is argued that there are some circumstances where it is most desirable and necessary to include fixed cost in stock valuations, for example, maturation processes, extended contracts, or long production cycles. This is quite valid but, rather than a principle of general application, it is a case of special pleading calling for exceptional treatment.

In practice, the full marginal costing philosophy is seldom adopted. However, thanks to the efforts of marginal costing enthusiasts, all management accountants recognize the importance of distinguishing between fixed costs and variable costs and appreciate the significance for profit performance of volume changes. There is also a widespread presentation of financial results in the marginal costing form to show the contribution earned by sales. Nowadays the term marginal costing tends to be applied to any accounting system which at one stage or another differentiates between fixed costs and variable costs and measures contribution from sales—whether or not the period costs are carried forward to another period.

Break-even Analysis

In a narrow sense, **break-even analysis** relates to a system of determining that level of activity at which total revenue will equal total costs. In a broader sense, break-even analysis refers to a system of analysing cost into its fixed and variable components to determine the probable profits at any given level of activity. In this latter sense, **break-even analysis is an extension of marginal costing** and provides a useful basis for business forecasting as well as for judging the results of past performance.

The Break-even Point

All costs must be met before a business can make any profit. Where the contribution from sales is less than the fixed costs, the company will incur a trading loss as there can be a profit only to the extent that the contribution exceeds the fixed cost. When the contribution exactly equals the fixed expenditure there will be neither a profit nor a loss and the company is then said to break even. That level of sales at which this occurs is known as the **break-even point** and can be derived from the formula:

$$£ B/E = F \; \frac{S}{S-V}$$

where F = total fixed expense, S = selling price, and V = marginal cost per unit.

Suppose that, in a given situation the fixed cost was £4,000; marginal cost is £1·80 per unit and the selling price is £2·60. Then B/E = £4,000 × 2·60 ÷ 0·80 = £13,000 (or 5,000 units). The significance of the B/E point firstly is, that it indicates the volume of sales necessary before profits begin. Secondly, **all contribution from sales above B/E point will be profit.**

Graphical Presentation

It is important that management understands the significance of the B/E point and is acquainted with the company's B/E volume. It is frequently desirable to use a graphical presentation for this purpose so that it is properly appreciated. There are three recognized advantages in a graphical presentation.

(1) It is particularly well suited to the needs of busy executives since the situation can be appraised at a glance.
(2) It avoids over much detail by presenting the essential features as simply as possible.
(3) The presentation is especially appealing to persons who have a non-accounting background.

Types of B/E Chart

There are several different forms of the B/E chart and each has its own advantages. However, because of the linear function ascribed to sales and costs, all are founded on the formula for a straight line that $Y = a + bX$. Y is the value on the vertical axis derived from a which is a constant (or fixed value), b is the value per unit of sales volume, and X is the volume or number of units.

The Simple B/E Chart

This is a construction of two linear curves intersecting at the B/E point and is illustrated by the following example (*see* Fig. 49). In a certain business the fixed expenses are £20,000 per annum; marginal cost is £12 per unit; the selling price is £20 per unit; and normal capacity is 4,500 units per annum.

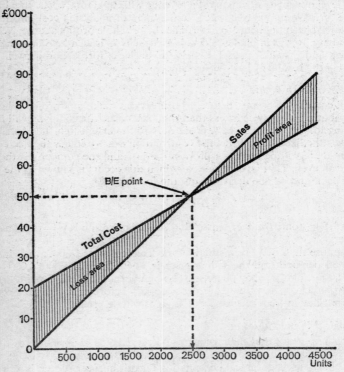

Fig. 49. The simple B/E chart

The sales curve intersects the total cost curve at the B/E point which is 2,500 units (on the X axis) or £50,000 sales (on the Y axis).

The Fantail Chart

It is sometimes useful to present accounting results in graphical form for the benefit of non-accountants and this is especially helpful in showing the analysis of revenue. The **fantail chart** in Fig. 50 shows the relative sizes of the various cost elements and the appropriation of the profit within the total revenue. Figure 50 is also arranged to show the marginal cost and the contribution. However, this is not strictly a B/E chart even though the B/E point is shown, but a **revenue analysis chart** as the B/E chart needs no more than the two curves for revenue and total cost.

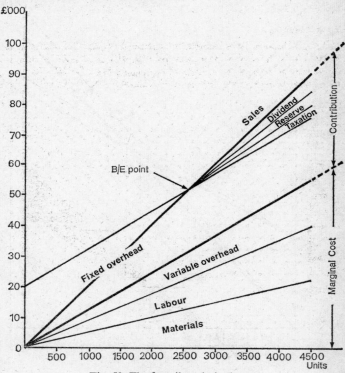

Fig. 50. The fantail analysis chart

The B/E Date Chart

Non-financial executives sometimes find the concept of a **B/E date** easier to accept than the break-even capacity. They seem to appreciate more readily the idea that the company will not begin earning profits until some time during the financial year. Figure 51 illustrates the B/E date of Omega Pans Limited where the annual sales are £500,000, marginal cost is £250,000 for the year, and the fixed cost is £150,000 per annum. This shows that the company should break-even about August 4. In using the date instead of units, it is not possible to extrapolate for activity changes since the X axis is *fixed* in length to accommodate twelve months. Furthermore, activity changes affect the B/E date but do not influence the B/E point. Should early sales suggest an annual total of £550,000 this will give a B/E date about July 15, although the B/E point remains unchanged at a sales volume of £300,000.

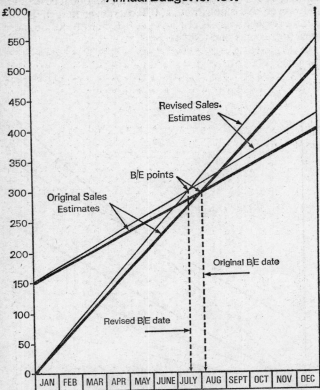

Omega Pans Limited
Annual Budget for 19..

Fig. 51. The B/E date chart

Seasonal Influence. Figure 51 was drawn on the assumption that sales accrue evenly from month to month throughout the year. This is an assumption that will be found wanting in most cases and will certainly not be valid in any seasonal trade. In this latter case it is necessary to plot an ogive (cumulative frequency curve) from month to month as in Fig. 52 prepared from the following budget:

AGRICOLA TOOLS LIMITED
BUDGET FOR YEAR TO SEPTEMBER 30, 19..

Month	Units	Month	Units	Month	Units
October	600	February	1,000	June	4,200
November	200	March	1,600	July	3,000
December	200	April	2,400	August	2,000
January	600	May	3,200	September	1,000

Selling price = £5; marginal cost = £2 per unit; fixed expenses = £35,000 per annum.

The B/E date is shown as June 15. The chart also indicates that using linear curves (on the assumption of equal monthly accruals) would give the wrong B/E date of April 30.

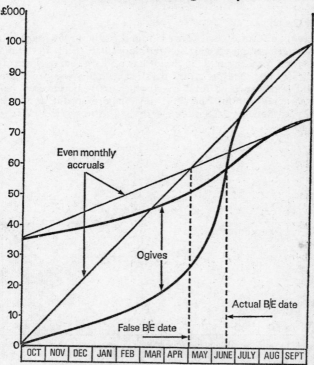

Agricultural Implements Limited
Budget for Year Ending 30 Sept 19..

Fig. 52. The seasonal B/E date

Margin of Safety

That proportion of the total sales volume which is above the B/E point is known as the **margin of safety (M/S)** for the normal or budgeted activity. Consequently, the margin of safety indicates the extent to which a fall in demand could be absorbed before the business begins to sustain trading losses. It is, therefore, advantageous to have a reasonably wide margin of safety. M/S is dependent, however, on the level of fixed costs, the rate of contribution and the normal level of sales; so that a change in any one or another of these three factors will induce a change in the margin of safety. The real significance of a given M/S is, therefore, influenced by the **profit/volume ratio**.

Profit/Volume Ratio

The contribution from sales when expressed as a percentage of sales value is known as the **profit/volume ratio (P/V)** and indicates that proportion of sales revenue which will be added to the trading profit once the B/E point has been reached. The P/V ratio is particularly useful when determining the effect on profits of volume changes and especially when considered in conjunction with the margin of safety.

The Profit Graph

An alternative form of B/E chart is found in the **profit graph** which has three advantages compared with the traditional B/E chart. In the first place, the profit graph is more simple in that it has only one curve (instead of two) which indicates the *contribution* from sales. Secondly the profit graph emphasizes the importance of fixed costs which must be covered before the company earns any profit. The third advantage of profit graphs is in the opportunity to show the M/S more clearly and to note the P/V ratio on the chart.

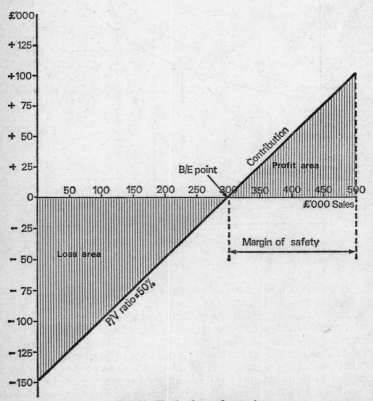

Fig. 53. The basic profit graph

The Basic Profit Graph

This is illustrated in Fig. 53 by using the data for Omega Pans Limited (*see* Fig. 51). The fixed costs are £150,000 and the contribution is £250,000 (a P/V ratio of fifty per cent). At a nil sales level the profit graph shows a loss of £150,000 which is equal to the fixed costs. As sales volume rises, this loss is diminished by the contribution from each successive unit sold. At sales of £300,000, the contribution is £150,000 (P/V = fifty per cent) and this is the B/E point which is shown on the chart as the point where the contribution curve intersects the *X* axis. Beyond the B/E point, all further contribution is clearly shown as incremental profit. The profit graph can be used also to indicate the B/E date by showing the calendar months or accounting periods on the *X* axis instead of the sales volume.

Relationship between P/V and M/S

A consideration of the relationship between the P/V ratio and the M/S for a given situation provides a valuable indication of the effect on profits generated by volume changes. In Fig. 54, (a) has low fixed costs with a small P/V (indicated by the narrow slope of the curve), but a good M/S at fifty per cent of the normal activity volume. This company will still make profits with significant falls in demand, and the low fixed cost limits the losses at volumes below the B/E point. Nevertheless, the small P/V ratio restricts the profit potential at high volumes. The position for (b) is quite different with its poor M/S as profits will cease much earlier than for (a) with falls in demand. The P/V ratio is also smaller for (b) so that profits could rise only slowly with volume increases. The position of (b) is very weak and calls for

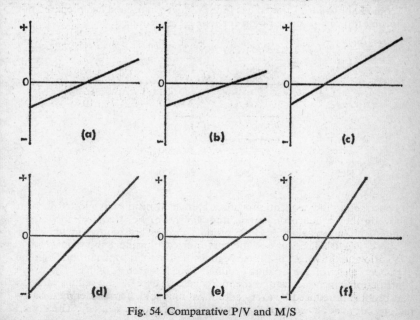

Fig. 54. Comparative P/V and M/S

a rigorous analysis of production and marketing to seek improvements. By contrast, (c) is strongly placed with a very good M/S and a high P/V. Company (d) has a similar M/S to (a) but a better profit performance through a higher P/V ratio despite the heavier fixed costs. This company is in a more satisfactory position. On the other hand, (e) is in a weak position with its low M/S and high fixed costs. Nevertheless it is better placed than (b) to make price cuts or advertise extensively to stimulate sales and improve the position because of its relatively better P/V ratio. Company (f) has a very high P/V ratio and a good M/S of about fifty per cent. However, its profit performance may be erratic since the high P/V makes profit highly sensitive for quite small volume changes.

The Sequential Profit Graph

Where a business manufactures several products of varying profitability, any change in the relative proportions of the sales of each product will affect the profit. B/E charts, however, represent either a single product (or a group of similar products) or else assume a constant sales mix between the products. The normal business situation is both dynamic and multi-product, but it is not possible to represent graphically the effects on profits of changes in the sales mix. The B/E chart is a static (snapshot) picture like the balance sheet. However, it is possible to indicate the *relative contributions* from different products (or product groups) by means of a **sequential profit graph** (Fig. 55).

Illustration

Scopic Fabrications Limited has four product groups and has prepared the following forecast in preparation for its next year budget.

Product	Sales £	Contribution £	P/V %
'A'	200,000	100,000	50
'B'	25,000	(5,000)	−20
'C'	60,000	40,000	$66\frac{2}{3}$
'D'	90,000	9,000	10
	375,000	144,000	
Fixed costs		100,000	
Net profit		£44,000	

In constructing the sequential profit graph, each product is plotted in turn following the sequence of diminishing P/V ratio. For Scopic Fabrications Limited this means that the four product groups are plotted in the order 'C', 'A', 'D', 'B'. The slope of the curve for each product shows its relative P/V ratio and the length of the curve indicates the total contribution from the expected sales volume of that product. Product group 'B' has a negative contribution which means that the marginal cost exceeds the selling value so that profits are reduced by every additional unit sold. This is clearly unsatisfactory but may be accepted as part of the total market strategy. The dotted curve is the collective contribution curve and shows the overall B/E point for this particular sales mix.

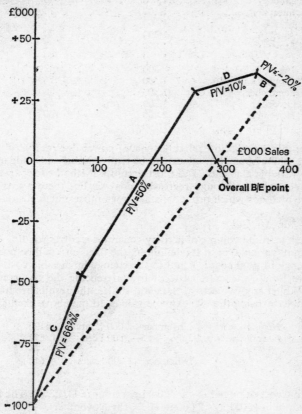

Fig. 55. The sequential profit graph

Separation of Fixed and Variable Costs

One is sometimes in the position of knowing the total costs at different levels of activity, but faced with the problem of separating the fixed overhead from the variable cost. This may be so in the case of a fellow subsidiary or of an autonomous operating division in the same company. It may also occur with service departments which have hitherto been deprived of management accounting services. Occasionally it may occur with a trade association in an anonymous exchange of cost data. A separation of total cost into its fixed and variable components adds significantly to an appreciation of the cost behaviour characteristics in the relevant situation.

The separation of fixed and variable costs is illustrated by using the following hypothetical example of the power consumption in the heavy press department of Blandish Holloware Limited:

Month	Machine hours	Power cost £
January	1,800	96
February	1,400	74
March	1,600	84
April	1,200	70
May	1,800	92
June	1,700	90
July	800	52
August	1,500	76
September	1,800	88
October	1,200	64
November	2,000	100
December	1,500	82

A study of this data discloses that the cost of power does not vary absolutely with the machine hours, but appears to be semi-variable and made up of both fixed and variable elements. The most accurate method of separating these two cost elements is through **regression analysis** but there are two simple alternative methods which prove satisfactory in most practical situations.

The High-Low Method

Any change in the volume of activity generates a corresponding change in the marginal (variable) cost. By definition, the fixed cost will be unaltered so that a change in total cost is equal to the change in variable cost. It is thus possible to isolate the marginal cost by differencing the cost and activity changes. Whilst any two sets of data will suffice, the results are likely to be more reliable by using the two extreme values. In the above example:

Highest activity:	November—2,000 hours	£100
Lowest activity:	July — 800 hours	£52
	Difference 1,200 hours	£48

The variable cost of power is then £0·04 per hour (£48/1,200). The fixed cost is £20 per month (£100 less 2,000 at £0·04 for November).

The Scattergraph

The separation may also be done graphically by means of a scattergraph. The series of observed data is plotted on a chart (*see* Fig. 56) as scatter points from each observation. The total cost curve is assumed to possess linearity (the formula for a straight line is $Y = a + bX$) and a straight line curve is drawn through the points by visual inspection. This line is known as the **line of best fit** and equally divides the scatter points. The line of best fit is then extrapolated to the Y axis which it intersects at the fixed cost interval. Drawn with care, the line of best fit gives quite good results.

Limitations of B/E Analysis

Break-even analysis has several limitations as has been indicated already. It represents a static picture of a dynamic situation which is a real disadvantage, but it is no worse in this respect than the balance sheet. There

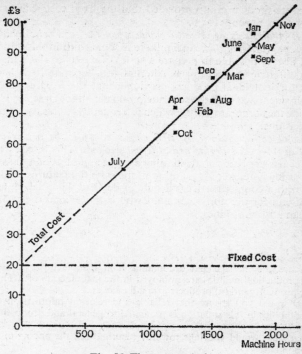

Fig. 56. The scattergraph

are several other criticisms made against B/E analysis in general and B/E charts in particular.

(1) *The total cost is not linear in practice*. Output does not usually fluctuate outside fairly narrow limits and within these limits a straight-line assumption is probably as accurate as a curvilinear function (*see* Chapter Three). However, if total costs are known not to have the characteristics of a straight line, they should be plotted accordingly (compare the use of a seasonal ogive for finding the B/E date). It should be noted also that B/E analysis does not depend on the assumption of linearity in total costs, but requires an ability to predict cost at different activity volumes.

(2) *The revenues are not linear*. In most cases the sales revenues are linear and vary directly with the number of units sold since each product has a single price. Where preferential discounts are given to special customers there will be effectively differential prices, but this is really no different from a given mix of products of varying profitability. A series of B/E charts may be helpful where alternative pricing policies are under consideration.

(3) *The X axis cannot measure units where unlike products are sold by the company*. This is true, but it is difficult to see any virtue in measuring the aggregate units manufactured or sold in multi-product businesses—especially with unlike products. It is frequently possible to prepare individual charts for

each separate product group provided that the fixed costs can be identified with the product groups.

(4) *B/E Analysis is of doubtful value when the firm sells many products with different profit margins*. Again, there is some truth in this criticism. It is, however, always possible to prepare a series of charts to show the results of adopting different product mixes. Alternatively, separate B/E charts can be prepared for individual products providing that the fixed expenses can be realistically identified with the separate products; although separate charts do not provide the corporate picture which is frequently necessary when reaching policy decisions.

(5) *The objectives gained by B/E charts can also be achieved by using schedules to report the profits and different volumes*. This is essentially valid, but B/E charts are better in facilitating a rapid appraisal of a given situation and permitting a quicker assimilation of the essential features than would be possible with a comprehensive schedule of detailed data. Schedules are also far less useful for the non-accountant who is more concerned with relative rather than absolute values.

Exercises

1. You are the management accountant in a manufacturing business where common production facilities are employed in the manufacture of: (i) high volume repetitive products; and (ii) products in small batches.
   (*a*) How would you ensure that reliable and relevant information on product profitability in this situation is presented to general and production management?
   (*b*) What steps would you take towards ensuring that the pricing of all work is economic? [C.M.A.]

2. Explain clearly what you understand by 'contribution', in a cost accounting sense. How is it related to profit? List three benefits that management can obtain from knowing the contribution from its cost units. [C.M.A.]

3. (*a*) What is a profit/volume ratio?
   (*b*) What does it measure?
   (*c*) On what does it depend with regard to a factory as a whole? and why could it alter from year to year? [C.M.A.]

4. 'The objectives of B/E analysis are concerned with financial planning, forecasting and policy-making. It is dependent on certain assumptions which limit its usefulness, nevertheless—whilst accepting the validity of the criticisms based on these limitations—it must be admitted that for most practical purposes B/E analysis is a useful exercise.'

Required:
   Explain carefully the objectives, assumptions, limitations and usefulness of B/E analysis. [C.A.A.]

5. The supporters of the technique are often heard to claim that standard marginal costing is the technique to solve the problems of product profitability and control over departmental operating costs. They argue that the profitability of a product should be determined by reference to its standard contribution rather than to its actual profit, while the involvement of a manager in cost control is best achieved by the use of standard costing, with emphasis on the departmental variable costs, over which he has control.
   Appraise and criticise the standard marginal costing techniques in these two circumstances. [C.M.A.]

6. In a company manufacturing aluminium diecastings there are three distinct product groups, pressure diecastings, gravity diecastings and sand castings. Each group is cast in a separate location and then passed through common fettling, finishing, and heat treatment operations. Administration, selling, and distribution functions and their costs are common to all product groups. Inevitably, the costs of metal and bought-out items are a significant part of sales turnover, averaging approximately fifty-five per cent.

(a) Detail the application of marginal costing in this company to determine product group and individual product profitability.
(b) In what circumstances do you consider absorption costing would provide more relevant information for management needs?
(c) Indicate the possible usefulness of added value calculations in the measure-ment of productivity and/or profitability. [C.M.A.]

7. Addit Calculators Limited manufacture a simple desk calculating machine, the direct material cost of which is estimated at £18. The machines are assembled by teams of three employees who are paid hourly rates of 50p, 40p, and 30p respectively. On average, each machine takes the team two hours to assemble. Variable overheads are estimated at £1·10 per machine.

When working at one hundred per cent capacity the factory is capable of producing 1,000 machines per week. 'Fixed' costs amount to £1,050 per week up to eighty per cent capacity. Production over eighty per cent of capacity attracts additional costs for canteen and other facilities of £55 per week, whilst production over ninety per cent and up to one hundred and ten per cent of capacity attracts further costs of £25 per week for materials handling and other works services.

Overtime working is necessary for production in excess of one hundred per cent capacity and an overtime premium of one-third of basic wage rates becomes payable. You are required:

(a) to calculate the unit costs at production levels of sixty per cent, eighty-five per cent and one hundred and ten per cent of capacity;
(b) to calculate the weekly profit at each of these production levels, assuming in each case no opening or closing stocks or work in progress and that all machines produced are sold at £30 each. [A.C.A.]

8. Using the information given below:
(a) prepare a simple graph to calculate the approximate amount of fixed cost in the delivery expenditure;
(b) give a formula for estimating delivery cost for the annual budget:

Month	Sales £'000	Delivery costs £
July	162	6,610
August	104	5,850
September	360	8,229
October	540	10,308
November	756	12,411
December	822	13,021
January	880	13,920
February	970	14,760
March	922	14,482
April	420	9,010
May	310	8,007
June	284	7,841

[C.M.A.]

9. Antarctic Frozen Produce Limited has prepared the following sales forecast for next year:

Month	£'000	Month	£'000
January	9	July	36
February	3	August	30
March	6	September	18
April	12	October	6
May	18	November	3
June	24	December	15

(i) Fixed costs are £64,000 per annum.
(ii) The company's profit/volume ratio is sixty per cent.

Required:
(a) What profit would you expect the company to make next year?
(b) At what sales value will the company break even during the year?
(c) Construct a profit graph (taking due account of the seasonal nature of the business) to show the *date* on which the company can expect to reach its B/E point.

[C.A.A.]

10. A manufacturing company produces and sells three products 'X', 'Y' and 'Z'. From the accounts of the past year, the following information is available:

Product	Selling price per unit £	Profit/ volume ratio %	Percentage of total sales by units
'X'	50·00	10	50
'Y'	37·50	20	40
'Z'	25·00	40	10

Total fixed costs £32,500

Management is concerned that the overall profit picture might be improved by selling a greater proportion of more profitable lines. After a full investigation it is found that the following sales mix should be possible in future.

	% by units
Product: 'X'	30
'Y'	50
'Z'	20

Present the following information to management:
(a) a B/E chart for the existing sales mix showing the combined units of sale in 1,000 unit intervals up to a maximum of 7,000 units;
(b) a profit/volume graph for both the existing and proposed sales mix over the same range as in (a) above.

[C.M.A.]

11. Middleford Engineering Limited makes up its accounts to September 30 in each year. The summarized trading results for 1968 and 1973 are given below. Between these two years there has been no significant change in product design nor in manufacturing techniques, but output has risen by forty per cent during the period.

	1968 £	1973 £	1973 Price index (1968 = 100)
Materials consumed	150,000	270,000	120
Direct wages paid	105,000	210,000	150
Variable overheads	60,000	102,000	125
Fixed overheads	187,500	214,500	112
Trading profits	97,500	127,500	—
Sales value of output	600,000	924,000	110

Required:
A statement showing those factors which have caused the variation in trading profits and the extent to which each of these factors has influenced the profit increase.

[C.A.A.]

12. The management of a manufacturing company wishes to produce two products 'R' and 'S'. Two processes are necessary for the production of each of the products. The first process 'M1' has a maximum capacity of 12,000 hours, and the second process 'M2' has a maximum capacity of 7,200 hours. One unit of product 'R' requires twelve hours processing by 'M1' and six hours processing by 'M2'. One unit of product 'S' requires eight hours processing by 'M1' and five hours processing by 'M2'.

The variable costs and sales values are as follows:

	Per unit	
	Product 'R'	Product 'S'
	£	£
Variable cost	20	16
Sales value	40	30

Demand is buoyant and maximized production can be sold at existing prices.

(a) From the data provided, determine graphically or by calculation the output level of 'R' and of 'S' which, in conjunction, will maximize the contribution to fixed cost and profit.

(b) What is the amount of the contribution?   [C.M.A.]

13. A. Former is in a small way of business manufacturing a single product the cost of the materials of which is £14. Operatives are paid on a piecework basis of £2 per unit completed. Machine power costs £2 per hour during which eight units can be produced. The rent of his workshop and sundry other expenses amount to £126 per week. The product sells for £18. You are required to calculate:

(a) the quantity to be produced and sold each week in order to break-even (i.e. make neither profit nor loss).

(b) the quantity to be produced and sold if a profit of £35 per week is desired.

[A.C.A.]

14. The information given below relates to a company making and selling five groups of standard products. Using the information supplied you are required to prepare for the sales manager a report on the results of the year ended November 30, 1972 and on the budgeted results expected for the three months ended February 28, 1973. In the report, schedules setting out details of the profitability of the various product groups should be shown, with any explanations you consider necessary. A profit volume chart supporting the information in the report for the year ended November 30, 1972 should be included.

Data:

Product group	Year ended November 30, 1972			Three months to February 28, 1973
	Sales	Variable costs	Fixed costs	Budgeted sales
	£'000	£'000	£'000	£'000
'L'	80	84	20	10
'M'	140	84	20	20
'N'	380	209	50	150
'O'	230	184	47	110
'P'	170	119	23	10

It is expected that the profit/volume ratios of the product groups and the total fixed costs will remain unchanged for 1973.   [C.M.A.]

15. The following results are reported by the Rotary Spandrel Company Limited.

Quarter	Sales £	Profits £	Output (units)
1 (actual)	20,020	3,008	6,400
2 (actual)	27,060	5,824	8,200
3 (actual)	24,750	4,900	7,500
4 (estimate)	22,770	4,108	6,900

Required:

From the above information calculate:
(*a*) The marginal contribution per unit.
(*b*) the profit/volume ratio.
(*c*) The margin of safety for the year.   [C.A.A.]

16. Spatial Limited manufactures three distinctive products and the following details are taken from the budget which has been prepared for 1973.

Product	'Tradex'	'Kentic'	'Longon'
Unit selling prices:	£5·0	£20·0	£2·0
Unit marginal costs:	£3·2	£8·0	£1·5
Sales volume (units)	10,000	2,000	40,000

Fixed expenses amount to £40,000 per annum.

Required:

Construct a sequential profit graph and indicate thereon the company's B/E point as a *percentage* of the budgeted activity.   [C.A.A.]

17. The monthly cost figures for production in a manufacturing company are:

	£
Variable costs	120,000
Fixed costs	35,000
Total	£155,000

The normal monthly sales figure is £200,000.

Actual sales figures for three separate months are:

First month	Second month	Third month
£	£	£
200,000	165,000	235,000

Under a system of marginal costing stocks are valued as follows:

	First month	Second month	Third month
	£	£	£
Opening stock	84,000	84,000	105,000
Closing stock	84,000	105,000	84,000

If the marginal costing technique were not used stocks would be valued as follows:

	First month	Second month	Third month
	£	£	£
Opening stock	108,500	108,500	135,625
Closing stock	108,500	135,625	108,500

Prepare *two* tabulations, side by side, to summarize these results for *each* of the three months, basing one tabulation on marginal cost theory and the tabulation alongside on absorption cost theory.

Comment on the tabulations.   [C.M.A.]

CHAPTER TWENTY

CAPACITY DECISIONS AND PROFITABILITY

Rational choice can be made only where a decision-maker has some know—ledge regarding the likely outcome of the available alternatives and, since the ultimate objective of a business is to make profits, managerial decision-making must be **profit oriented**. In the final analysis this means that in making its decisions management will choose the least-cost alternatives, all other things being equal. Managerial decisions, therefore, depend on the availability and use of relevant accounting data. In this context, marginal costing and contri-bution become highly significant for evaluating the decision alternatives. Profit *per se* can be a troublesome performance indicator for individual products or activities as it does not vary absolutely with volume changes, or with any other variable factor, because of the influence of fixed costs. Contri-bution, on the other hand, varies directly with the level of activity and changes in contribution indicate the absolute changes in profit.

Volume and Pricing Decisions

Volume and price are not really separate decisions but two inter—related aspects of the same problem. This is a familiar situation for the monopolist who has the choice of either setting the selling price of his product or of fixing the quantity to be marketed—he cannot do either independently of the other. If he sets a high price, the market will decide the quantity to be demanded; should he fix the quantity to be produced, the market will deter-mine the price at which that quantity will be sold. This will hold true as long as the consumer remains free to buy or not to buy a product. It follows from this that volume and pricing decisions must include a consideration of the **elasticity of demand** for the product and the significance of its **diminishing marginal utility** if the business is to optimize its production. In general, the demand tends to be inelastic at relatively high prices, but becomes increasingly elastic as the price falls. Finally, the demand again becomes relatively inelastic at very low prices because of the influence of diminishing marginal utility. The starting-point then for any volume/pricing decision is the demand schedule which needs to be complemented by the relevant cost schedule.

Optimum Output Level

The optimum output level occurs where marginal cost equals marginal revenue and this is shown in Table 29 which gives the demand schedule and the cost schedule for Batbrix.

The optimum output is seen to be within the price range of £30·00 to £32·50 where the profit is £114,000. It is also here that (incremental) marginal cost (+£60,000) equals marginal revenue (+£60,000) and the contribution reaches its peak of £150,000. It may well be worth while to make a more detailed analysis in this critical area to find a better optimal point. For example, a

Table 29. Demand and Cost Schedules for Batbrix

Batbrix demand schedule			Batbrix costs schedule		
Unit price	*Demand*	*Revenue*	*Marginal cost*	*Contribution*	*Profit*
£	(units)	£'000	£'000	£'000	£'000
50·00	1,000	50	20	30	(6)
47·50	1,200	57	24	33	(3)
45·00	1,600	72	32	40	4
42·50	2,400	102	48	54	18
40·00	4,000	160	80	80	44
37·50	6,000	225	120	105	69
35·00	8,600	301	172	129	93
32·50	12,000	390	240	150	114
30·00	15,000	450	300	150	114
27·50	18,000	495	360	135	99
25·00	20,000	500	400	100	64

Note: Marginal cost is £20 per unit and the fixed expenses are £36,000 per annum.

price of £32·00 might attract sales of 13,000 units yielding revenue of £416,000. The marginal cost is £26,000, yielding £156,000 in contribution and £120,000 in profit.

Competitive Pricing

Few businesses are in the position of Batbrix, since most businesses are very much in competition with the makers of similar products and those manufacturing near substitutes. In these circumstances, the market price can usually be taken as given for the product. The individual manufacturer thus maximizes his profit through the optimization of output at the given price with lowest costs. The existence of alternative brands or near substitutes makes the demand elastic for any single product or manufacturer, even where the demand is inelastic for the market as a whole.

The importance of this is in the opportunity it gives one manufacturer to adjust his prices relative to those of his competitors. For example, a price reduction might increase a manufacturer's share of the total (fixed or inelastic) market at the expense of his competitors. However, retaliation by other manufacturers in also reducing prices to maintain their shares of the market will erode the original price cutter's advantage. That would leave the individual supplier's shares of the market in their original proportions, but at lower prices and profit margins, possibly, to everyone's disadvantage.

It is vitally important, therefore, to know and understand one's market before indulging in suicidal price-cutting. This is a marketing function, not an accounting responsibility. Accountants should, however, be aware of market behaviour when preparing data which may too glibly suggest that a price reduction will generate increased sales and higher profits. Nevertheless, where a manufacturer can gain a real advantage in sales volume from price reductions, it will always pay him to do so as long as the incremental cost of the greater output is less than the additional revenue.

Sales Promotion and Pricing

Apart from price-cutting, it is possible to stimulate demand for a company's products by sales promotional activities which increase the total costs. The net result is the same in each case; a smaller profit per unit on more units. Advertising is the first example of this. Even where the total market is inelastic, one's share of that market can be increased through advertising which seeks to persuade the customer that your product is in some way superior to those of competitors. It is even possible sometimes to establish a reputation for one's products through advertising, which enables them to be sold at a premium above the prevailing market price.

More expensive packaging will increase costs and reduce the profit per unit at a given selling price. However, attractive packaging improves the product's image and increases the demand for it, so that increased volume more than compensates for the extra cost. In some instances, notably cosmetics, it is the packaging which is the vital feature in sales especially when supported by skilful advertising. It is generally true that the public judges the quality of a product by its presentation and packaging. In the relevant market, the packaging may cost much more than the contents, but many people willingly pay a far higher price for the expensively packaged product because they blithely assume that the contents are also correspondingly better in quality. It is thus possible for the manufacturers to spend far more on the package than on its contents and to charge a very much higher price to the customers.

Special Order Pricing

It is still a common fallacy amongst accountants that the selling price of a commodity is determined by the cost of producing that product. Nowhere is this misconception more widely held than in jobbing businesses, yet here, too, the price is determined by the market. Nevertheless, cost is an important factor in pricing policy, not because it determines price, but because it shows the management whether it is worth while to accept work at prevailing prices.

Jobbing Businesses

Pricing is always a problem in the genuine jobbing business because it is difficult to find comparable alternatives as a basis for price-setting. The estimated cost of production is essential to provide a **datum line** from which to start, when deciding on the price to be quoted. It is also essential for determining whether or not the price to be quoted is profitable. In some ways, the preparation of a jobbing quotation is not unlike budgeting.

Assuming the existence of a sound costing system, it is a relatively simple exercise to prepare an estimated cost for making the order to the stated specifications. The cost is then usually **marked up** by a standard percentage to provide the desired profit margin and also (sometimes) to include a contingency allowance to cover unexpected costs or delays during manufacture. The sales or marketing manager then assesses the probability that the customer would place an order at this price. The production manager also considers whether or not he would welcome this job in the context of the present work load for the factory. The 'price' would then be adjusted accordingly.

A factory which has a long order book and is confident of maintaining a flow of fresh orders will not welcome small or difficult orders without some compensation. The company may well quote a much higher price than that suggested by the normal mark-up so as either to lose the order (without losing the customer through a refusal) or to make above average profits if the customer accepts the quotation. Alternatively, the factory may be short of work with idle plant capacity. In this case the quotation may be priced very low in order to win the order from competitors and indeed may be less than the estimated cost. In the short run, this is sound practice provided that the selling price is above marginal cost (in other words, there must be some contribution to fixed costs) and the order is for additional work which would *not* be obtained otherwise.

Once Only Orders

Manufacturers of standard products are sometimes asked to quote for supplying a single order for a large quantity to some other company which is not a regular customer. This may be an export order or perhaps the products are to be used in the customer's own sales promotion as a **free gift offer**. Such orders are single opportunities and usually depend on the lowest possible price being quoted. The quoted price in these circumstances should be set by reference to the marginal cost rather than total cost. Provided that the selling price exceeds the marginal cost, some contribution will be gained and profits will be increased by that amount of additional contribution. The special circumstances of the order prevent it from establishing a precedent for the existing sales which could generate an all-round drop in prices.

Customer's Label Sales

Large retail outlets frequently sell various products under their own labels instead of the manufacturer's. This is widely practised by the major supermarket chains which offer such products at prices below the normal selling price of the manufacturer's brand. To do this, the retailer tries to buy on terms favourable to himself. The manufacturer's costs of production (especially marginal cost) become critical in setting prices under these conditions. It is also necessary to consider very carefully the extent to which the manufacturer's branded sales may be affected by the sales under the customer's own label. The acceptance of orders for customer's labelled products can only be justified where there is an overall net increase in the contribution.

Setting Sales Commission

In Chapter Twelve it was said that the payment of commission on sales to salesmen fulfils a dual function. It acts as an incentive to salesmen to win orders, by rewarding them for their efforts but, as an avoidable cost if no orders are booked, it diminishes the employer's cost risk. Traditionally, sales commission is a fixed percentage of selling value but in a multi-product business the P/V ratio can vary widely from one product to another. The company will reach a higher profit performance from the sale of products with high P/V ratios than from products with low P/V ratios. To the salesman receiving, say, ten per cent commission on sales, it is a matter of indifference whether he sells £100 of 'X' or £100 of 'Y', yet they may have considerably different P/V ratios.

Differential Commission Rates

The effect of flat-rate commission with differing P/V ratios is illustrated by the following example:

	Product 'J'	Product 'K'	Product 'L'
P/V ratio (before sales commission)	60%	40%	20%
	£	£	£
Contribution on £100 sales	60	40	20
Commission at 10%	10	10	10
Net contribution	50	30	10

Although the salesman is indifferent to selling 'J' or 'K' or 'L', the effect on the company's profits is very different. It is in the company's interests to sell as much as possible of 'J' and to only sell necessary quantities of 'L'. There is a real need here to offer differential commissions which will encourage salesmen to sell as much as possible of 'J', reasonable quantities of 'K', and minimum quanties of 'L'.

The rate of sales commission should be related to the P/V ratio, and the following formula provides an acceptable basis:

$$\text{Ratio of commission to sales} = \sqrt{\frac{\text{P/V}}{25}}$$

The sales commission payable on 'J', 'K', 'L' would then be sixteen per cent, thirteen per cent, and nine per cent respectively. The results would then be:

	Product 'J'	Product 'K'	Product 'L'
	£	£	£
Contribution on £100 sales	60	40	20
Less differential commissions	16	13	9
Net contribution	44	27	11

Sales Price Discretion

Salesmen are occasionally given discretion to vary the prices at which orders are accepted—especially in highly competitive markets. It is generally accepted that the salesman's reduced commission is adequate protection against offering over-generous discounts. There is reason to doubt that this is so. In the case of product 'K', for example, an order taken at a trade discount of ten per cent would have the following effect:

	Gross	Less 10%
	£	£
Sales value	100	90
Marginal cost	60	60
Contribution	40	30
Commission at 10%	10	9
Net contribution	30	21

As a result of taking this order the salesman has foregone £1 of income (but gained £9 he might otherwise have missed). The company, however, has lost

£9 of contribution—a fall of thirty per cent. Under the differential scheme outlined above, the results would be:

	Gross	Less 10%
	£	£
Contribution	40	30
Less commission	13	10
Net contribution	27	20

Now the salesman's offer of ten per cent discount has reduced his commission by £3 or twenty-three per cent compared with only £1 or ten per cent previously. The company's loss has also been mitigated to show a reduction of only £7 in the net contribution or twenty-six per cent of the full rate.

Intra-group Transfer Pricing

Companies or divisions within a group frequently 'buy' products of other members of the group—sometimes this happens on a reciprocal basis. This normally desirable practice can, however, create considerable conflict between the members of the group which demands major policy decisions from group management. Conflict from the trading between the members of a group is created by the attempts to obtain favoured treatment which would not ordinarily be available; because such favoured treatment can be gained only at the expense of another member of the group (*see* Chapter Eighteen).

Decentralized Control

Individual subsidiaries frequently operate as independent units as do some divisions of a large company. In these circumstances, central control is exercised through the measurement of the profit performance of subordinate units. R.O.C.E. is particularly useful for this purpose as it permits a realistic comparison of performance between the various members of the group. Profit-consciousness, however, creates an awareness of costs which seeks to obtain preferential prices in transfers between group members.

Independent Subsidiaries

The boards of directors for some groups recognize, when the subsidiaries are required to stand on their own feet, that they should be free to develop their own policies in both marketing and manufacturing. This freedom includes the right to choose to trade with fellow subsidiaries and to mutually agree the terms of trade. In general, this means that members of the group are placed on an equal footing with competitors from outside the group, so that one subsidiary buys from another only where there is a cost advantage in doing so rather than buying from a supplier outside the group. However taking the group as a whole this practice may lead to sub-optimization when one subsidiary buys from outside the group while another subsidiary which also makes the product has idle capacity and unabsorbed fixed costs. A similar situation arises where a part is purchased outside at a slightly lower price than that asked by the internal supplier. The price-saving in this case may be more than offset by the contribution lost to the subsidiary formerly supplying the part.

Group Considerations

As a general principle, it should be established policy to buy within the group (all other things being equal) at prevailing **market** prices. This still permits individual subsidiaries to go outside the group where they consider that there is a cost advantage in doing so. Then there should be created an **intra-group trading study team** composed of suitably qualified personnel. The team's function is to view trading between subsidiaries from a group standpoint and to seek ways of improving the overall profit performance through a rationalization of intra-group transfers. This will require a consideration of the available technology, the productive capacity, and the marginal costs of production. In this way it is possible to assess the overall group contribution from sales to customers outside the group.

R.O.C.E. Pricing Decisions

In vertically integrated groups those companies in the supply positions frequently sell most if not the whole of their output to the subsidiary next in the production chain. There is considerable difficulty in setting transfer prices for this situation, and the knowledge of marginal cost is of limited value since there is no selling price to give the contribution. This is not a competitive position and there is consequently no external pricing data. The use of R.O.C.E. for price-fixing is particularly appropriate for such situations and is illustrated in the following example:

Quintain Components Limited manufacture pressure diecastings. The whole of its output is sold to another company within the same group which makes durable consumer goods. It has recently been decided that the transfer price for diecastings should be set so that in the long run Quintain Components Limited will earn the desired return of fifteen per cent on its capital employed. The following estimates have been prepared from accounting data.

Marginal cost	£0·30 per unit
Fixed cost per annum	£500,000
Capital employed	£800,000
Budgeted annual output	1·6 million units

The selling price is calculated as follows:

Marginal cost	£480,000
Fixed cost	£500,000
Profit (15% R.O.C.E.)	£120,000
Selling value	£1,100,000
Selling price (per 100)	£68·75

R.O.C.E. pricing is essentially **cost based** and is usually unsuitable in competitive pricing because it ignores demand. It is helpful in the situation envisaged, but still suffers from the weakness that opportunities for cost reduction and control may be obscured by the perennial profitability of products priced in this way. Formal cost-reduction programmes or value analysis is needed to continually monitor the cost effectiveness of production practices in this situation.

Make or Buy Criteria

The choice between making or buying a given component is one which is likely to face all businesses at some time. It is often one of the most important decisions for management for the critical effect on profits that may ensue. The choice is critical, too, for the management accountant who provides the cost data on which the decision is ultimately based.

Technical Considerations

There are certain situations where the **make or buy decision** is not really a choice at all. There can be no alternative to **making** where product design is **confidential** or the methods of processing are kept secret. On the other hand, **patents** held by suppliers may preclude the use of certain techniques and then there is no choice other than **buying** or going without. The supplier who has developed a special expertise or who uses highly specialized equipment may produce better-quality work which suggests buying rather than making. In other cases, the special qualities demanded in the product may not be available outside and so making becomes necessary.

Comparative Cost Data

Where technical considerations do not influence the make or buy decision, the choice becomes one of selecting the least-cost alternative in each decision situation. Comparative cost data are necessary, therefore, to determine whether it is cheaper to make or to buy. In general this requires a comparison of the respective marginal costs or, in some cases, the incremental costs of each alternative. Incremental costs are relevant in decisions which include capacity changes. For example, a certain component has always been bought out because the plant and equipment for its manufacture has not been installed in the factory. When considering the alternative to buying, the cost of making comprises all the incremental costs (including additional fixed expenditure) arising from the decision. The incremental cost also includes the **opportunity cost** of the investment in capital equipment, that is, the expected return from an alternative investment opportunity. A decision to buy a part which has previously been manufactured may release capacity for other uses or for disposal so that the incremental cost of the decision also includes the relevant fixed-cost savings.

Relevance of Marginal Cost

Apart from the incremental costs of capacity changes, the least cost alternative in make or buy decisions is revealed by a comparison of the respective marginal costs. Extant fixed costs will be common to both alternatives and consequently can be safely omitted from the calculation. The make or buy decision, therefore, is essentially one of choosing the higher contribution. The following example illustrates the use of marginal costing in this context.

The output of assembly No. XJ321 is 20,000 units per annum and the costs are:

	£
Materials	0·65 per unit
Direct wages	0·25 per unit
Variable overhead	0·20 per unit
Fixed overhead	0·40 per unit
Total cost	1·50 per unit

The company's buyer has recently obtained a quotation to supply this assembly at £1·25 per unit from an outside supplier.

A comparison of the total cost of making (£1·50) against the outside purchase price (£1·25) leads to the conclusion that buying is cheaper than making. Unless there is an alternative use for the released production capacity, the apparent cost saving by outside purchase is quite illusory. The real cost of buying is £1·65 per unit as purchase will result in unabsorbed fixed costs of £0·40 per unit in addition to the price paid to the supplier. The valid comparison is between the marginal cost of making (£1·10) and the marginal cost of buying (£1·25) which indicates that making assembly XJ321 will yield £3,000 (20,000 units at £0·15) more in contribution per annum than would be obtained by buying out.

The demand for XJ321 may increase beyond the present capacity of 20,000 units per annum to, say, 25,000 units annually. The factory may be able to increase the capacity by working overtime without any increase in fixed costs. There will be an increase in the marginal (incremental) costs since labour will expect a proportionately greater reward for work done outside the normal working week. It may be assumed that overtime premium will be half the normal rate but that efficiency during overtime falls by ten per cent. Higher spoilage during overtime increases materials costs by six per cent of the extra materials' usage in making the additional units. The variable overhead during overtime is expected to be at a rate five per cent above that for normal working.

Table 30. Comparison of Normal and Increased Capacity

Cost elements	Normal capacity 20,000 units	Increased capacity 25,000 units	Capacity change + 5,000 units
	£	£	£
Materials	13,000	16,445	3,445
Direct wages	5,000	7,083	2,083
Variable overhead	4,000	5,050	1,050
Fixed overhead	8,000	8,000	—
Total costs	30,000	36,578	6,578
Unit costs	1·500	1·463	1·316

From Table 30 it can be seen that total cost has risen by about twenty-two per cent for an increase of twenty-five per cent in the output which has reduced the average unit cost to £1·463. The marginal cost is now £1·143 per unit, which is still below the outside purchase price of £1·250. However, the last column in Table 30 is the really significant data as this shows a *marginal cost of £1·316 per unit during overtime working*. It is now clear that the extra capacity of 5,000 units is more cheaply obtained with buying at £1·250 per unit than through overtime working at £1·316 per unit.

Alternative Methods of Manufacture

In most factories it is possible to manufacture individual products or components by any one of several methods. All other things being equal, it will be prudent to use that method which has the lowest marginal cost since the fixed costs are unaffected by the decision.

The Bratislong Engineering Company Limited uses a valve housing in several of its products. It purchases semi-machined castings and then further machines them to its own requirements on either machine 716 or machine 802. The comparative costs of using these machines is:

	Machine 716	*Machine* 802
	£	£
Castings	1·25	1·25
Direct labour	0·60	0·80
Variable overhead	0·50	0·40
Fixed overhead	0·65	0·40
Per unit	3·00	2·85

On the criterion of total cost, the choice would be machine 802, but the respective marginal costs (£2·35 and £2·45) indicate that machine 716 yields the higher contribution. Unless there is other work available, the cost of using either machine includes the opportunity cost (unabsorbed fixed cost) of not using the other machine. This gives total unit costs of £3·40 for machine 716 and £3·50 for machine 802.

The relative cost advantage of machine 716 may also apply to other components so that this machine has a very high order loading while the other machine(s) have an order loading below their normal capacity. High order loading on a single machine may create bottlenecks unless overtime is worked to extend the capacity. This would be a similar situation to that described for make or buy decisions. Before deciding to introduce overtime working on machine 716, the marginal cost in overtime should be compared with the marginal cost in normal hours of the alternative method of manufacture.

Abandonment Decisions

From time to time management will be faced with the problem of deciding to abandon an unprofitable activity. Again, this is really a least-cost alternative decision and so made on the criterion of relative marginal costs.

Ceasing Production of Certain Products

It is sometimes suggested, where a given product is apparently making a loss, that manufacture and/or marketing of this product should cease to improve the company's overall profit performance.

ZOOMBAR CYCLES LIMITED
PROFIT AND LOSS STATEMENT FOR YEAR ENDED 31.12.19..

	Model A16 £'000	Model E35 £'000	Model N40 £'000	Total £'000
Direct materials	110	100	150	360
Direct labour	50	40	80	170
Variable overhead	65	60	100	225
Fixed overhead	45	120	220	385
TOTAL COSTS	270	320	550	1,140
Profit/(loss)	45	65	(50)	60
SALES VALUE	315	385	500	1,200

Model N40 is incurring losses of £50,000 per annum, which is ten per cent of its sales value. The implication of this profit and loss statement is that the withdrawal of Model N40 from the market will avoid losing £50,000 and (by inference) raise profits to £110,000. This is faulty reasoning, but a risk which is inherent in the total cost form of presentation. The marginal presentation of the year's results would avoid the risk and give a more meaningful report.

ZOOMBAR CYCLES LIMITED
PROFIT AND LOSS STATEMENT FOR YEAR ENDED 31.12.19..

	Model A16 £'000	Model E35 £'000	Model N40 £'000	Total £'000
Sales value	315	385	500	1,200
Marginal cost	225	200	330	755
CONTRIBUTION	90	185	170	445
Fixed overhead				385
PROFIT/(LOSS)				60

Since Model N40 yields an annual contribution of £170,000, the abandonment of this product will lose this contribution and so turn the overall profit of £60,000 into a *loss* of £110,000. (The contribution from A16 and E35 is £275,000 towards the fixed costs of £385,000.) The marginal presentation shows that it is better to continue production of Model N40 rather than lose its contribution. As a general proposition it can be postulated that it is more profitable to continue marketing a product which yields some contribution rather than abandon it. (If possible, it would be better still to replace it with another product having a higher P/V ratio.)

Temporary Closure of Factory or Department

Here there is a similar situation to that of discontinuance of a product such as Model N40. A factory which is expected to earn some contribution should continue in operation rather than be shut down. However, if the factory is part of a group, the decision is quite different when the output from the closed factory is not lost but transferred to another factory in the group with spare capacity. For example, a temporary fall in the sales volume of a company's products may result in either of two factories being capable of satisfying the expected demand. In this situation the company can optimize its profits by concentrating production in that factory which has the lowest marginal costs. In reaching a decision, consideration should be given to predictable cost changes generated by the decision: such as additional distribution costs, care and maintenance of the closed premises, restarting costs, and any fixed cost savings such as salaries in the closed factory.

Permanent Abandonment of Premises

A company may find it more profitable to concentrate its output in some factories by closing down others. The decision, in this instance, is made on the basis of incremental costs and will depend on that combination of resources which yields the greater overall group profit. The permanent closure of a factory saves fixed cost expenditure and also frees capital (by the sale of assets) for alternative investment, as well as providing the opportunity to take advantage of low marginal costs elsewhere. It is possible that the sale of freehold land and buildings could provide considerable investment funds free of interest which would make the abandonment particularly attractive. This has been demonstrated effectively by **asset stripping** following a successful takeover.

There may be a high social cost in a factory closure which is difficult to evaluate, but in any case it will be borne by the whole community rather than the individual manufacturer. A growing awareness of the social consequences which follow factory closures may persuade politicians that the cost to the community represents a hidden subsidy to the profits of an individual company. A tax or other deterrent for such cases in the future would be an additional cost of abandonment decisions and so make it relatively less profitable to close a factory.

Evaluation of Limiting Factors

In discussing the considerations to be made for setting budgets (*see* Chapter Fifteen) reference was made to **limiting factors** and the constraints which they impose on budgeting. **A limiting factor in the activities of a business is one which will limit the volume of output at a given point in time or over a period of time.** Limiting factors are essentially short-term problems as they can usually be eliminated in the long term. However, a limiting factor implies an output constraint and the management must determine the optimum output within that constraint. To make the optimum use of resources requires that the limiting factor be properly evaluated.

Units of Limiting Factor

When a limiting factor has been identified, the *contribution* is expressed as a rate per unit of that limiting factor. Typical units of limiting factor include:

> **Per £ of materials, or labour, or overhead.**
> **Per hour of direct labour or machine time.**
> **Per unit of product, or floor space.**

A comparison of the contributions per unit of limiting factor made by alternative courses of action indicates the more profitable alternatives. This assists management decision-making towards optimal profit performance.

Illustration

TEPHRITE PRODUCTS LIMITED
SALES BUDGET FOR SEPTEMBER 19..

	Product group 'A' £'000	*Product group 'B'* £'000	*Product group 'C'* £'000	*Total* £'000
Direct materials	150	150	300	600
Direct labour	50	100	90	240
Variable overhead	50	150	150	350
Marginal cost	250	400	540	1,190
Contribution	150	200	360	710
Sales value	400	600	900	1,900
Contribution	£	£	£	
Per £ sales	0·375	0·333	0·400	
Per £ materials	1·000	1·333	1·200	
Per £ labour	3·000	2·000	4·000	

Limiting Factor—Materials

When the supply of materials is limited it is more profitable to use it for product group 'B' than for either 'A' or 'C'. Any materials surplus to requirements for 'B' should be applied in the manufacture of 'C'. To make the most profitable use of this limited material, product 'A' should be manufactured only after the demand for 'B' and 'C' has been satisfied (all other things being equal).

MATERIALS USED WHOLLY FOR ONE PRODUCT

	Product group 'A' £'000	*Product group 'B'* £'000	*Product group 'C'* £'000
Direct materials	600	600	600
Direct labour	200	400	180
Variable overhead	200	600	300
Marginal cost	1,000	1,600	1,080
Contribution	600	800	720
Sales value	1,600	2,400	1,800

To make as much as possible of product group 'B' will maximize the contribution of £800,000, an increase of £90,000 over the original budget for Tephrite Products Limited. However, compared with the budget figure of £240,000 for direct labour, this new output level for 'B' requires £400,000 of direct labour. An increase of two-thirds in the labour force may not be practical, especially in the short term, so that direct labour would then become the limiting factor.

Limiting Factor—Direct Labour

When there is a shortage of labour, Tephrite Products Limited should concentrate on manufacturing product group 'C' since this yields the highest contribution per unit of direct labour. Labour which is surplus to 'C' should first be applied to product group 'A' and then to product group 'B'.

LABOUR USED WHOLLY FOR ONE PRODUCT

	Product group 'A' £'000	Product group 'B' £'000	Product group 'C' £'000
Direct materials	720	360	800
Direct labour	240	240	240
Variable overhead	240	360	400
Marginal cost	1,200	960	1,440
Contribution	720	480	960
Sales value	1,920	1,440	2,400

To use the whole of the budgeted labour in producing 'C' would increase the contribution (and profit) by £250,000. It might be difficult to procure all the materials needed to produce 'C' and/or to realize sales of £2,400,000 (an increase of about twenty-six per cent over the budgeted sales for 'C').

Optimum Mix

It may be assumed that the supply of materials for September is limited to the budget figure of £600,000 and that in the same period the direct labour will not be more than £240,000. The optimum production mix with both these constraints will yield the best possible profit performance in the circumstances. The following calculation assumes that production of 'A' can be safely discontinued.

(a) **Greatest possible output of 'B'**
  Ratio of materials to labour is 3:2.
  Limited materials £600,000 requires labour £400,000.
  Limited labour £240,000 requires materials £360,000.

Greatest possible output of 'C'
  Ratio of materials to labour is 10:3.
  Limited materials £600,000 requires labour £180,000.
  Limited labour £240,000 requires materials £800,000.

Therefore, the maximum output of 'C' would use all the materials, but only £180,000 direct labour leaving for 'B' £60,000 direct labour but no materials.

(b) The total contribution can be increased by transferring materials to 'B' from the total allocation made to 'C'. Every £30 materials transferred releases £9 labour, but £30 materials on 'B' requires £20 labour. The remaining £11 can be obtained from the £60,000 surplus labour allotted to 'B'. Transfers to 'B' of 'parcels' (£30 materials; £9 labour) can continue until the whole of the 'surplus labour' has been absorbed.

(c) The total transfers from 'C' to 'B' are:

Materials: £30 × £60,000 ÷ £11   = £163,636.
Direct labour £9 × £60,000 ÷ £11 = £49,091.

The optimum mix, therefore, yields an extra £31,818 contribution.

Summary	Materials £	Labour £	Contribution £
Product group 'B'	163,636	109,091	218,182
Product group 'C'	436,364	130,909	523,636
TOTAL	600,000	240,000	741,818

Further Constraints

It may not be practicable to discontinue the manufacture and marketing of product group 'A' since customers who buy products 'B' or 'C' as well as 'A' may discontinue their orders for those items too. It is usually prudent, therefore, to continue offering the full range of products by specifying a minimum output quantity for product group 'A'—say, forty per cent of the budgeted quantity. The optimum product mix will then be obtained from the best mix of 'B' and 'C' using £540,000 materials ('A' requires £60,000) and £220,000 labour ('A' requires £20,000).

(a) The maximum output of 'C' would use £540,000 materials and £162,000 direct labour. The surplus of £58,000 direct labour is allotted to 'B'.

(b) Transfers from 'C' to 'B' are:

Materials: £30 × £58,000 ÷ £11   = £158,182.
Direct labour £9 × £58,000 ÷ £11 = £47,455.

(c) The optimum mix, therefore, yields an extra £19,090 contribution.

Summary	Material £	Labour £	Contribution £
Product group 'A'	60,000	20,000	60,000
Product group 'B'	158,182	105,455	210,910
Product group 'C'	381,818	114,545	458,180
TOTAL	600,000	240,000	729,090

Rather than arbitrarily reduce the output of product 'A' it may be preferable to use a selective price increase to damp down the demand and so release resources to increase the output of 'B' and 'C'. It should be noted that an increase of, say, five per cent in the price of 'A' (all other things being equal) will be wholly reflected in the contribution. In this instance, sales value and contribution will each increase by £20,000 for the period. The contribution ratios are changed too:

Contribution £170,000 = £0·425 per £ sales.
= £1·133 per £ materials.
= £3·400 per £ labour.

Assuming that the proposed price increase for 'A' reduced the physical number of units sold by twenty per cent, then the new budgeted contribution would be £732,364.

Summary	Material £	Labour £	Contribution £
Product group 'A'	120,000	40,000	136,000
Product group 'B'	152,727	101,818	203,636
Product group 'C'	327,273	98,182	392,728
TOTAL	600,000	240,000	732,364

Linear Programming

In practice, optimum mix decisions may include several variables and constraints. This is particularly noticeable when introducing substitute materials at higher or lower prices to augment the supplies of traditional materials. The exercise may also be complicated by overtime working to increase the supply of labour—but at higher rates of pay. The use of selective price changes can further complicate the situation. The more difficult calculations can be solved by the use of linear programming and for really complex problems it may be necessary to use a computer.

Exercises

1. A company manufactures a wide range of consumer hardware which is marketed through wholesalers and retailers. There is consternation amongst the top management in the company at the moment about declining profits. It is clear from cost investigations that although this is partly because of reduced volume, changes in product mix are also having a considerable impact.

In this connection, the management accountant has produced a statement showing contribution per product on a marginal cost basis. Two particular criticisms have been levelled at this, which are as follows:

 (a) That the product costs do not reflect properly the use by products of particular items of plant and the directly attributable fixed costs incurred by these, and that to this extent the statement does not give a correct picture of product profitability.

 (b) That the 'per unit of product' approach does not reflect the different sizes of batches of different products, some of which require a lengthy set-up for relatively a short production run.

How would you deal with these criticisms? [C.M.A.]

2. Because of the inadequacy of profit measurement on an absorption costing basis for the individual products made by your company, you have turned your attention to the presentation of product marginal costs, the determination of unit contributions, and the expression of these contributions in terms of the limiting factor within the business.

You are required to report to your managing director on the relevance this approach might have in cost-estimating and selling price-fixing. [C.M.A.]

3. The profitability of a business is often dependent in the long term upon the ability of its managers to innovate, and in particular, to find new products for new markets. A constant problem which arises in connection with this is that at any point in time there are many different products and product groups in manufacture at different points in their product life cycles.

Frequently there will be an outcry from some quarter that a particular product has slipped too far to be profitable any longer. It will be recognized that the product makes a contribution of some sort to profits, but it will be argued that this is not in any way commensurate with the facilities used and the expenditure of managerial effort.

What information would you, as management accountant, supply to give guidance on this problem?

[C.M.A.]

4. The buyer in your company has found a source of supply for a range of components which you currently make and which use some part of the company's facilities for ironfounding, machining and heat-treatment. It has been an argument in the company for a long time that these particular components are outside the ability of the plant and equipment to make, and that supply should be sought from a specialist manufacturer who is properly geared to produce this range of article.

The managing director has asked you, as management accountant, to advise him on the financial and cost implications involved concerning the supply of the components.

(a) Detail the information which you would expect to provide to enable a decision to be made.

(b) Suggest the steps that should be taken to provide a routine for the systematic review of the relevant facts when deciding whether to make or to buy components.

[C.M.A.]

5. A suggestion has been made that an evening shift should be introduced to increase production. Prepare a report to your managing director of the expected unit costs of items produced by the evening shift and on the comparative profitability of units produced by the day and evening shifts.

[C.A.A.]

6. The AB Job Engineering Company Limited, which was formed in 1926, had operated successfully until the late 1950s, but since then because of increased competition its profits had fallen until 1967 and 1968 when the position was as follows:

	Sales £	Profit and loss £	Fixed expenses £
1967	710,000	40,000 loss	340,000
1968	690,000	45,000 loss	342,000

In 1969 the company did not market a complete product range, but concentrated on the smaller sizes and as a result its product range consisted of only twelve main products, each of which would be built to the customer's own special requirements. In 1969 the managing director decided that policy must change and that because of the heavy incidence of fixed expenses the company must increase its product range so that sales income would increase. This policy was put into operation and the results achieved to date have been as follows:

	Sales £	Profit and loss £	Fixed expenses £
1969	828,000	11,240 loss	359,000
1970	993,600	50,298 profit	376,950
1971	1,242,000	13,540 loss	485,500
1972 (11 months actual) (1 month estimate)	1,552,500	62,675 loss	575,000

The managing director is convinced that his policy of expanding sales is still correct and feels that perhaps the main problem lies in the company's pricing policy. You are required to prepare a report:

(a) commenting on the situation to date in so far as it is disclosed by the information given above; and

(b) outlining the additional information you would require before you could advise on pricing policy.

[A.C.A.]

7. A company manufacturing one product has a quarterly production capacity of 20,000 units which are sold at £5 each. Its forecasts for the next three quarters are:

Quarters	1st	2nd	3rd
Volume of sales (% of capacity)	80%	70%	55%
Production overhead (per quarter)	£11,000	£10,500	£9,750
Selling and administration overhead (per quarter)	£7,200	£6,800	£6,200

Fixed overhead per quarter included in the above figures is £7,000 for production and £4,000 for selling and administration. Opening and closing stocks are expected to be equal. Direct wages cost is £1 per unit for all quarters. Direct material cost is £2·50 per unit for quarters 1 and 2 and £2 per unit for quarter 3 due to an abnormally favourable purchase in that quarter.

You are required to present a statement to highlight the effect on net profit of the declining volume of sales over the next three quarters. [C.M.A.]

8. A manufacturing company plans to make a profit of £40,000 in a year.

In compiling the budget for this year the following points are taken into consideration:

(*a*) Labour is the principal budget factor (or the limiting factor) and is estimated at 160,000 hours of direct labour for the year.

(*b*) Standard labour hour rates average 40p per hour.

(*c*) Variable overhead rates average 30p per direct labour hour.

(*d*) Fixed overheads are expected to total £70,000.

Owing to the wide variety of products, material content varies considerably, and may range between forty per cent and sixty per cent of sales.

Prepare figures to show the expected sales, costs and profits, if materials average forty per cent, fifty per cent or sixty per cent respectively of sales.

What contribution per labour hour is necessary to achieve the desired profit of £40,000? [C.M.A.]

9. Brandywine Limited has prepared the following forecast for the year ending June 30:

	Product 'F' £	Product 'G' £	Product 'H' £	Total £
Raw materials	16,000	6,000	8,000	30,000
Direct wages	8,000	4,000	6,000	18,000
Other variable costs	10,800	3,000	2,800	16,600
Fixed expenses	11,100	4,600	1,200	16,900
TOTAL COSTS	45,900	17,600	18,000	81,500
Budgeted net profit	8,100	4,400	6,000	18,500
SALES VALUE	54,000	22,000	24,000	100,000

(*a*) Management is dissatisfied with this forecast since it fails to yield the expected return of fourteen per cent on the capital employed of £150,000.

(*b*) There is some spare plant capacity but further labour cannot be recruited and will be limited to £18,000 in total although it is transferable between the various products.

(*c*) The raw material is common to all products and additional supplies are unlikely to be available beyond £30,000 in total for the year.

(*d*) Market research reveals that considerably larger quantities of each product could be sold without difficulty. However—in the interests of good customer relations—it is necessary to produce a minimum of each product equal to twenty-five per cent of the original budget quantities.

Required:

Prepare a report to the budget officer showing the optimum sales and production mix. Indicate whether this is likely to yield the desired return on capital employed.

[C.A.A.]

10. The annual flexible budget of a company is as follows:

Production capacity	40%	60%	80%	100%
Costs:	£	£	£	£
Direct labour	16,000	24,000	32,000	40,000
Direct material	12,000	18,000	24,000	30,000
Production overhead	11,400	12,600	13,800	15,000
Administration overhead	5,800	6,200	6,600	7,000
Selling and distribution overhead	6,200	6,800	7,400	8,000
	£51,400	£67,600	£83,800	£100,000

Owing to trading difficulties the company is operating at fifty per cent capacity. Selling prices have had to be lowered to what the directors maintain is an uneconomic level and they are considering whether or not their single factory should be closed down until the trade recession has passed.

A market research consultant has advised that in about twelve months' time there is every indication that sales will increase to about seventy-five per cent of normal capacity and that the revenue to be produced in the second year will amount to £90,000. The present revenue sales at fifty per cent capacity would amount to only £49,500 for a complete year.

If the directors decide to close down the factory for a year it is estimated that:
 (*a*) the present fixed costs would be reduced to £11,000 per annum;
 (*b*) closing down costs (redundancy payments, etc.) would amount to £7,500;
 (*c*) necessary maintenance of plant would cost £1,000 per annum;
 (*d*) on re-opening the factory, the cost of overhauling plant, training and engagement of new personnel would amount to £4,000.

Prepare a statement for the directors, presenting the information in such a way as to indicate whether or not it is desirable to close the factory.   [C.M.A.]

11. The Acca Refrigerator Company manufactures three models of refrigerator, viz. Standard, Super and De Luxe, the costs of which have been calculated as follows:

	Standard	Super	De Luxe
	£	£	£
Material	21	30	36
Labour	6	6	15
Variable overhead	3	4	9

The selling prices of the refrigerators are: Standard £50, Super £65 and De Luxe £75, and during the current year sales are expected to be 3,000, 2,500 and 1,000 respectively.

Whereas demand for the Standard and Super models has increased over the past few years, that for the De Luxe model has steadily declined, and the board have decided to discontinue manufacture of that model after the end of the current year.

The labour force released as a result of this policy decision is to be employed in the manufacture of the remaining models. Sixty per cent of the labour cost attributable to the De Luxe model during the current year is to be expended on the production of the additional Standard models, and forty per cent on the Super models. No difficulty is anticipated in selling the additional production at the current prices.

The company's fixed charges for the current year are expected to be £50,000 and are not expected to change during the forthcoming year.

You are required to prepare statements showing: (*a*) the expected results of the current year's operations; (*b*) the results to be expected during the following year.
       [A.C.A.]

CHAPTER TWENTY-ONE

CORPORATE PLANNING

Business Policy

In every aspect of economic activity there is one overriding influence of only limited resources being available to satisfy unlimited ends. Consequently, management is the art or science of making the fullest use of available resources. However, the resources are not only limited in supply but they also have alternate uses. Management is concerned with choosing between these alternate uses to make the best possible use of the limited resources available to them within the policy of the business. Decision-making, however, is related to future events and hence constrained by **future uncertainty**. At the *day-to-day level*, the degree of uncertainty in decision-making is negligible; but as the time scale extends, uncertainty increases to create the risk of ever widening margins of error in decisions. This risk can be diminished by reducing the degree of uncertainty or by making due allowance for it in decisions.

Reducing Uncertainty

It is clearly impossible to remove all uncertainty regarding future events, but the problem of uncertainty is that of the *unexpected*. Uncertainty can be reduced in so far as it is possible to **anticipate future conditions** and so predict the probable outcome of current decisions. The anticipation or forecasting of future events demands a careful study of the forces which shape them and of their influence on the fortunes of the business. In making such a survey it soon becomes apparent that the business can be affected in a number of ways—some good, some bad.

Business Planning

However, the forecasting of future events permits the business to plan its activities in such a way that it can fully exploit the changing conditions. There will still be risks inherent in the planning forecast, but they will be minimized to the extent that the *unexpected* is less likely to affect the business which has made an intelligent anticipation of the future. The plan must be prepared on a basis which views the company **as a whole** rather than as an aggregation of multitudinous plans for individual divisions, departments, and sections. It is also essential for a **long-term view** to be taken of the company in drafting a plan. Hence the use of the term **corporate planning** in this context to embrace these two fundamental requirements of studying the long-term influences on the company as a whole. Corporate planning, therefore, seeks to ensure that the means are available to achieve a given **business policy**.

Corporate Objectives

Every business, be it large or small, will have a policy which aims to achieve certain objectives. These objectives may be explicitly formulated or unspecified beyond a vague statement contained in the **Memorandum of Association**. If corporate planning is to be effective, the company's objectives must firstly be clearly defined. Planning cannot begin until the long-term objective for the company is formulated. Vague or ill-defined objectives can only produce vague plans which fail to properly co-ordinate all the various activities of the business and so give rise to conflicting decisions.

Corporate Philosophy

It is apparent from a perusal of current literature that there is no universally accepted concept of the long-term objectives which should form the basis of business policy. Furthermore, the determination of corporate objectives is very much a philosophical matter so that the definition of objectives will depend largely upon one's viewpoint. Objectives for a business are conditioned by accepted guidelines in human relationships. In other words, freedom of action in setting objectives is constrained within an already accepted code of practice for the company. This means that the objectives are set with regard to its relationship (real or assumed) with customers, employees, shareholders, and the general public. Corporate objectives must recognize the legitimate but conflicting claims of all these groups and seek some form of reconciliation between them.

Conflict of Interests

Nevertheless, in practice, one or other of these groups will be accorded priority or pre-eminence. Hence, some companies may claim that their primary objective is to serve society (the general public) or, more particularly, to satisfy its customers' wants; to provide employment; maximize long-term profits; to earn the best return for its shareholders; to contribute to the gross national product; and so on. It is extremely doubtful that all shades of opinion can be reflected in any single one of these objectives because of the inevitable conflict of interest between them: customers look for the lowest prices and highest quality; employees seek high earnings but short hours; shareholders want good dividends with growth prospects; society expects higher productivity, contributing to improved standards of living. Nevertheless, unless the company can define its objective as a company, there can be no useful purpose in attempting corporate planning.

Corporate Orientation

A thoughtful study of these conflicting interests shows that they fall into distinct groups reflecting the three principal divisions of a business—production, marketing and finance. A defined corporate objective will, therefore, be located in one or other of these areas. Once the corporate objective is defined, then the company will operate most efficiently when all its various activities are directed towards this total goal. It is a function of corporate planning to ensure that the different activities of the business are oriented towards the corporate objective. Consequently, every business will prepare a corporate plan which is **production oriented**, **market oriented**, or **profit oriented**.

Production Oriented

A business which has a special opportunity to exploit a certain resource will tend to be **production oriented** as will those companies which depend on a given resource for their survival and growth. The resource may be a particular mineral or other material; a special skill or expertise in manufacturing; unique environmental conditions or production methods. The production oriented business sees its function as one of converting its particular resource into **a marketable product or service**. Production orientation is practicable where the resource is genuinely scarce with little risk of substitutes; or where there is little or no competition from other producers; or where capital investment is so specific (or on such a large scale) as to deter new entrants into the industry.

Corporate planning in a production oriented business seeks to strengthen the company's control over the particular resource. It would attempt to ensure that the resource was used in the most profitable manner and **profit planning** would be directly related to the resource. Every effort would be made to develop new markets and fresh applications for the resource. Capital expenditure would be influenced by any proposed developments for the resource but planned growth would depend on its future availability.

Market Oriented

Where the production function is expected to produce what can be sold, the business will be **market oriented** as will those companies where a knowledge and understanding of the market environment is the basis for its survival and growth. The market-oriented business sees its function as one of **satisfying a particular need** and is appropriate where it is possible to forecast future market conditions, including the activities of competitors, with a reasonable degree of confidence.

Corporate planning would be directed towards an anticipation of future market needs as well as considering the opportunities for creating and stimulating demand for the company's products. The market-oriented business will sponsor product development and encourage technological innovation. Planned growth would be correlated with the expected growth rates of the market within the national economy, being adjusted for any changes in the company's share of the market arising from internal and external factors. Capital expenditures would be influenced by any resulting capacity changes necessitated by the predicted growth.

Profit Oriented

A business which has no overriding constraints in either resources or markets will see its **corporate objective** in terms of supplying goods or services with market values in excess of their production costs in order to make profits. Such a business is **profit oriented** since all its activities are directed towards achieving the most satisfactory profit performance. Throughout this book it has been argued that profit orientation is fundamental to every business in making the most effective use of its available resources. It is, however, particularly appropriate for businesses in highly competitive markets since it permits a flexible strategy in exploiting its strengths and eliminating its weaknesses. This flexibility also makes it suitable for a business with changing demand patterns which make it difficult to forecast future conditions within reasonable margins of error.

The profit-oriented business seeks to expand its production facilities, increase the range of its products, and extend its markets in any profitable direction. At the same time, any less profitable activities would be curtailed or even discontinued. Corporate planning would set targets which would yield an acceptable return on capital employed so that the targets would tend to be expressed in terms of profit rather than in specific plans of development. The survival and growth of a profit-oriented business depends on its managerial ability in directing the corporate efforts towards the most profitable activities.

The Growth Target

It is a truism that a business must either grow or fade since it cannot be static in a dynamic environment. Even if the management of the business wish to maintain their present position and determine to do so, their relative position will be affected by other groups which have moved ahead or fallen behind. It is not possible, therefore, to remain static in either absolute or relative terms. Consequently there can be no choice for a business but to plan for growth.

Acceptance of the growth principle for a business does, however, beg the question of the nature and measurement of growth. In a production-oriented company this might be measured in units of output; in market-oriented firms it could be seen in terms of more outlets; in profit-oriented businesses, growth would be indicated by turnover or capital employed. Real growth, however, must lie in additional cash resources for re-investment and to offset the effects of inflation by maintaining the capital intact. Despite a company's orientation, the only realistic growth target is then the net cash flow increase.

Setting the Growth Rate

At first sight it appears to be sensible to set the planned growth rate by reference to the company's future environment and the forecast prospects for growth. Unfortunately, this approach creates an awareness of future problems and difficulties which encourages the acceptance of low growth rates derived from forecasts of poor future growth prospects.

The alternative is to start by setting a desired, but realistic, growth rate in real terms and comparing this with a forecast of the company's prospects. Any divergence between the forecast and the planned growth rate calls for a careful study of the situation to find some means of closing the gap. Corporate planning seeks to achieve the corporate objective and *closing the gap* is an essential part of the exercise. The company, therefore, sets a satisfactory growth rate and then searches for the means of achieving it.

There is no universally acceptable growth rate but there appears to be a general consensus of opinion that the average company should aim for earnings growth of about five per cent per annum in real terms. This would mean eight to ten per cent annually in money values in the long run. It is suggested, therefore, that the average business should use this growth rate in its long-range corporate planning.

Long-range Forecasting

All forecasting is necessarily hazardous because of uncertainty regarding future events. Nevertheless, despite rapidly increasing margins of error as the time-scale lengthens, long-range forecasting is a fundamental part of corporate planning. Opinions differ considerably regarding the definition of **long term** and to some extent it will vary from one industry to another. In many cases, one year is the practical limit for reliable forecasting, but corporate planning obliges management to gaze much further into the future. The changes that can come about within a period of five years can often be quite dramatic, if not revolutionary. Nevertheless, such changes do not occur 'in the twinkling of an eye' but are the eventual outcome of a continually dynamic environment and, therefore, can often be largely anticipated in one way or another.

The Need for Forecasting

The need to predict future conditions arises from the inevitable time-lag in implementing major decisions, and this is especially true for planned growth. Sales promotion campaigns take many months to organize, particularly when varying forms or techniques of sales promotion have to be correlated and integrated: publicity material must be well designed and printed or made; space must be booked in the various media and product stocks must be built up and delivered to distributors. The development and design of new products may require several years of research covering materials, functional design, appearance and quality, manufacturing processes, packaging and distribution.

Capital expenditure programmes are especially critical in corporate planning, and their acceptance relies heavily on long-range forecasting. On the decision to go ahead with such a plan, the architect will be commissioned to prepare the plans. It will usually be necessary to obtain planning permission for the building which may require reference back two or three times before permission is granted. In some cases it may even be eighteen months before building can begin. A major development scheme may well cover a period of up to five years hence—sometimes very much longer indeed.

Future Conditions

Generally speaking, today's environment is largely irrelevant to today's decisions. The important factor is the nature of the expected environment on completion of the project, that is, when the decision has been fully implemented. For example, there may currently be a high level of demand for a particular product with certain design features. A decision may be taken to build and equip a new factory to manufacture the new product, but it will be five years before the first units roll off the production lines. In that period there may be significant changes in taste or fashion or social acceptability which erode the market; or competitors may introduce more attractive alternatives; or technological innovation may make the product obsolete or outdated. The decision needs to be made in the context of the expected conditions of the period five to ten years ahead and not those currently prevailing.

The Future Environment

Corporate planning requires a consideration of the company's operating conditions in the future with special emphasis on both the expected opportunities and the anticipated difficulties. The consideration of the future environment goes beyond the customers and competitors for there are many other groups which may influence future conditions—workers, government, investors, suppliers, and so on. The long-range forecaster must assess the merits and potential of likely developments outside his own firm, outside the industry of which it is a part, outside manufacturing in general, and outside national boundaries. Long-range forecasting demands an awareness of changes and developments throughout the whole fields of economic, social, and scientific activity.

The Economic Environment

The long-range planner must study both national and world-wide economic trends as a preparation for predicting the future economic environment. There is a great mass of statistical data on economic trends published by most governments as well as by various international organizations such as U.N.O., E.E.C., W.H.O., and so on. An analysis of this data provides valuable information on the probable economic environment of the future. With this information it becomes possible to forecast the growth prospects for our own national economy, for our traditional overseas markets, and for any other country. It is also feasible to predict the extent to which investment is likely to be encouraged or discouraged in particular areas or regions.

In the context of the economic environment it is also desirable to study the supply of commodities and the possibility of changes in the quantities available. Outputs may be increased through improved methods of production —crops and other natural commodities may give higher yields; minerals may be extracted from hitherto uneconomic deposits, but many natural resources are limited and will ultimately be exhausted. The forecast risk of exhaustion in a natural material prompts a timely search for natural or synthetic substitutes. Current research and exploration may indicate the possibility of new sources of raw materials, alternative materials, or cheaper methods of reclaiming used materials.

The ever-increasing dependence on power supplies in a modern technological society may also suggest future risks or advantages to the corporate planner. Here, too, there may be significant implications for many businesses. The search for and exploitation of natural gas deposits has provided the classic example of this in modern times. Not only has this affected the supply and cost of gas, but in many ways it has replaced coal, oil, and electricity as industrial and domestic fuels. This affects the users of basic fuels and the manufacturers of fuel-burning equipment as well as the distributors and producers of fuels.

The Social Environment

A study of the social environment should consider social attitudes of the population in general as well as of those who are potential customers. Great Britain, like most countries in Western Europe, is a welfare state and this influences our attitudes towards work and unemployment. There are business implications in social attitudes to trades unions, social mobility, working mothers, and so on. Attitudes to education are particularly important for the effects of educational change are usually not experienced until after several years. (The consequences of the *1944 Education Act* have taken some twenty-five years to reach full fruition.)

The results of social change are frequently reflected in modified demand patterns for both consumer and capital goods. These are seen in varying fashions, developing cults, and changing tastes. The fashion industries, especially the clothing industry, are very conscious of change which is often quite rapid and even fickle, but the less glamorous industries are also subject to change albeit slower and less dramatic. The once-popular iron bedstead was ousted by the wooden bedstead which has now given place to the divan bed. It is worth while to note that, once they were completely out of favour and no one outside certain institutions ever slept in them, the uniqueness of iron bedsteads could create a new but limited market amongst the 'trendies'. Improved standards of living and the wider availability of different foods has sharply curtailed the consumption of bread and potatoes. The popularity of ice-cream and the greater availability of fresh cream have eroded the previously buoyant market for custard powder. The growth in domestic central heating has influenced the markets for home-heating fuels.

Environmental pollution is a growing problem of an industrial society. Waste materials, slag, and refuse are often dumped in the open to create a health hazard as well as making offensive eyesores. Industrial effluents and sewage are allowed to pollute rivers, lakes, and coastal waters. Toxic fumes are emitted into the atmosphere—often with a reckless disregard for their effect on either humans or the flora and fauna of the area. Throughout the world there is a growing reaction against the ever-increasing pollution of the environment. Pollution control will increase production costs and may stop certain previously accepted manufacturing processes. Conversely, this may also provide new opportunities for chemical plant makers and other manufacturers of industrial equipment in home and overseas markets. Long-range planning should help companies to anticipate such changes and prepare to exploit them.

The Political Environment

Governments of all shades of political opinion increasingly exert their influence on the economic and social environments. Legislation is passed to curb anti-social practices; to control the use of toxic and other dangerous materials; to regulate the relationships between conflicting groups; and to protect life and property. Statutory regulations may become a serious constraint in some cases and, in others, lead to cost increases. Typical examples are easily found in the *Industrial Relations Act*, social security regulations, and the Government health warning on cigarette packets.

Government action is often designed to bring about a more equal distribution of wealth through graded taxation. Changes in taxation may also be used to regulate the economy by stimulating or damping down in general or for certain items in particular. Taxation may be used to modify the relative economic or bargaining strengths of different social groups or areas. The encouragement to open factories in areas of high unemployment through grants, low-cost rents, or loans and tax allowances provides a typical example of this. It may also be considered to be in the national interest that certain industries should be supported when they have ceased to be economically viable; that some industries should be encouraged to expand and others allowed to contract. Examples of this are found in the nationalized industries, aircraft and shipbuilding, farming and cotton textiles.

Overseas markets, too, can be dramatically influenced by domestic Government actions, the effect of these on United Kingdom industries may be direct or indirect; sometimes it influences the supply of raw materials and sometimes the marketing of finished goods. Traditional markets may be closed by legislation to protect **infant industries**, or diminished through high import duties to give a cost advantage to the home producer. Tariff barriers or quotas may discriminate for or against particular nations, trades, or products, and balance of payments difficulties may lead to the imposition of import or export restrictions. Weak economies or unstable political conditions may lead to arbitrary discrimination in trade.

The Technological Environment

Corporate planning should take account of technological developments within the industry and outside it. Pure and applied research is continually leading to developments and refinement in existing materials and products which open up new opportunities for growth. High profit margins encourage a search for substitutes and ways of enabling the marginal producer to compete more effectively. The potentially high gains from new inventions encourage research into new products such as synthetic materials to replace traditional ones and into improved production techniques.

Reports of research projects are usually available from Government research stations, universities, private research units, and (in some cases) from large manufacturers. Current technological research seldom indicates the *precise* nature of future developments, but it does show likely trends and the possibilities that may be available. This is usually adequate within the context of long-range planning. For example, developments in plastics may threaten traditional materials such as iron or porcelain for bathroom furniture and equipment; further research into the hovercraft principle may suggest new applications in transport; further sophistication in computers may open completely new opportunities in many areas.

Seemingly quite irrelevant discoveries may have far-reaching repercussions with important ramifications for traditional producers or manufacturers. A good example of this is shown by the first splitting of an atom in the Cavendish Laboratory at Cambridge University. At the time, this must have been of little interest to most people and seen as no more than an academic exercise of little relevance to normal life. In retrospect it was an event of considerable significance. Currently, British research is in the forefront of developing practical equipment for the de-salination of sea water on a commercial scale. Success here could generate considerable social and economic consequences from its application at home and abroad.

Forecasting Techniques

A number of highly sophisticated techniques have been developed in recent years to improve the reliability of forecasting. Econometricians and mathematicians have made significant progress in **model-building** as an aid to predicting the future environment. The use of mathematical models encourages a scientific approach to long-range forecasting which diminishes the level of uncertainty in predictions. However, it is necessary to guard against a too ready acceptance of the precision and reliability of numerical data implied by the supporting algebraic relationships. Even the most sophisticated economic models depend on the accuracy of the input data, and available measuring techniques are seldom so reliable that historical data can be assumed, without some qualification, to provide an accurate reflection of the truth. Indeed, the uncertainty which is present in all predictions calls for a high degree of judgment in both preparing and interpreting forecasts.

Trend Analysis

Change seldom comes suddenly although the difference may be highly significant between two periods which are several years apart. Change will occur inevitably but it tends to be relatively small from one year to the next. The past is, therefore, a useful guide to the future because of the inertia to change.

It is desirable to analyse the underlying influences of any trend pattern so that possible changes can be anticipated as early as possible. A falling trend may well level off at some minimum point; a rising trend may start to taper off because of new influences. In this latter case, the output of motor cars is expected to continue its upward trend and on the face of things there is no early limit as we move into the era of the two- or three-car family. Road congestion, however, may now begin to escalate sharply and discourage continued growth in the home market.

Trend analysis is also useful for isolating both seasonal and cyclical variations and this, too, contributes to more reliable forecasting. The identification of **cyclical patterns** is especially valuable for forecasting and for long-run extrapolations of the trend. Cyclical fluctuations are more widely experienced than is popularly supposed. The British motor industry has experienced a five-year cycle in the output of motor cars, a characteristic which appears to be unique amongst the world's major car-producing countries. Some years ago the writer discovered a previously unknown cycle of about three and a quarter years in a particular engineering company's sales pattern—a phenomenon that was never satisfactorily explained. The knowledge of a cyclical pattern is invaluable for corporate planning and especially in the timing of capital expenditures or modifying plant layouts. Nevertheless, there is still some uncertainty regarding *future* cyclical patterns which calls for caution in forecasting and planning.

Correlation Analysis

It is helpful in forecasting if movements in one's own industry are found to be in sympathy with other events. This is especially valuable where the other event precedes one's own as the time-lag provides a valuable early warning system. In using correlated data it is vital to establish that there is genuine correlation through related causation. A few years ago it was demonstrated that the level of United Kingdom unemployment tended to vary with the price of sugar in the Caribbean. This was a coincidence rather than correlation, since it would be difficult to find even a remote cause which influenced both series. Spurious correlation is dangerous as it can so easily lead to faulty decision-making.

Correlation analysis is complementary to trend analysis rather than being an alternative technique. Both techniques together provide a valuable check on each other which improves the reliability of forecast data. Since either may be used to predict future events, when both are used the two forecasts can be compared and deeper analysis undertaken should there be a significant discrepancy between them. On the other hand, confidence in a forecast is enhanced by a similar result from an independent source.

Company Profile

Corporate planning also requires some measure of introspection or self analysis for the company. The present strengths and weaknesses of the company should be objectively studied and clearly identified. They should then be viewed in the context of the forecasts made about the future environment in which the company is expected to operate. In other words, corporate planning also includes the assessment of future organizational needs to meet changed conditions. This organizational study may indicate the need to recruit certain specialist staff such as chemists, engineers, economists, or accountants. It may be necessary to re-structure the company organization to deal with new conditions or to improve communications. By its very nature, corporate planning is a **total concept** which covers every aspect of company activity both internal and external and seeks to achieve the firm's corporate objective which forms the basis of its business policy.

Exercises

1. (a) Enumerate and explain the important contributions a management accountant should make to a company's long-range planning procedure.
   (b) Once a long-range plan has been chosen and put into action, the management accountant would be expected to monitor its progress. Explain how this problem differs from that of monitoring progress against short-term budget targets. [C.M.A.]

2. Effective corporate planning depends on the prior formulation of a business policy with long-term objectives for the company which will lead to a co-ordination of all the various activities and their orientation towards the corporate objective.

Required:

Discuss carefully the factors which need to be considered in defining the corporate objective.

3. Corporate planning must recognize the importance to a business of future growth since the alternative would be decline—at least in relative terms, at worst in absolute terms.

Required:

Discuss the considerations required to determine the nature and measurement of business growth.

CHAPTER TWENTY-TWO

SOURCES OF BUSINESS CAPITAL

Savings

The primary source of all capital is **savings** or postponed consumption. Basically, people save (that is, forgo the satisfaction of immediate consumption) because they believe that they will gain thereby an even greater satisfaction. One reason for saving is to provide a safeguard against future shortages, famine, disease, or disaster, etc. Another reason is to allow something to mature and so increase the total satisfaction, as with timber, wine, and tobacco.

Capital

Savings set aside as a means of increasing future production are known as **capital**. A simple illustration of capital is seen in the **seed corn** of the farmer in a primitive agricultural society. It is possible to harvest one year's crop and grind the whole output into flour for bread-making. However, if a proportion of the crop is *saved* for sowing in the following spring, there will be less bread to eat before the next harvest, but the new spring planting yields far more corn for harvesting than was originally saved. Furthermore, without saving this seed corn there would be nothing at all to harvest in the next year.

In a more sophisticated society a similar phenomenon occurs in that business capital is postponed consumption although it will be expressed in money terms as money is the means of exchange. There is, of course, another feature of the developed economy, that the savings (or surplus) of the producer may be 'invested' in another producer's business rather than his own. Further, some owners of capital (savings) cease to be producers but lend capital to other producers and receive a share of their output as the reward for postponed consumption.

Business Savings

Some industrial or commercial concerns are firmly established and may be able to generate sufficient savings from their profits to meet all their requirements for fresh capital. Such companies are said to depend on **autonomous savings** for capital expansion—that is, they look to *internal sources* for the savings which will finance their expansion. Other companies may be quite unable to generate their own savings sufficiently to meet new capital requirements. This is especially true of the young growth companies and those seeking major expansion programmes. In this latter case, the companies must look to *external sources* of savings. Many companies, of course, use internal savings but also supplement this with external savings from time to time.

Investors

Savings, *per se*, will not increase output as was ably demonstrated by Keynes. Savings which are in effect withdrawals from the economy slow down or retard economic growth and to be really effective savings must be invested or re-invested. The normal 'saver' in any case wishes to see his savings grow by lending them to someone who needs more capital and will pay for their use. The problem is to put *savers* in touch with **investment opportunities**, but first it is necessary to consider the motives for saving and investment by individuals and companies.

Capital Security

Investors who seek to maintain their money capital intact are, generally speaking, concerned with meeting some future commitment. The commitment itself may be more or less certain although its extent may be known or uncertain; or it may be seen as a completely unexpected occurrence for which the capital is a safeguard. (The *saving for a rainy day* concept.) Such an investor prefers his savings to be free of the risks which attend commercial enterprises.

Amongst others, this category of investor includes the small saver. That is, the individual who makes deposits in trustee savings banks and building societies; those who subscribe to the various forms of National Savings; and those who take out life assurance policies. Institutional investors such as banks and insurance companies will also keep at least some of their funds in this type of security. It will also appeal to business firms with surplus funds which need to be easily reconverted into cash at an early date. In general, investors who look for capital security also tend to prefer the opportunity of *near liquidity* to taking profits.

Income Security

Another group of investors will seek to secure a steady income for themselves from their investment. The size of income desired may influence to some extent the particular form of investment which is chosen. There are varying degrees of capital risk in different forms of investment, but the dominant characteristic of such investors is that a steady income is preferred to the security of money capital. Nevertheless, in many cases, the capital risk will merely reflect the income risk so that a secure income is more likely with low capital risk investments. The continuing effects of strong inflation has introduced a further very real risk for this class of investor. Although the money value of income remains intact, the continuing fall in the purchasing value of money has steadily diminished fixed investment income in real terms.

Speculative Gains

There are investors who aim to make **capital profits** from buying and selling securities. They may buy specific securities whose price they expect to rise for one reason or another. The intention is to resell later at the higher price to show a capital profit. Such investors are known on the Stock Exchange as **bulls** and may not even handle the securities when they buy at the start of the *account period* and resell before the end of the account.

Speculators are known as **bears** when they sell specific securities in anticipation of a price fall and then re-purchase them later at a lower price. Quite often bears do not own the securities which they have offered to sell but hope to buy them more cheaply before the end of the account. The Stock Exchange **stags** apply for new issues of securities at the offer price in the hope that, when dealing commences, the particular security will prove popular and quickly be sought at a premium.

Obviously, speculative operators take considerable risks as future price movements can seldom be forecast with any degree of certainty because of the many varied factors which influence stock market prices. It is doubtful that they can seriously be described as *investors* since they have no intention of holding their securities for a reasonable length of time; nor do they introduce fresh capital into the market but in a sense *manipulate* the market to their own advantage.

Job Security

Many people are willing to invest capital in trading ventures of one kind or another where they can also participate in the business management. The classical example is seen in the economic concept of an *entrepreneur*—a man who adds his capital to his skills and experience. Sole traders and partnerships fall into this category and include retailers, wholesalers, and professional people such as accountants, solicitors, and architects. Such people use their capital to strengthen their job or career prospects as well as becoming *their own boss*.

Large shareholders in family businesses are also in this category and often participate in the management as executive directors. The executive directors of public companies also invest in the company's shares; indeed, it is often a condition of their appointment. Their shareholding combined with a directorship gives them similar opportunities to those of sole traders and business partners. There is the satisfaction of managing a business and involvement in decision-making; they receive high incomes as senior executives; they are accorded an enhanced prestige and social status. Investors in this group are seldom willing (or able) to change their investments as their intention is really to secure the continuation of the business and their job with it.

Investment Choice

Individual investors cannot be classified so easily and neatly as the above four groups suggest. The majority, in fact, probably belong in two or more groups by diversifying their investments. Such people build up an investment portfolio which seeks to minimize most of the risks. However, all of them tend to consider investment opportunities from three aspects—capital risk, negotiability, investment income.

Capital Risk

All business ventures include some element of risk. It is difficult, therefore, to be assured of the security of capital invested in any but the most solid and firmly established undertakings. Companies which are *household names* are recognized as being 'safe' investments where they are long established, manufacture products in great demand, and have the benefits of good management. Even so, these **blue chip companies** are not immune from the vicissitudes of economic life; nor from the influence of security market fluctuations. New products, new fashions, and new competitors can all take their toll; not to mention the costs and risks inherent in advanced technologies as was shown by the Rolls-Royce collapse.

At the other end of the scale are the mining and prospecting companies. The search for oil and natural gas in the North Sea is a good example, but prospecting for rare or precious minerals in many parts of the world is an ever-growing activity. In such companies the capital risk is very high, but the possibility, however remote, of success leading to capital gains and high yields is sufficient inducement for some investors to disregard capital security.

The security of capital invested in a limited company may be assessed by calculating the tangible net assets value which covers the investment. The following example illustrates the calculation for different kinds of securities.

THE REVANCHIST COMPANY LIMITED

CAPITAL STRUCTURE

	£
Ordinary shares of 40p each	700,000
8% preference shares of £1 each	200,000
10% debentures of £100 each	100,000
	£1,000,000
Tangible net assets	£1,500,000

Tangible net assets per £ invested:

$$10\% \text{ debentures } \frac{1,500,000}{100,000} = £15$$

$$8\% \text{ preference } \frac{1,500,000 - 100,000}{200,000} = £7$$

$$\text{Ordinary shares } \frac{1,500,000 - 300,000}{700,000} = £1\cdot71$$

It should be noted that these values do not represent the current market prices of these securities; but the extent to which they are 'protected' by the net tangible assets. The book value of the assets may also be relatively high or low for 'policy reasons'.

Negotiability

Most investments need to be converted into cash at some time, but it is not always possible to predict when this becomes necessary. Where there is no ready market for his securities, an investor may be obliged to take what he can get on a forced sale—regardless of either a fair price or of their cost to him. A ready market, on the other hand, ensures (even in a quick sale from necessity) that he will receive what the market currently thinks his securities to be worth.

Negotiability depends largely on the safety of the investment, the regularity of income from it, and the turnover of the particular security. Investors are usually less willing to buy high-risk shares and/or those with irregular earnings. Also, securities held by a large number of investors (such as the shares of large public companies) have a much wider market than those held by a relatively small number of investors. At any one time, the turnover of a particular share may be influenced by the prospects for increased dividends, bonus issues, take-over bids, and so on.

The existence of a wide market for the securities, at all times, is the criterion of negotiability. The Stock Exchange provides such a market for securities and securities which are *officially listed* on a stock exchange are, therefore, presumed to be more readily negotiable without the risk of fortuitous loss than is the case with *unlisted* securities.

Investment Income

All investors are interested in the yields from their investments; but this will be especially true of those who seek a steady income, who in purchasing a security are really buying an **income expectation**. In deciding on the adequacy, or otherwise, of investment income there are two criteria. Firstly there is the magnitude of the income and secondly there is the security of the income.

Investors tend to buy those securities which yield the highest return on their investment. This criterion is considerably modified by the inherent risks in the investment so that, by and large, higher average yields are expected for higher risks. Also, securities showing high returns are more attractive than similar investments yielding less and this induces the potential investor to offer a higher price to secure it. This is precisely what happens with stock exchange securities, so that they change hands at prices which are markedly different from the **par value**.

Equity Yields

It is important to distinguish between **dividend** and **yield**. The earnings rate is related to the **nominal value** of the share, whereas the yield is calculated on the **market value**. This can be illustrated by reference to two different companies, each of which is currently paying a dividend of fifty per cent on the par value of its £1 shares. Company 'A' is a well-established business with good management and a steady growth. The market value of its shares is quoted at £7·50 and consequently the shares yield $50\% \div 7\cdot50 = 6\frac{2}{3}\%$ on the investment. Company 'B' manufactures semi-luxury goods and has an erratic profit record. Dividends have fluctuated widely and the management is generally weak. Its shares are quoted at £2·50 each to yield $50\% \div 2\cdot50 = 20\%$ on the investment.

Dividend Cover

Income security is partly reflected in the stability of profits since income risk is greater where earnings fluctuate from year to year. The security of investment income is also indicated by the relationship between **after tax profits** and **dividends distributed** to shareholders. The **dividend cover** is the number of times that the dividend could be met from the profits available for distribution (net profit after taxation). The following data illustrate this in relation to Companies 'A' and 'B' mentioned above.

	Company 'A'	Company 'B'
Issued equity	£600,000	£800,000
Profit after tax	£800,000	£500,000
Dividend at 50%	£300,000	£400,000
Dividend cover	2·67 times	1·25 times

Not only does Company 'A' earn steadier profits but the current dividend has the security of being supported by earnings which could fall considerably before dividends need be affected. This is not so with 'B' which offers more risk in the income expectation from its shares.

Price/Earnings Ratio

The confidence of the market in a particular equity is indicated by the share's **price/earnings ratio** (P/E ratio) which is a comparison of the market value of issued capital against the company's annual profits after taxation. The P/E ratio may be obtained by taking the reciprocal of the product of yield and dividend cover. Using the above information, therefore, Company 'A' has a P/E ratio of 5·625 and Company 'B' has a P/E ratio of 4·000. A high P/E ratio indicates that the market is expecting long-term growth with the prospects of higher future earnings and perhaps capital gains. A low P/E ratio suggests a lack of confidence in the company's long-term prospects.

Availability of Capital

The source of all capital is savings, but people's motives for saving vary widely as do their motives for investing their savings. Consequently, it is apparent that a particular investment opportunity will appeal to some people but not to others. Therefore, an industrial or commercial undertaking may find it necessary *to attract capital in different forms* if it is to find sufficient for its needs. This requires a consideration of two further aspects—the **term** for which capital is provided and the **price** or income rate of capital.

Issuing Houses

In making an issue of securities, the directors of a public company have to decide:

(*a*) The type and denomination of securities to be issued.
(*b*) The price of the securities—par, premium, or discount.
(*c*) The manner of making the issue to the public.

It is clear that these are *highly technical decisions* and it is generally desirable that the directors should seek expert advice before committing themselves. This need has led to the emergence of **issuing houses** (the Issuing Houses Association was formed in 1945) which advise on business capital and assist in raising it.

The issuing house will offer its expert advice on the form in which capital should be raised.

(i) Long term, medium term, short term.
(ii) The particular type of security relative to the term—ordinary shares, preference shares, debentures, and so on.
(iii) The appropriate manner for appealing to the public. The issuing house will also offer its experience and expertise in preparing the prospectus; obtaining a stock exchange quotation and so on.

Share Issues

New issues of shares to the public may be made through an issuing house in three ways.

(a) **Public issues** through the agency of the issuing house which receives a fee for its services. The proceeds of the issue go directly to the company and not the issuing house.

(b) **Offers for sale** to the public by an issuing house of a block of shares which they have already purchased from the company raising the capital.

(c) **Placings** whereby the issuing house puts the shares into the hands of interested investors. They may either buy the securities first or simply act as an agency.

Long-term (or Permanent) Capital

The obvious manner of raising *permanent* capital is to issue shares. The capital subscribed for shares will remain in the business and cannot be withdrawn by investors whether or not they give notice to do so. (There are occasions when capital can be repaid but this is most unusual.) There are considerable advantages to the directors of a company in raising permanent capital. There is no need to make provisions against possible withdrawals of capital and this helps to promote the financial stability of the company. The apparent drawback to the investor of an inability to withdraw sums invested is removed where the shares are quoted on a stock exchange as this provides a ready market for re-selling securities as desired.

Ordinary Shares

Ordinary shares represent the *risk capital* in a business and are usually referred to as **equity capital**. The two characteristics of ordinary shares are:

(1) They always come last in the queue for payments.
(2) After all preferential rights have been satisfied, the remainder belongs to the equities.

When profits are low the ordinary shares may receive little or no dividends; but in a really successful venture, the dividends may be very high. In the event of a company being wound up, there may be little or no payment to ordinary shareholders after the preferential rights have been satisfied. However, there could be a large repayment of capital on winding up, although this is unlikely since the most probable cause is business failure.

Ordinary shares appeal to the investor who is prepared to risk his capital for the chance of high returns. Even so, there are varying degrees of risk in different industries and between separate companies in the same industry. Prospecting companies may end in a total loss with never a dividend, although profits could be phenomenal with a *lucky strike*. New industries may give promise of above average growth yet not succeed. The distribution trade, on the whole, is a fairly safe investment and offers relatively small but regular dividends. However, equities are *risk capital* and thus have only a limited appeal to the potential investors.

Rights Issues. A rights issue of shares is an invitation to the existing shareholders to subscribe for a new issue of shares to be made by the company. The price at which the shares are offered is fixed by the directors and should be *lower* than the current market price of the shares being offered. This will discount the likely fall in market prices following the issue; it will offer the shareholders some benefit as members and also encourage them to take up the issue. It is normally better to undervalue the shares than otherwise since the offer is to *existing shareholders* who have a right to any advantages which may be going.

The number of shares which each shareholder may obtain is proportional to his present holding—for example, one for one; two for five; three for two; and so on. There is, of course, *no compulsion* on the shareholder to buy against his wishes and he may not have the cash available to do so. This could be especially the case when the rights issue is large relative to the existing shares. A shareholder may willingly buy *one for ten* where *one for one* would be less attractive. It is usual to allow the shareholder to **sell the rights**; that is, to renounce the *letter of acceptance* in favour of others. In this way he transfers the shares at a profit without actually buying them.

If it can be assumed that the return on the fresh capital will be the same as that on the present capital so that the *dividend rate* can be sustained, then the new market price will settle at about the weighted average of new and old shares. Eventually after payment of an unchanged dividend, the market price may rise because of the *higher yield*, although it may be retarded if there is a smaller *dividend cover*. Rights issues are popular with directors because of their simplicity, cheapness, and quickness when compared with a public issue of shares.

Scrip Issues. Directors occasionally issue fully paid ordinary shares to their shareholders free of charge which are known as **bonus shares**. The cost of these bonus shares is met by transfers from **reserves** into **issued capital** and the scrip issue is, therefore, sometimes also referred to as a **capitalization issue**. Generally speaking, the ordinary shareholder will be in the *same* relative position *after* a scrip issue as he was *before* it. His relative position in respect of dividend rights, capital rights, and voting rights is quite unchanged. However, when the company's prospects for growth are good, he will find that his investment steadily increases its market value.

A scrip or bonus issue of shares brings the value of **issued capital** much closer to the value of **net assets** used in the business. The **market value** of the shares is also brought closer to the **par value** of those shares. The capitalization of reserves may also be made as a ploy to ward off the risk of a *take-over bid* since the increased confidence of the shareholders encourages retention of the shares. Furthermore, any gain in the market value of the shares may preclude a 'generous' offer from outside. Scrip issues may facilitate the payment of larger dividends to shareholders without raising the dividend rate. This may be considered prudent where the company is under pressure from trades unions.

The immediate effect on the share prices of a bonus issue is for them to fall to a point where the total value of an investment remains unchanged. For example, the market value of a given share may be £2·00 before a scrip issue of *one for four*. The market value per share would then tend to be £1·80 (£2·00 × 4/5) after the scrip issue. In practice, a bonus issue is often judged by the market as a sign of good future prospects; so that the post issue market price tends to be slightly higher, say, £1·85 per share.

Preference Shares

Some investors who wish to invest in business undertakings are unwilling to face the capital risks or income risks which are present in equities.

Preference shares diminish this risk by taking precedence before ordinary shares in the payment of dividends and in the repayment of capital. Thus, in any given year, provided that sufficient profits are available—the profit is applied in paying the full stated dividend on the preference shares before any dividend becomes payable on equities. Consequently, even when profits are low, the preference shareholders may still receive dividends. Nevertheless, the profits may be too low to meet the preference dividend, so that there remains some risk. However, the company may make exceptional profits and pay high ordinary dividends, but the preference shareholders receive no more than the stated amount. In practice there are several classes of preference shares; all of which have priority over equities but also have their own order of precedence.

Cumulative Preference Shares. These shares are entitled to a fixed rate of dividend and, in addition, when in one year the profits are inadequate to meet this dividend, the **arrears** of unpaid dividend have priority in future years before the payment of dividend to the other classes of share. The payment of arrears thus reduces the risk of losing dividends due in poor trading years. Sometimes these shares have priority of capital repayment over other preference shares.

Participating Preference Shares. The holders of these shares are entitled to a fixed rate of dividend (provided that adequate profits are available). Additionally they receive a **bonus dividend** when profits are high provided that the ordinary shareholders have first received a stated minimum dividend. Participating preference shares usually take precedence **after** all other classes of preference shares.

Redeemable Preference Shares. A company's *Articles of Association* may allow the issue of **redeemable preference shares.** Strictly speaking, the limited term makes these shares a **loan** rather than equity capital and *medium-term capital* rather than permanent capital. Their advantage to the directors is that the agreed rate of *dividend* (as distinct from *interest*) is dependent on profits. In other words, if trading is difficult, the company will not have to meet the charge as it would with interest.

Medium-term (or Loan) Capital

There are considerable differences of opinion on the limits for the various *terms* of capital. Some authorities prefer only two groups whereas others suggest three categories. Most classifications observe arbitrary time-spans which depend on the writer's opinions; for example, short term is up to one year; medium term is from one to five years; long term is over five years. In this work the distinction between long term and medium term is not time-based but classified according to the need (or otherwise) to repay the investor at some future date apart from a winding up. Therefore, medium-term capital is represented by long-term *borrowing* and so redeemable. Short-term capital is that which is repayable on demand, at short notice or at a fixed date within two years.

Debentures

A debenture is a **bond** given in exchange for a loan by which the company agrees to pay a stated rate of *interest* for its use throughout an agreed term. Debentures are normally redeemable on a specified date or the redemption may proceed by stages within an agreed number of years when the early redemptions are decided annually by lot. Rarely, a company may issue **irredeemable (or perpetual) debentures** which cannot be 'paid off' or cancelled, although they are sold on the Stock Exchange. These really form a part of the *long-term capital*.

Debenture bonds are usually issued in values which are multiples of £50 or £100. Sometimes a large company may issue more than one series of debentures which are termed successively *first*, *second*, and so on; or A, B, C, etc. These various debentures rank in security according to their priority of issue. Debenture interest is a charge upon the company and must be met in full whether or not any profits are made. Debenture holders always rank for payment in full before shareholders of any class even if *unsecured*.

Debentures may be **unsecured loans**; that is, a simple promise to pay; or **secured** by a charge upon the whole or part of the company's assets.

Mortgage Debentures

These are secured on specified assets of the business. The property constituting the security is *vested in trustees* and held by them for the debenture holders who become the virtual owners of the property. No dealing in the property or change in its constitution can be effected without the prior consent of the trustees.

Floating Debentures

These are secured by a floating charge (*or general lien*) upon the total assets of the business. In other words, it is secured on all assets in general but on none in particular. A general lien does not prevent the company from dealing with its assets in the normal course of business.

Finance Corporations

A feature of the post-war era has been the creation of a number of specialized financial agencies to meet a demand for capital which cannot be easily satisfied through traditional channels. Some of these finance corporations serve industry generally, whereas others are designed to aid a specific industry, but all of them are either directly, or indirectly, sponsored by the Government through the Bank of England.

Finance Corporation for Industry Limited (F.C.I.)

The capital of F.C.I. is held by the Bank of England, certain insurance companies, and some investment trusts. It also has the support of the English and Scottish banks through substantial borrowing facilities. F.C.I. investments by way of advances are subject to a *minimum* of £300,000. Loans are repayable over a period from ten to twenty years and the rate of interest fluctuates with *bank rate*. F.C.I. does not supplant, but supplements the money market so that it is normally only willing to help companies which are unable to obtain their finance requirements elsewhere. The corporation has made substantial advances to the steel industry and also some **venture investment** in new projects with rights of conversion into equities.

Industrial and Commercial Finance Corporation Limited (I.C.F.C.)

The purpose of I.C.F.C. is to assist the business man who requires finance for expansion or development which it is not practicable or convenient to raise by way of banking facilities, or a public issue. Finance is provided in several forms, including long-term loans and/or share capital, in amounts ranging from £5,000 to £300,000.

The terms on which finance is provided are settled by negotiation but every effort is made to meet the customer's particular situation and wishes. Loan periods normally range between ten and twenty years with annual repayment instalments. A fixed rate of interest is generally quoted for the entire period, but charged on the outstanding balances.

Estate Duties Investment Trust Limited (E.D.I.T.)

The serious impact of death duties on the small family business has long been a matter for concern. Existing finance organizations and investment trusts can help to some extent, but there are difficulties where a private company is too small for Stock Exchange dealings. E.D.I.T. was formed in 1953 as an I.C.F.C. associate company with an initial capital of one million pounds.

Its objects are to provide a reliable and neutral means of **acquiring, and holding as an investment**, a minority interest in the share capital of family businesses whose shares are privately held. It thus meets the needs of shareholders (and executors or others), who from time to time may wish to dispose of a part of their holding. The trust's activities are not confined to cases where a death has already occurred, but it is prepared to consider the provision of funds to meet estate duty which may become payable in the future by existing proprietors.

Commonwealth Development Finance Company Limited (C.D.F.)

The principal function C.D.F. is to assist in the provision of financial assistance for development projects within the Commonwealth, and in particular those designed to increase resources and also to strengthen the sterling area's **balance of payments**.

Agricultural Mortgage Corporation Limited (A.M.C.)

The primary objective of A.M.C. is to grant long-term loans for periods not exceeding *sixty years* against **first mortgages** on agricultural land and buildings. Its secondary objective is to make loans to landowners for carrying out **improvements** to agricultural land and buildings.

Ship Mortgage Finance Company Limited

This is another associate company of I.C.F.C. and exists to assist British shipowners by providing finance, upon completion of construction, for ships being built, or to be built, in the United Kingdom yards against the security of a first mortgage. Loans may also be made on first mortgage of existing ships built in the United Kingdom. Normally, the size of loan does not exceed fifty per cent of the building cost (or current valuation for existing tonnage) and is repayable at six-monthly intervals within a period of from five to ten years.

Air Finance Limited

Air Finance assists United Kingdom aircraft manufacturers to increase their exports of aircraft and aero-engines by granting credit terms to overseas buyers. The manufacturer is expected to arrange for its customers to pay sixty per cent on or before delivery, the balance is then financed over a maximum of three years.

Other Sources of Medium-term Capital

Investment and Merchant Banks

The merchant banks are finance houses outside the main commercial banking structure. Their present form has arisen, in part, from their origins as merchants trading with different parts of the world. Consequently, the primary business of merchant banks is in financing international trade, although they also engage in many other financial activities including the provision of permanent capital through their activities as *Issuing Houses*. They arrange finance for the export of capital goods where the terms of payment require extended credit over several years and also provide loans or overdrafts for longer periods than do the commercial banks.

In recent years the merchant banks have increasingly developed their activities in an important area of medium-term finance through the financing of hire-purchase transactions, credit sales, and leasing facilities. Several finance companies which were originally formed to provide this form of finance have now developed their activities to the point where they are now recognized as merchant banks. The significance of these activities lies in the financial assistance they give to both vendor and purchaser with the resultant stimulus to the production of capital goods and consumer durables.

Insurance Companies

The insurance companies are very large investors and exert great influence on the capital market. The bulk of their funds come from life assurance premiums and pension funds so that they prefer medium to long-term investments with a high degree of security. They subscribe for well-balanced portfolios which include equities, gilt-edged securities, and debentures. Another important form of medium-term capital from insurance companies is in the provision of property mortgages at about two-thirds of the property valuation. The sums advanced are in excess of £10,000 up to about £250,000 (in special cases more) for periods of twenty to twenty-five years.

Government Assistance

The Department of Trade and Industry (D.O.T.I.) is authorized to provide financial assiatance to business concerns which are setting-up or expanding in the **Development Areas** where D.O.T.I. considers that the resulting employment created will be proportionate to the assistance provided. In the provision of buildings, D.O.T.I. will finance the construction and offer a lease (usually twenty-one years) at something below the economic rent, as related to the current local market values of similar properties. Buildings of a specialist nature are not leased but sold on deferred terms together with a grant of twenty-five to thirty-five per cent for either new buildings or for adapting existing ones. There are also substantial grants (up to forty per cent) for new plant and machinery in industrial undertakings.

Loans against capital expenditure are also available from D.O.T.I. for business in the development areas. The size of the advance may be up to seventy-five per cent of the capital expenditure involved and is available in respect of premises, plant, equipment, and working capital. The interest is slightly above *bank rate* and may be waived for the first year or two in the case of new businesses. Repayment is spread over a reasonable period, usually up to ten years but exceptional cases may be twenty years.

D.O.T.I. also administers a **Revolving Loan Fund** to provide medium-term loans to small- and medium-sized industrial concerns. The primary objective is to raise productivity and any project is eligible for consideration. In practice, as the funds are very limited, loans are normally given to projects which are likely to contribute quickly to the expansion of exports or to increased efficiency in meeting essential domestic needs. There are no limits to the size of loan but first consideration is given to sums below £30,000. Further assistance is available to all businesses through loans for the installation of **fuel-saving equipment**. Sums of up to £30,000 are available for individual firms with repayments spread over a maximum of twenty years.

Short-term Finance

The principal source of short-term finance is the **commercial banks**, although the **merchant banks** also make an important contribution in this area. Trade credit is another important source of short-term capital and is discussed in some depth below.

Overdrafts

The commercial banks most commonly make advances by permitting their customers to have their current accounts in debit within an agreed limit, which is reviewed from time to time. Overdrafts are technically **repayable on demand**, but in practice they are allowed to continue if the account is conducted satisfactorily. Bank advances of this kind are usually the cheapest form of borrowing since interest is relatively low (normally one or two per cent above bank rate) and charged on the fluctuating daily balance.

Loan Accounts

Loans for periods up to two years (occasionally three years) are available from the commercial banks or from most of the merchant banks. Interest charges are usually higher than those on overdrafts and the borrower is usually expected to make regular repayments at agreed intervals. They are less popular with borrowers but the banks sometimes insist on this form of advance in cases of marginal security.

Discounting Bills of Exchange

This is an important form of short-term finance—especially in foreign trade. A bill of exchange is an unconditional promise to pay a certain sum of money on a specified future date so that the banks will pay to the holder of a bill its value less a discount in advance of its maturity. In effect, the bank lends the value of the bill to its holder for the unexpired term; the discount being the interest charged on the loan. The discount rate fluctuates from day to day and is influenced by **bank rate**, the state of the **money market**, and the credit-worthiness of the **acceptor**. In accepting a bill of exchange the purchaser can postpone payment for goods, but the vendor can obtain his money straight away by discounting the bill. The commercial banks provide this service but foreign bills are usually discounted by merchant banks, whose special know-ledge of particular foreign trading enables them to offer better terms.

Acceptance Credits

The banks also provide a valuable service to their customers by **accepting bills of exchange** on their behalf. Bills accepted by a reputable bank will be readily discounted and at a lower rate than those accepted by unknown businesses. Consequently, **bank bills** are preferred by the vendors and en-courage them to sell goods against such bills. The bank knows its customers and thus takes little risk. Although the accepting bank does not advance money, it is as good as a loan to the purchaser since he really buys the goods on short-term credit.

Export Credits Guarantee Department (E.C.G.D.)

This is a Government department which encourages exports so as to improve the United Kingdom balance of payments. It issues insurance policies, providing cover (or guarantees) against the major risks of foreign trading, not available from commercial insurance. Although E.C.G.D. **does not provide business finance** in the sense of loans, it **reduces the need** for businesses to obtain additional finance to cover the risks of overseas trade. The premium rates are assessed separately for each country according to the risks involved, but with an overall average of one per cent.

Trade Credit

The granting and taking of trade credit is an important aspect of business finance because of the extent to which it occurs. This is illustrated by Table 31.

Table 31. Quoted Companies in Manufacturing, Building and Distribution for 1956

	£ millions		£ millions
Issued share capital	3,739	Fixed assets (net)	4,972
Capital and revenue reserves	4,193	Goodwill, etc.	324
Future tax reserves	592	Trade investments	283
Debs. and minority interests	1,379	Current assets	7,928
Current liabilities	3,604	Stocks and W.I.P.	3,963
Overdrafts and loans	444	Trade debtors	2,609
Trade creditors	2,050	Other debtors	12
Other creditors	76	Securities	470
Current taxation	740	Tax reserve certs.	225
Provisions, etc.	294	Cash and Bank	649
TOTAL LIABILITIES	£13,507	TOTAL ASSETS	£13,507

Source: Radcliffe Report (Committee on the Working of the Monetary System).

From Table 31 it can be seen that *trade creditors* represent over fifteen per cent of the total liabilities and *trade debtors* form over nineteen per cent of the total assets. However, it is frequently argued that trade credit does not provide additional funds for business purposes since what is advanced by a vendor cannot be used by himself, therefore, trade credit should be **netted out.** (In Table 31 this would reduce the significance of trade credit to four per cent of the total.) The validity of the netting-out argument can be challenged on the grounds that it confuses a source of capital (trade creditors) with the use of capital (trade debtors). This was cogently argued in the following passage:

> It might seem reasonable, at first sight, to dismiss trade credit as an element in the monetary system on the grounds that what is owed and what is owing cancel one another out, or that a business cannot manufacture credit but merely conveys to others credit that it has itself obtained elsewhere. It is, however, no more reasonable to net out commercial credit in this way than it would be to net out bank loans and bank deposits. All financial assets are simultaneously liabilities, but this does not make them any less important from the point of view of the monetary authorities. Any expansion of trade credit, for example, is unlikely to affect every sector of the economy in exactly the same way: some sectors find themselves net takers and others net givers of credit, and the resulting change in relative liquidity may reinforce or thwart the policy of the authorities, especially if the two groups are not equally dependent on bank and other forms of credit (*Radcliffe Report*, paragraph 299).

Granting of Trade Credit

Short-term trade credit helps to smooth business transactions in three ways. Delivery can be made as soon as the goods are ready instead of storing them while arrangements are made for payment. It is also possible to settle complaints, make exchanges, and accept returns before payment is due. Credit transactions require a fuller documentation than is needed for cash transactions so that more complete records are available and internal check is facilitated.

Long-term trade credit may be offered to assist customers with limited financial resources. There can be no strong objection to this practice provided that adequate investigation is made into the customer's credit rating. Many businesses, however, are forced by competitive pressures to grant longer periods of credit than they would wish. In cases where the market is highly competitive quality, price, and delivery may be very finely balanced so that longer credit is the only competitive advantage remaining to the supplier. This practice, if undertaken regularly, usurps the banking function with potential dangers for the trader as an 'amateur financier'.

Net Receivers of Trade Credit

Retail traders generally are net receivers of credit as they purchase on credit, but mainly sell for cash out of which they pay their suppliers. This is especially true of small retailers. Small manufacturers, too, are dependent on credit from their suppliers to strengthen their finances. The seasonal trades —particularly farming and farm equipment—look for credit from their suppliers to help them in financing their operations during the *slack* periods.

Trade credit is more important in small firms than in large, and small firms are on the whole more likely than large to be net receivers of credit. The same is true of young firms and rapidly growing small firms. When a firm is big enough to have access to the new issues market, however, this apparently no longer applies and the rapidly growing larger firms extend more credit than they are given. These are, however, very broad generalizations and the pattern is by no means clear-cut. The representatives of the Engineering Industries Association, for example, told us that in their experience 'the small firm comes off worst in engineering' and cited 'some very big firms in the Midlands that owed their sub-contractors in the Spring of 1958 for at least one more month's supplies than two years earlier (*Radcliffe Report*, paragraph 313).

Capital Requirements

This quotation provides an interesting example of the power of large businesses to obtain **free finance**, from small firms by extended credit obtained through the **slow payment** of outstanding debts. One can dispute the ethics of this practice, but it is undeniably cheaper than running up an overdraft and clearly avoids the need to obtain short-term accommodation elsewhere.

It is possible, therefore, to start a business with *less capital* than would be necessary if stocks, supplies, or raw materials had to be paid for on delivery. In other words, in the absence of trade credit, a business man would need to raise additional capital from other sources to finance his purchases. Trade credit is, then, clearly a source of business finance and recognized as such (at least tacitly) by the business community.

Exercises

1. List and briefly describe the main sources of long- and short-term capital available in the United Kingdom.

Briefly discuss the factors which will influence the decision by a company whether or not to replace short-term with long-term capital.   [C.A.A.]

2. 'The decline in volume of Preference share issues over the past years has been more than made good by the increased supply of Debenture capital.'

Comment on this statement paying particular attention to why you think the transition has occurred and what relative advantages and disadvantages such a movement has to both company and investor.   [C.A.A.]

3. Your company exports machine tools and has agreed to provide extended credit for an overseas customer.

(*a*) What arrangement would you make?

(*b*) How can your company cover itself against the risks involved in granting credit to overseas customers?   [C.M.A.]

4. The following data relates to B Limited:

        Issued capital 500,000 ordinary shares of £1 each
        No fixed interest capital

	£
Earnings before tax	120,000
Corporation tax (assumed at 45%)	54,000
Earnings after tax	66,000
Price/earnings ratio: 16	

It is intended to raise further capital amounting to £600,000 by one of the following methods:

  (i) an issue of twenty-year debenture stock at six per cent per annum;

 (ii) a one-for-one rights issue priced at £1·20 per share;

(iii) a three-for-four rights issue priced at £1·60 per share;

(iv) a three-for-five rights issue priced at £2·00 per share.

You are required to answer the following questions:
- (a) for a shareholder who had purchased his existing holding at the current market price, at what level of earnings before interest and tax would a rights issue be more beneficial than the debenture issue;
- (b) assuming the price/earnings ratio remained unchanged, what level of earnings before tax would be needed to ensure that the shareholder did not suffer a capital loss;
- (c) what factors would be taken into account in deciding which scheme of rights issue should be adopted? [C.M.A.]

5. The following list represents a few alternative methods of raising capital:
- (a) a placing of ordinary shares;
- (b) a rights issue of ordinary shares;
- (c) a debenture issue;
- (d) a convertible loan stock issue.

Required:

Contrast the relative advantages and disadvantages of each of them from the point of view of the business requiring the money. [C.A.A.]

6. A company decides to raise additional capital by a rights issue to existing shareholders. It is stated that earnings per share will be increased as a result of the issue. Would you advise a shareholder to subscribe for his rights? [C.M.A.]

7. Using the information given below relating to an industrial company you are required to:
- (a) calculate: (i) earnings per share; (ii) earnings yield; (iii) price earnings ratio;
- (b) express an opinion on the significance of the P/E ratio calculated above for a prospective investor under current market conditions;
- (c) explain in general terms the significance of a P/E ratio in the context of take-over bids.

Extract from consolidated profit and loss account

	£
Group profit before taxation	244,623
Taxation	140,302
Group profit after taxation	£104,321

	£	
Proportion applicable to :		
Minorities	3,763	
Group	100,558	
	£104,321	

	£	
Appropriations:		
Retained in the business:		
Minorities	2,928	
Revenue reserves	31,780	
		34,708
Transfer to sinking fund for redemption of debenture stock		22,578
Dividends paid and proposed:		
To minority shareholders		835
To preference shareholders in holding company, net	27,142	
Income tax	19,058	
		46,200
		£104,321

The balance sheet of the holding company shows 6,453,000 ordinary shares of £0·25 each issued and fully paid. The current market value of the ordinary shares is £0·20 each. [C.M.A.]

8. The balance sheet of Trojan Limited shows the following capital structure:

Ordinary shares of £1 issued and fully paid	£160,000
8% preference shares of £1 issued and fully paid	£100,000

It is proposed that the preference shares be converted into an equivalent amount of debentures.

During the past year the dividend rate of the ordinary shares has been one and a half times that on the preference shares and retained profits have been equal to the total amount paid as ordinary dividends.

Corporation tax rate is 45%.

Required:

(a) The maximum rate which could be paid on the new debentures assuming gross earnings, before allowing for taxation or interest, remains the same.

(b) Summarized profit and loss accounts showing the position: (i) as at present; (ii) after the changeover. [C.A.A.)

CHAPTER TWENTY-THREE

CAPITAL STRUCTURE

Capital Gearing

The capital required to run a business undertaking may be computed from an assessment of the necessary fixed assets, current assets, and non-recurring charges. Against this total requirement, an estimate is made of the short-term finance available so that the balance represents the amount to be raised as long-term capital and medium-term funds. The **capital structure** of a business is the way in which its long-term and medium-term liabilities are distributed between the various classes of contributors. The relationship between equities and fixed income securities is referred to as **capital gearing**.

Capital Gear Ratio

The capital gear ratio (or leverage) indicates the amount of issued ordinary share capital per £ of fixed income securities. This is illustrated by reference to the following alternatives for a company having a total of £900,000 capital.

	1 £'000	2 £'000	3 £'000	4 £'000
Ordinary shares	300	400	600	900
6% preference	200	300	300	—
10% debentures	400	200	—	—
TOTAL CAPITAL	£900	£900	£900	£900
Gear ratios	0·50	0·80	2·00	∞

Assuming this company earns pre-tax profits of £160,000 per annum before charging debenture interest and, for the sake of simplicity, that no profits are retained but that the equity holders receive all that is available after meeting prior claims, the effects of capital gearing in this situation are demonstrated as follows:

	1 £'000	2 £'000	3 £'000	4 £'000
Earnings	160	160	160	160
Debenture interest	40	20	—	—
Pre-tax profits	120	140	160	160
Taxation at 45%	54	63	72	72
Shareholders	66	77	88	88
Preference dividend	12	18	18	—
Ordinary dividend	£54	£59	£70	£88
Ordinary dividend rate	18·0%	15·0%	11·7%	9·8%

The significant feature of these results is the fall in the rate of ordinary dividend as the gear ratio increases.

Earnings Changes

Because the fixed income liabilities remain constant for a given capital structure, the rate of ordinary dividend will fluctuate with changes in earnings. Any increase or decrease in post-tax income will be wholly applicable to equities so that equity income fluctuates more widely than the earnings change. Initial earnings of £200,000 before tax and interest would increase equity income by (£40,000 less tax at forty-five per cent) £22,000. Similarly, initial earnings of £120,000 would reduce equity income by £22,000.

	1	2	3	4
	£'000	£'000	£'000	£'000
Initial earnings	200	200	200	200
Ordinary dividend	76	81	92	110
Ordinary dividend rate	25·3%	20·2%	15·3%	12·2%
Initial earnings	120	120	120	120
Ordinary dividend	32	37	48	66
Ordinary dividend rate	10·7%	9·2%	8·0%	7·3%

Fixed Income Investors

Gearing is not only important for equity shareholders but also to the holders of debentures or preference shares. **A low-geared company** (one with a high gear ratio) is more likely to be successful in making an issue of debentures or preference shares than would a company having **high gearing** (that is, a low gear ratio). There are two reasons for this. A low-geared company has a greater assets backing for the issue which enhances the **capital security**. Furthermore, the prior charges against income would be less so that there is also a greater **income security**.

Composition of Authorized Capital

The authorized capital stipulated in the company's *Memorandum of Association* should be sufficient to provide for reasonable growth. Consequently, most companies are usually registered with more capital than is needed initially. The consequences of making an additional issue of shares may affect the various classes of shareholders in different ways. This is illustrated by reference to the following example.

	Company 'F' £	*Company 'G'* £
AUTHORIZED CAPITAL		
£1 ordinary shares	400,000	600,000
6% preference shares	100,000	400,000
	£500,000	£1,000,000
ISSUED CAPITAL		
£1 ordinary shares	150,000	600,000
6% preference shares	100,000	100,000
	£250,000	£700,000

In the event of either company needing additional capital for expansion this can be obtained by offering to the public all or part of the unissued capital.

In the case of 'F' this can only be an issue of ordinary shares which will increase the gear ratio. The preference shares would then form a smaller proportion of the issued capital with the result that the preference shareholders have improved capital security and earnings security. By the same token, the relative position of the existing shareholders has worsened.

In the case of 'G', the company can only issue more preference shares—unless it takes steps to change its authorized capital. In this instance the existing preference shareholders will be in a relatively weaker position, whereas the lower gear ratio indicates that the equities will be greatly strengthened by the new capital earnings in excess of six per cent.

Denominations of Securities

English company law requires shares to have a stipulated nominal (or par) value, although there is no regulation regarding the amount of the nominal value. Most companies adopt the basic currency unit of £1, although there are many issues with higher or lower par values. The par value may have an important influence on the market for the share, especially with very high values: a par value of £500, for example, is likely to severely restrict the market share's. Consequently, many shares are issued in small denominations of fractions of £1 to allow for both inflation and company growth.

Par Value and Market Price

A **share** entitles the holder to a proportionate interest in the company's income and in the assets on a winding up. Once a business is established, however, **par value** may become very misleading when the **market value** is quite unrelated to it as the market value depends on income prospects and assets backing. In a profitable business, where the directors have consistently retained profits to finance growth and regularly paid high dividends, the market value would be so high as to render the nominal value meaningless.

Advantages of Par Values

Shareholders may compute their proportionate interest in corporate assets and income with relative ease. The creditors also may judge the extent to which their claims are covered by the ownership interests. It is easy to trace in the accounts the treatment of differences from par when shares are issued at a premium or a discount. Nevertheless, the loss of these advantages would not really be serious if shares were issued without a nominal value.

Shares of no Par Value

Management could issue shares at any price it wished depending on current market conditions, without the accompanying overtones in premiums and discounts. It would avoid the presumed relationship between par values and market values and so prevent the attachment of misleading interpretations by uninformed observers including buyers, sellers, and workers. However, greater knowledge nowadays, of the factors which influence market value, tends to reduce misunderstandings.

Capitalization

The capital structure of a business is greatly influenced by its expected average earnings. When buying securities, the investor is really buying **income expectations** so that the yield on an investment should be comparable with the yields from similar risk investments. There is a need, therefore, for companies to *balance* the amount of capital against the earning potential to prevent inadequate yields. A potential investor makes a careful study of any *prospectus* issued in connection with a share offer and he will not make an application for the shares unless he is satisfied that the expected yield is adequate. Consequently, the success of a new issue depends on the company's ability to earn sufficient profits to give the desired yield.

Earnings and Yield

The *amount* of capital which a company can raise is very much dependent upon its potential earnings and the yield expected by investors from that type of investment. Let it be supposed that it is intended to form a company to manufacture a new product from which the distributable earnings are estimated to be £40,000 per annum. On the assumption that the yield on ordinary shares in similar ventures is eight per cent, this company could reasonably issue ordinary shares up to £500,000. In other words, the expected income of £40,000 is capitalized at eight per cent to give £500,000. If the market looked for a yield of ten per cent, then the capitalized earnings would be £400,000 only.

Capital Requirement

The capitalized earnings, however, may be more or less than the directors' estimate of the capital needed to finance the business. If the prospective earnings are high by comparison with the funds considered necessary for the venture, the company will seldom have any difficulty in raising the necessary capital from an issue of equities. On the other hand, there are obvious problems in a situation where the capitalized earnings fall short of requirements. It is in this context that **capital gearing** becomes important.

Suppose, in the preceding example, the directors had estimated that the formation of the company demanded capital of £640,000. The earnings of £40,000 represent only six and a quarter per cent of £640,000 which is patently inadequate for equities. However, it may be possible to issue six per cent preference shares which would improve the amount available for a correspondingly smaller number of ordinary shares. Six per cent on preference shares is half a per cent *below* the average, and eight per cent on ordinary shares is one and three-quarter per cent above the average; therefore, the ratio of ordinary shares to preference shares would be 1:7. The claims on income are:

Ordinary shares:	£80,000 at 8% =	£6,400
Preference shares:	£560,000 at 6% =	£33,600
TOTAL	£640,000	£40,000

A gear ratio of 0·143 in this situation is unlikely to commend itself to potential investors in preference shares.

Capital Structure

An alternative combination of securities could include debentures at, say, nine per cent since this would 'cost' the company only 4·95 per cent after **corporation tax** at forty-five per cent. The problem may now be tackled by an arbitrary decision on the amount to be raised in *one* of the categories of securities—ordinary, preference, debentures. Let it be assumed that £240,000 will be raised in equities to give a gear ratio of 0·6. Then, the ordinary share-holders claims against income are £19,200 (eight per cent of £240,000), leaving an income of £20,800 for the fixed income securities of £400,000 giving an average yield of five and one-fifth per cent. The ratio of six per cent preference shares to nine per cent debentures is then (5·20 − 4·95 : 6·00 − 5·20) = 5:16. The company's capital structure and claims against income are then:

Ordinary shares:	£240,000 at 8%	= £19,200
6% preference:	£95,238 at 6%	= £5,714
9% debentures:	£304,762 at 4·95%	= £15,086
TOTAL	£640,000	£40,000

In practice the six per cent preference shares would probably be set at £100,000 and the ten per cent debentures at £300,000. In a situation such as this it would be essential to carefully review the proposed programme to find ways of improving the forecast earnings by revised manufacturing techniques, alternative materials, modified quality standards, or an amended selling price structure.

Rate of Capitalization

The rate at which potential earnings are capitalized will vary widely from one given situation to another. Generally, a particular capitalization rate is influenced by five factors.

(1) **Capital risk** is crucial and, therefore, the rates will vary between different industries all other things being equal.

(2) **Earnings regularity** indicates the measure of income risk. Businesses producing necessary consumer goods or those with steady earnings profiles will have a lower rate than businesses with erratic profit performances and those in speculative ventures.

(3) **Period of establishment** helps in assessing the above risks. A new company still has to prove itself and will tend to have a higher rate than similar ones which are well established with a proven past record.

(4) **Economic conditions** being currently experienced influence the income expectations of investors. When the economy is slack there is a greater risk of dividends being passed and of capital losses than in brisk trading periods. Thus, a given company may be capitalized at ten per cent in prosperous periods but at fourteen per cent in slack ones.

(5) **Prevailing interest rates** influence the rate of capitalization because of the yields which are available in alternative investment opportunities. This often runs counter to (4) since interest rates tend to be higher in boom periods and lower in depressions.

Over-capitalization

A business is said to be *over-capitalized* when its earnings are insufficient to pay the expected rates on its securities. That is, earnings will not cover the contracted rates on fixed income securities *plus* the expected yield on equities. Over-capitalization may well go unnoticed during boom periods when above average earnings are possible, but it becomes all too obvious where profits begin to fall under conditions of falling demand. Over-capitalization arises from either too much capital for the earnings potential of the company or an earnings level which is too low to support the capital employed. This condition may be the result of faulty estimating in the first instance or of unpredictable circumstances.

Over-funding

In companies which have over-estimated their capital needs the management will be relieved of many financial worries especially during the early years of the business when recourse to short-term advances is sometimes necessary. The company's ability to withstand early set-backs is also greatly strengthened by over-funding. The funds may be used to expand the business and increase its earnings which will offset the over-capitalization. However, if there are no such opportunities for expansion and growth, the company may use its resources inefficiently simply because they are at hand.

Inadequate Earnings

When profits fail to reach the expected level, dividends may fall and reduce the yield on equities. This will make it more difficult to raise fresh capital, especially in equities. Raising fresh capital will be almost impossible if the market value of issued securities is below the issue price. Under conditions of over-capitalization, management may be tempted to boost the reported income by short-term considerations. These could include arbitrary increases in selling prices, manufacturing poorer-quality products, dubious decisions regarding stock valuation and depreciation.

The low yield may be seen as a **storm signal** by the company's suppliers and other creditors. If they lose confidence in the business, they may restrict or withdraw their credit facilities. On the other hand, the low yield may bring an advantage to the company by discouraging competition, even though this may be seen as a 'social' disadvantage.

Under-capitalization

Under-capitalization is said to exist when a company earns sufficient income to meet its fixed interest and fixed dividend charges *and* to pay on its ordinary shares a rate which is better than that prevailing on equities in similar businesses. The causes of under-capitalization are either inadequate capital to match the company's earnings potential, or an earnings level which is capable of supporting a greater amount of capital.

Inadequate Funding

The company with too little capital will need to exercise restraint in the use of funds. It may not be able to take advantage of quantity discounts by buying in bulk and increasing investment in stocks. It may even be unable to benefit from cash discounts through an inability to pay promptly. In this condition it is, of course, relatively easy to obtain short-term accommodation —especially a bank overdraft. Nevertheless, short-term credit can be expensive especially if frequently resorted to. A more serious disadvantage may lie in the restriction on growth and expansion or in the inability to adapt readily to changing circumstances.

High Earnings

A company which earns higher profits than has been expected will appear to be more successful than the average which reflects favourably on its future prospects and on the ability of its management. Such a company will see the market price of its shares rise and the raising of additional capital will be greatly facilitated. Furthermore, in so far as any connection with an unusually profitable organization is valued, the company may experience little difficulty in obtaining services of many kinds. Employees, suppliers, creditors, and even customers may be ready and anxious to deal with it.

The Adequacy of Funds

Over-capitalization does not relate to a mere *surplus* of funds any more than under-capitalization relates to a *shortage* of funds. These two concepts relate to **investment yields**; that is, they involve a comparison of distributable income with issued capital. A company which has larger funds than it really needs could *not* be described as over-capitalized if its earnings are adequate to meet the reasonable expectations of its shareholders. Similarly, the available funds may be quite inadequate for the company's needs, but if the earnings were relatively low the company may not be under-capitalized.

Under-capitalization with Adequate Funds

This situation provides a useful illustration of the forces and pressures to which all undertakings are subject in some measure. The prospect of high earnings may induce competitors to enter the field and employees to make claims for higher wages. The company's customers may seek lower prices or longer credit while suppliers force harder bargains for higher prices. The market price of the company's share may go so high as to **limit the market** with the result that shares may be traded at prices below their true worth. In extreme cases, political pressure may urge the socialization of the firm or even of the whole industry.

Internal Finance

Retained profits are a common method of increasing the scale of business operations. In fact, they form the greatest single source of fresh capital (**savings,** *see* Chapter Twenty-two) and it has been estimated that about seventy-five per cent of all new investment (in both the U.K. and the U.S.A.) comes from the **autonomous savings** or retained profits. They provide reserves against business contingencies and also funds for growth which are free of the constraint imposed by the money market.

Merits of Autonomous Savings

Business savings may be used without incurring the obligation to pay interest or dividends. This makes it possible for a business to undertake activities when the earnings cannot be easily forecast. A company may also be willing to risk a project on a speculative basis if the chances of success are reasonable even where there is the risk that earnings might not cover current interest rates. If such projects had to be financed by external funds they would probably never be attempted.

Autonomous savings may be used to finance activities for which bankers and financial institutions would not provide funds, or those which do not inspire sufficient confidence in investors. The retained profits also avoid the difficulties which occasionally arise from market 'nerves' when investors are temporarily reluctant to finance even normal business investments.

Criticism of Retained Profits

Projects financed from internal savings will not necessarily be the most profitable investment of the funds when considered within the context of the national economy. The seriousness of this is emphasized by the fact that seventy-five per cent of all new investment comes from internal sources. This has led to the suggestion that all companies should be required by law to distribute all their earnings to the shareholders. However, although this idea has much to commend it, it does also contain the seeds of two other problems. There can be no certainty that investors would re-invest the extra dividends rather than consuming them; so that a chronic shortage of finance might occur. Distribution of greatly increased dividends could also lead to dissatisfaction amongst employees unless wage awards were offered also.

Extent of Plough Back

The extent to which profits are re-invested in a business depends on three factors. **The current level of earnings** is, of course, a crucial factor for there can be no *plough back* where there are no profits. The margin which can be retained is influenced by the directors' **dividend policy**. The modern tendency is to stabilize dividends and so avoid fluctuations in the market prices of shares arising from varying dividend rates. Recent years have also witnessed a reversal of earlier low dividend policies which could encourage take-over bids. The company's access to **other sources of funds** can also influence the extent to which profits are retained. Private companies and unincorporated businesses cannot appeal to the public for funds and, consequently, they must depend more heavily on autonomous savings than would a large public company.

Reserves

Retained profits are transferred from the appropriation account to a *reserve account* so that the sums involved are clearly set aside for use in the business. These savings are made for the same basic reasons that influence all savings—to increase future outputs or to meet future commitments.

Increased Outputs

Savings made to increase future outputs are referred to as *capital*. Reserves provide an internal source of capital funds for expanding the company's activities by increasing capacity or by enabling the business to diversify its activities. Internal savings put into reserves may also increase future outputs by improving technical efficiency, and through the introduction of new products or processes. Annual provisions for depreciation are seldom adequate to meet the needs of growth and many innovations are too conjectural for external sources of capital.

Future Commitments

It is desirable to build up reserves to meet long-term obligations on maturity, such as debentures and redeemable preference shares. Reserves also provide insurance against abnormal trading losses as shortages of raw materials, interrupted power supplies, industrial unrest, unexpected competition, changes in economic conditions, taxation, or Government policies. Adequate reserves cushion the effect of these situations and help the company to withstand them. Reserves may also be used to equalize dividend payments and as a protection against any erosion of capital through inflation.

External Effects

The attitudes of investors and creditors also are influenced by the reserve as an indicator of the company's underlying financial strength. The reserves provide a measure of the security for investors of both capital and income while assuring creditors of the safety of their debts. The creditors' interests are bound up with the retention of profits as the payment of dividends reduces the liquidity of their debtors. A company which pays regular dividends and also steadily builds up its reserves will find it relatively easy to raise fresh capital as well as being able to obtain the maximum credit facilities from its suppliers.

Exercises

1. Two companies, A Limited and B Limited are quoted companies in a similar line of business. The average P/E ratio for this type of company is 12. Both companies have made dividend proposals such that the dividends are covered twice by earnings. A summarized balance sheet for year ended June 30, 1973, in respect of both companies, together with their profit record for the last three years, is given below:

Fixed assets	A Limited	B Limited
	£	£
Land and buildings	250	100
Plant and machinery	650	325
	900	425
Current assets	2,400	1,000
	3,300	1,425
Less		
Current liabilities		
Creditors including current taxation and dividends	850	375
	£2,450	£1,050
Represented by:		
Share capital		
£1 shares issued and paid up	500	200
£1 preference shares	—	200
Reserves and surplus	1,000	600
Loan capital	800	—
Future taxation	150	50
	£2,450	£1,050
Profits—after taxation, debenture interest and preference share dividends		
Year ended June 30, 1971	75	25
1972	75	30
1973	75	35

Required:

(a) In respect of both companies:
   (i) estimated market value per ordinary share; (ii) dividend rate; dividend yield; earnings yield; gear ratio.

(*b*) Comment, in so far as possible, as to which company you consider the better investment for a prospective investor. [C.A.A.]

2. 'Dividend, capital investment, and financing policies are all inter-dependent.'
What do you understand by this statement, and what do you consider should be the objects of a dividend and retentions policy under current economic conditions?
[C.M.A.]

3. Three companies—'A', 'B', 'C'—have the same total capital but made up from the sources indicated below:

	'A'	'B'	'C'
	£	£	£
Ordinary shares of £1 each	400,000	600,000	1,000,000
8% preference shares of £1 each	400,000	400,000	—
8% mortgage debentures	200,000	—	—
	£1,000,000	£1,000,000	£1,000,000
Profit before providing for corporation tax, interest, or dividends	150,000	150,000	150,000

(*a*) State what you understand by the term 'capital gearing' and illustrate your answer by calculating the appropriate ratios from the above data.

(*b*) Assuming all profits after tax are distributed, calculate the market price of ordinary shares in EACH company if the expected yield for this type of business is nine per cent. (Take corporation tax to be forty per cent.) [C.A.A.]

4. You are given the following information concerning Z Limited and are required to:

(*a*) forecast the operating capital required at sales values per annum of:
(i) £4,250,000; (ii) £1,800,000;

(*b*) comment on the internal availability of capital as sales rise or fall;

(*c*) review the profit effectiveness of capital employed in the business and suggest methods of improving it.

The amounts of capital in use at various annual sales values are as follows:

Annual sales value (in £000's)	£2,150	£2,500	£2,850	£3,200
Average capital employed:				
Current assets:	£	£	£	£
Cash	122,455	134,250	146,045	157,840
Accounts receivable	223,075	251,250	279,425	307,600
Stock and work in progress	420,900	465,000	509,100	553,200
	766,430	850,500	934,570	1,018,640
Current liabilities	226,360	251,000	275,640	300,280
Net working capital	540,070	599,500	658,930	718,360
Fixed assets at cost	676,170	684,500	692,830	701,160
Total operating capital	£1,216,240	£1,284,000	£1,351,760	£1,419,520

The following information is taken from the profit and loss account:

Variable cost per £100 of sales:	£
Direct labour	10·80
Direct material	46·88
Indirect salaries	5·00
Other indirect costs	14·67
	£77·35

Fixed costs, per annum   £478,500   [C.M.A.]

CHAPTER TWENTY-FOUR

INVESTMENT APPRAISAL

Capital Productivity

A predicament which is common to all organizations is the one of allocating **limited investment funds** between competing projects for increasing the company's earnings potential. This difficulty arises from the fact that the **claims to funds** for potential projects greatly exceed the **funds available**. The quandary also tends to be aggravated by the many alternate uses of liquid resources. The resultant problem is then one of equating the **demand** for capital with the **supply** of capital.

Supply of Capital

There are two principal sources of capital which have been discussed in the preceding two chapters. Companies will probably do best by adopting some prudent combination of both sources to suit their needs.

Internal finance is usually *fixed* for a given budget period and companies, which depend wholly on these **autonomous savings,** will be obliged to restrict their capital expenditure to this fixed sum. Although internal finance has the advantage of being free from the whims of the money market, total dependence on retained profits for capital expenditure funds may impede a company's long-term growth. Worthwhile projects may be held back in some years for lack of funds, while in other years the availability of funds may permit the acceptance of less profitable projects.

External finance is not always readily available as the supply tends to be affected by conditions in the money market. Furthermore, the **price** of capital also fluctuates and at times will be high enough to disqualify otherwise useful projects. External funds are also unpopular with some companies because investors are prone to impose restrictions on the uses of their funds—albeit indirectly.

Demand for Capital

Demand is always at a **price** since price measures the intensity of demand. Many people have *needs* which never become *demands* because their scale of preferences allocates such resources as they have to satisfy more urgent needs. It is equally true of capital for businesses. A works manager may feel he *needs* a new item of plant; or the sales director may *need* additional warehousing, but it is necessary to measure objectively the intensity of these needs. In the case of demand for capital, it is not sufficient simply to know the current rates of borrowing, although this is a necessary part of the exercise. The justification for any capital expenditure must be its potential contribution to company earnings, and, therefore, it is only acceptable where the increased earnings exceed the cost of capital. Consequently, as a general rule, the **demand for capital** is measured by the **capital productivity**; that is, the expected profitability of the project. Capital productivity, then, provides an objective measurement of the demand for capital.

Estimation of Capital Earnings

The calculation of project profitability requires to be made with the utmost care and skill. Indeed, the difference between good investment decisions and poor ones depends very largely on the meticulous estimation of earnings. It is vital to recognize that capital earnings are generated in *future* periods and, therefore, it is the future profits, future costs and future revenues which are relevant to investment decisions. This theme was developed in *Corporate Planning* (Chapter Twenty-one) where it is pointed out that past or current performance is only valid as a *guide* to the future. That is equally pertinent in capital expenditure decisions since the stream of earnings only begins after some future completion date for the project.

Source of Capital Earnings

The additional earnings generated by an investment project arise from two sources—**cost savings** and **added revenue**. The source of earnings in a given investment will depend on the nature of the project but some projects will yield earnings from both sources. Generally speaking, investment in plant replacement, modernization of equipment, and new buildings will yield cost savings. Increased revenue stems from a greater sales volume or a more profitable sales mix. It is generated, therefore, by an investment which expands the productive capacity whether from new or existing products.

Indirect Earnings

Earnings estimates should consider any possible **indirect earnings** resulting from the proposed investment. Naturally, these indirect earnings are often difficult to recognize and their measurement calls for considerable care and judgment. Incremental costs and revenues on a corporate basis provide the relevant data for this purpose but their measurement often contains wide margins of error which should be clearly recognized. **Cost savings** may come from the fuller utilization of a particular piece of equipment or the release of certain plant for more profitable work. Factories which have *standby* equipment to minimize interruptions to output will retain the existing equipment for future standby and dispose of the former standby equipment. There would then be *indirect savings* from the new use of the current equipment. **Added revenue** may come from a wider market for existing products through the introduction and promotion of a new product.

Earnings Erosion

Highly profitable situations indicate opportunities for high yield investments. Such opportunities continue to attract capital until increasing costs become so high that eventually economic marginal cost equals the marginal revenue. Together with falling prices as the supply increases, this results in steadily narrowing profit margins which erode the high profitability. Consequently, any attempt to exploit opportunities for above average earnings tends to erode the margin of super-profits. In preparing estimates of capital productivity it is crucial to consider the wider effects of making a given investment and especially to allow for any risks of earnings erosion which may be induced by the investment.

Price Differentials

Good examples of earnings erosion may be found in seasonal trades—especially where the prices of a commodity show wide variations at different times of the year. During the summer months, the demand for coal falls away quite sharply but the National Coal Board is anxious to keep output reasonably steady throughout the year. In periods of slack demand, the N.C.B. stockpiles the output which is in excess of sales. This requires an investment by N.C.B. in production costs and storage facilities, so that there would be a real cost advantage from reducing prices to stimulate summer sales and avoid storage costs. Coal merchants who could provide their own storage sites have an opportunity to buy all their requirements at summer prices but sell at winter prices. The price differential may show a high yield on an investment in purchasing additional storage space. However, if the practice became widespread, summer prices would rise to reflect increased demand while winter prices would be *pared* with a diminished demand.

The Frozen Food Industry

The remarkable growth in the output of frozen foods is a classic illustration of **earnings erosion**. Prior to deep freezing, the supply of fresh peas lasted only a few weeks at harvest time. For about one week there would often be a glut with prices falling to about one penny per pound. During the greater part of the year, none were available unless specially imported and dried or canned peas provided the only real alternative to going without. Small quantities were imported by air (especially at Christmas or Easter) and sold at very high prices by the more exclusive fruiterers.

The price range between the 'harvest' prices (at 1p per lb) and the 'imported' prices (at 40p per lb) indicated a very highly profitable investment opportunity. The purchase of the crop, plus the building and operation of the factory, plus the distribution costs still left a generous profit margin at prices below the imported prices. However, rapidly increasing capacity by the innovators and competitors steadily eroded the profits. In the first place, the 'pick of the crop' is now bought by the frozen food firms which leaves a small proportion for the market at harvest time. Consequently, the retail price of fresh peas seldom falls below 4p or 5p nowadays while the 'glut' of frozen peas is available throughout the year at prices around 15p per lb.

Uncertainty in Estimates

All forecasting and prediction is hazardous because there can never be absolute certainty concerning future events. Estimates of capital productivity are, therefore, subject to ever-widening **limits of error** as the time-scale extends. Consequently, if the capital productivity of a potential investment is to be realistically estimated, some **allowance for uncertainty** becomes an essential part of the exercise. Making allowance for uncertainty can be challenged on the grounds that it is no better than guesswork. That may be so, but for the sake of objectivity it is essential to explicitly make some such allowance for uncertainty, otherwise the risk is greatly increased of making poor investment decisions.

Allowances for Uncertainty in Estimates

Apart from using **informal judgement** (pure guesswork or 'playing a hunch') there are three possible methods of allowing for future uncertainty in preparing estimates of capital productivity. In effect, each of these methods diminishes the forecast earnings by adopting the lower limit of error in each case. Therefore, should the investment be justified at this estimate of minimum earnings, it is more likely than not to prove successful.

Modified Life Expectancy

The actual economic life of an asset may be more or less than the original estimate prepared for investment appraisal purposes. Risk subsists in *over-estimation* of the earnings period which would lead to over-statement of the expected profits. This could make a project appear to be more successful than it really is; so that the project is evaluated on the estimated earnings for some shorter period of operation. The reduction in asset life may be made arbitrarily for each individual project or some attempt at objectivity may be introduced by all forecast life periods of assets being reduced by a given proportion; say, one eighth or twelve and a half per cent. Therefore, in evaluating a project with an expected life of sixteen years, only the earnings of the first fourteen years would be counted. Alternatively, a maximum allowed life may be set for each class of asset such as four years, seven years, or twelve years, and so on.

The Probability Multiplier

This method recognizes in the first place that errors can be plus or minus and that the risk of error is related to the remoteness in time of a given forecast. The estimated earnings for a given year, therefore, are adjusted by using a probability multiplier derived from the following formula:

$$P_n = 1 \pm r(n-1)$$

where P = the probability multiplier;
$\quad n$ = the year of expected life;
$\quad r$ = the rate of uncertainty.

In practice, it is the **lower limit** which is significant so that:

$$P_n = 1 - r(n-1).$$

It will usually be found satisfactory to adopt a five per cent rate of uncertainty so that $r = 0.05$. Consequently,

for $n =$	1	2	3	4	5	etc.
then $P =$	1.00	0.95	0.90	0.85	0.80	etc.

In evaluating a proposed capital expenditure project, where $r = 0.05$; the first year's forecast earnings would be included as originally estimated; the second year's forecast would be ninety-five per cent of the original estimate; the forecast for year ten would be included at fifty-five per cent of the original estimate; and so on. Consequently, as earnings become less remote so does their influence on the decision. This is probably the most satisfactory method of allowing for uncertainty in predicted earnings.

Accelerating Discount

This method is similar to the **probability multiplier** with the difference that it recognizes that uncertainty increases with time at an accelerating rate. In other words, the uncertainty rate is compounded by using the following formula:

$$R_n = 1 - r(n-1)(1+r)^{(n-1)}$$

where R = the discount rate of earnings;

n = the year of expected life;

r = the rate of uncertainty.

Once again, a five per cent rate of uncertainty may be chosen so that $r = 0.05$; consequently,

for $n =$	1	2	3	4	5	etc.
then $R =$	–	5·25%	10·25%	17·36%	24·13%	etc.

The discount R is the proportionate reduction in the estimated earnings to allow for uncertainty. The **accelerating discount method** will give lower values of earnings in a given year than does the *probability multiplier*. Nevertheless, this is probably an unnecessary refinement—especially as the probability multiplier can be obtained by simple arithmetic.

Project Selection

The rationing of funds between competing projects requires the establishment of selection criteria in the allocation of scarce resources. For some kinds of investment projects it is unnecessary or impractical to make any estimate of earnings. The destruction of a key section in production such as a power-producing unit or a vital process will halt the whole factory. Its immediate replacement is made without any question of first evaluating the **return** on investment before making a decision. In this case, the profitability of the capital expenditure is so obviously the total factory profit potential that it is beyond doubt. The 'earnings' from some investments defy measurement since they are so uncertain and scattered throughout the company. This is particularly true of capital expenditure on canteens, works hospitals, sports grounds, and so on, as well as investment in research and development activities. The measurement of capital productivity is really only valid for choosing between marginal investment opportunities.

Postponability

To choose between alternative projects, it is necessary to establish some order of **priority ranking**, so that available funds are first allocated to those projects with the highest priority rating. The criterion of **postponability** is used to determine those projects which can be deferred until the next budget period. Funds are then allocated to those projects which are considered to be **perishable investment opportunities**; that is, opportunities which will expire shortly, such as lease options. The justification for using postponability as the criterion of selection is that the earnings from a perishable investment opportunity will be lost if the investment is not made, whereas the earnings from the 'rejected' projects are not lost but simply postponed.

Considered in the context of a single budget year, postponability appears to be **not unreasonable** as a simple means of deferring certain projects when funds are inadequate to satisfy all the demands for capital. However, a project which can be deferred in one year may well be postponable in the following year, too, and maybe the year after that, and so on indefinitely. For example, the replacement of plant and machinery by improved models can lead to considerable cost savings which would fully justify the additional capital expenditure involved. However, the replacement can be safely postponed since the plant is currently giving satisfactory service.

Profitability

There are many investments capable of yielding significant cost savings or even increased revenues which could be postponed almost indefinitely because production is already 'flowing'. The consequences of using postponability for investment decisions are that technological innovation is slowed down and the company's growth rate may be virtually brought to a standstill. Unless there are special circumstances, a company should be *profit-oriented* (*see* Chapter Twenty-one) so that the only valid criterion of investment selection is **profitability**. In other words, the choice of an investment is dependent on its estimated earnings potential.

Nevertheless, there are several methods of choosing between alternative projects on the basis of earnings potential, and to illustrate these different methods the following example will be used.

The Latentworth Chemical Company Limited is currently considering the following proposals for capital expenditure and the Budget Committee has been asked to determine the priority ranking for each project.

| Project | Capital cost £'000 | Estimated annual earnings | | | | |
		Year 1 £'000	Year 2 £'000	Year 3 £'000	Year 4 £'000	Year 5 £'000
'A'	200	200	20	—	—	—
'B'	200	100	100	100	100	—
'C'	200	30	60	80	100	120
'D'	200	180	120	60	—	—
'E'	200	100	80	120	80	—

Note: Earnings are taken after taxation but before depreciation.

Pay-back Period

The pay-back period of an investment is defined as the length of time required for the stream of cash flows generated by the investment to equal the original cash outlay. It should be noted that this definition requires the earnings to be taken **after taxation** since tax payments diminish the net cash inflow, but **before depreciation** since the provision for depreciation is purely a *book-keeping transaction* and, therefore, has no effect on cash flow. The question here is, quite simply, 'How soon can we expect to recover the capital invested in the project?'

Capital Recovery

It is important in this context to avoid the *negative attitude*, which sees depreciation as asset consumption and, therefore, as an erosion of capital. The *positive attitude*, on the other hand, recognizes the annual provision for depreciation as a partial **recovery of capital** invested in the asset. Here, too, by and large, is the difference between **net cash flow** and **net profit**. The return on an investment is represented by the earnings which are surplus to the capital repayment—in receiving a loan, there is a commitment to repay the capital sum as well as meeting the agreed interest for the term of the loan. Consequently, depreciation represents annual repayments of the capital sum so that the net earnings (net profit) represent the return on the investment. The recovered capital is, of course, **re-invested** in the business. Considering the many uncertainties in all forecasting, straight-line depreciation provides a reliable estimate of annual capital recovery, and is often superior to methods giving unequal annual increments.

Pay-back Ranking

In calculating the length of a *pay-back period*, it is similar to charging depreciation at the rate of earnings until the asset value is fully recovered. Hence the need to take the earnings before providing for depreciation. The priority ranking for the Latentworth Chemical Company Limited projects when based on pay-back periods is as follows:

Project	Pay-back years	Priority ranking
'A'	1·00	1
'B'	2·00	3
'C'	3·30	5
'D'	1·17	2
'E'	2·17	4

Advantages of Pay-back Ranking

(1) It is **simple** to calculate, but also simple in concept and, therefore, easily understood by *non-financial* executives.

(2) It indicates the **timing** of the investment being available for re-investment. (Project 'B' will be available after two years.)

(3) By concentrating on the earliest pay-back date it recognizes that **early returns are preferable** to those which accrue later.

Limitations of Pay-back Ranking

(1) It fails to give any consideration at all to those earnings which accrue **after** the pay-back date. In some instances the subsequent earnings can be very high or very low. In the example, project 'A' has only £20,000 earnings after pay-back whereas project 'C' subsequently earns £190,000.

(2) Furthermore, *pay-back* ignores the **timing** of earnings prior to the pay-back date. 'E' earns £100,000 by the end of year one whereas 'C' does not reach this figure until early in the third year.

The Annual Rate of Return

This method of capital priority ranking measures the average annual net earnings (that is, after capital recovery) throughout the estimated life of the project. On the whole, the incidence of taxation makes no difference to the ranking of projects but the return will usually be preferred on post-tax earnings since this represents the funds at the disposal of the company. In calculating the **average** annual R.O.C.E., the net earnings are obtained by total depreciation (original cost less residual value) being deducted from the aggregate earnings less tax throughout the estimated asset life. The calculations for the Latentworth Chemical Company Limited are shown in Table 32.

Table 32. Average R.O.C.E. for Projects Ranking

LATENTWORTH CHEMICAL COMPANY LIMITED
Investment Projects Priority Ranking Schedule

Project	Life years	Aggregate earnings	Capital cost	Total net earnings	Net earnings Per annum	Net earnings Per £ invested	Net earnings R.O.C.E.	Priority ranking
		£'000	£'000	£'000	£'000	£	%	
'A'	2	220	200	20	10	0·050	10	5
'B'	4	400	200	200	50	0·250	50	2
'C'	5	390	200	190	38	0·190	38	4
'D'	3	360	200	160	53	0·265	53	1
'E'	4	380	200	180	45	0·225	45	3

Average Capital Employed

The annual R.O.C.E. is calculated on the **average capital employed** through-out the life of the asset. In this example, the Latentworth Chemical Company Limited assumes that each project has a nil residual value so that the average capital employed in each asset is equal to half the original investment. The reason for this is that the annual provision for depreciation represents a repay-ment of capital thereby steadily reducing the amount invested in the original project. The capital recovered from gross earnings in this way is now available for re-investment elsewhere in the business and, to that extent, the original investment should be relieved of the necessity to contribute to its earnings.

Advantages of Average R.O.C.E.

(1) The calculation is easy to make but (unlike pay-back) it gives considera-tion to the total earnings throughout the life of the asset.

(2) The average R.O.C.E. provides a reasonable basis of comparison for earnings with alternative investment opportunities and especially with the external cost of capital.

(3) It is possible to introduce a **Rejection Rate** (or **cut-off point**) as a means of segregating those projects whose profitability is too low to merit consideration.

Weaknesses of Average R.O.C.E.

(1) It fails to recognize the **timing** of cash flows. For example, two similar investments (**P** and **Q**) require the same capital sum of £4,500 and each yields earnings of £7,500 over a period of five years. However, their **earnings profiles** are completely different as shown below:

Project	Year 1	Year 2	Year 3	Year 4	Year 5
P	£500	£1,000	£1,500	£2,000	£2,500
Q	£3,000	£2,200	£1,400	£600	£300

Although equally desirable in other respects, **Q** has the more favourable *earnings profile* since it yields £2,500 more in year 1 which can be re-invested and generate additional earnings.

(2) Since it is an *average*, it gives no weight to the **duration of the earnings**.

Project	Total earnings	Capital	Net earnings	Life	Average
X	£10,000	£8,000	£2,000	1 year	£2,000
Y	£28,000	£8,000	£20,000	10 years	£2,000

The two projects are equally desirable on the basis of average R.O.C.E., yet *Y* yields ten times the total earnings from a similar sum invested in *X*.

The Rejection Rate

The rejection rate is the minimum acceptable rate of R.O.C.E. for new projects. Its purpose is to discard at an early stage those projects which are not expected to yield an acceptable rate of return. It avoids the allocation of capital to marginal projects in periods of slack investment, and thereby preserves the funds for more profitable investments. The use of rejection rates, by sifting the various proposals, saves the time of executives who do not need to study unprofitable proposals.

Calculating the Rejection Rate

The rejection rate may be set at the current rates of external borrowing as providing an acceptable minimum. Clearly, in this position, a business would be better off in investing surplus funds outside the business if a project could not cover the cost of capital. Even so, this is generally considered to be too low as a rejection rate. It is suggested that a more satisfactory cut-off point would be the company's overall average R.O.C.E. on the grounds that all new investment should do at least as well as the existing sunk investments. On the other hand, a company will be better off from any investment yielding a higher return than the cost of capital. The *return to equities* may be significantly improved in such cases despite a fall in the R.O.C.E.

Significance of the Cut-off Point

It is difficult to formulate a general rule for establishing the rejection rate, but in most businesses it can probably be taken as the mid-point between the rate of external borrowing and average R.O.C.E. Although failure to reach the cut-off point leads to the complete rejection of a proposal, there is no corresponding guarantee that every project exceeding the rejection rate will be adopted. Those proposals which satisfy the rejection criterion still have to compete for available funds with all the other such projects. The *cut-off point*, therefore, is not the criterion of selection but the screen which removes the less profitable proposals for capital expenditure.

Discounted Cash Flow

The allocation of capital funds requires a method of evaluating the relative profitability of capital projects. However, such a method should satisfy three criteria—it should take into account the earnings over the life of the project; give due weight to the duration of the earnings; and also make allowance for the timing of the cash flows. This can be achieved by the use of the **discounted cash flow (D.C.F.)** technique in either of two ways—the **net present value method** and the **yield method**.

Principle of D.C.F.

The D.C.F. technique recognizes that **£1 received today is more valuable than £1 receivable in (say) five years' time**. The reason for this is that today's £1 could be invested for those five years at (say) five per cent compound interest when it would be worth £1·2763. Alternatively, £1 receivable in five years' time has a **present value** of £0·7835 at five per cent *discount*; that is, £0·7835 invested today at five per cent will equal £1 in five years' time.

Present Value Tables

D.C.F. discounts the future proceeds of an investment by evaluating them at their **present values** which are obtained from *tables* (*see* Appendix 1). It is apparent that the present value of a given sum diminishes as the period lengthens so that larger discounts are applied to the more remote earnings.

> Present value of £1 at eight per cent
> After one year   £0·9259
> After two years   £0·8573
> After five years   £0·6806
> After ten years   £0·4632

The use of D.C.F. thus gives due weight to the **timing** of cash flows and consequently overcomes the principal drawback to the other methods of project priority ranking.

Relevance to Inflation

It is a popular misconception that the purpose of D.C.F. is to make due allowance in forecasting for the effects of inflation. That is not so! The confusion arises from the diminishing present value (because of the earnings potential in an investment) being equated with the diminishing purchasing power of a given sum through inflation. In the context of investment appraisal, **inflation is a self-correcting** phenomenon since costs and revenues tend to be equally affected by changes in the general level of prices. All other things being equal, ten per cent inflation will increase prices and income by ten per cent, but also costs so that profits, too, rise by ten per cent in money terms. However, the fall in the purchasing power of money leaves the **profits unchanged in real terms**. It is for this reason that inflation is usually ignored in investment appraisal. The principal exception to this rule is dealt with later.

Net Present Value (*N.P.V.*)

N.P.V. is the balance of the present values of annual earnings after the recovery of the capital invested. This is illustrated in Table 33 by using present values of eight per cent for the Latentworth Chemical Company Limited.

Table 33. Net Present Values at Eight Per Cent

LATENTWORTH CHEMICAL COMPANY LIMITED
Investment Appraisal Priority Ranking Schedule

		A		B		C		D		E	
Year	Present value at 8%	Annual proceeds £'000	P.V. earnings £'000	Annual proceeds £'000	P.V. earnings £'000	Annual proceeds £'000	P.V. earnings £'000	Annual proceeds £'000	P.V. earnings £'000	Annual proceeds £'000	P.V. earnings £'000
1	0·9259	200	185·18	100	92·59	30	27·78	180	166·66	100	92·59
2	0·8573	20	17·15	100	85·73	60	51·44	120	102·88	80	68·58
3	0·7938			100	79·38	80	63·50	60	47·63	120	95·26
4	0·7350			100	73·50	100	73·50			80	58·80
5	0·6806					120	81·67				
Total			202·33		331·20		297·89		317·17		315·23
Capital			200·00		200·00		200·00		200·00		200·00
N.P.V.		£	2·33		£131·20	£	97·89		£117·17		£115·23
Ranking			5		1		4		2		3

In this example of the Latentworth Chemical Company Limited each project has been given the same capital cost of £200,000 so that comparisons of the projects can be made under different methods of ranking without too many variable factors. In practice, competing projects are likely to require differing amounts of capital; so that the N.P.V. for each project can be misleading unless reduced to a coefficient or ratio for the purposes of comparison. In most cases it will be sufficient for this purpose to express the N.P.V. as a ratio of the capital outlay.

Choosing the Discount Rate

The choice of the discount rate may be critical under the N.P.V. method since the **priority ranking can differ** at varying discount rates. Nevertheless, this only becomes really important for significant rate differences (*see* Table 34).

Table 34. Net Present Values at Sixteen Per Cent

LATENTWORTH CHEMICAL COMPANY LIMITED
Investment Appraisal Priority Ranking Schedule

Year	Present value at 16%	A Annual proceeds £'000	A P.V. earnings £'000	B Annual proceeds £'000	B P.V. earnings £'000	C Annual proceeds £'000	C P.V. earnings £'000	D Annual proceeds £'000	D P.V. earnings £'000	E Annual proceeds £'000	E P.V. earnings £'000
1	0·8621	200	172·42	100	86·21	30	25·86	180	155·18	100	86·2
2	0·7432	20	14·86	100	74·32	60	44·59	120	89·18	80	59·4
3	0·6407			100	64·07	80	51·26	60	38·44	120	76·8
4	0·5523			100	55·23	100	55·23			80	44·
5	0·4761					120	57·13				
Total			187·28		279·83		234·07		282·80		266·7
Capital			200·00		200·00		200·00		200·00		200·
N.P.V.			£(12·72)		£ 79·83		£ 34·07		£ 82·80		£ 66·7
Ranking			5		2		4		1		3

At sixteen per cent discount, projects 'B' and 'D' change places in the priority ranking order. Other changes in ranking may occur at different discount rates. As a general rule, the discount rate chosen will also be the **rejection rate** so that most projects showing a *surplus* will be adopted. The N.P.V. method is appropriate where there are adequate funds available but it is desired to avoid the relatively less profitable projects.

The D.C.F. Yield

This method is based upon the proposition that the best investment is that which yields the highest return from equating the present values of earnings and capital invested. In other words, that rate at which the discounted earnings are equal to the present value of the capital expenditure; that is, a form of **break-even point** where there is neither a surplus nor a deficit. D.C.F. yield is superior to the N.P.V. method from the point of view of project ranking. Consequently, it is the method to use for *rationing capital*; that is, putting strictly limited funds to the most profitable uses.

Searching

The D.C.F. yield rate is found by **searching** (that is, *trial and error*) with the help of *present value tables*. Initially, some discount rate is chosen and the

N.P.V. is computed. If the N.P.V. at this rate is positive, the exercise is repeated at a higher rate—or a lower rate is selected for negative N.P.V. at the original rate. The *searching* continues until the approximate actual yield rate is identified and the precise actual rate is then obtained by **interpolation**.

Illustration

A certain investment costing £50,000 is expected to generate the following earnings after tax and before depreciation.

Year 1	£8,000
Year 2	£12,000
Year 3	£18,000
Year 4	£24,000
Year 5	£30,000

(1) N.P.V. at fifteen per cent

Year	Earnings £	P.V.	D.C.F. £
1	8,000	0·8696	6,957
2	12,000	0·7561	9,073
3	18,000	0·6575	11,835
4	24,000	0·5718	13,723
5	30,000	0·4972	14,916
Total	£92,000		£56,504

Since there is a *surplus* of £6,504 at fifteen per cent, it is necessary to try a higher rate—say, twenty per cent.

(2) N.P.V. at twenty per cent

Year	Earnings £	P.V.	D.C.F. £
1	8,000	0·8333	6,667
2	12,000	0·6944	8,333
3	18,000	0·5787	10,417
4	24,000	0·4823	11,575
5	30,000	0·4019	12,057
Total	92,000		49,049

This time the *deficit* of £951 indicates that the actual rate is just below twenty per cent. The rate could be obtained by interpolation at this point in the following manner:

$$\text{Actual rate} \simeq 15\% + \frac{(£56,504 - £50,000)}{£56,504 - £49,049} \times (20\% - 15\%)$$

$$\simeq 15\% + \frac{£6,504}{£7,455} \times 5\%$$

$$\simeq 15\% + 4·37\%$$

$$\simeq 19·37\%$$

Interpolation Range

The rate can be obtained more precisely by interpolating between nineteen and twenty per cent when the actual rate would be found to be 19·235 per cent

(N.P.V. at nineteen per cent = £50,416). The **interpolation range** is a matter of choice depending on the required degree of precision in the answer. However, it is vital to keep the interpolation range as narrow as possible and five per cent is normally the acceptable maximum range. To avoid a large number of calculations in *searching* for the rate, students are particularly prone to interpolating between a very low rate and a very high rate. This is quite unsatisfactory because of the wide margin of error in the answer. For example, interpolation between ten per cent and twenty-five per cent in the above example gives an 'actual' rate of 20·36%—one whole point difference.

Capital by Instalments

It has been assumed so far that all capital expenditure was made **in advance** —that is, on or before the first day of *year 1*. In many cases, especially with very large projects, the total capital expenditure may be spread over several of the early years—even concurrently with the first earnings. There may also be cash inflows from the capital recovery in residual values or the liquidation of working capital. All capital related cash flows must be expressed in *present value* terms to obtain the correct D.C.F. yield or N.P.V. of a project.

Illustration

Metronic Components Limited is currently considering a proposal to increase production capacity to which the following data relate. The company has adopted a rejection rate of fifteen per cent before taxation and wishes to know whether this project satisfies that criterion. Capital expenditure on plant is expected to cost £38,000 payable as to £18,000 in advance, £12,000 at the end of the first year and £8,000 at the end of the second year. The project is expected to have a residual value of £1,000 at the end of the fifth year. In addition, an investment of £2,000 in working capital will be required at the commencement of the project. Pre-tax earnings in each of the five years of the project are forecast as respectively £2,000, £6,000, £12,000, £20,000, £30,000.

Year	Capital cash flow £	Earnings cash flow £	Net cash flow £	P.V. at 15%	D.C.F. £
0	(20,000)	—	(20,000)	1·0000	(20,000)
1	(12,000)	2,000	(10,000)	0·8696	(8,696)
2	(8,000)	6,000	(2,000)	0·7561	(1,512)
3	—	12,000	12,000	0·6575	7,890
4	—	20,000	20,000	0·5718	11,436
5	3,000	30,000	33,000	0·4972	16,408
	£(37,000)	£70,000	£33,000		£5,526

The project satisfies the company's criterion of fifteen per cent minimum before taxation since it yields a surplus at that rate. In making this calculation it is assumed that all cash flows are generated on the last day of each year and also that the investment in working capital is liquidated in the fifth year. (The *D.C.F. Yield* on this project is twenty per cent before charging taxation.

Influence of Taxation

Payments of corporation tax diminish the earnings available for the company, so that it is post-tax earnings which are relevant for investment decisions. However, the D.C.F. yield will not be reduced in proportion to the prevailing rate of *corporation tax*—indeed, in some cases the earnings profile may be such as to show a higher yield after taxation. The first reason for this is that the whole of the earnings are not subject to taxation since the taxpayer can set certain allowances against his tax liability. Secondly, these allowances tend to be much higher in the early years of the project. Thirdly, the **basis of assessment** on the previous year's accounts has the effect of making tax payments lag one year behind the earnings.

Illustration

The Latentworth Chemical Company Limited is considering the purchase of new plant to manufacture a recently developed range of new products. The cost of this plant is £260,000 payable in year 0—the plant has a residual value of £10,000 in year 10. The pre-tax yield on this project is approximately eight and a half per cent as shown below:

Year	cash flow £	PV at 8½%	D.C.F. £
0	(260,000)	1·000	(260,000)
1	10,000	0·921	9,210
2	20,000	0·849	16,980
3	30,000	0·783	23,490
4	40,000	0·721	28,840
5	50,000	0·665	33,250
6	60,000	0·613	36,780
7	70,000	0·565	39,550
8	80,000	0·519	41,520
9	40,000	0·479	19,160
10	25,000*	0·442	11,050
			£170

*Earnings £15,000 plus residual value £10,000.

Corporation tax is chargeable at forty per cent; an investment grant of £50,000 is payable at the end of the first year and an annual allowance of twenty-five per cent is available on the reducing balance. Any balancing allowance or balancing charge should be taken in the tenth year.

Year	Cash flow £	Taxation allowance £	Taxable earnings £	Taxation payable £	Net cash flow £	Present value at 8½%	D.C.F. £
0	(260,000)	—	—	—	(260,000)	1·000	(260,000)
1	60,000*	(52,500)	(42,500)	—	60,000	0·921	55,260
2	20,000	(39,375)	(19,375)	17,000	37,000	0·849	31,413
3	30,000	(29,531)	469	7,750	37,750	0·783	29,558
4	40,000	(22,148)	17,852	(188)	39,812	0·721	28,704
5	50,000	(16,612)	33,388	(7,141)	42,859	0·665	28,501
6	60,000	(12,458)	47,542	(13,355)	46,645	0·613	28,593
7	70,000	(9,344)	60,656	(19,017)	50,983	0·565	28,805
8	80,000	(7,008)	72,992	(24,262)	55,738	0·519	28,928
9	40,000	(5,256)	34,744	(29,197)	10,803	0·479	5,175
10	25,000	(5,768)	9,232	(13,897)	11,103	0·442	4,908
11	—	—	—	(3,693)	(3,693)	0·408	(1,507)
	£215,000	£200,000	£215,000	(£86,000)	£129,000		£8,782

* The cash flow in year 1 includes the investment grant of £50,000.

The surplus at eight and a half per cent on the **pre-tax cash flows** was £170, whereas the **post-tax cash flows** is £8,338, which indicates a higher yield because of the **investment grant** and the modified cash flow profile through the taxation structure.

Finance through Borrowing

Projects which are financed through external borrowing will often show an improved rate of return despite the payment of interest. This is partly due to the fact that interest charges are allowable against taxation, but mainly to the fact that the capital sum is repayable at the termination of the project. Consequently, the present value of the capital is very much lower because, in effect, the company does not finance the project in year 0 but in the last year.

Suppose that in the above example that the project was financed by the issue of ten-year debentures at ten per cent for £260,000. This would mean a cash *inflow* of £260,000 in year 0 from the debenture holders; this would then be redeemable in year 10. The difference in N.P.V. at 8·5% is:

Year 0	£260,000 at 1·000 =	£260,000
Year 10	£260,000 at 0·442 =	£(114,920)
INCREASE IN SURPLUS		£145,080

The debentures will cost £26,000 per annum in interest charges, and the present value of the interest is equal to **an annuity** of £26,000 for ten years at eight and a half per cent. Such an annuity would cost £26,000 × 6·557 = £170,482. This will be reduced by the savings in corporation tax at £10,400 per annum. The total saving will be equal to an annuity for ten years (commencing in year two) at eight and a half per cent, which is £10,400 × 6·044 = £62,858. Consequently, the present value of the net interest cost is £170,482 less £62,858 which is £107,624.

Increase in surplus	£145,080
less interest charges	£107,624
NET GAIN FROM BORROWING	£37,456

Clearly, this represents a very substantial increase in the yield of the project when compared with a surplus of £8,338.

Effect of Inflation

It has already been pointed out that inflation is a **self-correcting phenomenon** within the context of investment appraisal. Therefore, it can be assumed that cash flows are expressed in **real terms**. The single exception to this is finance through borrowing since loans are always repayable in **money terms**. The effect of inflation then is to make money debts diminish in real terms.

Suppose that throughout the ten-year period of the above project that inflation is expected to run at an average of four per cent per annum. This means a *depreciation* in money values of approximately four per cent annually. The £260,000 debentures will be repaid in real terms as £260,000 × 0·676 = £175, 760. (The figure of 0·676 has been taken from the *present value* tables for four per cent as giving an acceptable value.)

This means that the *present value* of the debentures on redemption in **real terms** is £175,760 × 0·442 = £77,686 compared with the redemption value of £114,920 given above. This is a further increase in present value of £37,234 to give a net gain from borrowing in real terms of £74,690 present value at eight and a half per cent.

Summary of Investment Cost in Real Terms

Debenture redemption	= £77,686
Interest charges (net)	= £107,624
TOTAL COST OF £260,000	= £185,310

Conclusion

The financing of investment projects through borrowing is by far the most economical method—even at relatively high interest rates—and especially after making allowances for loan redemption in real terms. The above example has been worked through at eight and a half per cent N.P.V., but the savings increase as the discount rate rises which makes potential projects show rising yields as the N.P.V. is raised.

Exercises

1. Schedule the management accounting information requirements of a machine replacement decision in the circumstances where:
    (*a*) the proposed new machine will produce roughly the same per shift as the existing machine;
    (*b*) the proposed new machine will produce fifty per cent more per shift than the existing machine.
Assume that in both instances the existing machine has not completed its useful life and is not fully depreciated. [C.M.A.]

2. The Alpha Company Limited are considering the purchase of a new machine which will cost £40,000. It is estimated that the machine will have a life of seven years at the end of which it will have a scrap value of £1,000. This will also involve an investment in working capital of £10,000. The net pre-tax cash flows which this will produce are as follows:

	£
Year 1	10,000
2	10,000
3	14,000
4	13,000
5	11,000
6	12,000
7	10,000

The company has a target return on capital of fifteen per cent and on this basis you are required to prepare a statement evaluating the above project.
Taxation: Assume the following:
    (1) Income tax 40p in the £ (ignore Profits Tax).
    (2) Investment allowance thirty per cent. Initial allowance ten per cent.
    (3) Annual allowances twenty-five per cent.
The company carries on other trading activities from which it derives taxable profits. [A.C.A.]

3. Various machining operations on rough castings are performed in the machining department of a factory. The equipment in use has still several years of useful life, but methods study has shown that investment in equipment of a new type would yield savings in operating cost.

Two alternative models of equipment are available. For the purpose of this question each has an effective life of three years with no salvage value.

Model I would require an investment of £5,000 and would yield a saving of £1 per unit of production, constant at all foreseeable volumes.

Model II would require an investment of £12,000 and would yield a saving of £2 per unit.

Current production volume is 2,000 units per annum, but new market opportunities might increase the volume to 4,000 units per annum.

Using both: (*a*) present value, and (*b*) D.C.F. rate of return calculations, you are asked to advise which investment would be financially preferable. You should assume that:

   (i) the opportunity cost of capital is eight per cent after taxation;

  (ii) for taxation purposes the annual allowance is twenty per cent per annum on a straight line basis with no initial allowance;

 (iii) the effective rate of corporation tax is forty per cent. [C.M.A.]

4. Your company installed on January 1, 1972, a special moulding machine at a cost of £85,000 for producing a new product. It is anticipated that the product and the machine would have a life of four years. The disposal value of the machine at the end of the four-year period was estimated to be £5,000. Cash operating costs are at present £100,000 per annum.

Your company has now received a firm offer from a reputable machine tool manufacturer for the supply of a technically superior machine at a cost of £97,500 with immediate delivery. It is estimated that the new machine would save your company £30,000 per annum in cash operating costs and that it would have a disposable value at the end of three years of £7,500. On December 31, 1973 the book value of the existing machine will be £65,000 and its disposable value £35,000.

You are required to prepare a report for your chief production engineer, using the information given above, to advise him of:

   (*a*) the comparative total costs of the present and the proposed methods so that he may decide whether serious consideration should be given to the proposal;

   (*b*) further information which should be considered before a decision is made;

   (*c*) any factor given which you would not take into consideration in making the decision. [C.M.A.]

5. A company is buying a special-purpose machine tool for £120,000. A final decision must be made as to how the purchase is to be financed.

There are three available methods:

   (i) Outright purchase using bank overdraft facilities at an interest rate of nine per cent per annum.

  (ii) Loan from a finance house, covered by a specific debenture. The loan would be repayable by annual instalments of £20,000 with interest at eleven and a half per cent per annum on the reducing balance.

 (iii) Leasing agreement with a finance house who would buy the machine and rent it to the company for £18·30 per £1,000 per month.

The machine attracts an Investment Grant of twenty-five per cent and the rate of annual allowance for taxation purposes is twenty per cent. The rate of Corporation Tax may be taken as forty per cent. All taxation adjustments are made one year in arrear. It may be assumed that the company is making adequate profits to absorb any 'loss' adjustments within this project.

The savings, before tax, arising from the use of the machine are estimated at £15,000 in the first year, and £30,000 per annum thereafter.

It may be assumed that the bank overdraft and accrued interest would be repaid out of savings and tax benefits received.

You are required to show by calculations:

   (*a*) which method of financing would be financially preferable over the first six years (ignoring taxation adjustments in the seventh year) if the opportunity cost of capital employed is ten per cent. Use annual rests:

(*b*) the opportunity cost of capital at which the ranking of the overdraft alternative and the debenture alternative would be reversed. [C.M.A.]

6. Prepare a report for management commenting on the advantages and disadvantages of the discounted cash flow approach to the evaluation of investment opportunities compared to the more traditional approach such as payoff or return on original investment. [A.C.A.]

7. The management committee of your company is considering the introduction of a new product and has before it the following *alternative* proposals.

	Product 'A' £	Product 'B' £
Pre-production costs (already incurred)		
Market Research	1,000	1,000
Prototype	2,000	6,000
New machinery required not yet purchased	8,000	10,000
Variable Costs (each)		
Materials	2·50	3·00
Labour	1·50	1·00
Expenses	0·50	0·50
General fixed costs (per annum)—all allocated	4,000	4,000
Production (per annum) for first 3 years	1,000 units	1,000 units
Production (per annum) for next 2 years	2,000 units	2,000 units

The plant will last for five years and has no residual value.

The cost of capital is nine per cent per annum.

If product 'A' is produced and sold the patentees will charge a royalty of £0·5 per item sold.

If product 'B' is produced and sold a licence costing £500 per annum must be obtained or a cancellation fee equivalent to five years licence paid immediately.

Taxation to be ignored.

Required:

(*a*) Evaluate the merits of the alternative proposals:
 (i) on the assumption that all costs must be considered;
 (ii) omitting any costs or making other adjustments you consider are relevant to the decision.

(*b*) Comment on your findings. [C.A.A.]

8. Your company's required rate of return on investment projects is twenty per cent before tax, calculated on a discounted cash flow basis.

The following project for the design, development, and exploitation of a new product is submitted, and accepted on the grounds that it satisfies the above criterion:

Year:	1 £	2 £	3 £	4 £	5 £	6 £	7 £	8 £
Design	5,000	500						
Drawing	700	2,500						
Prototypes		300	8,500					
Production drawings			500	1,000				
Manufacturing costs				45,000	67,500	67,500	65,000	65,000
Sales income				50,000	75,000	75,000	75,000	75,000
Net cash flow	(£5,700)	(£3,300)	(£9,000)	£4,000	£7,500	£7,500	£10,000	£10,000

By the end of the first year £5,000 has been expended on design work.

At this stage the project controller reports that he has made new estimates, and that the probable course of the project will now be as follows:

Year:	1	2	3	4	5
	£	£	£	£	£
Design	5,000	1,000	500		
Drawing		250	750	2,300	
Prototypes				700	9,000
Production drawings					500
Net cash flow	£5,000)	(1,250)	(1,250)	(3,000)	(9,500)

Year:	6	7	8	9	10
	£	£	£	£	£
Production drawings	1,000				
Manufacturing costs	36,000	58,000	80,000	71,000	63,000
Sales income	40,000	65,000	90,000	80,000	75,000
Net cash flow	£3,000	£7,000	£10,000	£9,000	£12,000

These new estimates are probably reliable within plus or minus twenty per cent.

You are required to evaluate the revised project, and to advise the board with full reasons what action you now recommend. [C.M.A.]

9. The D.C.F. (discounted cash flow) method of evaluating capital expenditure projects has been criticised on the following grounds:

(a) it rarely takes into account the deterioration in the value of money;

(b) it distorts the present value of continuous cash flow, by reckoning interest only once a year;

(c) it could mislead if the required rate of return on loan capital is calculated on an after tax basis, for an increase in the standard rate of tax could convert an unacceptable or marginal project into an acceptable one.

Discuss the practical validity of these criticisms and illustrate your answer to point (c) given above by reference to the following project:

	£
Initial outlay	1,000
Return, cash flows in years 1, 2, 3, and 4, per annum	200
Taxed in years 2, 3, 4, and 5.	
Investment grant receivable in year 1	250

Annual allowances twenty per cent per annum on reducing balance, commencing in year 2.

Rate of tax, say, forty per cent.

Alternative rate of tax, to be assumed for the purpose of your illustration sixty per cent.

Current cost of loan capital, before tax, say, fifteen per cent per annum. [C.M.A.]

10. The discounted cash flow methods of evaluating investment opportunities do not explicitly take account of uncertainty. Discuss the factors which you would consider in assessing uncertainty and how discounting can be used to take account of these. [A.C.A.]

11. The XYZ Company Limited is considering the replacement of three of its present machines with a single machine which has just come on to the market. Consideration of this proposition has arisen because of the necessity to spend £5,000 on exceptional maintenance on the present machines. The three machines which would be replaced were purchased two years ago for £1,500 each, and are being depreciated over twelve years on a straight-line basis with an estimated final scrap

value of £600 each. The current second-hand market value of each of the machines is £1,000.

The annual operating costs for *each* of the existing machines are:

		£
Material		60,000
Labour—1 operator at 1,800 hours		1,350
Variable expenses		925
Maintenance (excluding any exceptional expenditure)		2,000
Fixed expenses:	£	
Depreciation	75	
Fixed factory overhead absorbed	2,700	
		2,775

The new machine has an estimated life of ten years and will cost £100,000 as follows:

Purchase price (scrap value in ten years £4,500)	£87,000
Installation costs	£13,000

The estimated annual operating costs for all the existing output on the new machine are:

		£
Material		162,000
Labour:	£	
2 operators at 1,500 hours	3,000	
1 operator's assistant at 1,500 hours	900	
		3,900
Variable expenses		2,275
Maintenance		4,500
Fixed expenses	£	
Depreciation	9,550	
Fixed factory overhead absorbed	7,800	
		17,350

The company's cost of capital is ten per cent and products are evaluated in rate of return terms. In addition to satisfying the profitability test, projects must also satisfy a financial viability test, in that they must pay for themselves within a maximum period of five years.

You are required to:

(a) Advise management on the profitability of this proposal by applying the discounted cash flow—trial and error yield technique.

(b) Subject the proposal to a financial viability test and

(c) Comment briefly on two other factors that could influence this decision.

Notes:

(1) Taxation is to be ignored.

(2) Assume that residual value is received on the last day of a machine's working life. [A.C.A.]

12. The management of William Brown Limited has the following two projects under consideration:

	Project 'A'	Project 'B'
	£	£
Cost of new buildings	5,000	—
Cost of new plant	25,000	30,000
	£30,000	£30,000

Forecast additional earnings (before tax and depreciation)

	£	£
Year 1	12,000	4,000
Year 2	16,000	10,000
Year 3	14,000	15,000
Year 4	11,000	18,000
Year 5	7,000	20,000

The supplier of the new machinery for project 'B' offers to take some existing plant valued £6,000 in part exchange.

The managing director is particularly keen on project 'A', and says he is prepared to advance the money required for the buildings immediately—interest free—from his own resources provided we guarantee repayment at the end of five years. It is proposed that this could be done by setting up a loan redemption fund providing equal annual provisions at the end of each year. Interest will be allowed on this fund at the rate of four per cent thus requiring an annual sum of £923 to be so provided.   [C.A.A.]

13. (a) In evaluating investment projects, X Limited normally uses a D.C.F. rate of return of ten per cent as the cut-off point for acceptability. It is considered however that greater attention should be given to the degree of risk involved in certain points.

What methods can you suggest of compensating for the element of uncertainty in the basic data; and what would be the advantages and disadvantages of each?

(b) In simplified form, two alternative investment opportunities show the following prospects.

Which of the two alternative projects would you recommend for acceptance and what further analysis of the figures would be desirable?

		Project 'A'	Project 'B'
Life of project		5 years	5 years
		£	£
Initial investment		2,500	2,500
Average annual cash inflow, net		650	700

Possibility of average annual cash net flow differing from figures given above:

One chance in			£	£
20	⎫	at least	800	—
50	⎪	not more than	450	—
25	⎬ of being ⎨ at least	—	1,700
12½	⎪	a loss of	—	(200)
100	⎭	a loss of	—	(600)

The chance of a loss on project 'A' is considered to be insignificant.   [C.M.A.]

14. A machine with a purchase price of £14,000 is estimated to eliminate manual operations costing £4,000 per year. The machine will last five years to have no residual value at the end of its life.

You are required to calculate:

(a) the discounted cash flow (D.C.F.) rate of return;
(b) the level of annual saving necessary to achieve a twelve per cent D.C.F. return;
(c) the net present value (N.P.V.) if the cost of capital is ten per cent.   [C.M.A.]

15. (a) Discuss the significance of cash flow in management accounting:

(b) (i) The AB Company Limited is proposing to make a capital investment of £200,000 which it is estimated will produce the following profit figures after allowing for depreciation over five years on a straight-line basis:

Year 1	£30,000	Profit
2	£30,000	Profit
3	£20,000	Profit
4	£10,000	Profit
5	£15,000	Loss

To undertake this, the company will require to issue loan stock at six per cent per annum. Over the past few years the company's profits have been of the order of twenty per cent on the equity interest. You are required to prepare a statement for management indicating the apparent profitability or otherwise, of this proposal and to state, giving reasons, whether you think that management are acting in the best interests of the shareholders in undertaking this. *Note:* taxation can be ignored.

(ii) In present-day circumstances do you think that taxation can be ignored when investment opportunities are being considered? Give reasons for your answer.

[A.C.A.]

16. As projects officer your function is to ensure the financial soundness of proposals for capital expenditure. State briefly what information you would expect to receive in financial justification of the following proposals:

(a) installation of plating shop, to eliminate the existing need to sub-contract plating operations;

(b) new press tool to implement a change in product design;

(c) replacement of general purpose drilling machine;

(d) additional oven for works canteen. [C.M.A.]

17. A company operates two foundries, primarily to supply castings for its own machine shops, but also undertaking work for outside customers in order to maintain a capacity throughput.

The foundry manager has submitted to the board a proposal to:

(a) centralize all the foundry operations in one building having the same total capacity as the two existing buildings;

(b) sub-contract the heavier castings required by the company; and

(c) increase the sales of smaller castings in order to maintain his own tonnage output.

The second building would become vacant, and the company has no prospective use for it. It might eventually be sold for about £300,000.

You are also given the following information:

Costs of reorganization

	To be capitalized £	Associated revenue expenditure £
As detailed in proposal	424,600	22,000

Cost savings attributable to the reorganization

	First year £	Sunsequent years £
Direct labour	85,000	92,500
Indirect labour	50,000	67,000
Establishment expenses	20,000	20,000
Internal transport	1,000	1,500

The additional cost of sub-contracting heavy castings is exactly balanced by the contribution from increased outside sales.

Investment grant	25%
Annual allowance (on reducing balance)	20%
Rate of corporation tax	40%

You are required to:

(a) discuss briefly whether or not the prospective sales proceeds of £300,000 have any bearing on a D.C.F. assessment of the proposal;

(b) excluding any consideration of the £300,000 prospective sales proceeds, calculate the D.C.F. rate of return yielded by the proposal over a five year period only. [C.M.A.]

18. The financial director of a holding company calls for budgets of capital expenditure for the forthcoming year from each subsidiary company. At the same

time he points out that expenditure on approved projects will be rationed in proportion to the profits made by the various subsidiaries in the current year.

The managing director of a subsidiary which has incurred a loss objects. This he considers is tantamount to saying that because a company has not made a profit in the past, it shall not be given the opportunity to do so in the future. He suggests that it is probably the unprofitable company which requires the biggest infusion of new finance.

Do you agree? [C.M.A.]

PRESENT VALUE TABLE

The table shows the value today of £1 to be received or paid
after a given number of years

Rate ⟶ No. years	1%	2%	3%	4%	5%	6%	7%	8%	9%	10%	11%	12%
1	0·99	0·98	0·97	0·96	0·95	0·94	0·93	0·93	0·92	0·91	0·90	0·89
2	0·98	0·96	0·94	0·92	0·91	0·89	0·87	0·86	0·84	0·83	0·81	0·80
3	0·97	0·94	0·92	0·89	0·86	0·84	0·82	0·79	0·77	0·75	0·73	0·71
4	0·96	0·92	0·89	0·85	0·82	0·79	0·76	0·74	0·71	0·68	0·66	0·64
5	0·95	0·91	0·86	0·82	0·78	0·75	0·71	0·68	0·65	0·62	0·59	0·57
6	0·94	0·89	0·84	0·79	0·75	0·70	0·67	0·63	0·60	0·56	0·53	0·51
7	0·93	0·87	0·81	0·76	0·71	0·67	0·62	0·58	0·55	0·51	0·48	0·45
8	0·92	0·85	0·79	0·73	0·68	0·63	0·58	0·54	0·50	0·47	0·43	0·40
9	0·91	0·84	0·77	0·70	0·64	0·59	0·54	0·50	0·46	0·42	0·39	0·36
10	0·91	0·82	0·74	0·68	0·61	0·56	0·51	0·46	0·42	0·39	0·35	0·32
11	0·90	0·80	0·72	0·65	0·58	0·53	0·48	0·43	0·39	0·35	0·32	0·29
12	0·89	0·79	0·70	0·62	0·56	0·50	0·44	0·40	0·36	0·32	0·29	0·26
13	0·88	0·77	0·68	0·60	0·53	0·47	0·41	0·37	0·33	0·29	0·26	0·23
14	0·87	0·76	0·66	0·58	0·51	0·44	0·39	0·34	0·30	0·26	0·23	0·20
15	0·86	0·74	0·64	0·56	0·48	0·42	0·36	0·32	0·27	0·24	0·21	0·18

Rate ⟶ No. years	13%	14%	15%	16%	17%	18%	19%	20%	30%	40%	50%
1	0·88	0·88	0·87	0·86	0·85	0·85	0·84	0·83	0·77	0·71	0·67
2	0·78	0·77	0·76	0·74	0·73	0·72	0·71	0·69	0·59	0·51	0·44
3	0·69	0·67	0·66	0·64	0·62	0·61	0·59	0·58	0·46	0·36	0·30
4	0·61	0·59	0·57	0·55	0·53	0·52	0·50	0·48	0·35	0·26	0·20
5	0·54	0·52	0·50	0·48	0·46	0·44	0·42	0·40	0·27	0·19	0·13
6	0·48	0·46	0·43	0·41	0·39	0·37	0·35	0·33	0·21	0·13	0·09
7	0·43	0·40	0·38	0·35	0·33	0·31	0·30	0·28	0·16	0·09	0·06
8	0·38	0·35	0·33	0·31	0·28	0·27	0·25	0·23	0·12	0·07	0·04
9	0·33	0·31	0·28	0·26	0·24	0·23	0·21	0·19	0·09	0·05	0·03
10	0·29	0·27	0·25	0·23	0·21	0·19	0·18	0·16	0·07	0·03	0·02
11	0·26	0·24	0·21	0·20	0·18	0·16	0·15	0·13	0·06	0·02	0·01
12	0·23	0·21	0·19	0·17	0·15	0·14	0·12	0·11	0·04	0·02	0·008
13	0·20	0·18	0·16	0·15	0·13	0·12	0·10	0·09	0·03	0·013	0·005
14	0·18	0·16	0·14	0·13	0·11	0·10	0·09	0·08	0·03	0·009	0·003
15	0·16	0·14	0·12	0·11	0·09	0·08	0·07	0·06	0·02	0·006	0·002

Note: The D.C.F. calculations in Chapter Twenty-four have been made with
the use of four-figure present value tables: these tables are generally recommended for solving practical business problems. The two-figure present
value table above minimizes the arithmetical calculations and these are
normally best for practice exercises, as well as being suitable for examination
problems.

INDEX

INDEX